Dragon Knights

Written and Illustrated by
Mineko Ohkami

Volume 8

TOKYOPOP®

Los Angeles • Tokyo • London

Translator - Agnes Yoshida
English Adaption - Stephanie Sheh
Associate Editor - Tim Beedle
Retouch and Lettering - Ronnel Papa
Cover Layout - Anna Kernbaum

Senior Editor - Luis Reyes
Managing Editor - Jill Freshney
Production Coordinator - Antonio DePietro
Production Manager - Jennifer Miller
Art Director - Matthew Alford
Editorial Director- Jeremy Ross
VP of Production & Manufacturing - Ron Klamert
President & C.O.O. - John Parker
Publisher & C.E.O. - Stuart Levy

Email: editor@TOKYOPOP.com
Come visit us online at www.TOKYOPOP.com

A  Manga
TOKYOPOP® is an imprint of Mixx Entertainment, Inc.
5900 Wilshire Blvd. Suite 2000, Los Angeles, CA 90036

ISBN: 1-59182-112-6

First TOKYOPOP® printing: June 2003

10 9 8 7 6 5 4 3 2 1

Printed in the USA

From the Chronicles of Dusis, the West Continent...

The Beginnings: Nadil and Lord Lykouleon

When the Yokai Nadil, the leader of the Demon Forces, kidnapped the Dragon Queen Raseleane, the Dragon Lord Lykouleon ventured to the Demon Realm to rescue her. He defeated Nadil by cutting off his head, but not before the demon leader rendered Raseleane barren, unable to give Lykouleon a child... and the Dragon Kingdom an heir. Now the Demon and Yokai Forces, under the command of Shydeman and Shyrendora, plot to attack Draqueen, the Dragon Kingdom, and retrieve their leader's head in the hopes of reviving him. But other shady characters such as Master Kharl the Alchemist and the rogue Yokai Bierrez have also entered the contest for control of all Dusis. The Dragon Officers and Lord Lykouleon desperately try to ready the Dragon Palace to repel an assault by the Demon Forces.

The Dragon Knights: A Motley Trio

The Dragon Knights are three specially-chosen warriors granted the power of the various elemental dragons for the protection of the Dragon Realm. They have been dispatched on three separate missions. The human/demon Rath is the Dragon Knight of Fire and has gone out of his way to accompany the fortuneteller Cesia to Mt. Emphaza. However, his reluctance to be entirely forthcoming about his motives may be a point of concern. Thatz, a human thief, is the Dragon Knight of Earth and is currently engaged in a search for the mysterious Three Treasures. The Elfin prince Rune, the Dragon Knight of Water, has left the Dragon Palace to investigate reports that the Faerie Realm, his home, has been destroyed.

Rath and Cesia

Now partners, these two have always had a strained relationship, primarily because each doesn't trust the fact that the other is part demon. But they care about each other tremendously. When Cesia-prone to curses as she is-finds herself the victim of dark magic, it is Rath who helps her through each crisis. And when Rath becomes consumed with anger-as he is prone to do-it is Cesia that coaxes him back into calm. Now back on track, the two head for Mt. Emphaza to find a power that will revive the fallen Demon Dog Crewger, but they may be in for more than they realize.

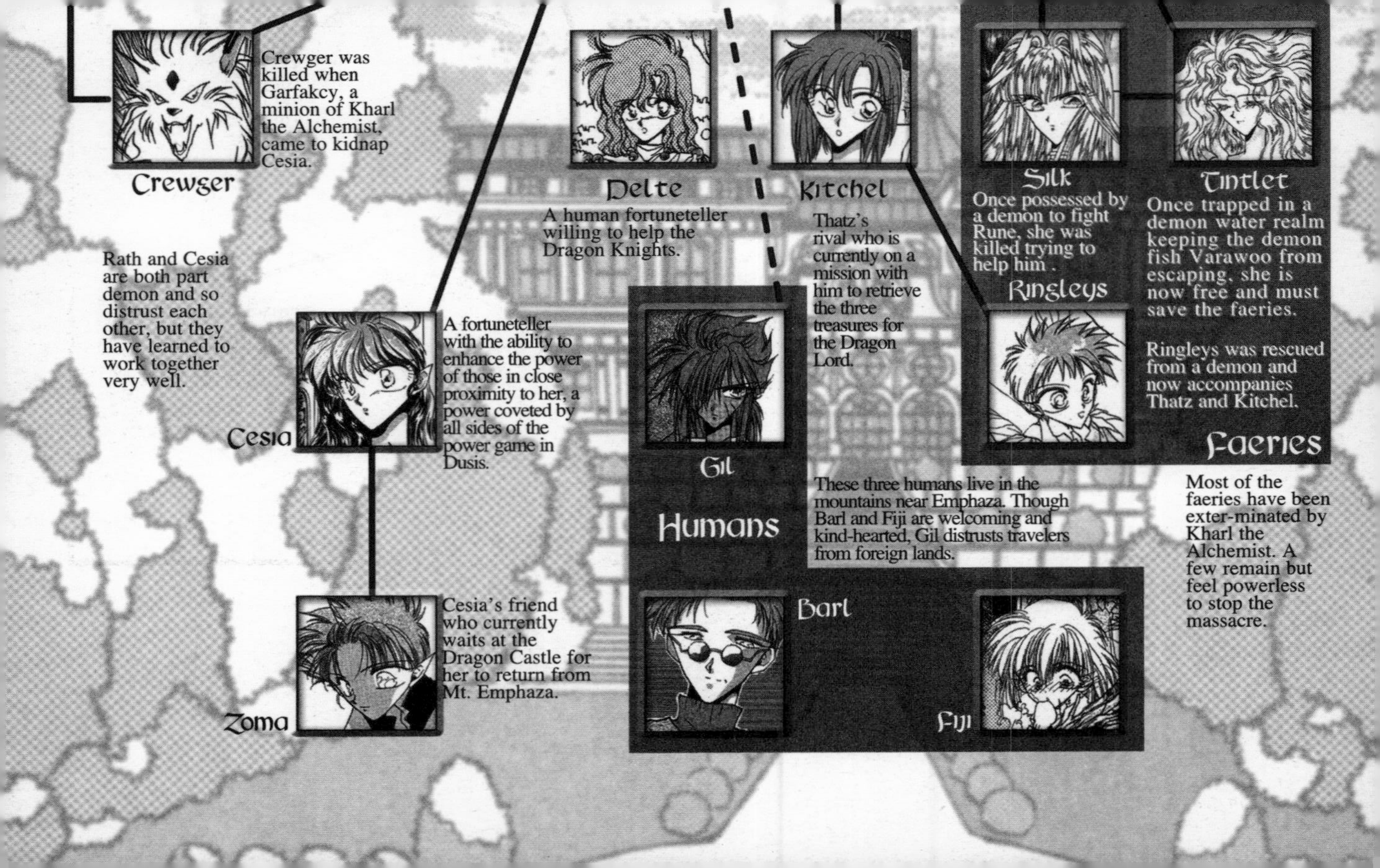
Crewger
Crewger was killed when Garfakcy, a minion of Kharl the Alchemist, came to kidnap Cesia.
Rath and Cesia are both part demon and so distrust each other, but they have learned to work together very well.
Cesia
A fortuneteller with the ability to enhance the power of those in close proximity to her, a power coveted by all sides of the power game in Dusis.
Zoma
Cesia's friend who currently waits at the Dragon Castle for her to return from Mt. Emphaza.
Delte
A human fortuneteller willing to help the Dragon Knights.
Kitchel
Thatz's rival who is currently on a mission with him to retrieve the three treasures for the Dragon Lord.
Humans
Gil
Barl
Fiji
These three humans live in the mountains near Emphaza. Though Barl and Fiji are welcoming and kind-hearted, Gil distrusts travelers from foreign lands.
Silk
Once possessed by a demon to fight Rune, she was killed trying to help him .
Tintlet
Once trapped in a demon water realm keeping the demon fish Varawoo from escaping, she is now free and must save the faeries.
Ringleys
Ringleys was rescued from a demon and now accompanies Thatz and Kitchel.
Faeries
Most of the faeries have been exter-minated by Kharl the Alchemist. A few remain but feel powerless to stop the massacre.

The Cast of Dragon Knights

The Dragon Knights and the Dragon Officers, under the command of Lord Lykouleon, are positioning themselves to face the Demon Forces in the defense of Dusis. But they will have to rely on the help of others to see them through. This is an overview of the Dragon Clan and their allies.

Royalty

Lord Lykouleon

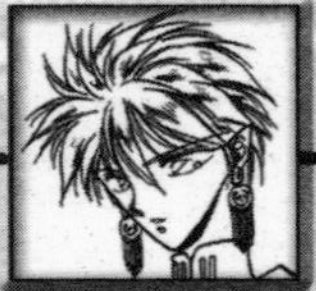

Raseleane

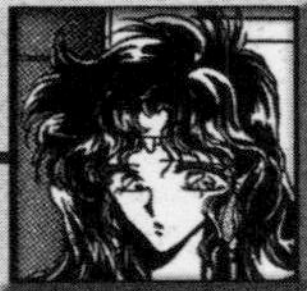

Dragon Officers

Kai-Stern

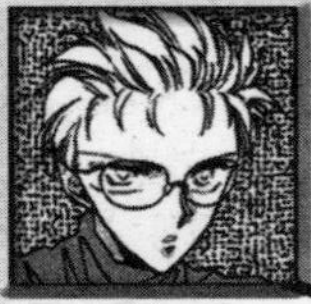

Blue Dragon Officer-Secretary of Foreign Affairs

Alfeegi

White Dragon Officer-Chief Secretary

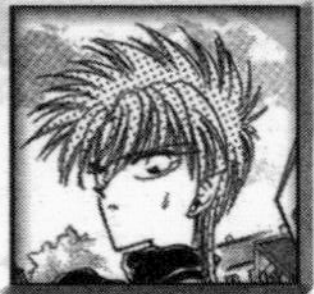

Ruwalk

Yellow Dragon Officer-Secretary of State

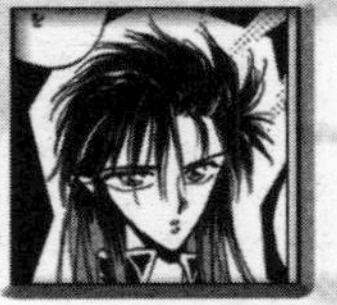

Tetheus

Black Dragon Officer-Secretary of Security

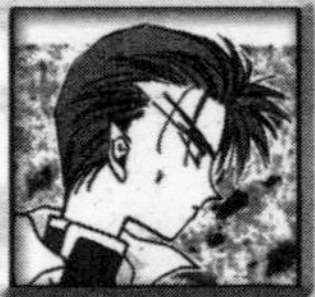

Cernozura

Dragon Castle Administrator

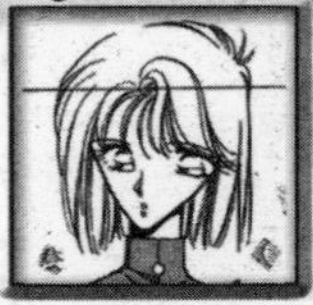

Illuser

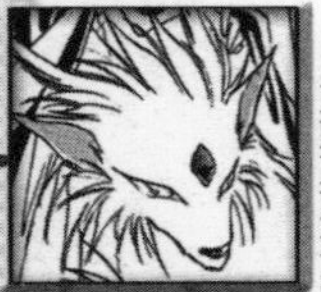

Illuser was killed when Lord Lykouleon faced Nadil to save his Queen Raseleane.

Drgon Knights

Rath

Rath is very close to Kai-Stern and was to the late Demon Dog Crewger.

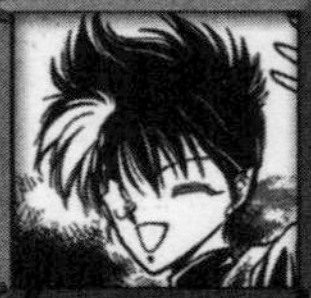

Thatz

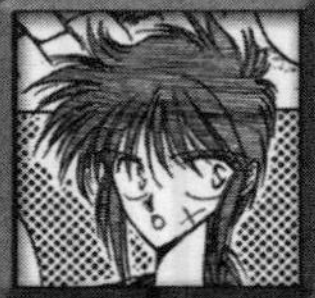

Rune

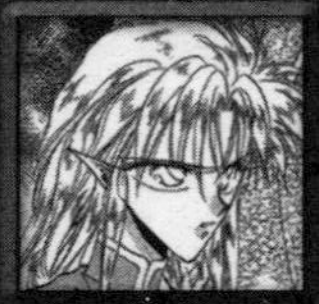

Nohiro

A human with a love for Faeries.

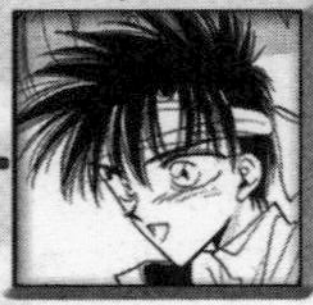

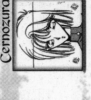

The Villains of Dragon Knights

Nadil

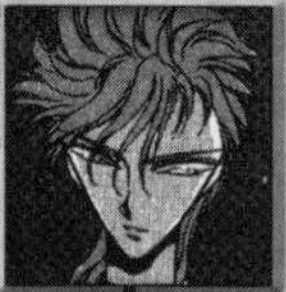

Leader of the Demon Forces who was decapitated by Lykouleon. His army is trying to retrieve his head and resurrect him.

Shydeman

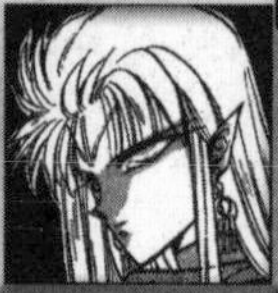

Shyrendora

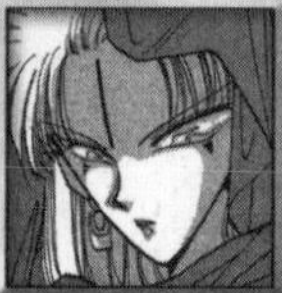

Current leaders of Nadil's army. They are fortunetellers with the express goal of reviving Nadil and destroying the Dragon Tribe.

Bierrez

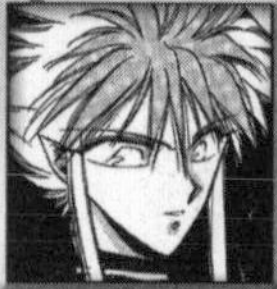

The only Yokai who can penetrate the shield of the Dragon Castle. Though a demon, he isn't a loyal follower of Nadil.

Lady Medicinea

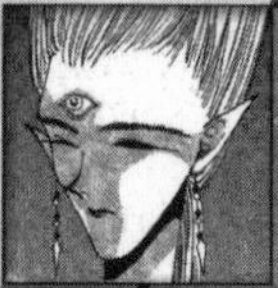

A demon leader in Nadil's army responsible for the Black Smoke in Dusis. Has a competative relationship

Jilge

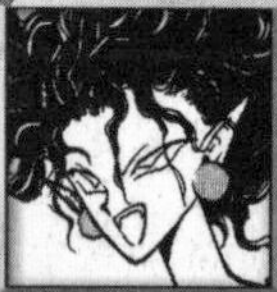

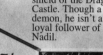

A witch who worked for Nadil's forces until her untimely death at the hands of the Dragon Knights.

Fedelta

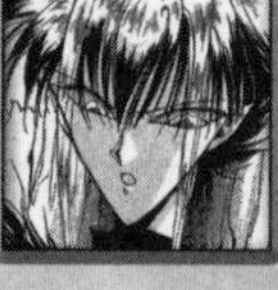

One of the leaders in Nadil's army. Answers to Shydeman and is competative with Medicinea.

Kharl

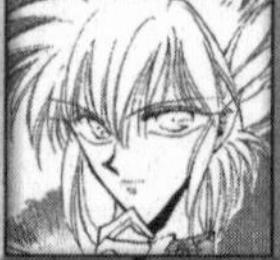

Kharl is an Alchemist and a Renkin Wizard who can create demons. He longs to control Dusis himself but sometimes assists Nadil's army. Garfakcy is sneaky, vicious and serves Kharl, but harbors a desire to be a demon himself.

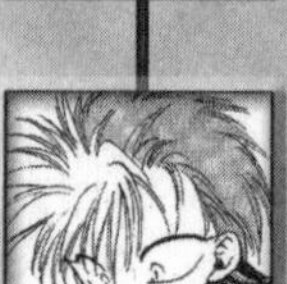

Garfakcy

Kirukulus

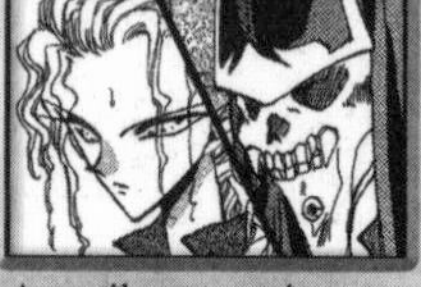

An evil sorcerer intent on capturing Cesia and using her to make him stronger. Was defeated by Rath but still lives and is determined to control Dusis.

Kingdom of Glaciosa

At the northern-
most point of the
northern town of
Yuba lies...

...Emphaza.

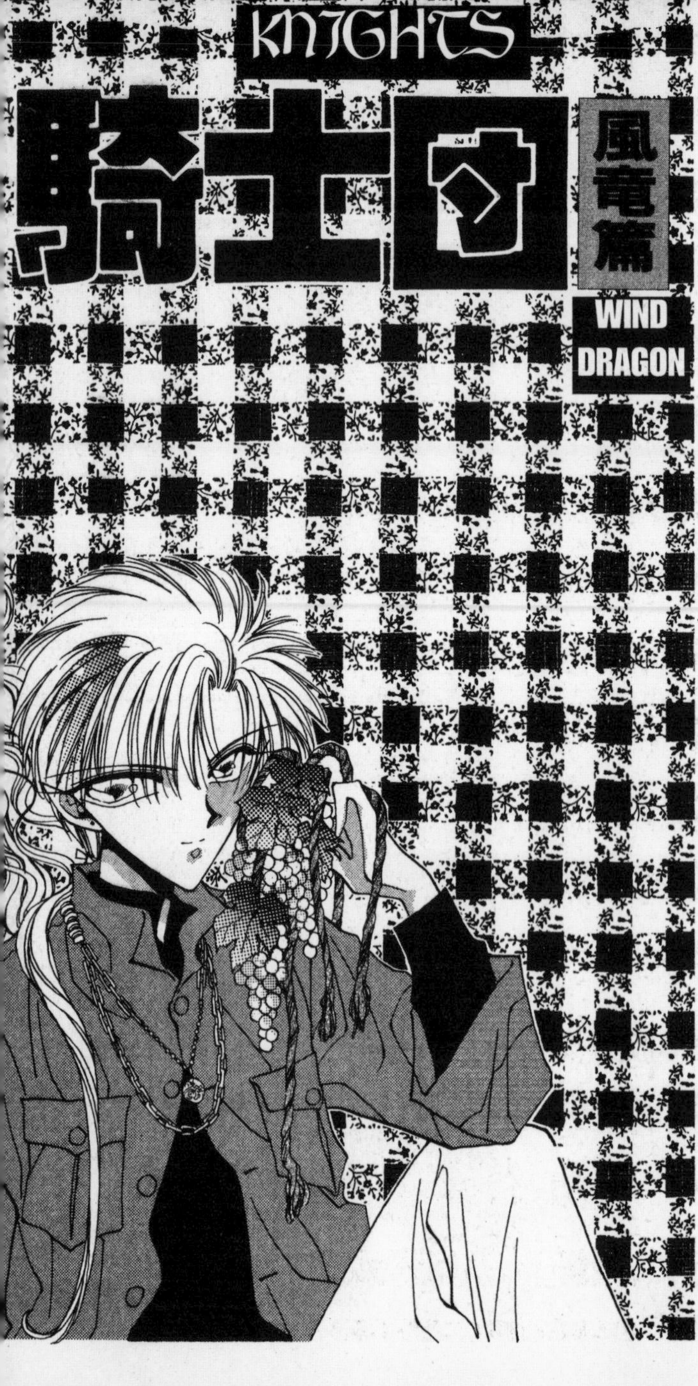
KNIGHTS
騎士団
風竜篇
WIND DRAGON

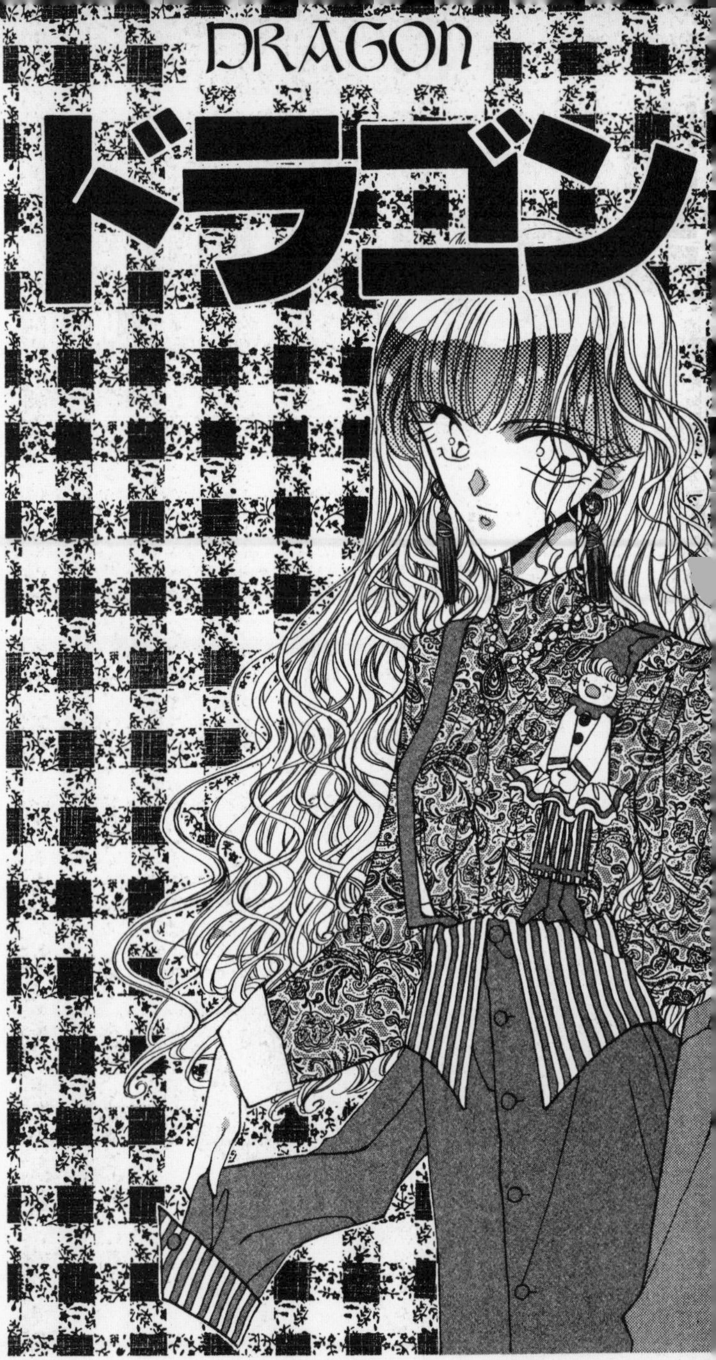
DRAGON
ドラゴン

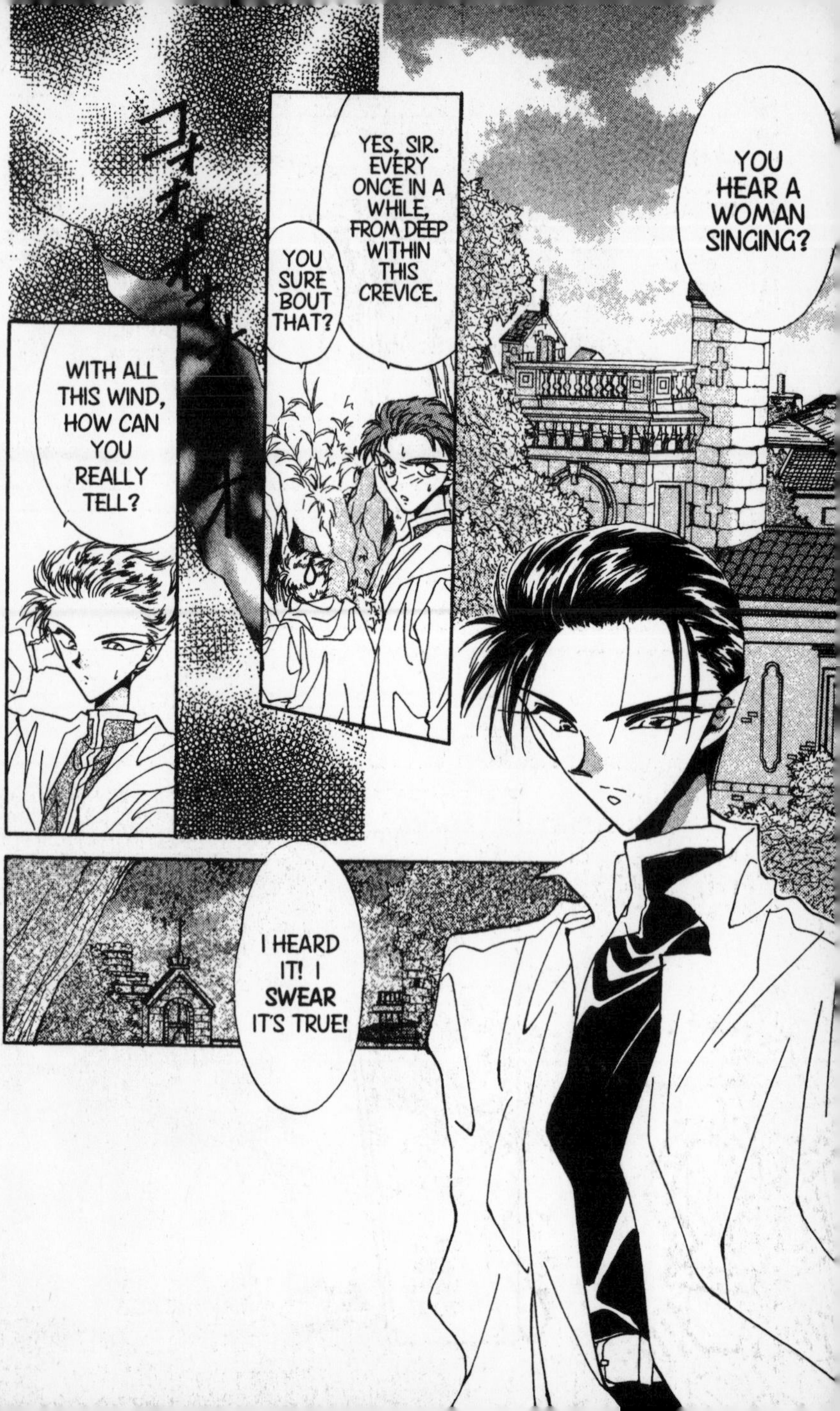
YOU HEAR A WOMAN SINGING?
YES, SIR. EVERY ONCE IN A WHILE, FROM DEEP WITHIN THIS CREVICE.
YOU SURE 'BOUT THAT?
WITH ALL THIS WIND, HOW CAN YOU REALLY TELL?
I HEARD IT! I SWEAR IT'S TRUE!

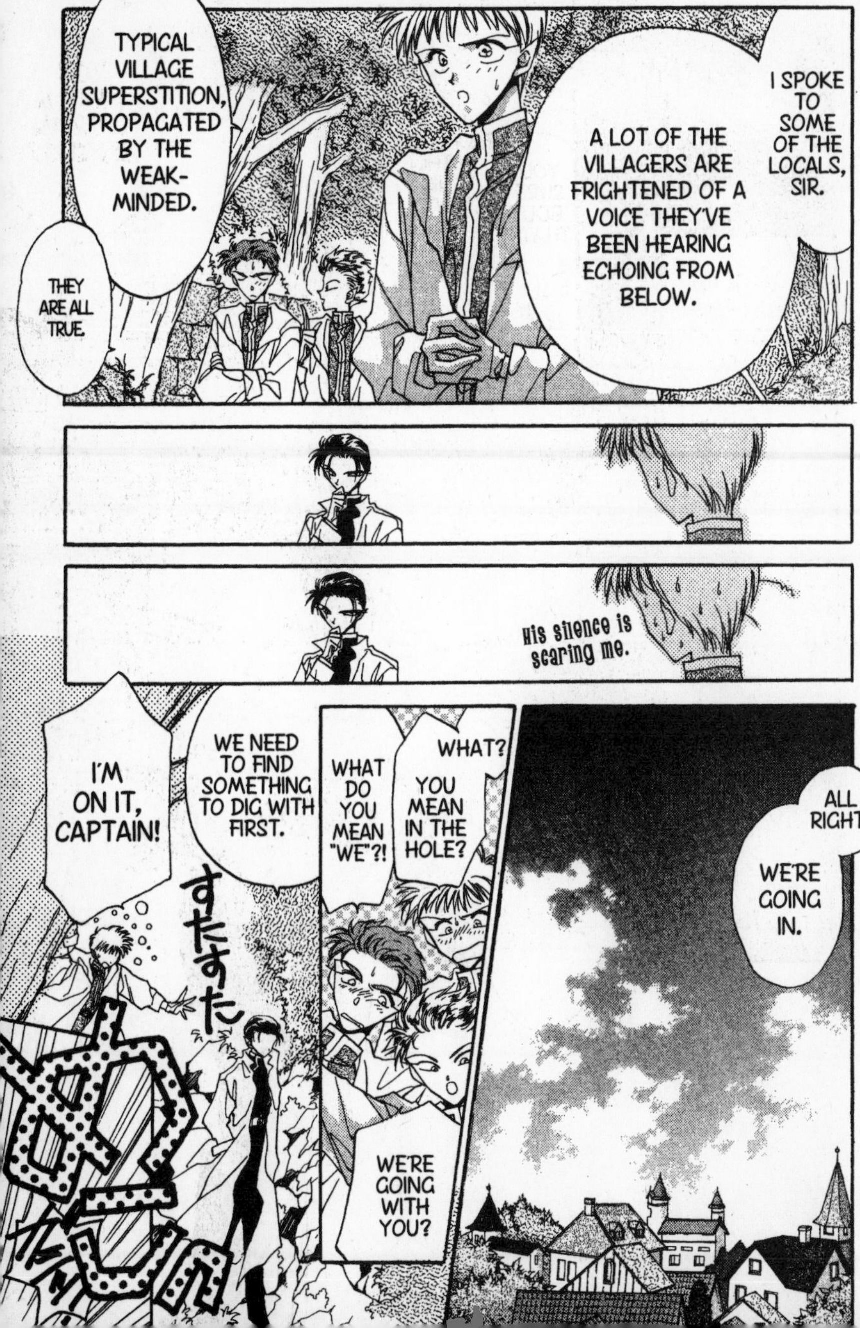
I SPOKE TO SOME OF THE LOCALS, SIR.
A LOT OF THE VILLAGERS ARE FRIGHTENED OF A VOICE THEY'VE BEEN HEARING ECHOING FROM BELOW.
TYPICAL VILLAGE SUPERSTITION, PROPAGATED BY THE WEAK-MINDED.
THEY ARE ALL TRUE.
His silence is searing me.
ALL RIGHT,
WE'RE GOING IN.
WHAT?
YOU MEAN IN THE HOLE?
WHAT DO YOU MEAN "WE"?!
WE'RE GOING WITH YOU?
WE NEED TO FIND SOMETHING TO DIG WITH FIRST.
I'M ON IT, CAPTAIN!
すたすた

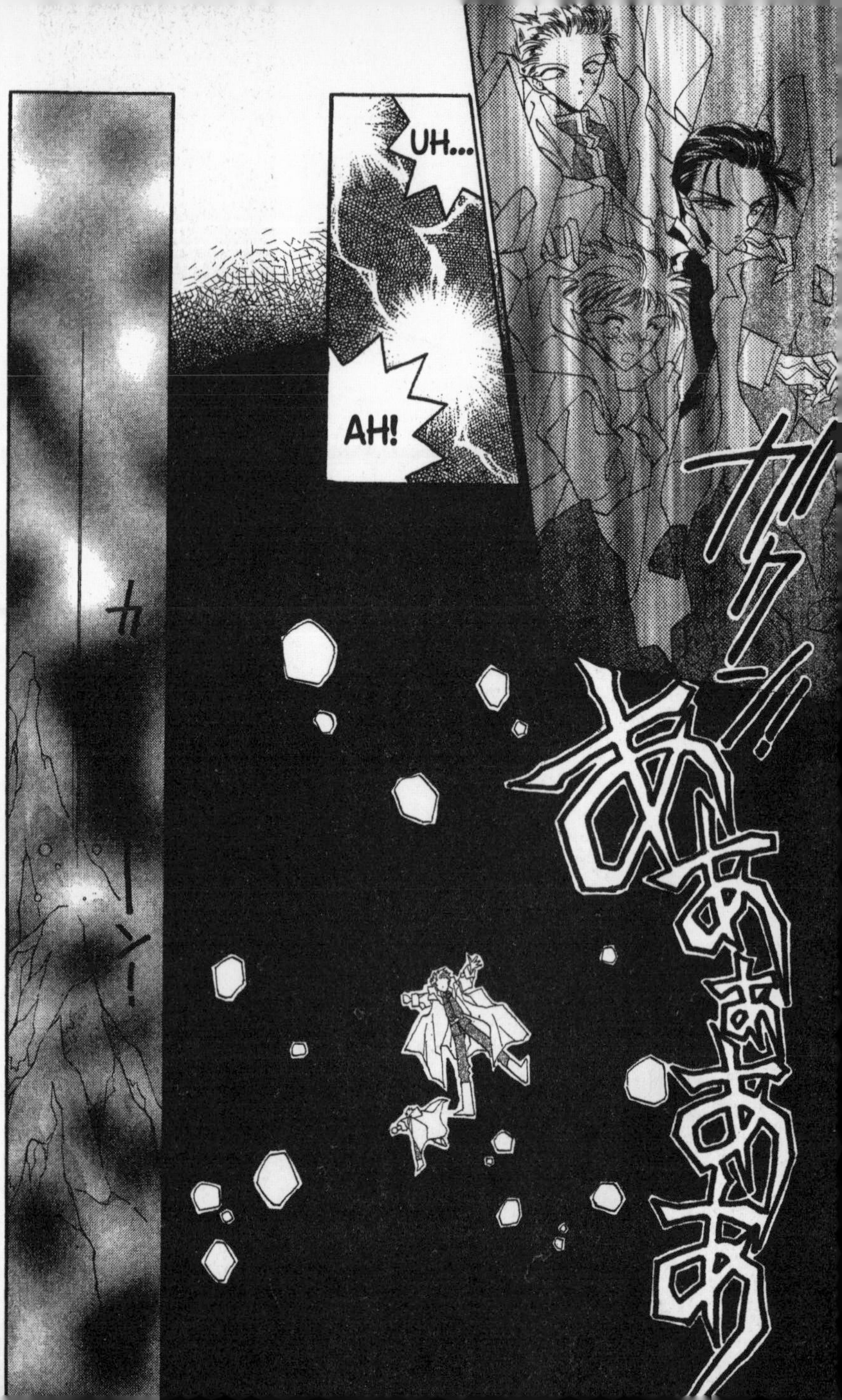
ガクン!!
UH...
AH!

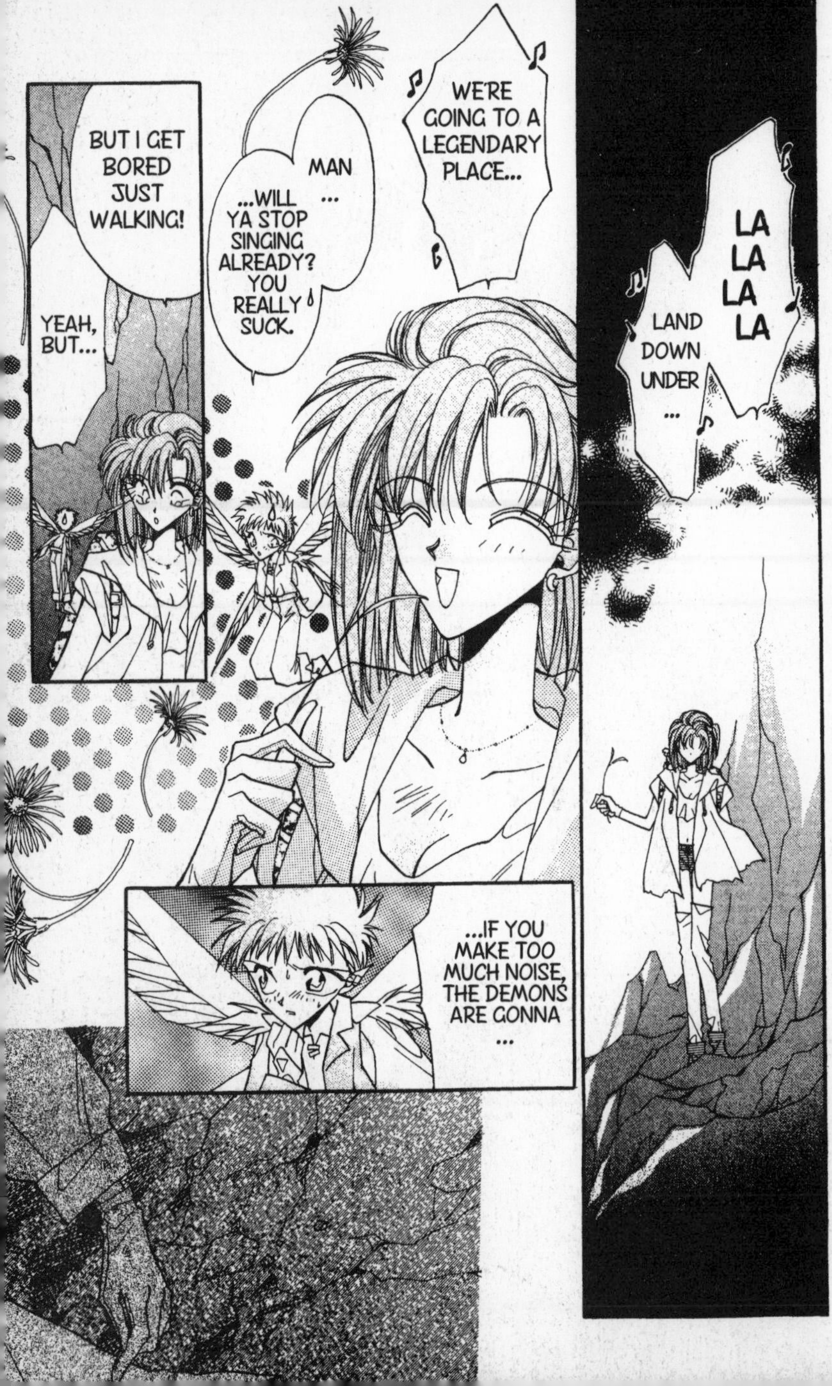
LA LA LA LA
LAND DOWN UNDER ...
WE'RE GOING TO A LEGENDARY PLACE...
MAN ...
...WILL YA STOP SINGING ALREADY? YOU REALLY SUCK.
BUT I GET BORED JUST WALKING!
YEAH, BUT...
...IF YOU MAKE TOO MUCH NOISE, THE DEMONS ARE GONNA ...

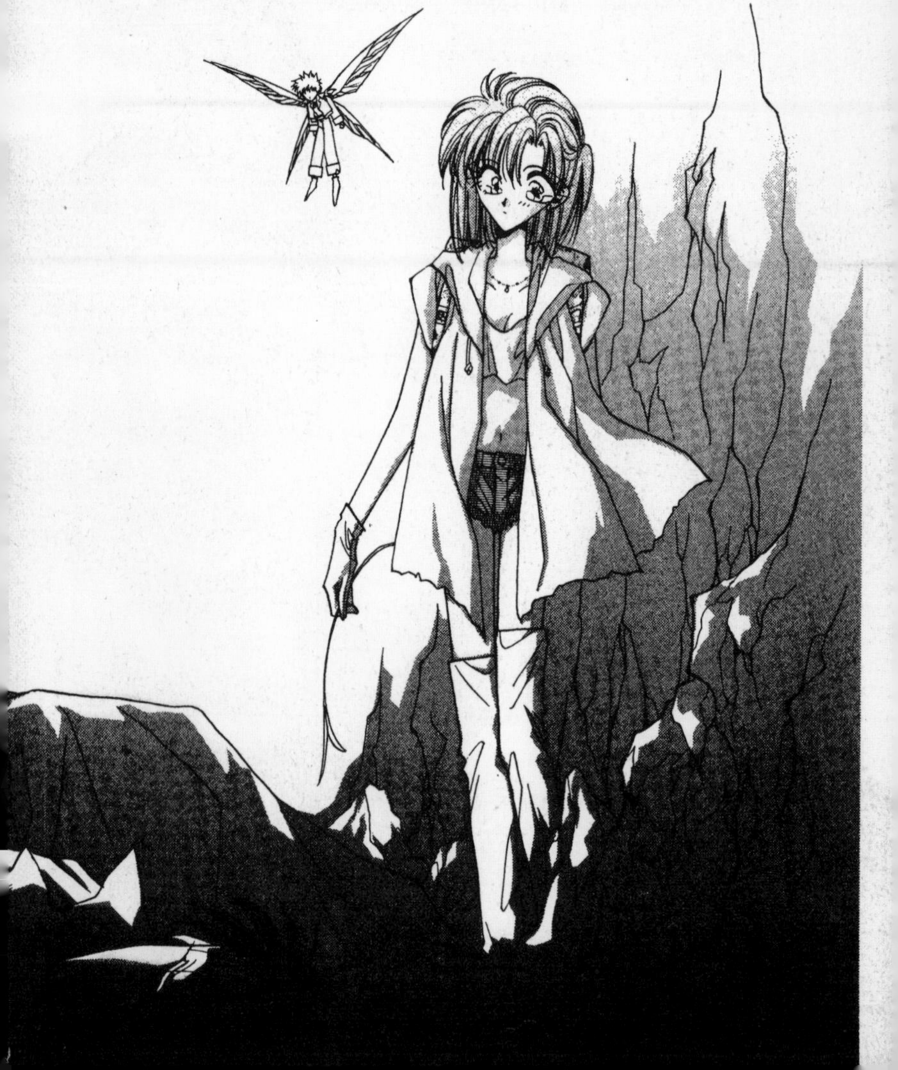

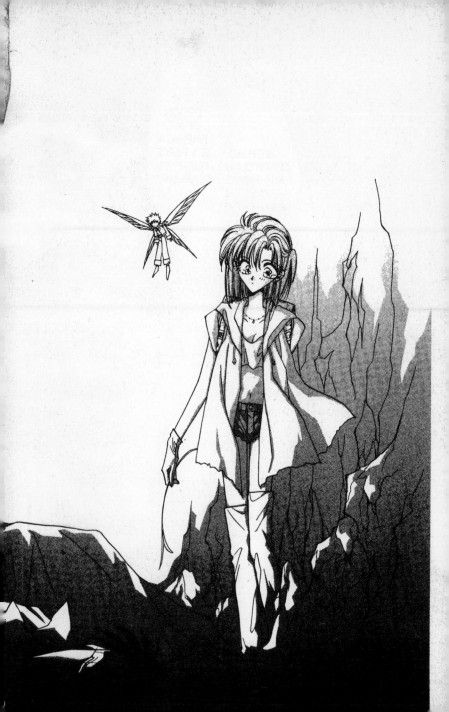

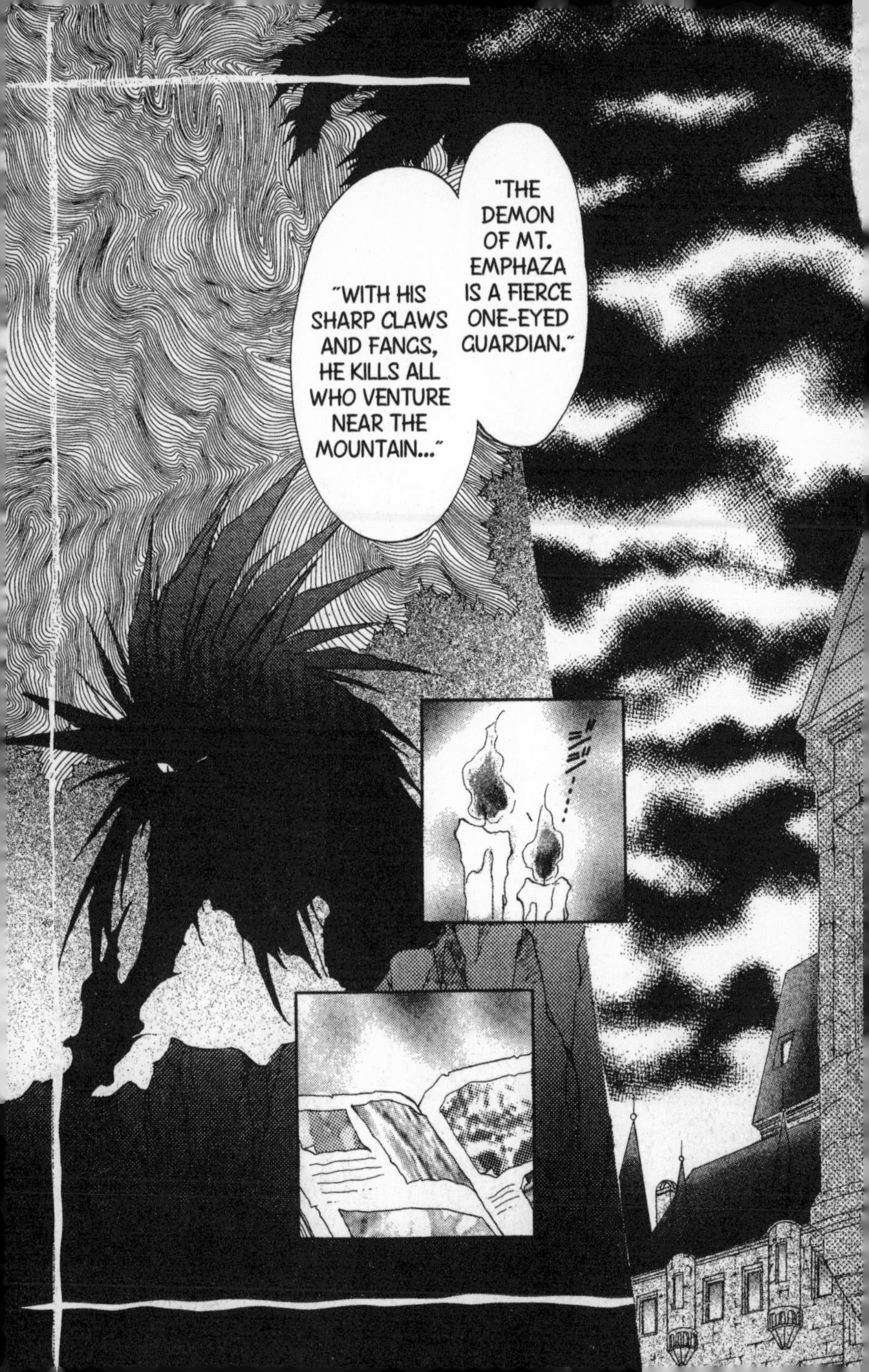
"THE DEMON OF MT. EMPHAZA IS A FIERCE ONE-EYED GUARDIAN."
"WITH HIS SHARP CLAWS AND FANGS, HE KILLS ALL WHO VENTURE NEAR THE MOUNTAIN..."

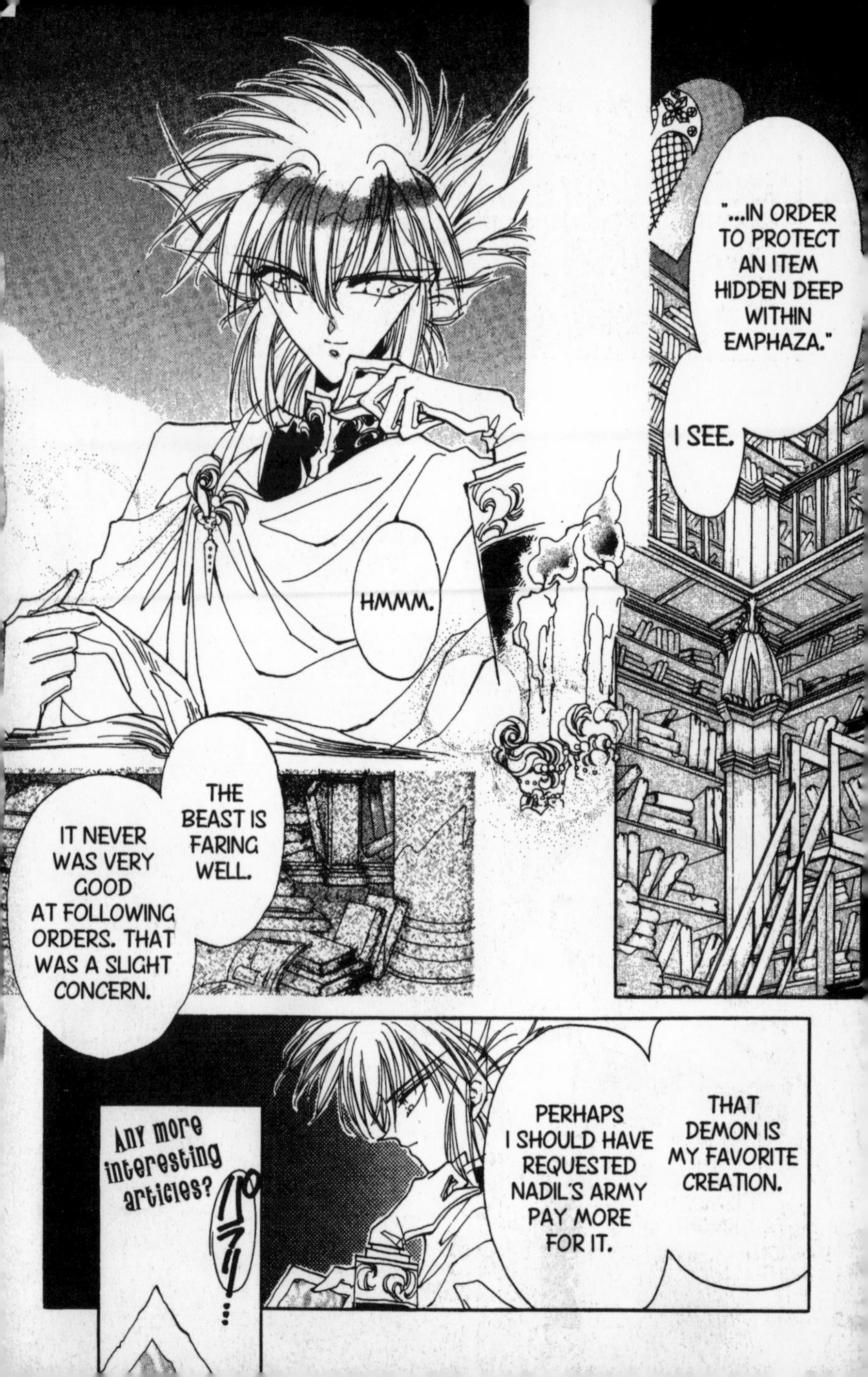
"...IN ORDER TO PROTECT AN ITEM HIDDEN DEEP WITHIN EMPHAZA."
I SEE.
HMMM.
THE BEAST IS FARING WELL.
IT NEVER WAS VERY GOOD AT FOLLOWING ORDERS. THAT WAS A SLIGHT CONCERN.
THAT DEMON IS MY FAVORITE CREATION.
PERHAPS I SHOULD HAVE REQUESTED NADIL'S ARMY PAY MORE FOR IT.
Any more interesting articles?

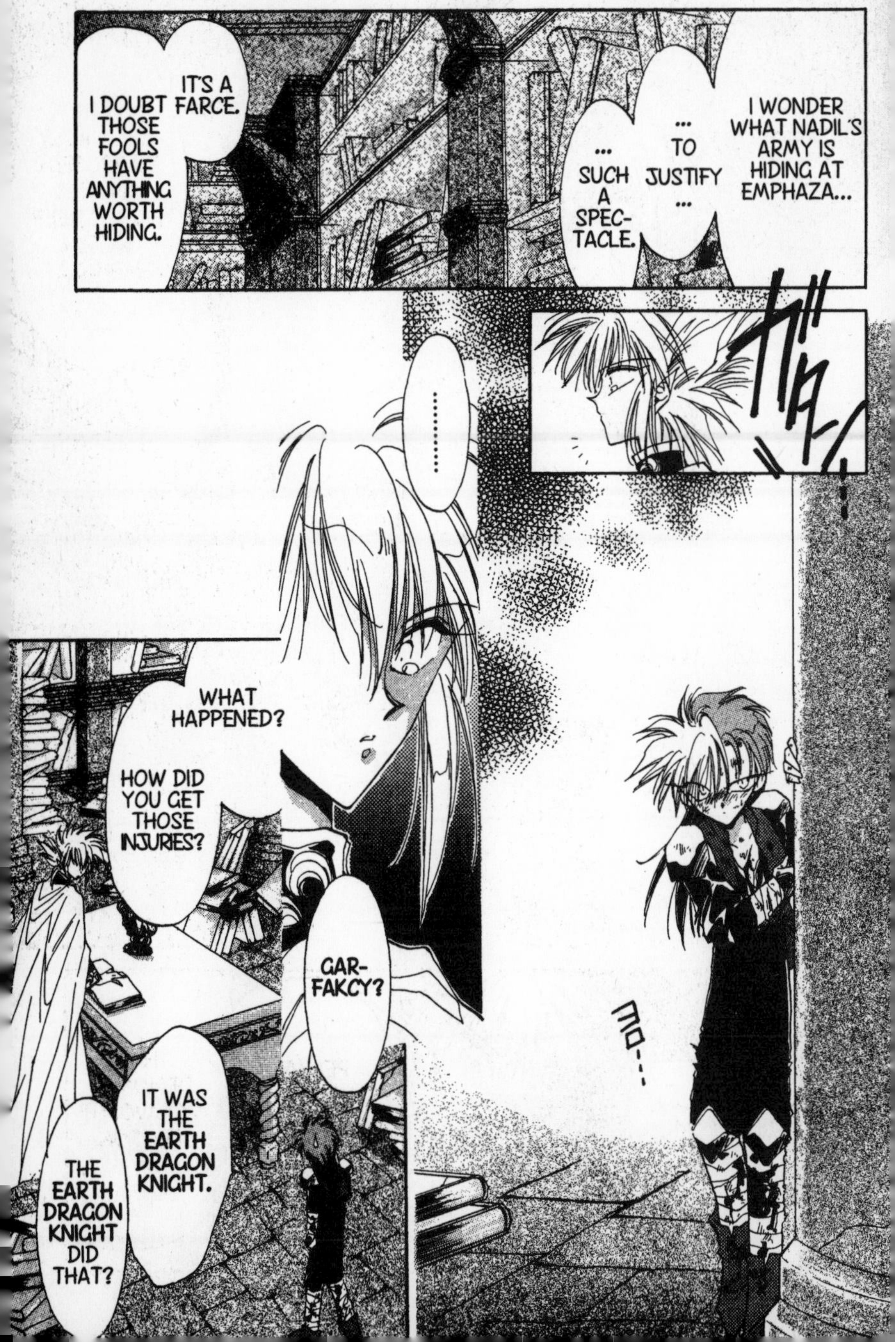
I WONDER WHAT NADIL'S ARMY IS HIDING AT EMPHAZA...
... TO JUSTIFY ...
... SUCH A SPECTACLE.
IT'S A FARCE.
I DOUBT THOSE FOOLS HAVE ANYTHING WORTH HIDING.
....
GAR-FAKCY?
WHAT HAPPENED?
HOW DID YOU GET THOSE INJURIES?
IT WAS THE EARTH DRAGON KNIGHT.
THE EARTH DRAGON KNIGHT DID THAT?

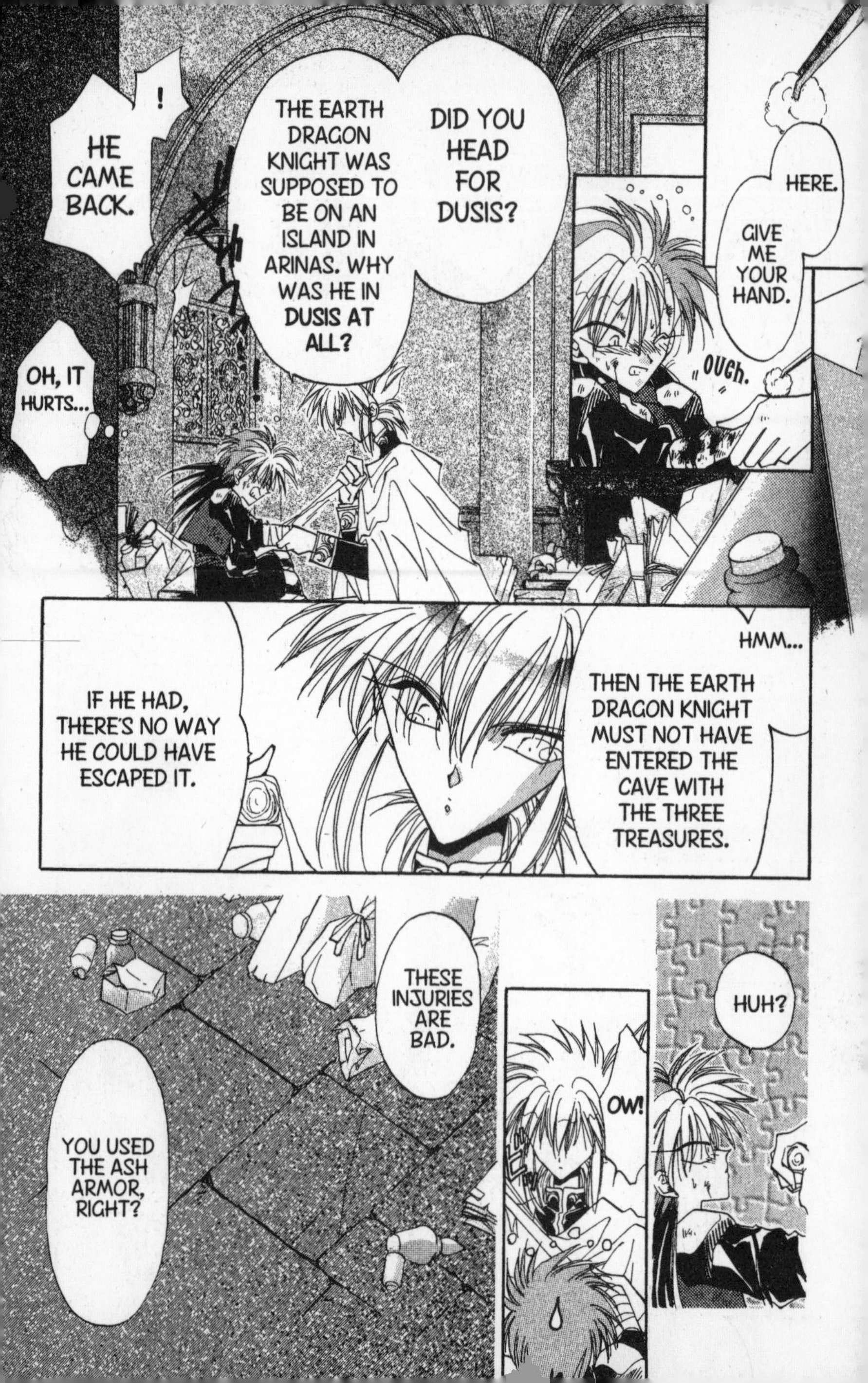
HERE.
GIVE ME YOUR HAND.
OUCH.
DID YOU HEAD FOR DUSIS?
THE EARTH DRAGON KNIGHT WAS SUPPOSED TO BE ON AN ISLAND IN ARINAS. WHY WAS HE IN DUSIS AT ALL?
!
HE CAME BACK.
OH, IT HURTS...
HMM...
THEN THE EARTH DRAGON KNIGHT MUST NOT HAVE ENTERED THE CAVE WITH THE THREE TREASURES.
IF HE HAD, THERE'S NO WAY HE COULD HAVE ESCAPED IT.
HUH?
OW!
THESE INJURIES ARE BAD.
YOU USED THE ASH ARMOR, RIGHT?

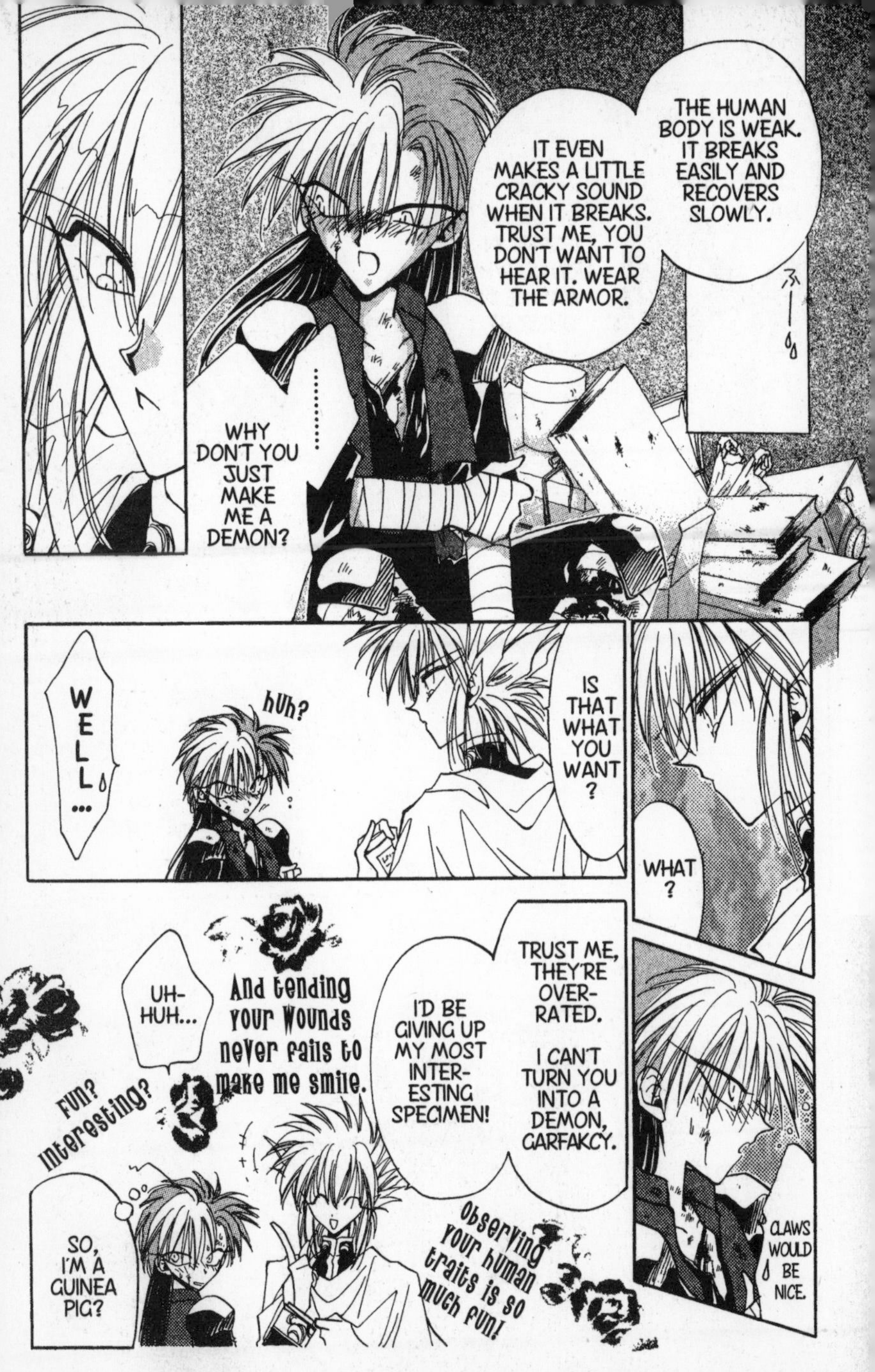
THE HUMAN BODY IS WEAK. IT BREAKS EASILY AND RECOVERS SLOWLY.
IT EVEN MAKES A LITTLE CRACKY SOUND WHEN IT BREAKS. TRUST ME, YOU DON'T WANT TO HEAR IT. WEAR THE ARMOR.
......
WHY DON'T YOU JUST MAKE ME A DEMON?
WHAT?
IS THAT WHAT YOU WANT?
huh?
WELL...
CLAWS WOULD BE NICE.
TRUST ME, THEY'RE OVER-RATED.
I CAN'T TURN YOU INTO A DEMON, GARFAKCY.
I'D BE GIVING UP MY MOST INTER-ESTING SPECIMEN!
UH-HUH...
And tending your wounds never fails to make me smile.
Fun? Interesting?
Observing your human traits is so much fun!
SO, I'M A GUINEA PIG?

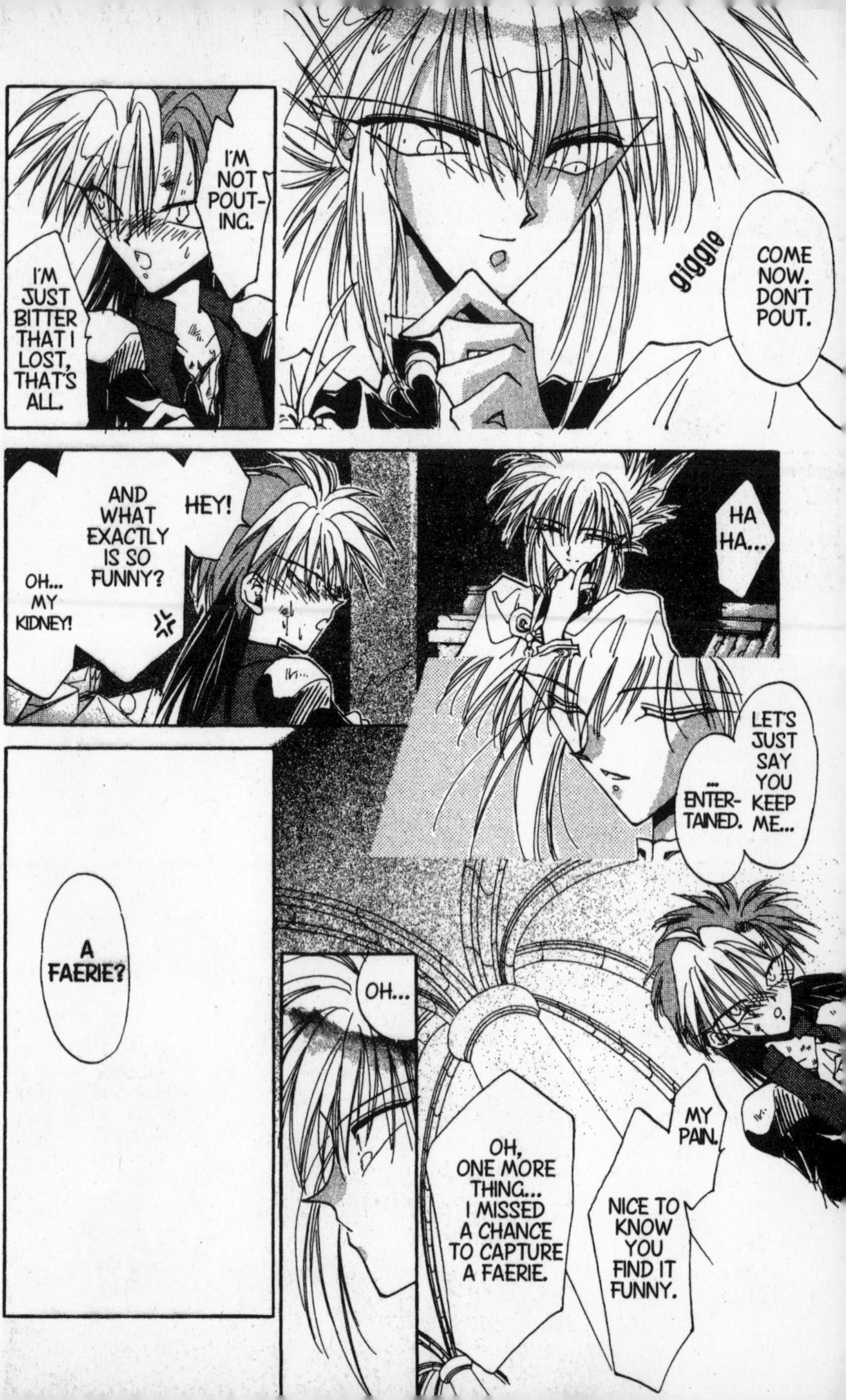
COME NOW. DON'T POUT.
giggle
I'M NOT POUT-ING.
I'M JUST BITTER THAT I LOST, THAT'S ALL.
HA HA...
HEY!
AND WHAT EXACTLY IS SO FUNNY?
OH... MY KIDNEY!
LET'S JUST SAY YOU KEEP ME...
...ENTER-TAINED.
MY PAIN.
NICE TO KNOW YOU FIND IT FUNNY.
OH, ONE MORE THING... I MISSED A CHANCE TO CAPTURE A FAERIE.
OH...
A FAERIE?

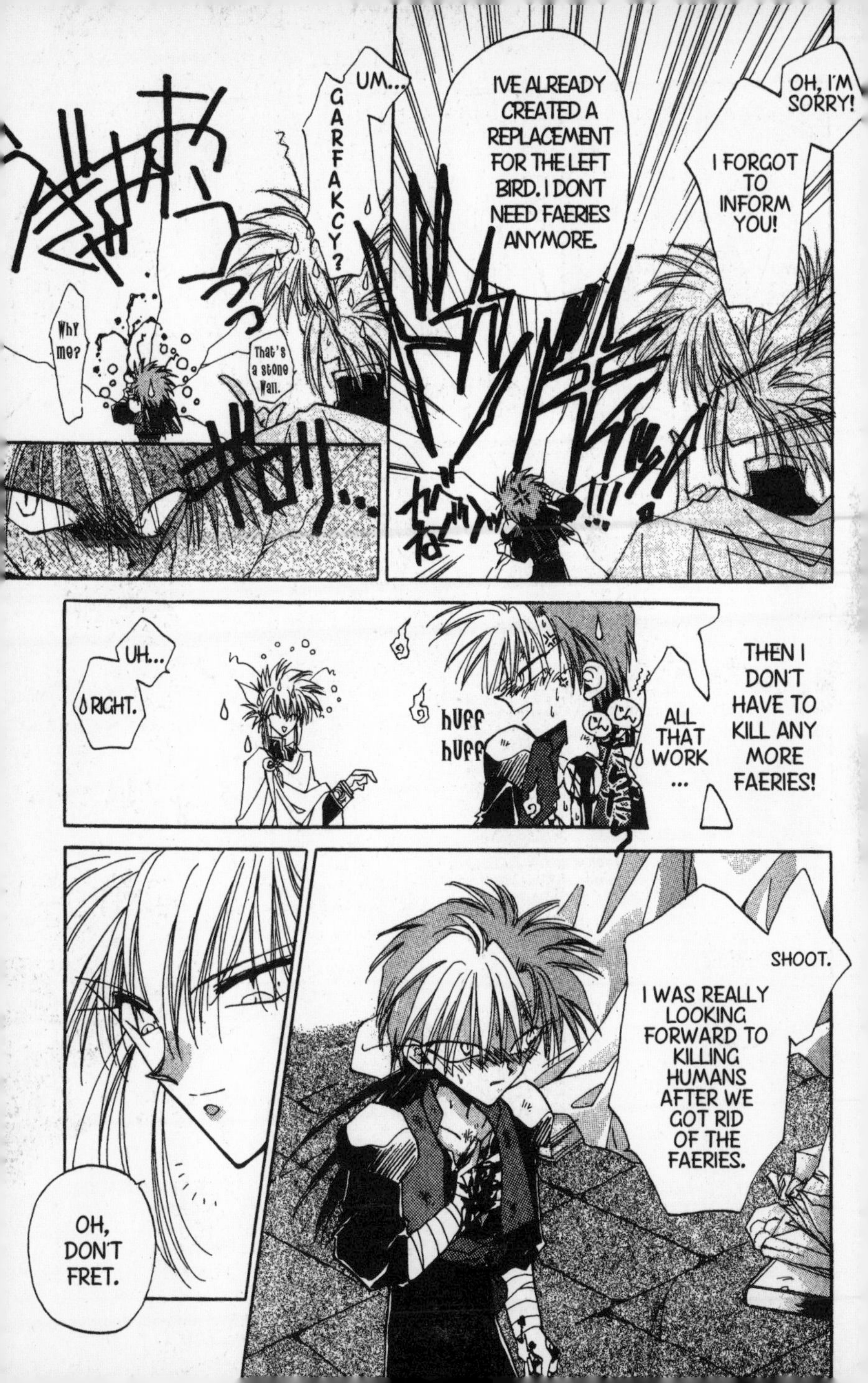
OH, I'M SORRY!
I FORGOT TO INFORM YOU!
IVE ALREADY CREATED A REPLACEMENT FOR THE LEFT BIRD. I DONT NEED FAERIES ANYMORE.
UM...
GARFAKCY?
That's a stone Wall.
Why me?
THEN I DON'T HAVE TO KILL ANY MORE FAERIES!
ALL THAT WORK ...
huff huff
UH... RIGHT.
SHOOT.
I WAS REALLY LOOKING FORWARD TO KILLING HUMANS AFTER WE GOT RID OF THE FAERIES.
OH, DON'T FRET.

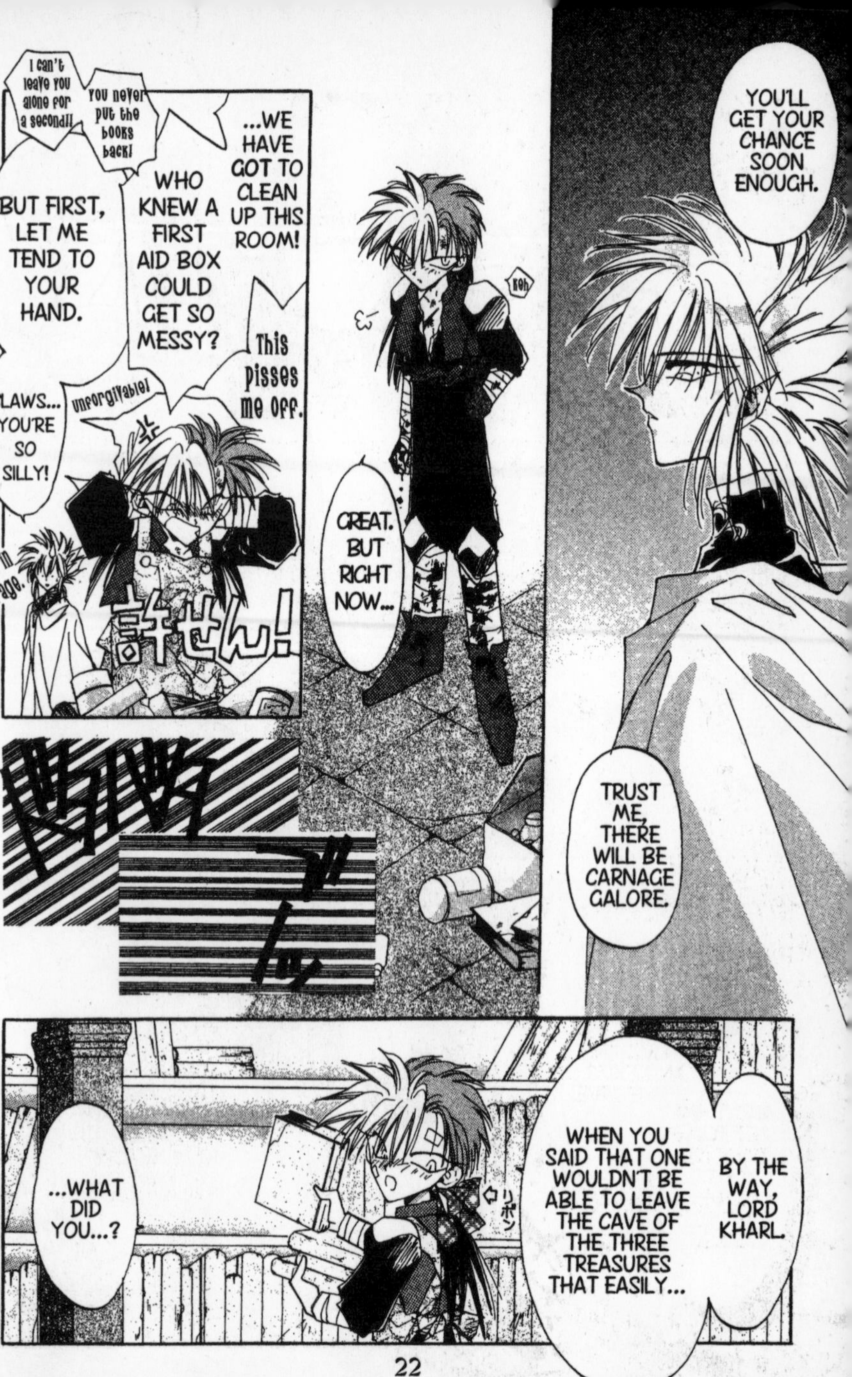
YOU'LL GET YOUR CHANCE SOON ENOUGH.
TRUST ME, THERE WILL BE CARNAGE GALORE.
Keh
GREAT. BUT RIGHT NOW...
...WE HAVE GOT TO CLEAN UP THIS ROOM!
This pisses me off.
WHO KNEW A FIRST AID BOX COULD GET SO MESSY?
You never put the books back!
I can't leave you alone for a second!!
Unforgivable!
BUT FIRST, LET ME TEND TO YOUR HAND.
CLAWS... YOU'RE SO SILLY!
許せん!
He's in a rage.
BY THE WAY, LORD KHARL.
WHEN YOU SAID THAT ONE WOULDN'T BE ABLE TO LEAVE THE CAVE OF THE THREE TREASURES THAT EASILY...
リボン
...WHAT DID YOU...?

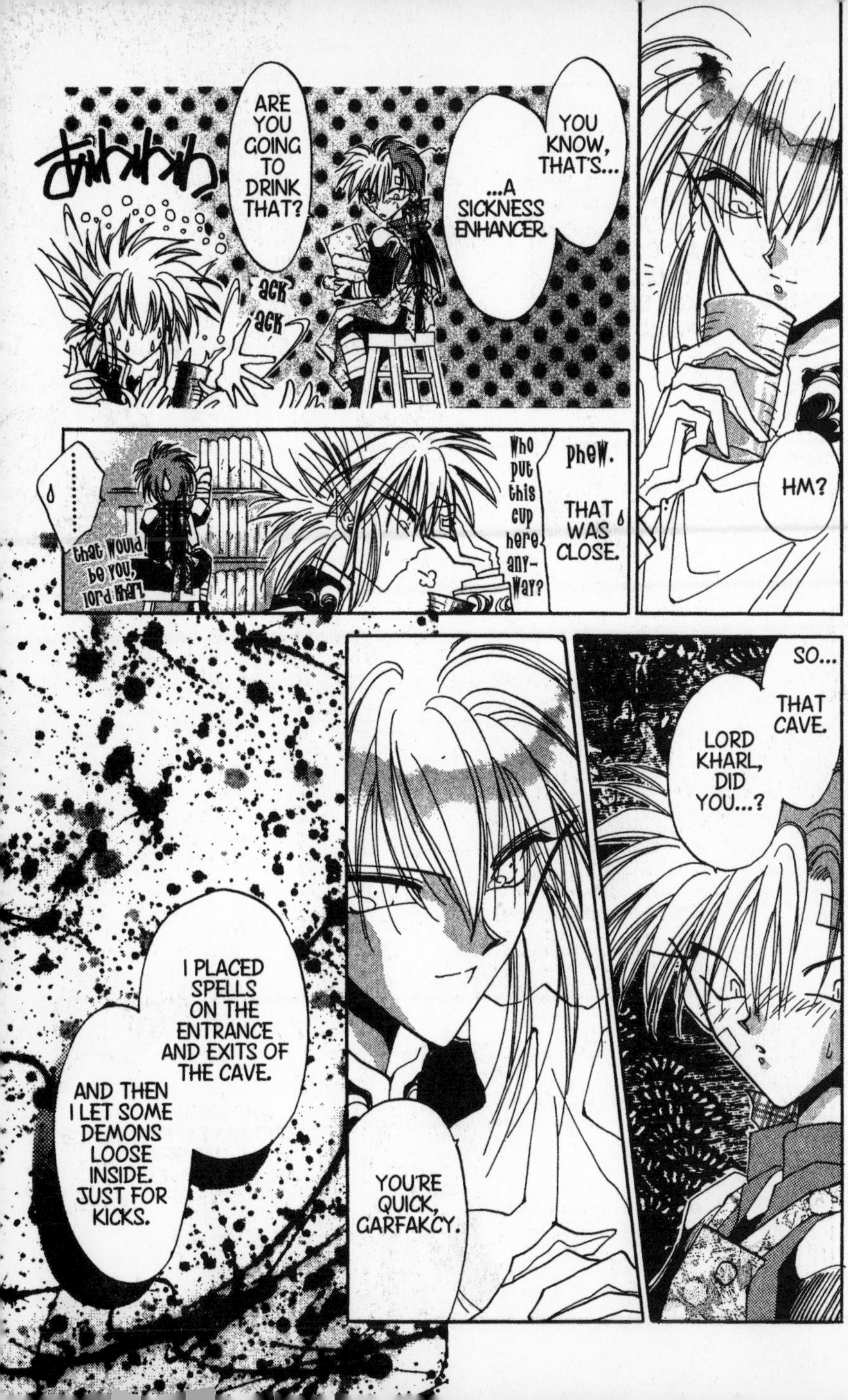
HM?
YOU KNOW, THAT'S...
...A SICKNESS ENHANCER.
ARE YOU GOING TO DRINK THAT?
ack ack
あわわわ
phew.
THAT WAS CLOSE.
Who put this cup here any-way?
......
that would be you, lord kharl
SO...
THAT CAVE.
LORD KHARL, DID YOU...?
YOU'RE QUICK, GARFAKCY.
I PLACED SPELLS ON THE ENTRANCE AND EXITS OF THE CAVE.
AND THEN I LET SOME DEMONS LOOSE INSIDE. JUST FOR KICKS.

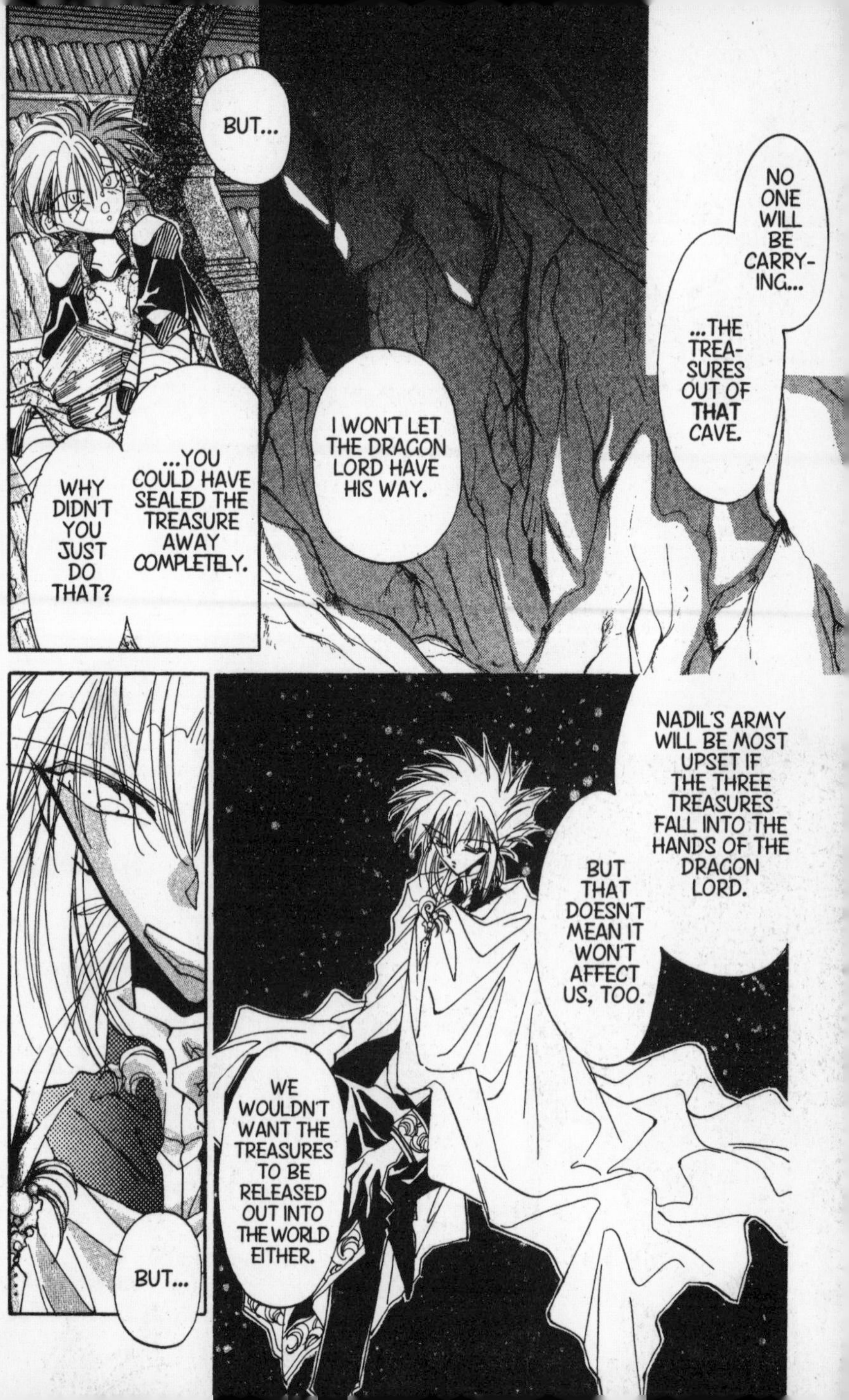
NO ONE WILL BE CARRYING...
...THE TREASURES OUT OF THAT CAVE.
I WON'T LET THE DRAGON LORD HAVE HIS WAY.
BUT...
...YOU COULD HAVE SEALED THE TREASURE AWAY COMPLETELY.
WHY DIDN'T YOU JUST DO THAT?
NADIL'S ARMY WILL BE MOST UPSET IF THE THREE TREASURES FALL INTO THE HANDS OF THE DRAGON LORD.
BUT THAT DOESN'T MEAN IT WON'T AFFECT US, TOO.
WE WOULDN'T WANT THE TREASURES TO BE RELEASED OUT INTO THE WORLD EITHER.
BUT...

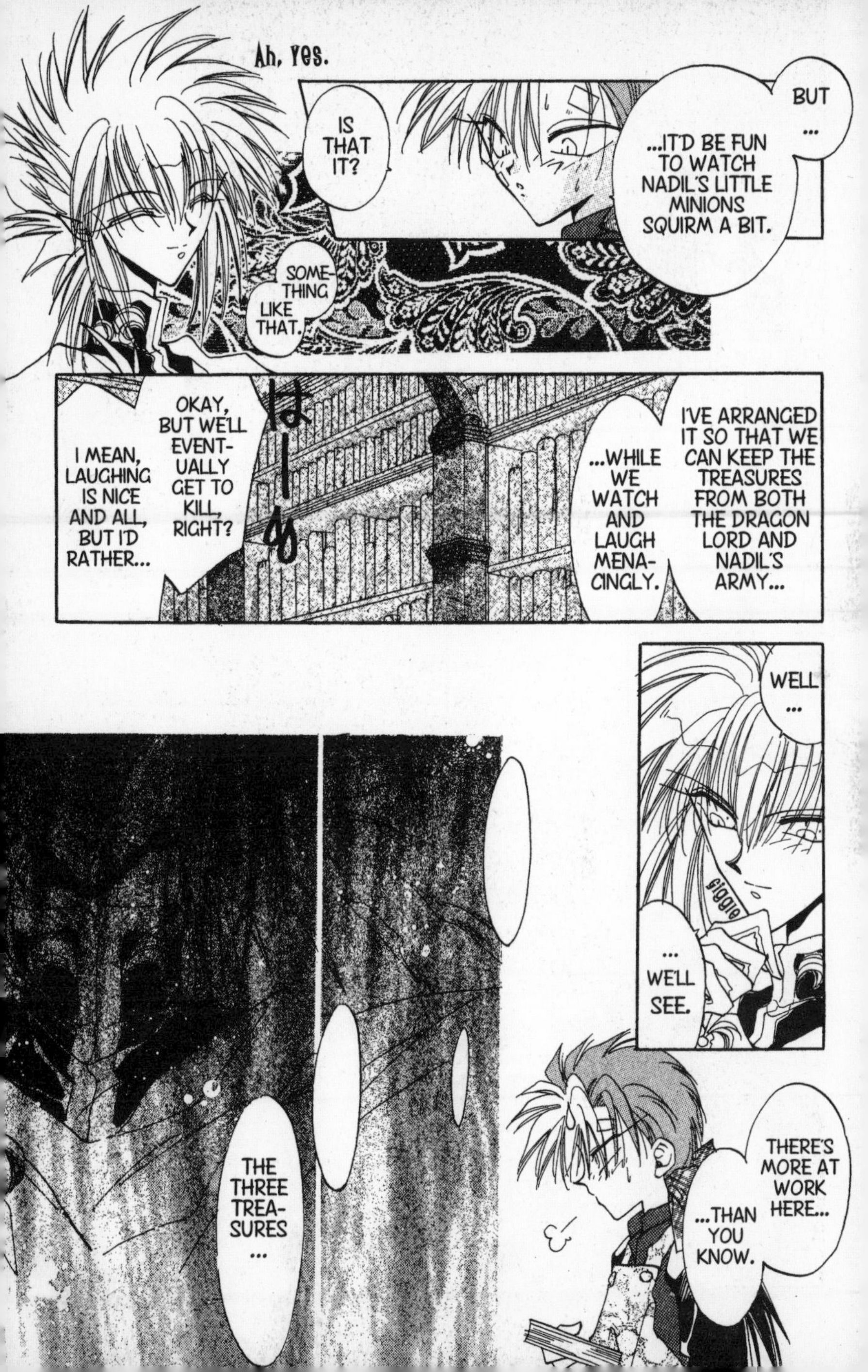
BUT ...
...IT'D BE FUN TO WATCH NADIL'S LITTLE MINIONS SQUIRM A BIT.
IS THAT IT?
Ah, yes.
SOME-THING LIKE THAT.
I'VE ARRANGED IT SO THAT WE CAN KEEP THE TREASURES FROM BOTH THE DRAGON LORD AND NADIL'S ARMY...
...WHILE WE WATCH AND LAUGH MENA-CINGLY.
はーぁ
OKAY, BUT WE'LL EVENT-UALLY GET TO KILL, RIGHT?
I MEAN, LAUGHING IS NICE AND ALL, BUT I'D RATHER...
WELL ...
giggle
... WE'LL SEE.
THERE'S MORE AT WORK HERE...
...THAN YOU KNOW.
THE THREE TREA-SURES ...

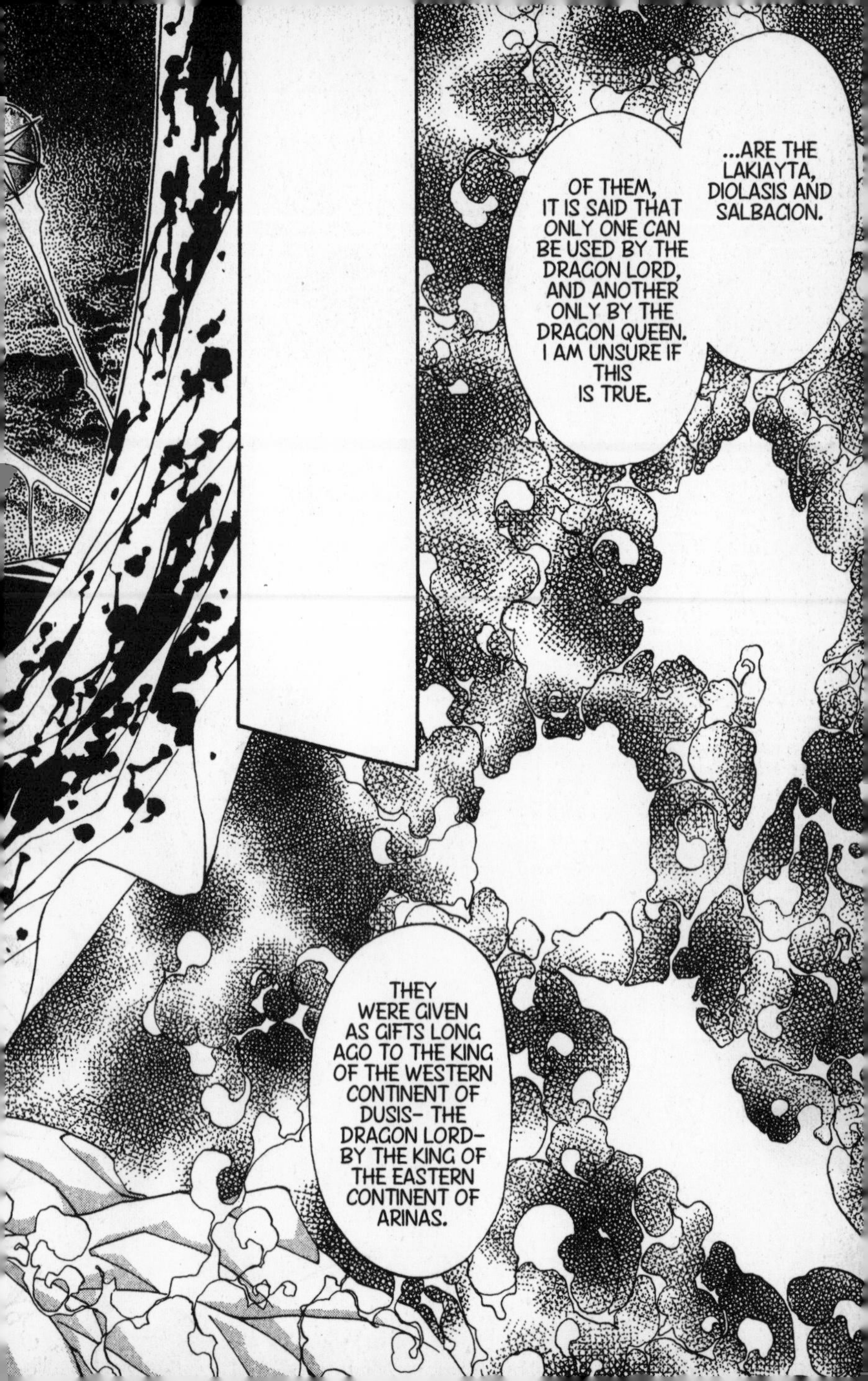
...ARE THE LAKIAYTA, DIOLASIS AND SALBACION.
OF THEM, IT IS SAID THAT ONLY ONE CAN BE USED BY THE DRAGON LORD, AND ANOTHER ONLY BY THE DRAGON QUEEN. I AM UNSURE IF THIS IS TRUE.
THEY WERE GIVEN AS GIFTS LONG AGO TO THE KING OF THE WESTERN CONTINENT OF DUSIS- THE DRAGON LORD- BY THE KING OF THE EASTERN CONTINENT OF ARINAS.

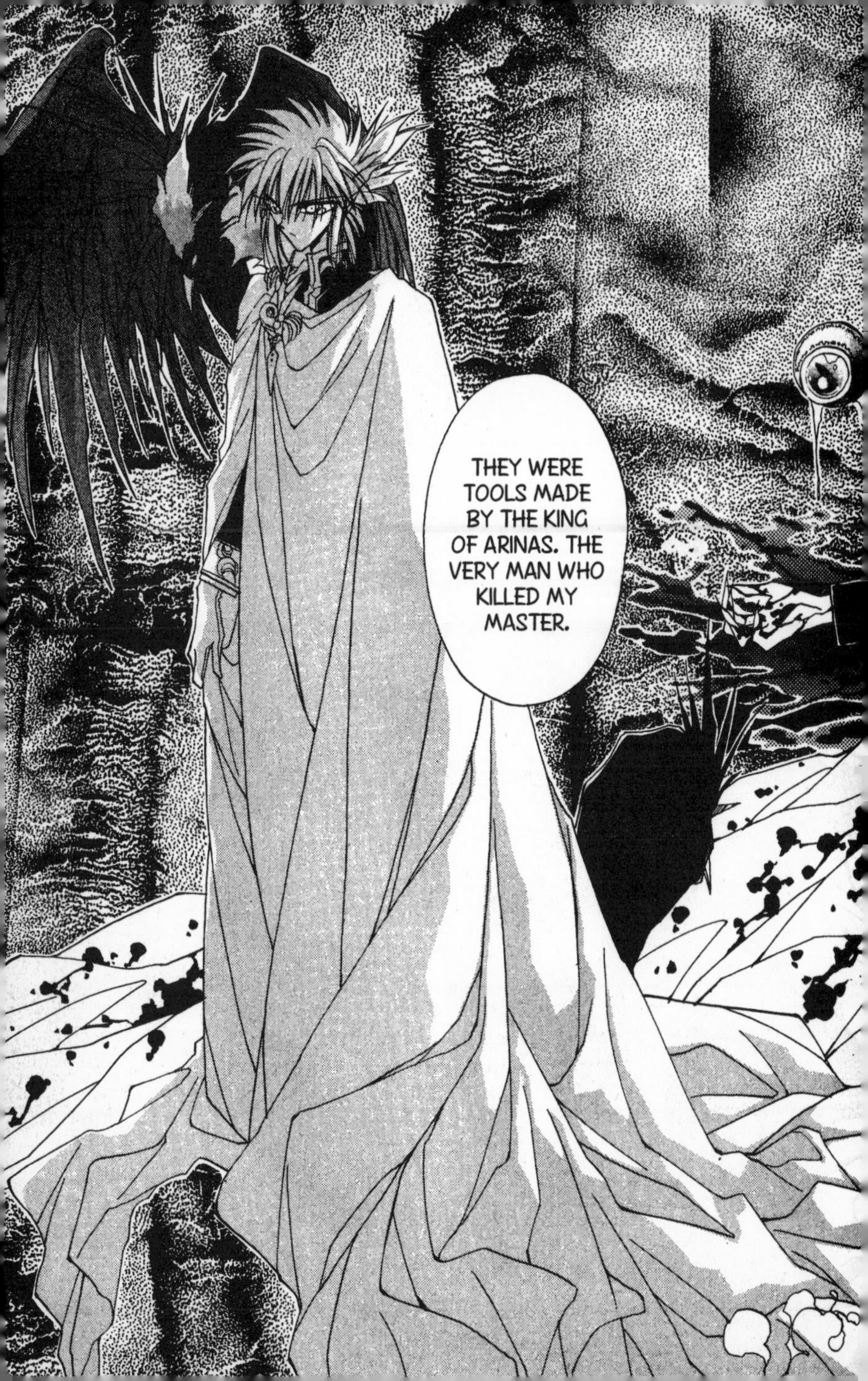
THEY WERE TOOLS MADE BY THE KING OF ARINAS. THE VERY MAN WHO KILLED MY MASTER.

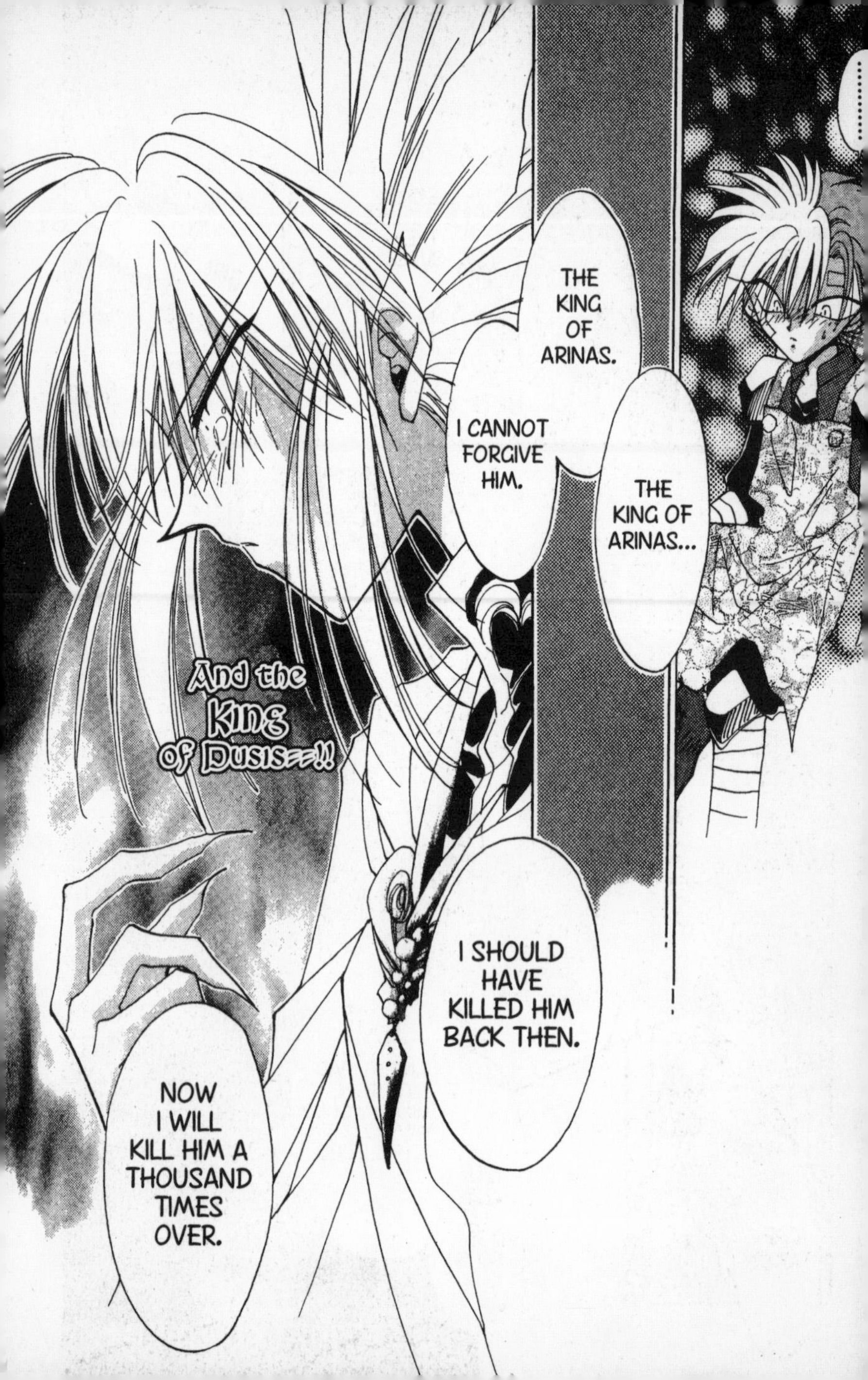
......
THE KING OF ARINAS...
THE KING OF ARINAS.
I CANNOT FORGIVE HIM.
And the King of Dusis——!!
I SHOULD HAVE KILLED HIM BACK THEN.
NOW I WILL KILL HIM A THOUSAND TIMES OVER.

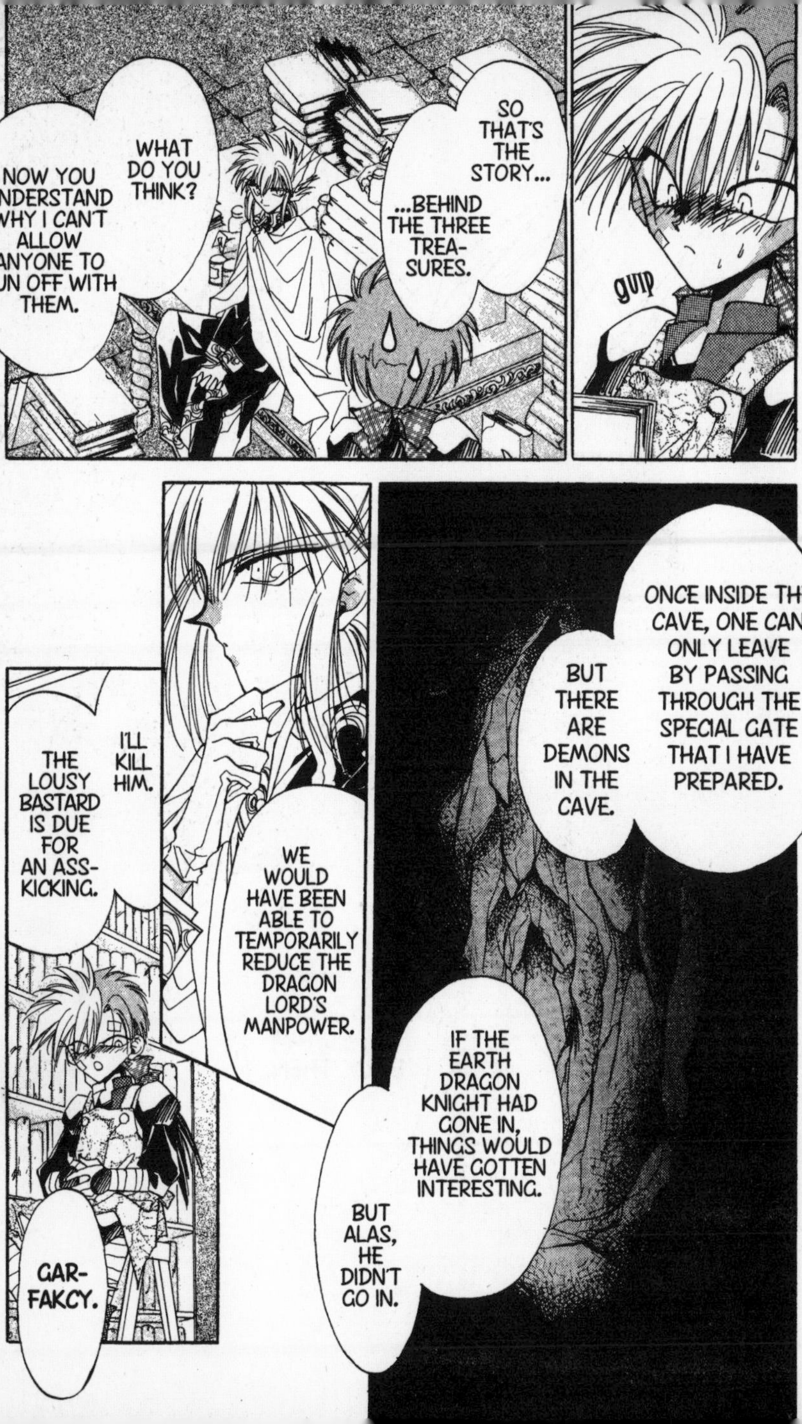
gulp
SO THAT'S THE STORY...
...BEHIND THE THREE TREA-SURES.
WHAT DO YOU THINK?
NOW YOU UNDERSTAND WHY I CAN'T ALLOW ANYONE TO RUN OFF WITH THEM.
ONCE INSIDE THE CAVE, ONE CAN ONLY LEAVE BY PASSING THROUGH THE SPECIAL GATE THAT I HAVE PREPARED.
BUT THERE ARE DEMONS IN THE CAVE.
IF THE EARTH DRAGON KNIGHT HAD GONE IN, THINGS WOULD HAVE GOTTEN INTERESTING.
BUT ALAS, HE DIDN'T GO IN.
WE WOULD HAVE BEEN ABLE TO TEMPORARILY REDUCE THE DRAGON LORD'S MANPOWER.
I'LL KILL HIM.
THE LOUSY BASTARD IS DUE FOR AN ASS-KICKING.
GAR-FAKCY.

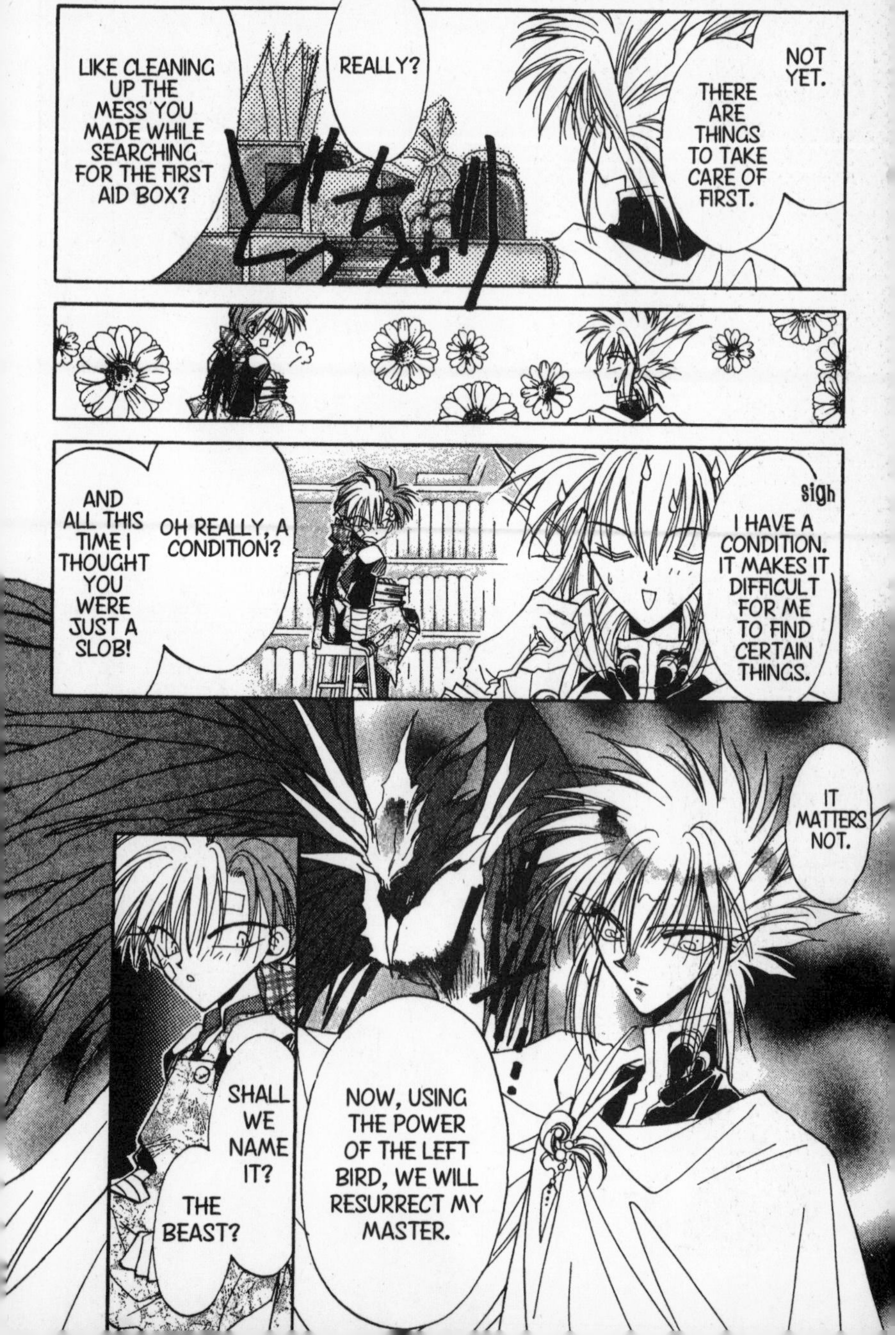
NOT YET.
THERE ARE THINGS TO TAKE CARE OF FIRST.
REALLY?
LIKE CLEANING UP THE MESS YOU MADE WHILE SEARCHING FOR THE FIRST AID BOX?
sigh
I HAVE A CONDITION. IT MAKES IT DIFFICULT FOR ME TO FIND CERTAIN THINGS.
OH REALLY, A CONDITION?
AND ALL THIS TIME I THOUGHT YOU WERE JUST A SLOB!
IT MATTERS NOT.
NOW, USING THE POWER OF THE LEFT BIRD, WE WILL RESURRECT MY MASTER.
SHALL WE NAME IT?
THE BEAST?

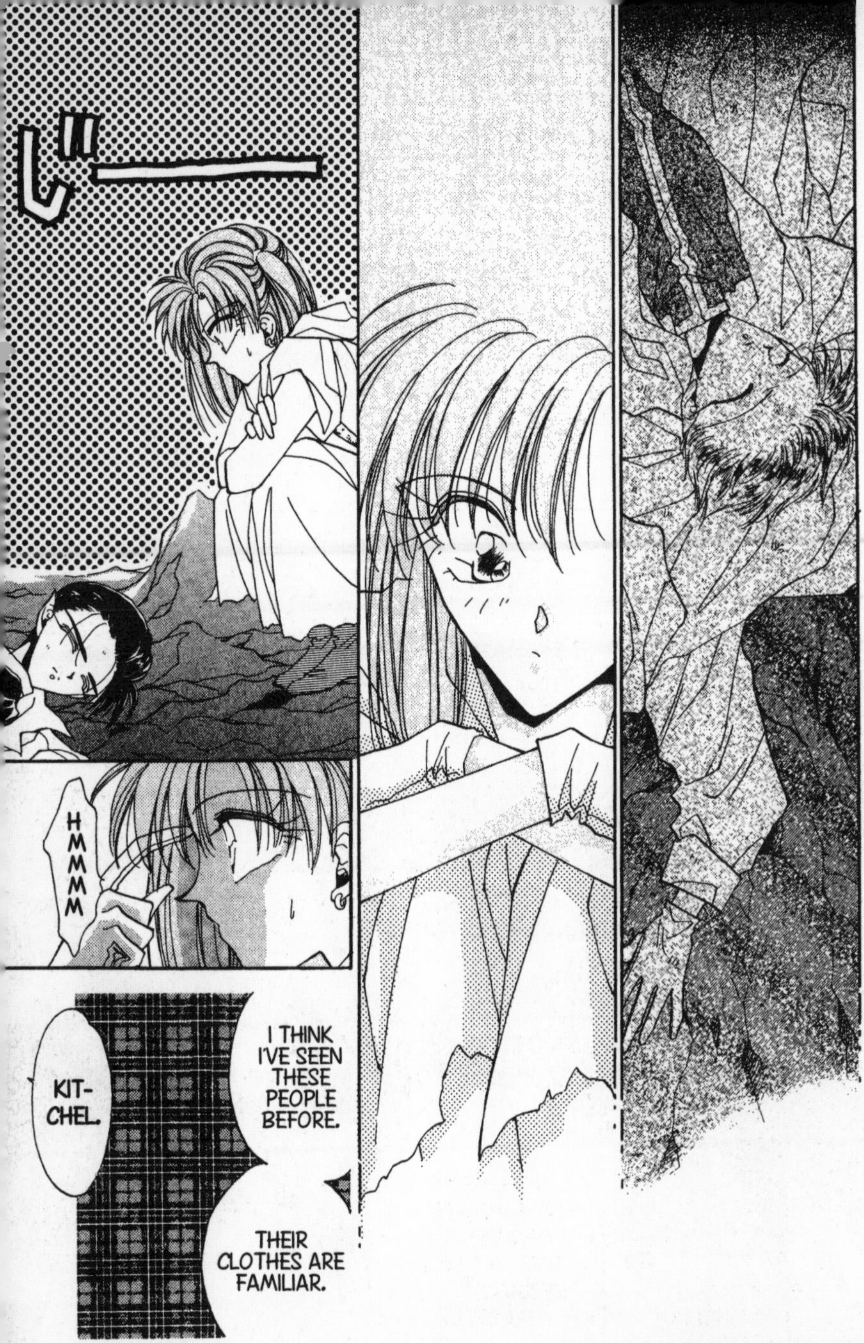
じー
HMMMM
I THINK I'VE SEEN THESE PEOPLE BEFORE.
KIT-CHEL.
THEIR CLOTHES ARE FAMILIAR.

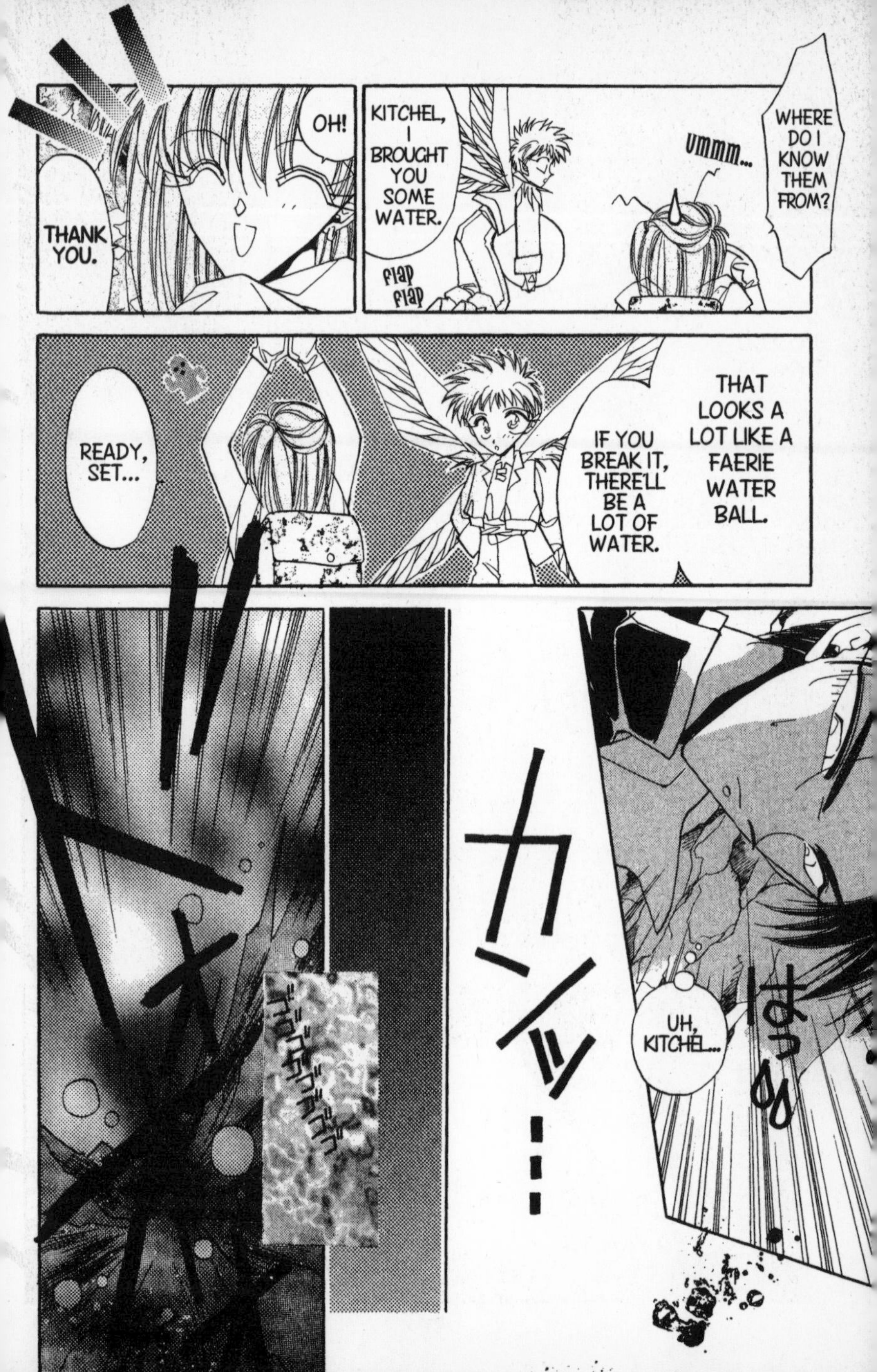
WHERE DO I KNOW THEM FROM?
UMMM...
KITCHEL, I BROUGHT YOU SOME WATER.
FLAP FLAP
OH!
THANK YOU.
THAT LOOKS A LOT LIKE A FAERIE WATER BALL.
IF YOU BREAK IT, THERE'LL BE A LOT OF WATER.
READY, SET...
UH, KITCHEL...

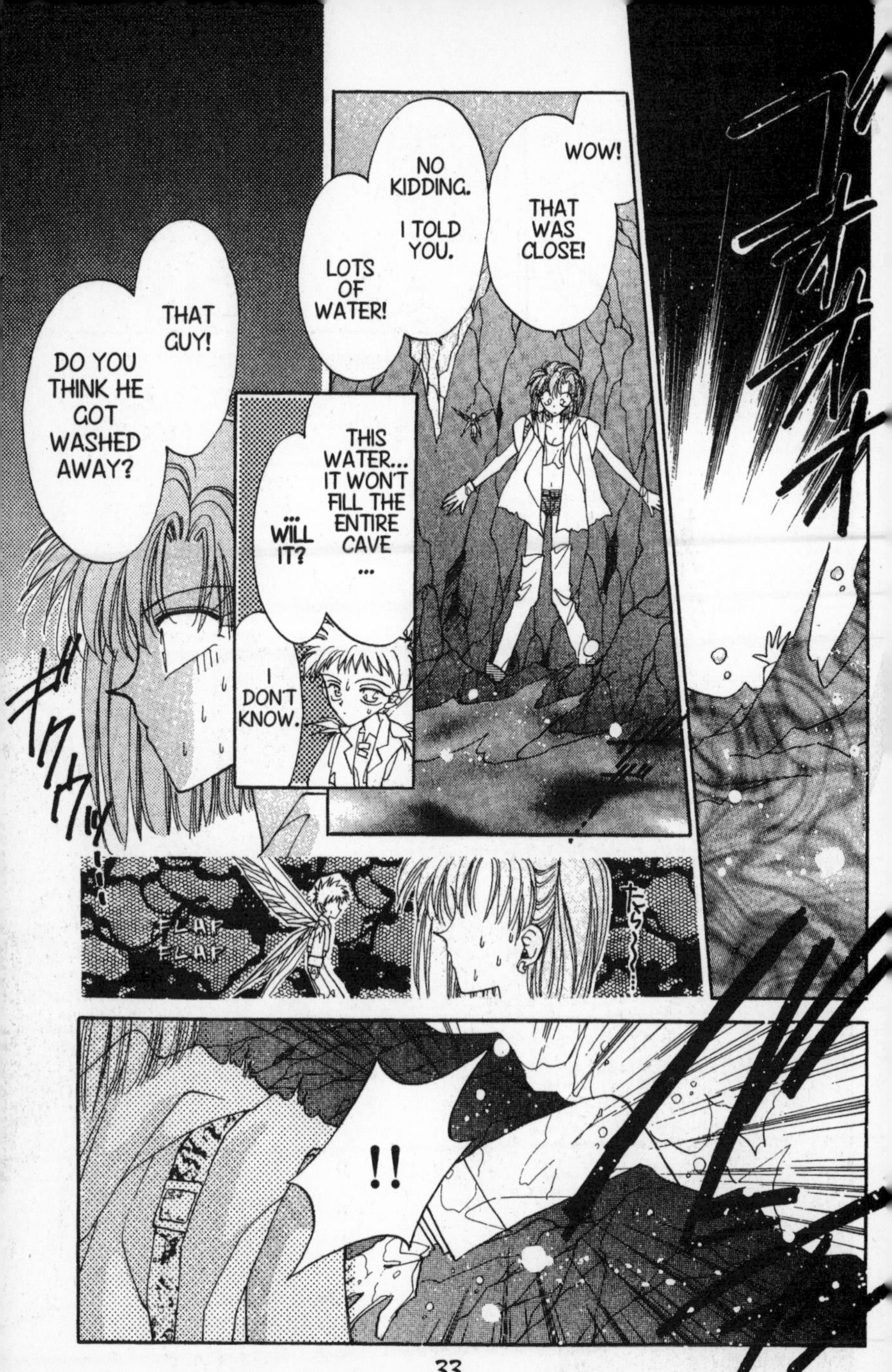
WOW!
THAT WAS CLOSE!
NO KIDDING.
I TOLD YOU.
LOTS OF WATER!
THIS WATER... IT WON'T FILL THE ENTIRE CAVE ...
... WILL IT?
I DON'T KNOW.
THAT GUY!
DO YOU THINK HE GOT WASHED AWAY?
たら~
FLAP FLAP
!!

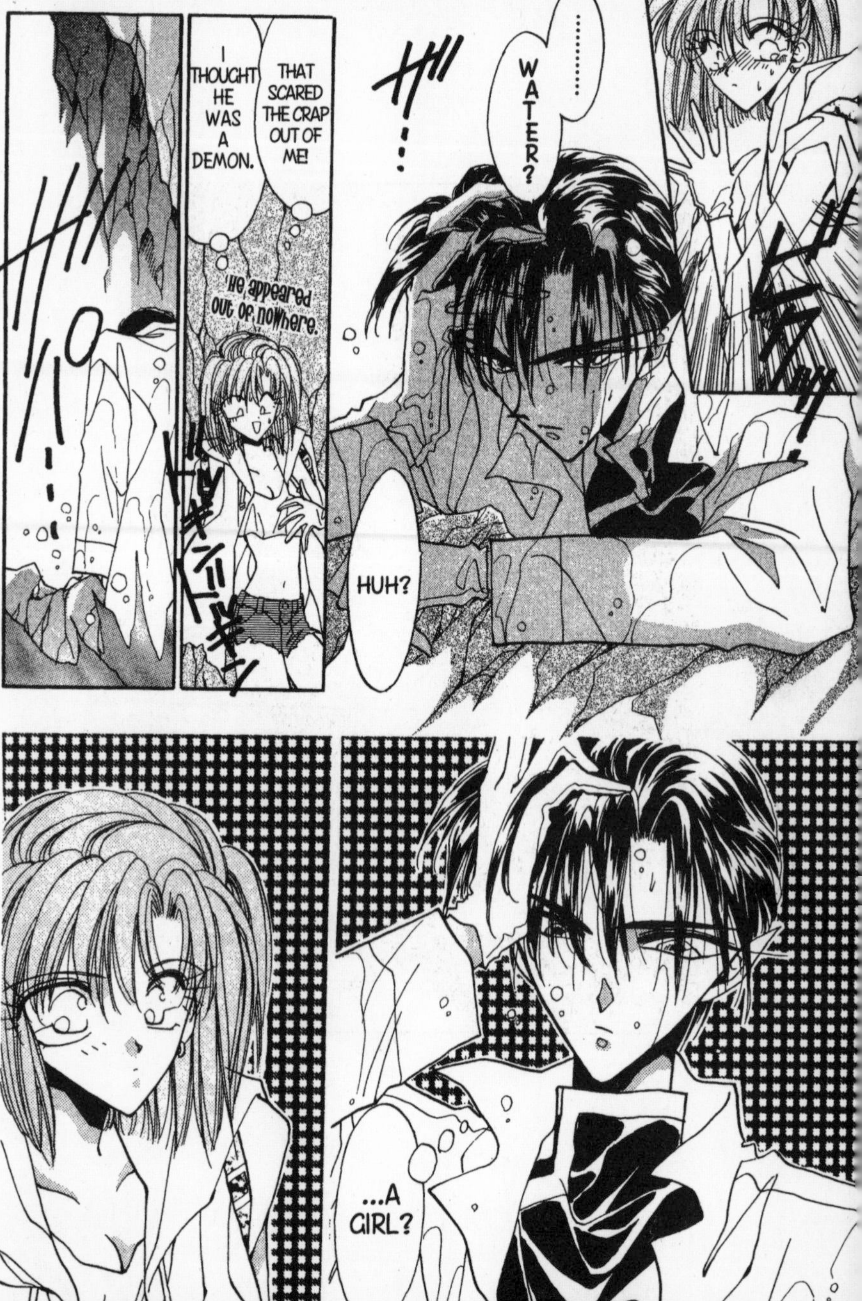
......
WATER?
HUH?
THAT SCARED THE CRAP OUT OF ME!
I THOUGHT HE WAS A DEMON.
He appeared out of nowhere.
...A GIRL?

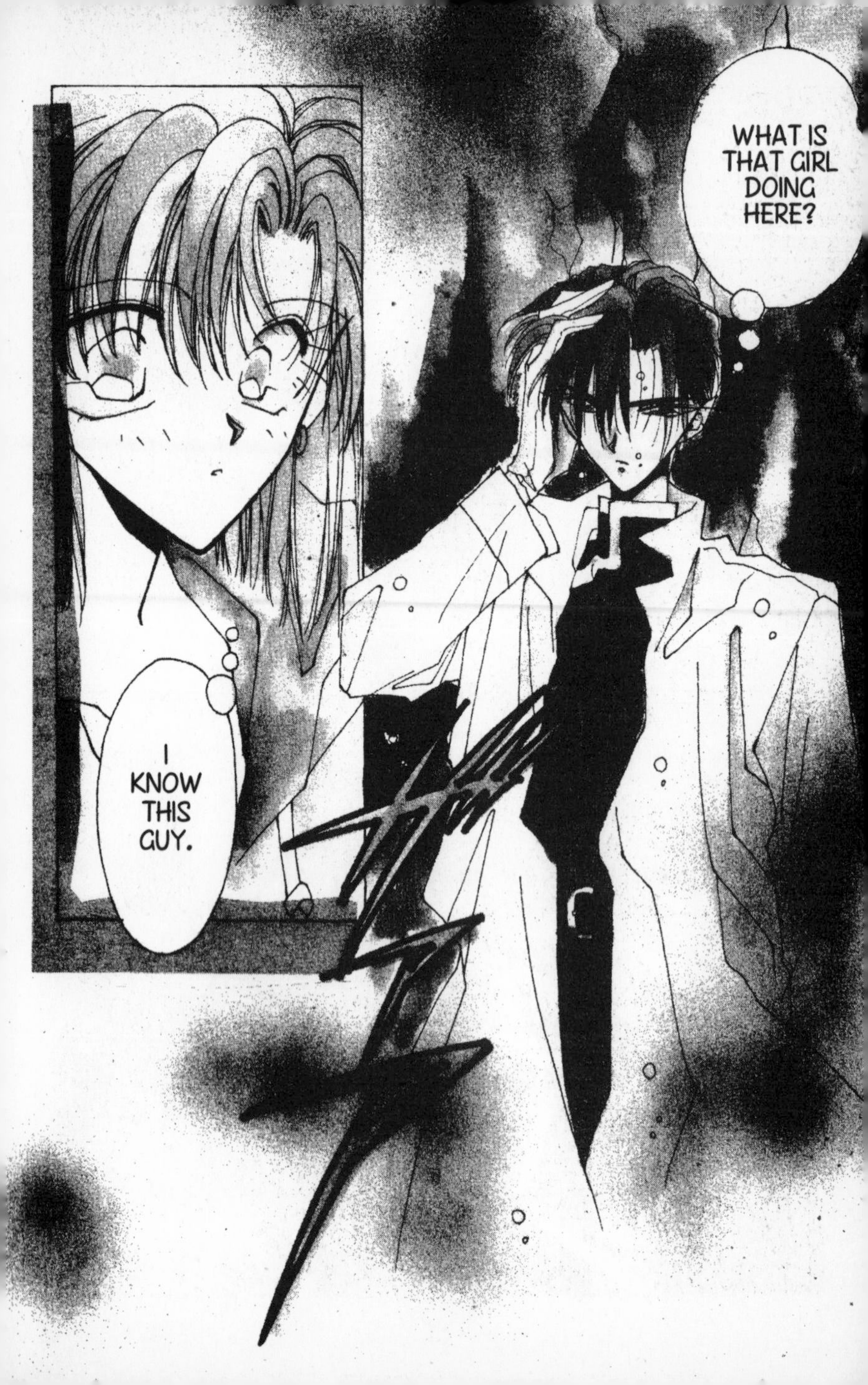
WHAT IS THAT GIRL DOING HERE?
I KNOW THIS GUY.

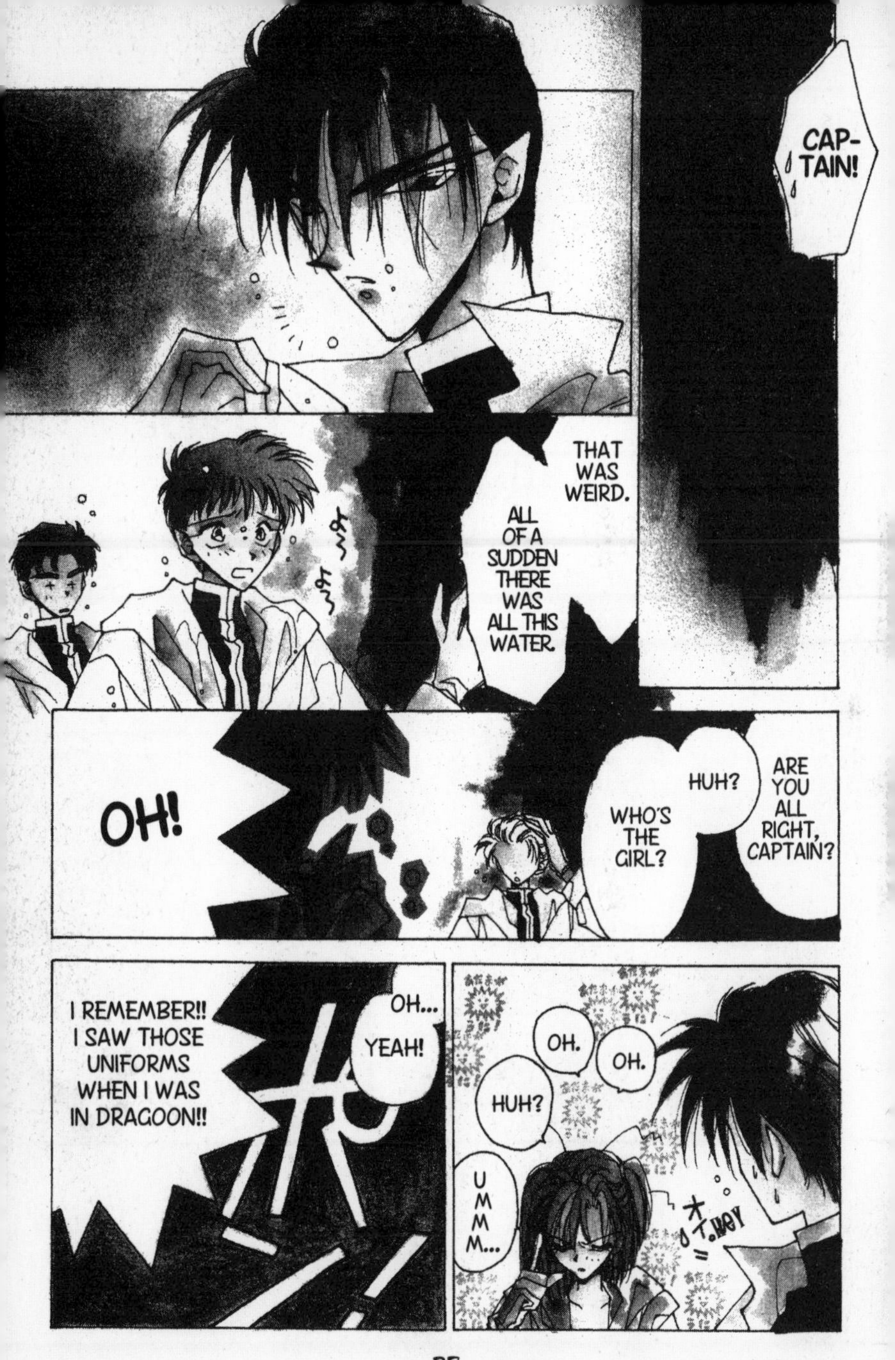
CAP-TAIN!
THAT WAS WEIRD.
ALL OF A SUDDEN THERE WAS ALL THIS WATER.
ARE YOU ALL RIGHT, CAPTAIN?
HUH?
WHO'S THE GIRL?
OH!
OH.
OH.
HUH?
UMMM...
HEY
OH...
YEAH!
I REMEMBER!! I SAW THOSE UNIFORMS WHEN I WAS IN DRAGOON!!

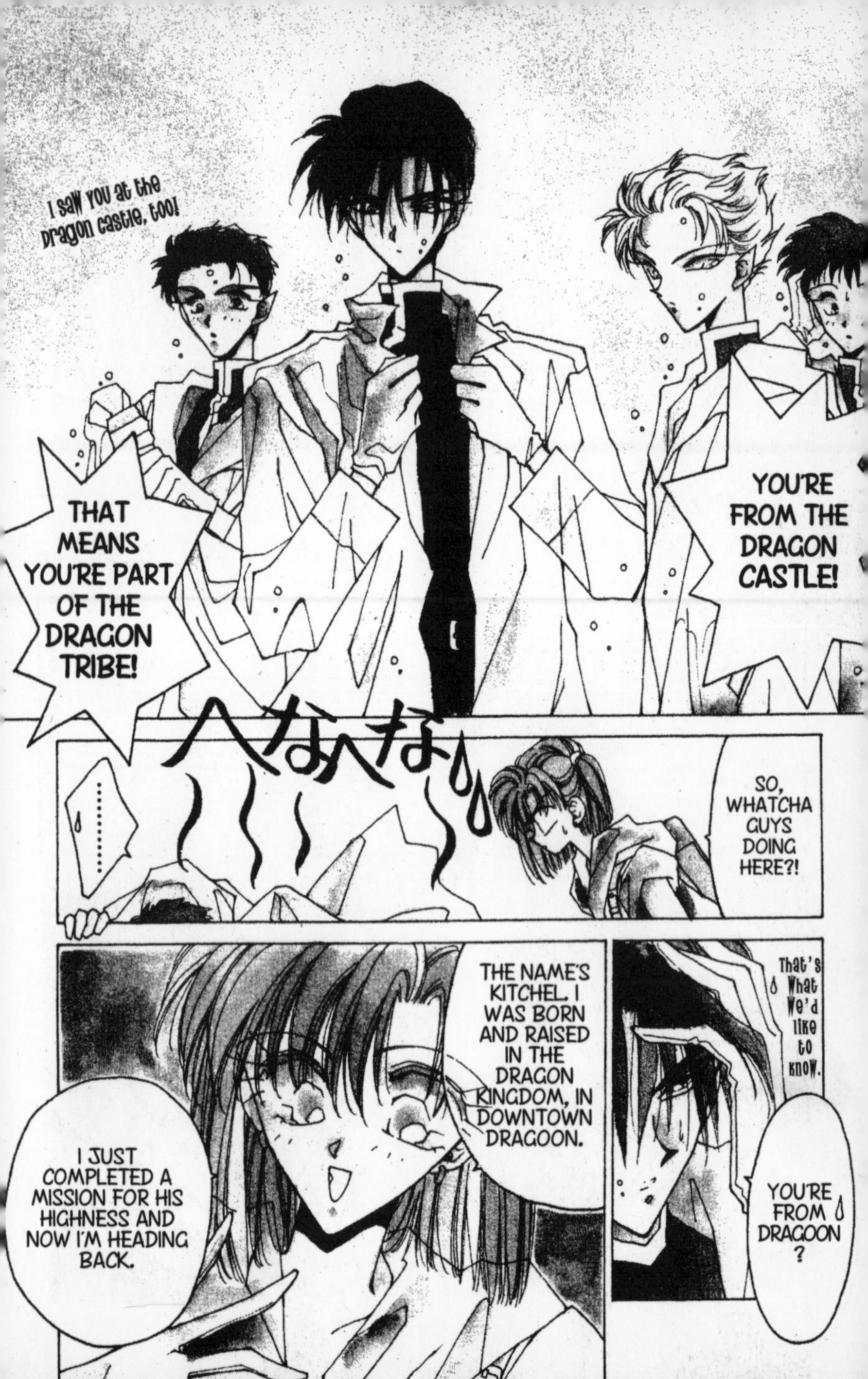
YOU'RE FROM THE DRAGON CASTLE!
I saw you at the Dragon castle, too!
THAT MEANS YOU'RE PART OF THE DRAGON TRIBE!
SO, WHATCHA GUYS DOING HERE?!
へなへな
......
That's what we'd like to know.
YOU'RE FROM DRAGOON?
THE NAME'S KITCHEL. I WAS BORN AND RAISED IN THE DRAGON KINGDOM, IN DOWNTOWN DRAGOON.
I JUST COMPLETED A MISSION FOR HIS HIGHNESS AND NOW I'M HEADING BACK.

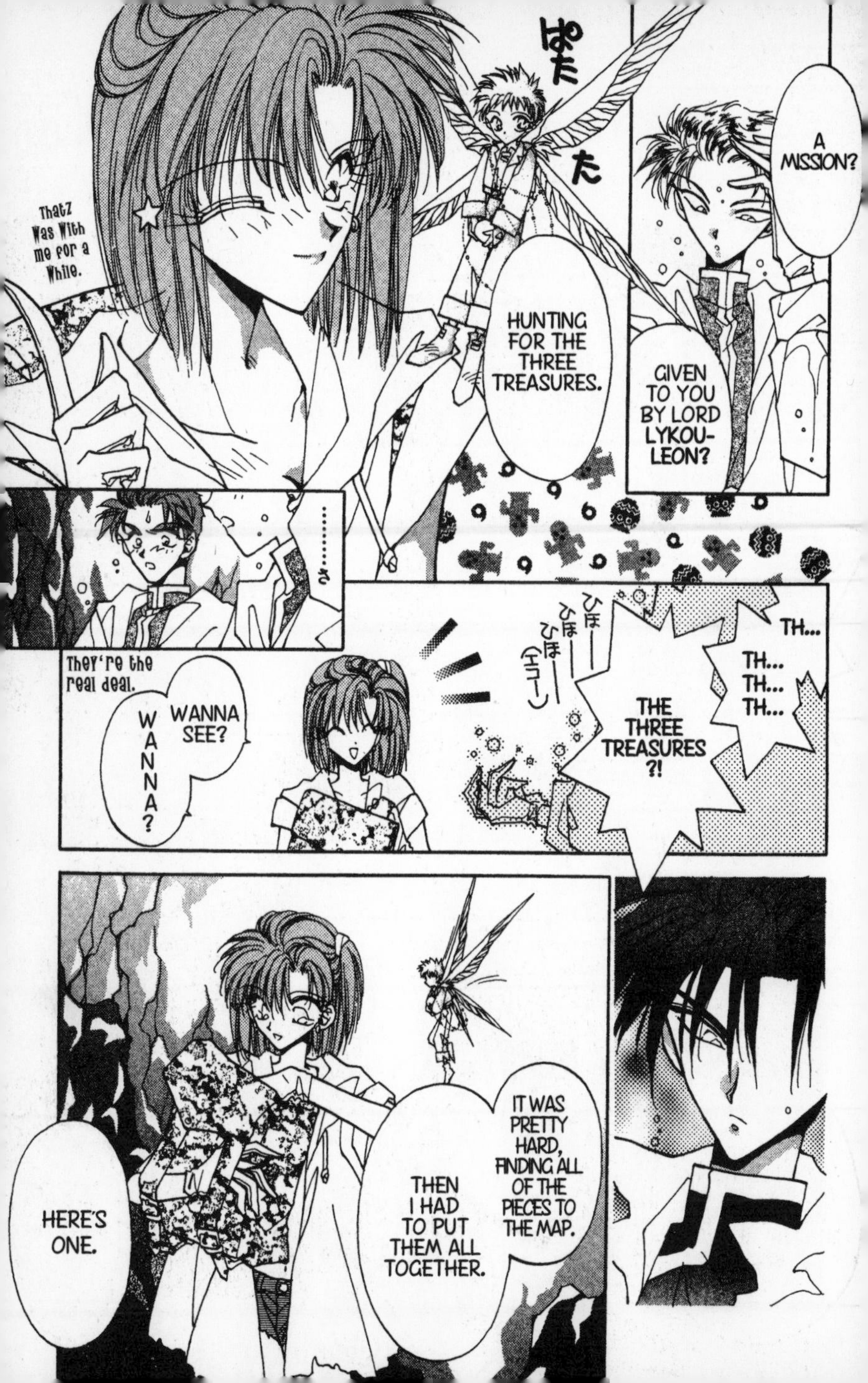
A MISSION?
GIVEN TO YOU BY LORD LYKOU-LEON?
ぱた
た
HUNTING FOR THE THREE TREASURES.
Thatz was with me for a while.
......さ
TH...
TH... TH... TH...
THE THREE TREASURES?!
ひほー ひほー ひほー (エコー)
They're the real deal.
WANNA SEE?
WANNA?
IT WAS PRETTY HARD, FINDING ALL OF THE PIECES TO THE MAP.
THEN I HAD TO PUT THEM ALL TOGETHER.
HERE'S ONE.

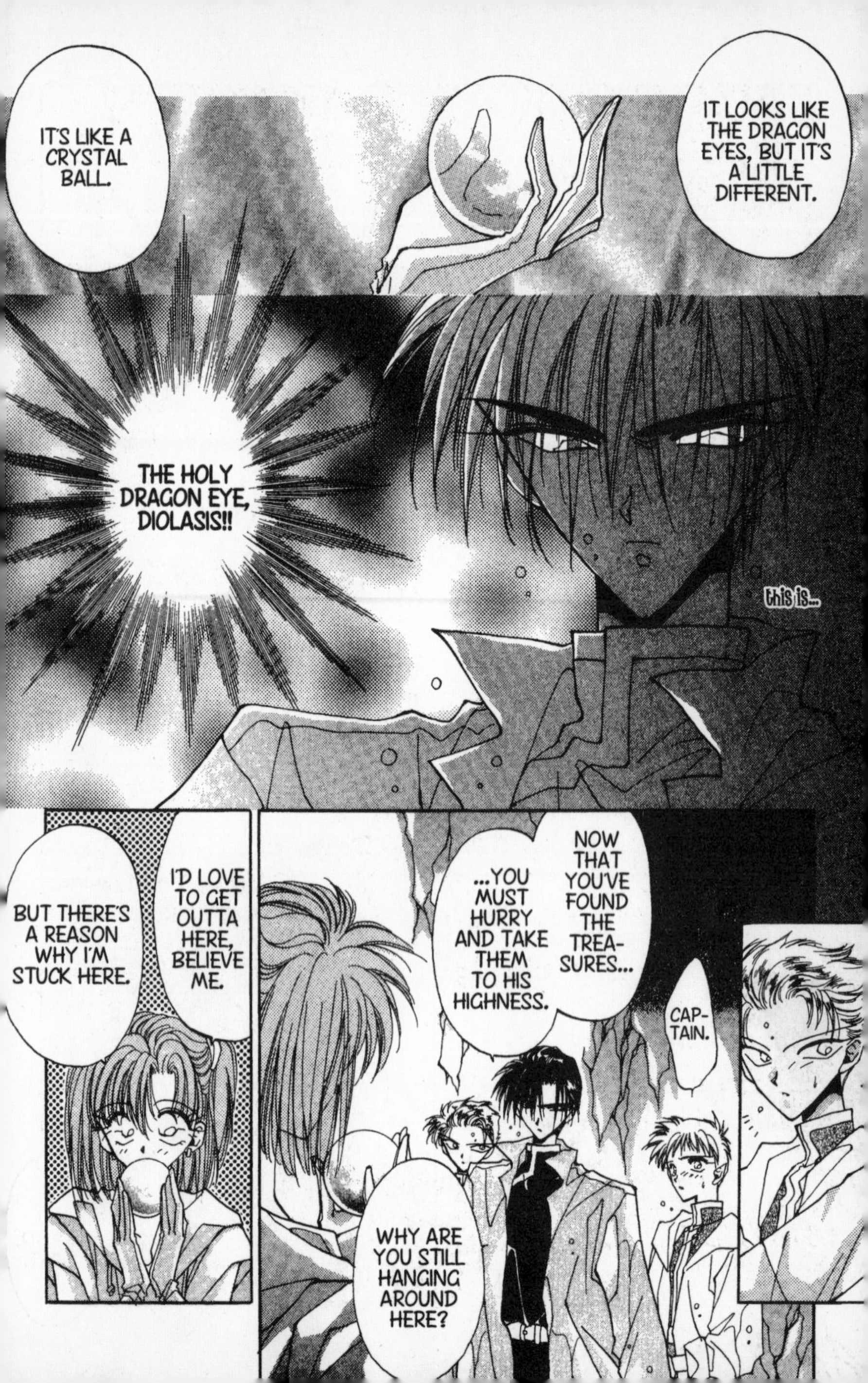
IT LOOKS LIKE THE DRAGON EYES, BUT IT'S A LITTLE DIFFERENT.
IT'S LIKE A CRYSTAL BALL.
this is...
THE HOLY DRAGON EYE, DIOLASIS!!
NOW THAT YOU'VE FOUND THE TREA-SURES...
...YOU MUST HURRY AND TAKE THEM TO HIS HIGHNESS.
CAP-TAIN.
WHY ARE YOU STILL HANGING AROUND HERE?
I'D LOVE TO GET OUTTA HERE, BELIEVE ME.
BUT THERE'S A REASON WHY I'M STUCK HERE.

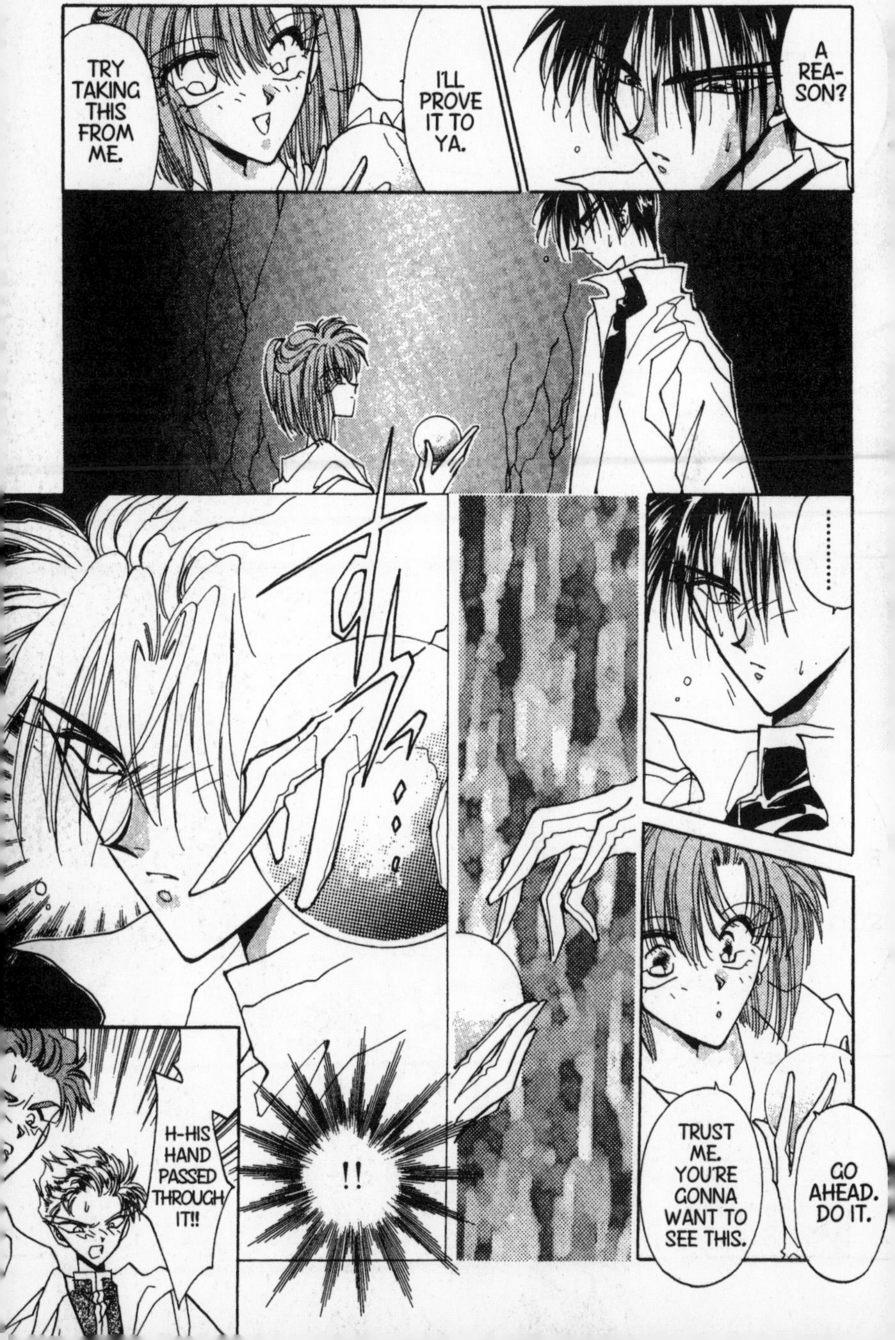
A REA-SON?
I'LL PROVE IT TO YA.
TRY TAKING THIS FROM ME.
GO AHEAD. DO IT.
TRUST ME. YOU'RE GONNA WANT TO SEE THIS.
!!
H-HIS HAND PASSED THROUGH IT!!

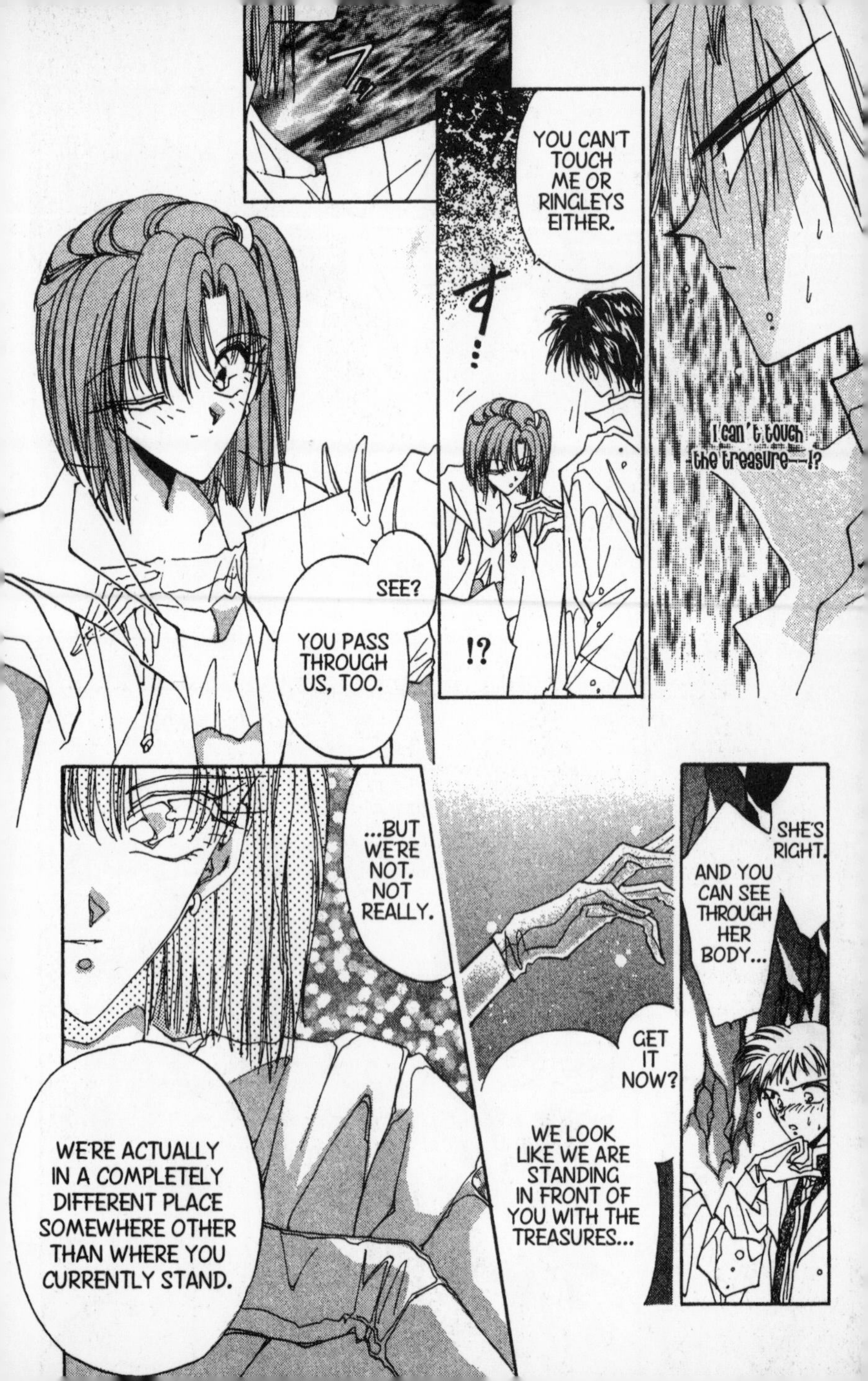
I can't touch the treasure--!?
YOU CAN'T TOUCH ME OR RINGLEYS EITHER.
す
!?
SEE?
YOU PASS THROUGH US, TOO.
SHE'S RIGHT.
AND YOU CAN SEE THROUGH HER BODY...
GET IT NOW?
WE LOOK LIKE WE ARE STANDING IN FRONT OF YOU WITH THE TREASURES...
...BUT WE'RE NOT. NOT REALLY.
WE'RE ACTUALLY IN A COMPLETELY DIFFERENT PLACE SOMEWHERE OTHER THAN WHERE YOU CURRENTLY STAND.

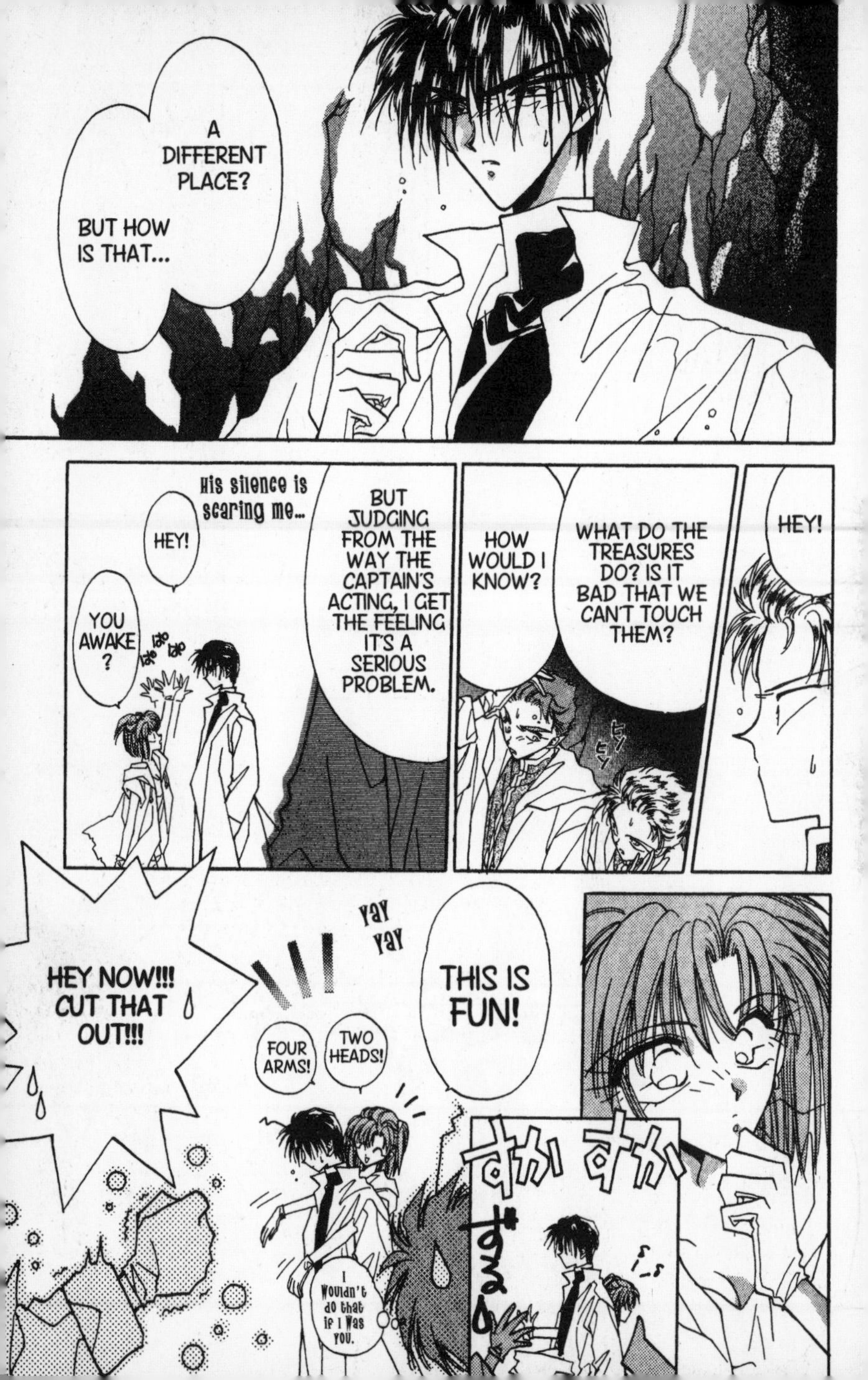
A DIFFERENT PLACE?
BUT HOW IS THAT...
HEY!
WHAT DO THE TREASURES DO? IS IT BAD THAT WE CAN'T TOUCH THEM?
HOW WOULD I KNOW?
ヒソ ヒソ
BUT JUDGING FROM THE WAY THE CAPTAIN'S ACTING, I GET THE FEELING IT'S A SERIOUS PROBLEM.
His silence is scaring me...
HEY!
YOU AWAKE?
すか すか
ずる
THIS IS FUN!
yay yay
TWO HEADS!
FOUR ARMS!
I wouldn't do that if I was you.
HEY NOW!!! CUT THAT OUT!!!

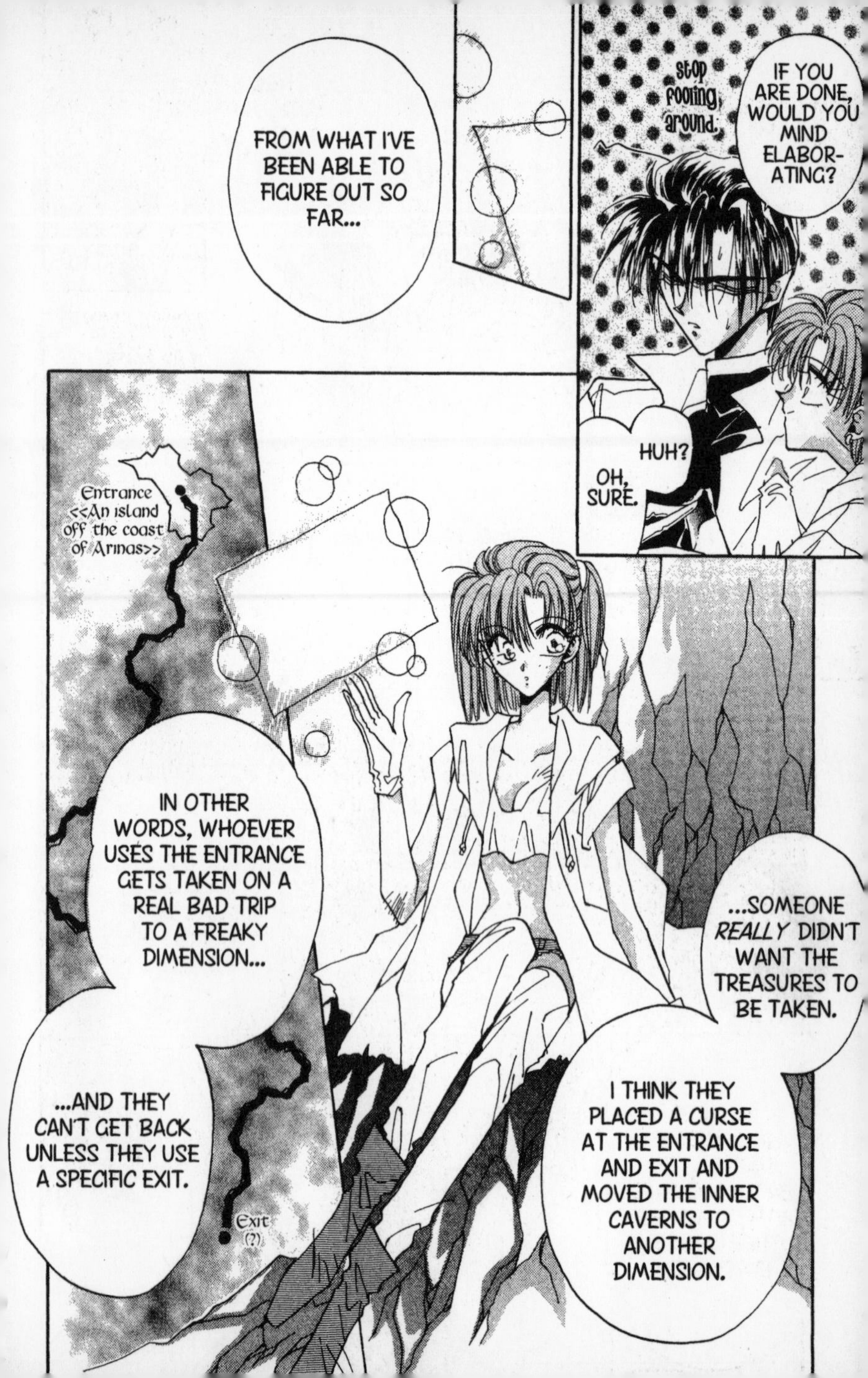
IF YOU ARE DONE, WOULD YOU MIND ELABOR-ATING?
stop fooling around.
HUH?
OH, SURE.
FROM WHAT I'VE BEEN ABLE TO FIGURE OUT SO FAR...
I THINK THEY PLACED A CURSE AT THE ENTRANCE AND EXIT AND MOVED THE INNER CAVERNS TO ANOTHER DIMENSION.
IN OTHER WORDS, WHOEVER USES THE ENTRANCE GETS TAKEN ON A REAL BAD TRIP TO A FREAKY DIMENSION...
...AND THEY CAN'T GET BACK UNLESS THEY USE A SPECIFIC EXIT.
...SOMEONE *REALLY* DIDN'T WANT THE TREASURES TO BE TAKEN.
Entrance <<An island off the coast of Arinas>>
Exit (?)

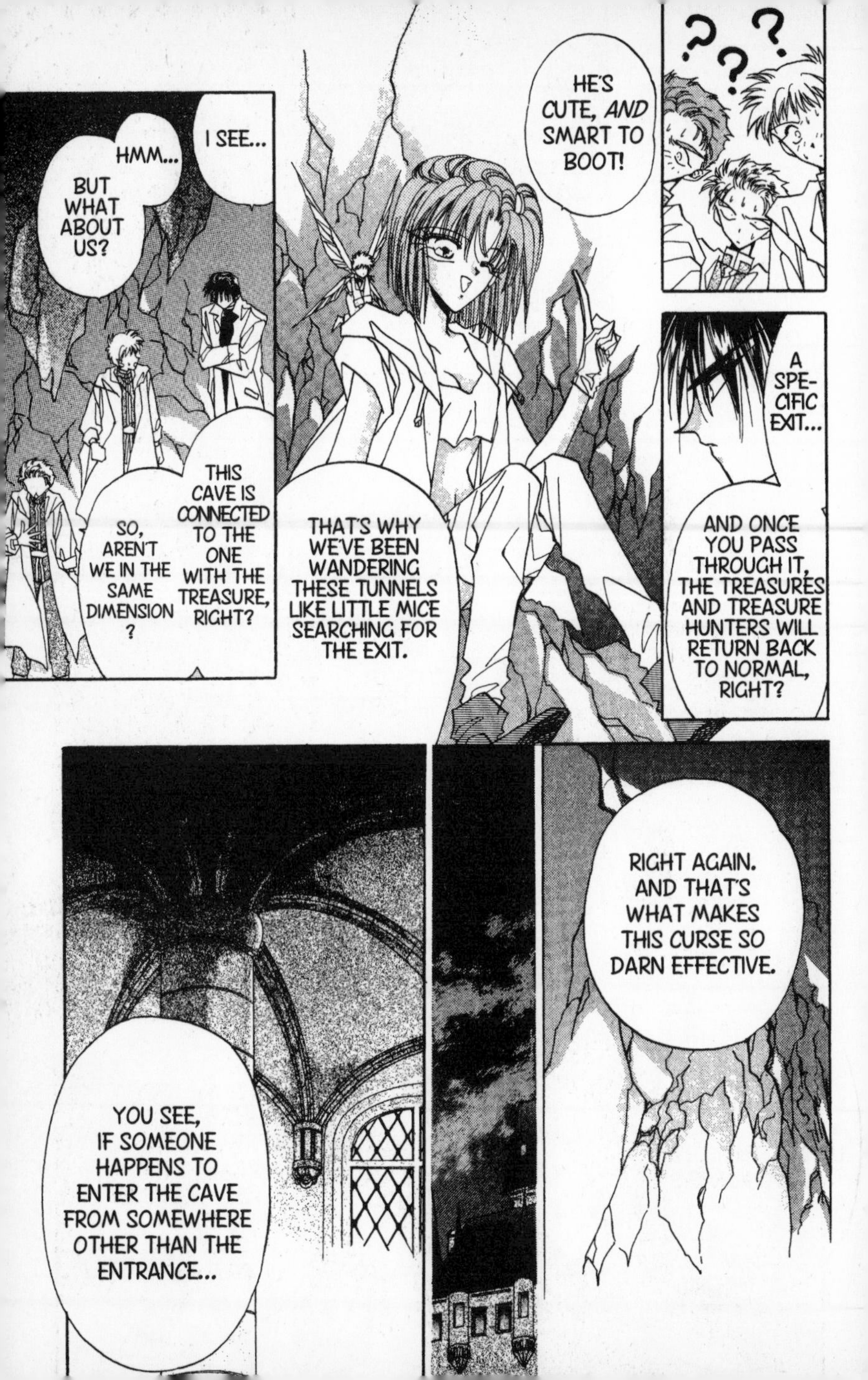
? ? ?
A SPE-CIFIC EXIT...
AND ONCE YOU PASS THROUGH IT, THE TREASURES AND TREASURE HUNTERS WILL RETURN BACK TO NORMAL, RIGHT?
HE'S CUTE, *AND* SMART TO BOOT!
THAT'S WHY WE'VE BEEN WANDERING THESE TUNNELS LIKE LITTLE MICE SEARCHING FOR THE EXIT.
I SEE...
HMM...
BUT WHAT ABOUT US?
THIS CAVE IS CONNECTED TO THE ONE WITH THE TREASURE, RIGHT?
SO, AREN'T WE IN THE SAME DIMENSION ?
RIGHT AGAIN. AND THAT'S WHAT MAKES THIS CURSE SO DARN EFFECTIVE.
YOU SEE, IF SOMEONE HAPPENS TO ENTER THE CAVE FROM SOMEWHERE OTHER THAN THE ENTRANCE...

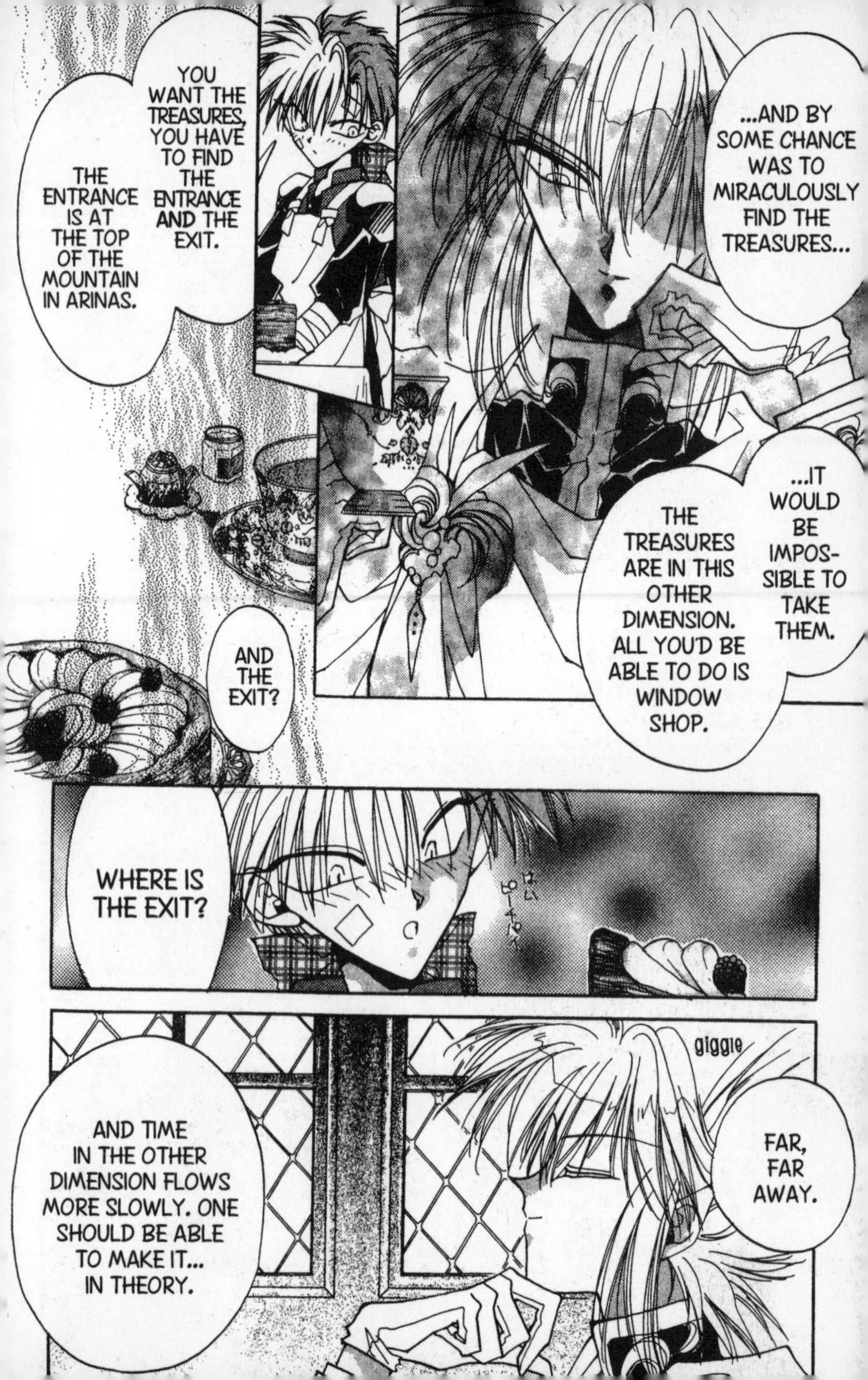
...AND BY SOME CHANCE WAS TO MIRACULOUSLY FIND THE TREASURES...
...IT WOULD BE IMPOS-SIBLE TO TAKE THEM.
THE TREASURES ARE IN THIS OTHER DIMENSION. ALL YOU'D BE ABLE TO DO IS WINDOW SHOP.
YOU WANT THE TREASURES, YOU HAVE TO FIND THE ENTRANCE AND THE EXIT.
THE ENTRANCE IS AT THE TOP OF THE MOUNTAIN IN ARINAS.
AND THE EXIT?
WHERE IS THE EXIT?
giggle
FAR, FAR AWAY.
AND TIME IN THE OTHER DIMENSION FLOWS MORE SLOWLY. ONE SHOULD BE ABLE TO MAKE IT... IN THEORY.

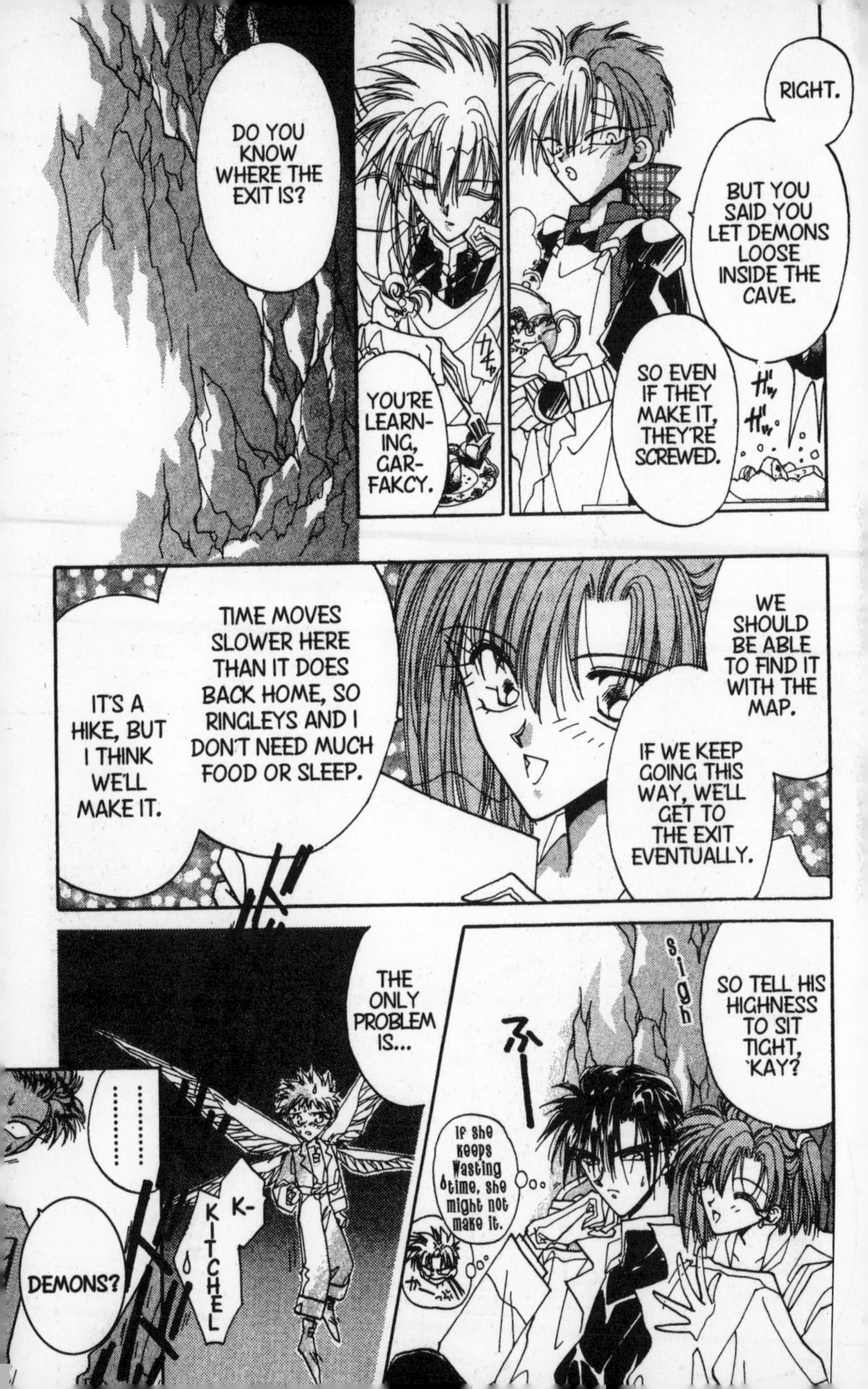
RIGHT.
BUT YOU SAID YOU LET DEMONS LOOSE INSIDE THE CAVE.
SO EVEN IF THEY MAKE IT, THEY'RE SCREWED.
YOU'RE LEARNING, GARFAKCY.
DO YOU KNOW WHERE THE EXIT IS?
WE SHOULD BE ABLE TO FIND IT WITH THE MAP.
IF WE KEEP GOING THIS WAY, WE'LL GET TO THE EXIT EVENTUALLY.
TIME MOVES SLOWER HERE THAN IT DOES BACK HOME, SO RINGLEYS AND I DON'T NEED MUCH FOOD OR SLEEP.
IT'S A HIKE, BUT I THINK WE'LL MAKE IT.
SO TELL HIS HIGHNESS TO SIT TIGHT, 'KAY?
sigh
ふー
If she keeps wasting time, she might not make it.
THE ONLY PROBLEM IS...
......
K-KITCHEL
DEMONS?

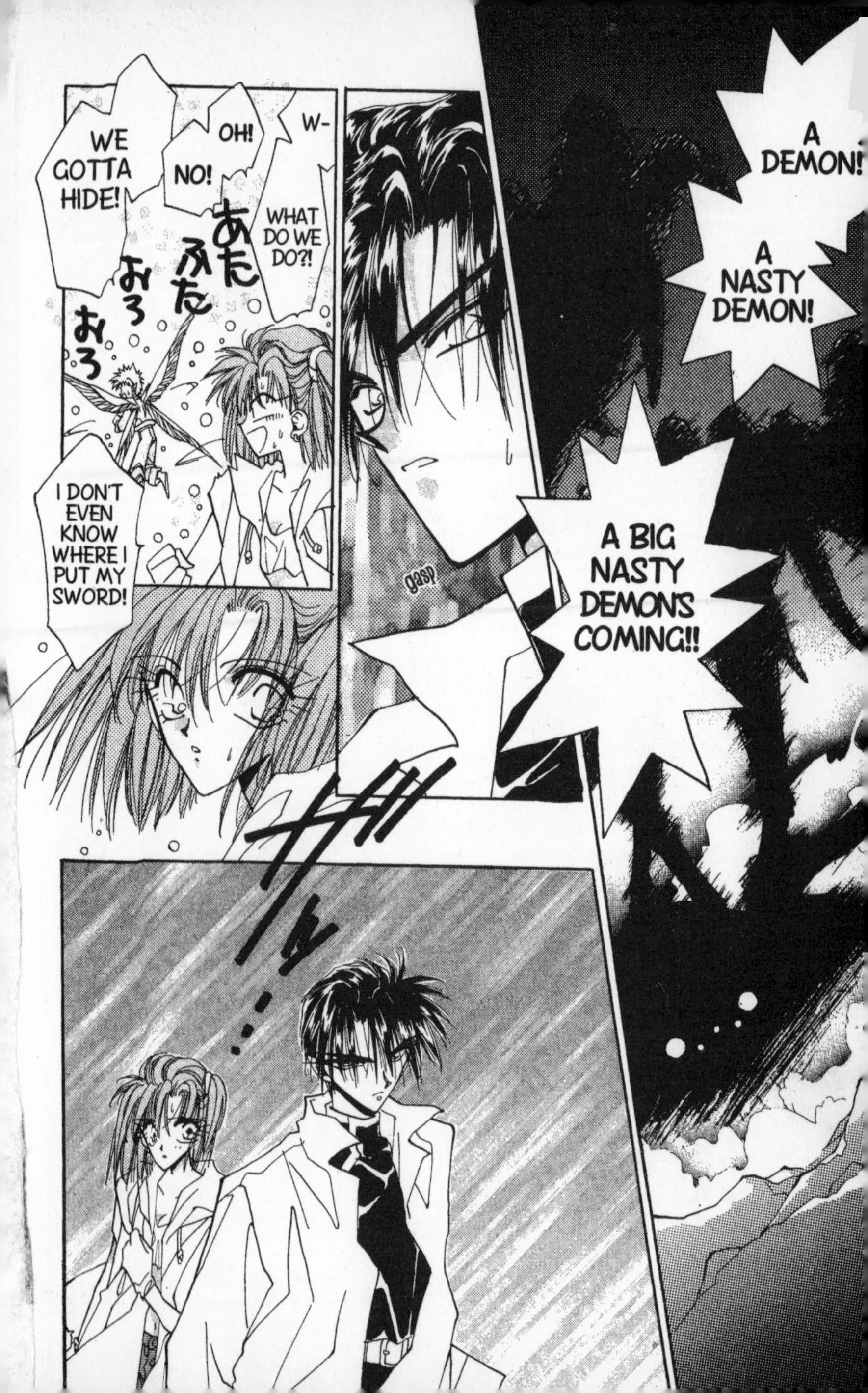
A DEMON!
A NASTY DEMON!
A BIG NASTY DEMON'S COMING!!
gasp
W-
OH!
NO!
WE GOTTA HIDE!
WHAT DO WE DO?!
あたふた
おろおろ
I DON'T EVEN KNOW WHERE I PUT MY SWORD!

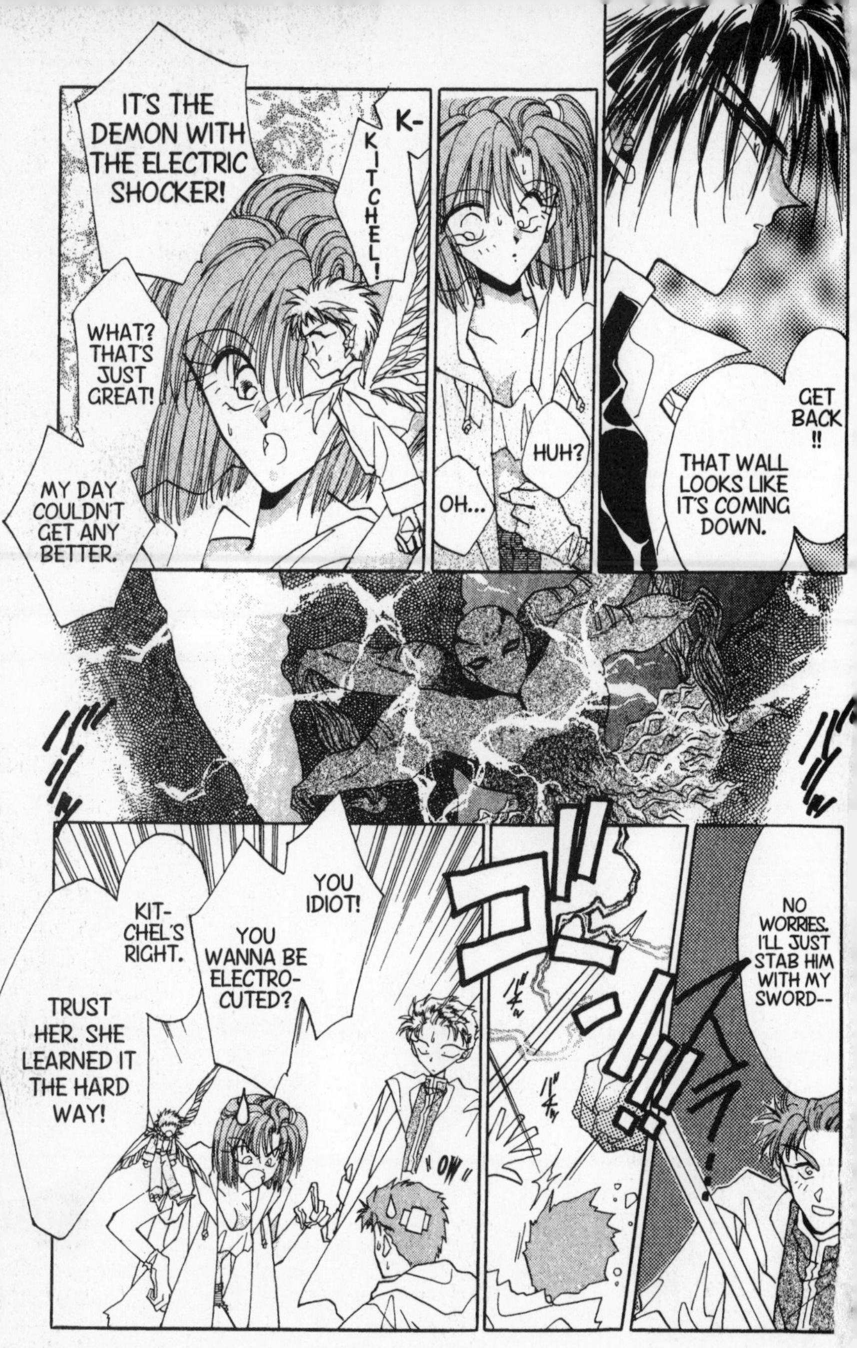
GET BACK!!
THAT WALL LOOKS LIKE IT'S COMING DOWN.
HUH?
OH...
IT'S THE DEMON WITH THE ELECTRIC SHOCKER!
K-KITCHEL!
WHAT? THAT'S JUST GREAT!
MY DAY COULDN'T GET ANY BETTER.
NO WORRIES. I'LL JUST STAB HIM WITH MY SWORD--
YOU IDIOT!
YOU WANNA BE ELECTROCUTED?
KIT-CHEL'S RIGHT.
TRUST HER. SHE LEARNED IT THE HARD WAY!
"OW"

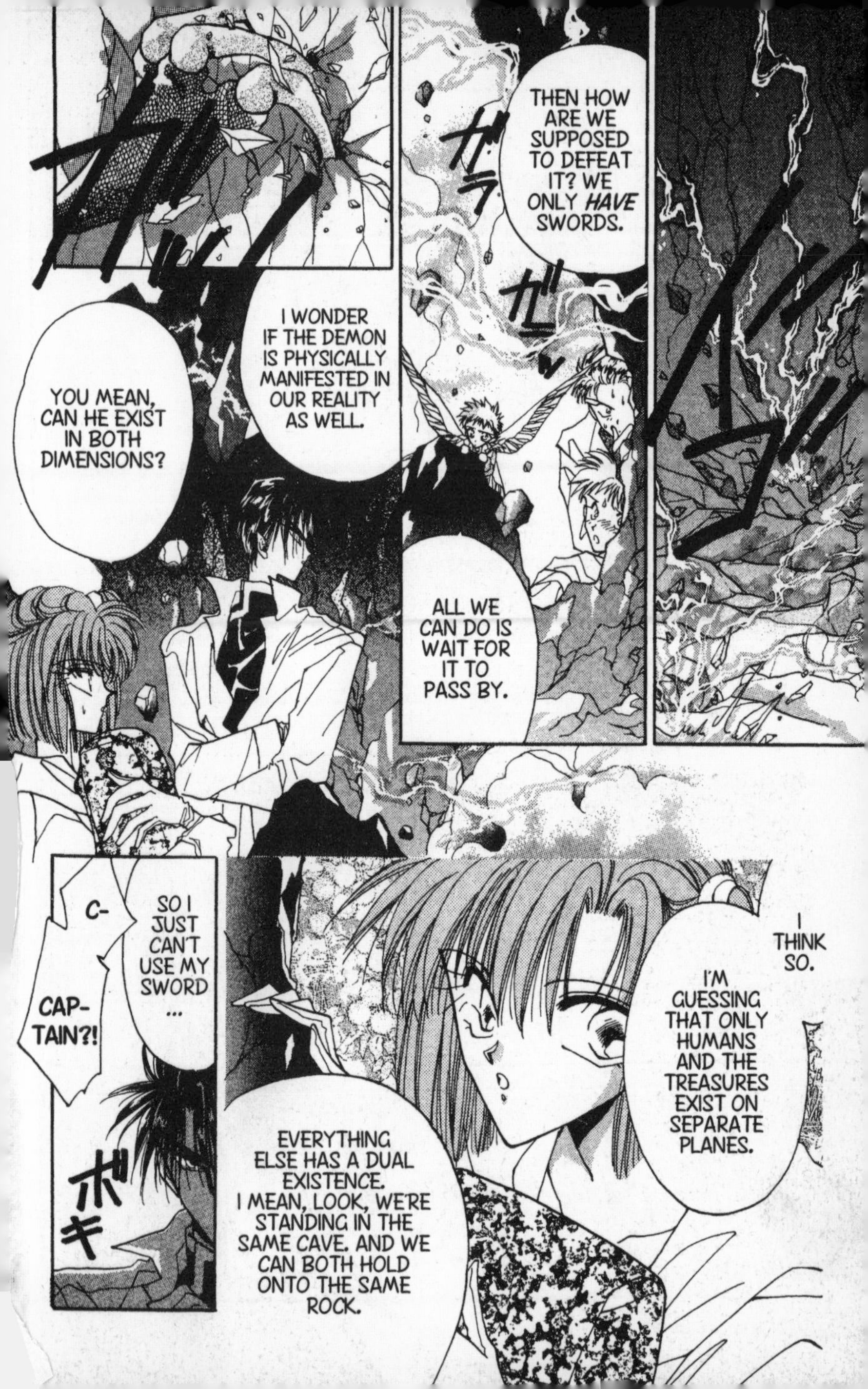
THEN HOW ARE WE SUPPOSED TO DEFEAT IT? WE ONLY *HAVE* SWORDS.
ALL WE CAN DO IS WAIT FOR IT TO PASS BY.
I WONDER IF THE DEMON IS PHYSICALLY MANIFESTED IN OUR REALITY AS WELL.
YOU MEAN, CAN HE EXIST IN BOTH DIMENSIONS?
I THINK SO.
I'M GUESSING THAT ONLY HUMANS AND THE TREASURES EXIST ON SEPARATE PLANES.
EVERYTHING ELSE HAS A DUAL EXISTENCE. I MEAN, LOOK, WE'RE STANDING IN THE SAME CAVE. AND WE CAN BOTH HOLD ONTO THE SAME ROCK.
SO I JUST CAN'T USE MY SWORD ...
ボキ
C- CAP- TAIN?!

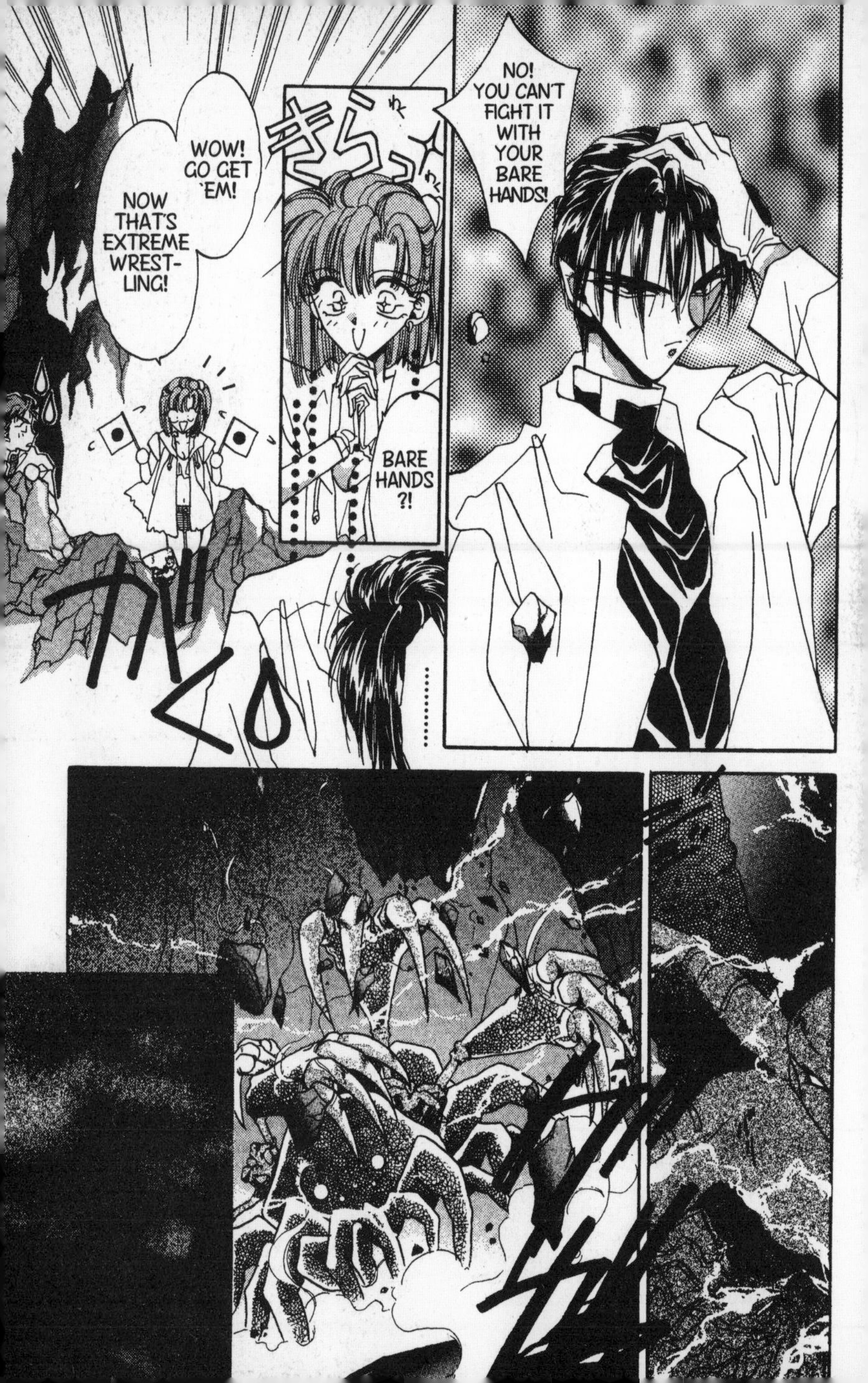
NO! YOU CAN'T FIGHT IT WITH YOUR BARE HANDS!
きらっ
BARE HANDS ?!
WOW! GO GET 'EM!
NOW THAT'S EXTREME WREST-LING!

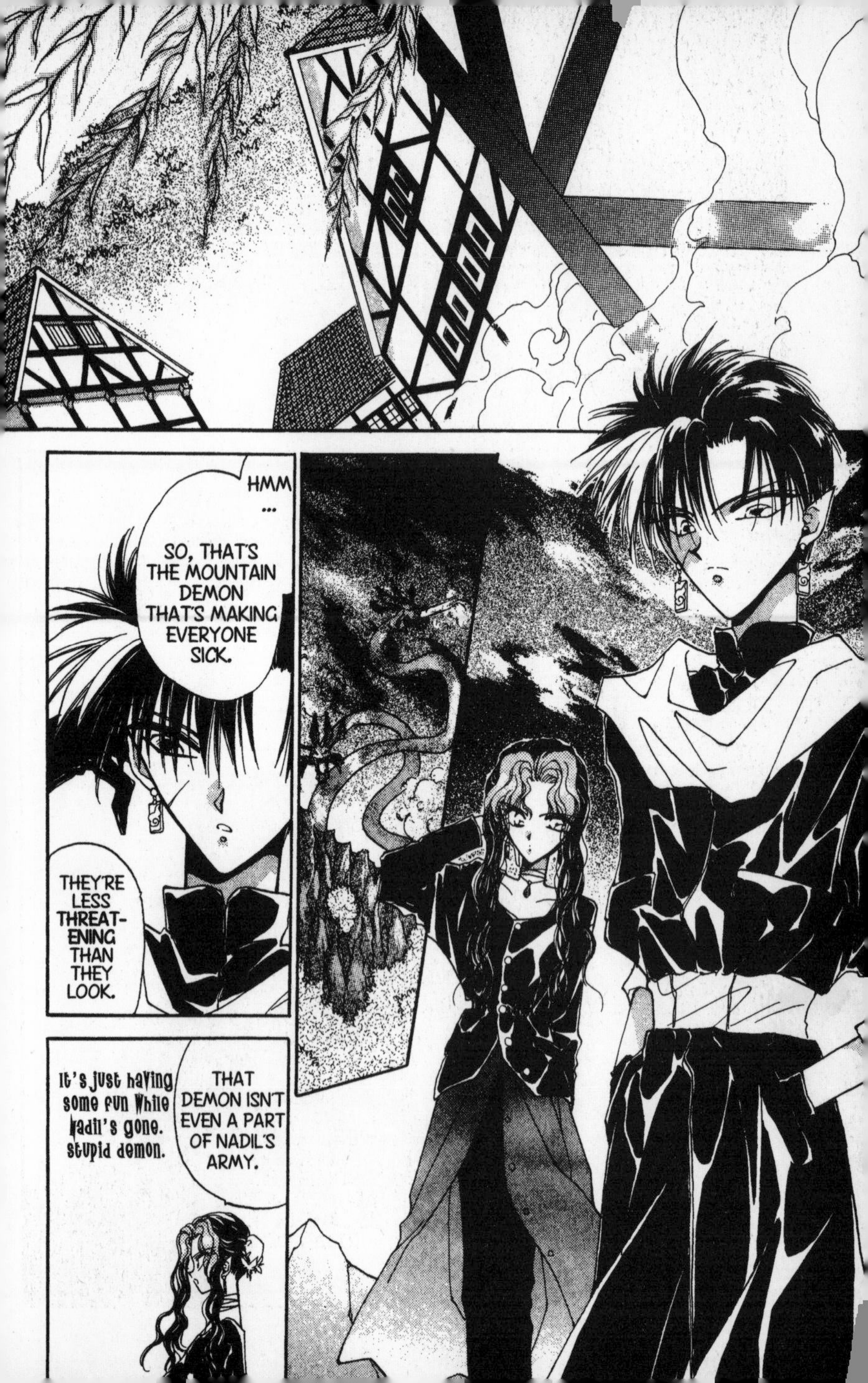

HMM ...
SO, THAT'S THE MOUNTAIN DEMON THAT'S MAKING EVERYONE SICK.
THEY'RE LESS THREAT-ENING THAN THEY LOOK.
THAT DEMON ISN'T EVEN A PART OF NADIL'S ARMY.
It's just having some fun while Nadil's gone. stupid demon.

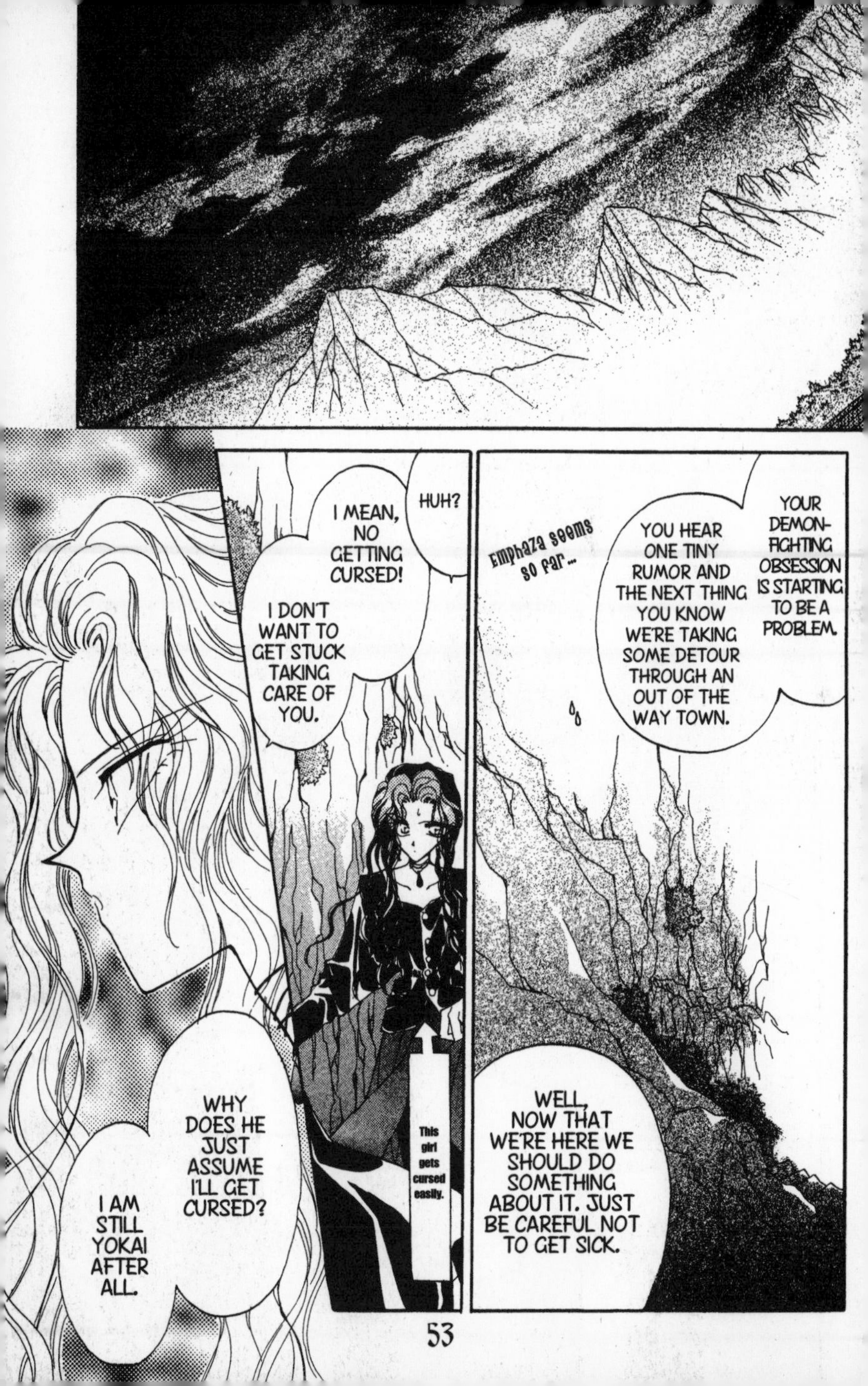
YOUR DEMON-FIGHTING OBSESSION IS STARTING TO BE A PROBLEM.
YOU HEAR ONE TINY RUMOR AND THE NEXT THING YOU KNOW WE'RE TAKING SOME DETOUR THROUGH AN OUT OF THE WAY TOWN.
Emphaza seems so far...
WELL, NOW THAT WE'RE HERE WE SHOULD DO SOMETHING ABOUT IT. JUST BE CAREFUL NOT TO GET SICK.
HUH?
I MEAN, NO GETTING CURSED!
I DON'T WANT TO GET STUCK TAKING CARE OF YOU.
This girl gets cursed easily.
WHY DOES HE JUST ASSUME I'LL GET CURSED?
I AM STILL YOKAI AFTER ALL.

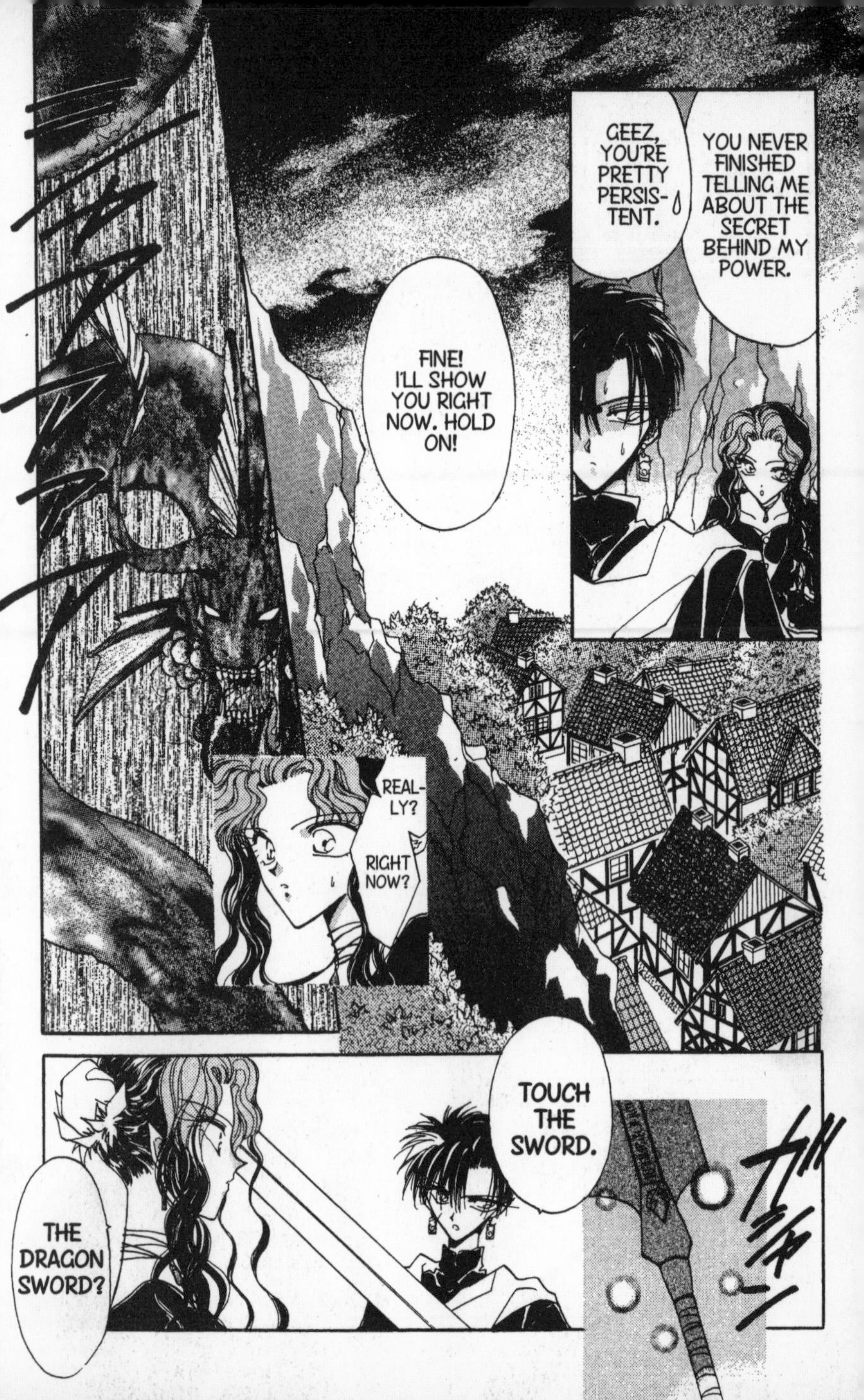
YOU NEVER FINISHED TELLING ME ABOUT THE SECRET BEHIND MY POWER.
GEEZ, YOU'RE PRETTY PERSIS-TENT.
FINE! I'LL SHOW YOU RIGHT NOW. HOLD ON!
REAL-LY?
RIGHT NOW?
TOUCH THE SWORD.
THE DRAGON SWORD?

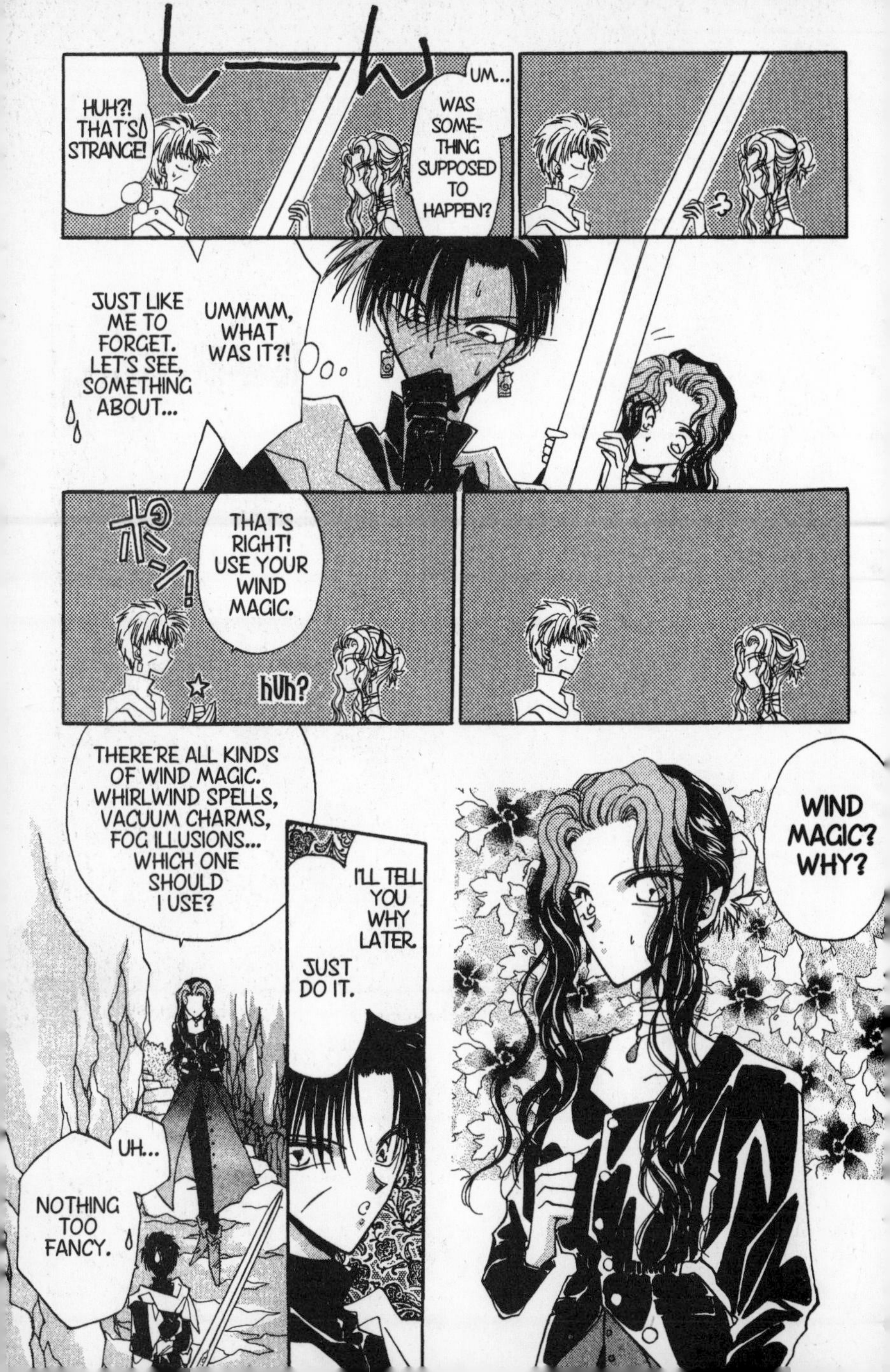
しーん
UM... WAS SOMETHING SUPPOSED TO HAPPEN?
HUH?! THAT'S STRANGE!
UMMMM, WHAT WAS IT?!
JUST LIKE ME TO FORGET. LET'S SEE, SOMETHING ABOUT...
THAT'S RIGHT! USE YOUR WIND MAGIC.
ポン!
hUh?
WIND MAGIC? WHY?
I'LL TELL YOU WHY LATER.
JUST DO IT.
THERE'RE ALL KINDS OF WIND MAGIC. WHIRLWIND SPELLS, VACUUM CHARMS, FOG ILLUSIONS... WHICH ONE SHOULD I USE?
UH...
NOTHING TOO FANCY.

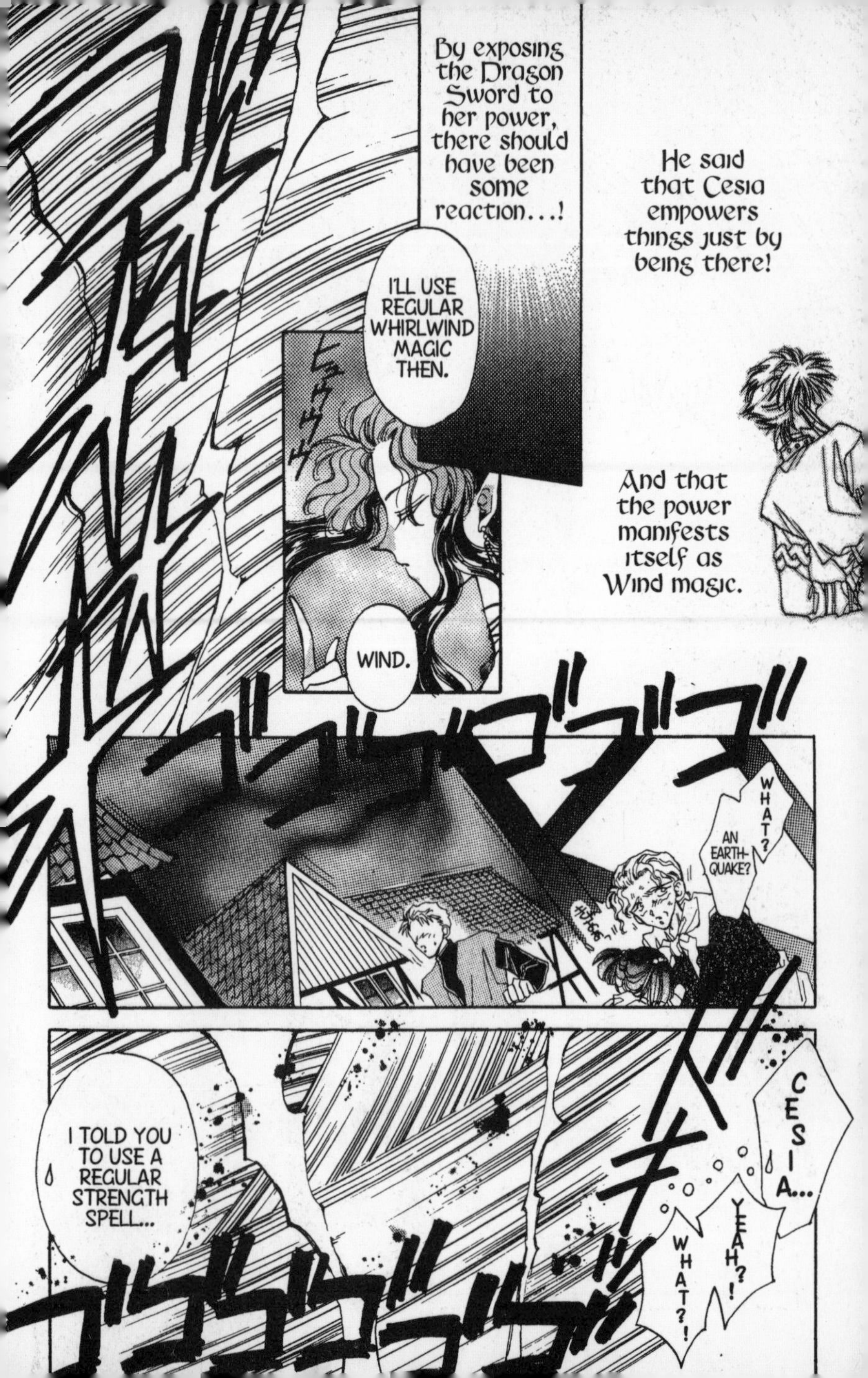
He said that Cesia empowers things just by being there!
And that the power manifests itself as Wind magic.
By exposing the Dragon Sword to her power, there should have been some reaction...!
I'LL USE REGULAR WHIRLWIND MAGIC THEN.
WIND.
WHAT?
AN EARTHQUAKE?
CESIA...
YEAH?!
WHAT?!
I TOLD YOU TO USE A REGULAR STRENGTH SPELL...

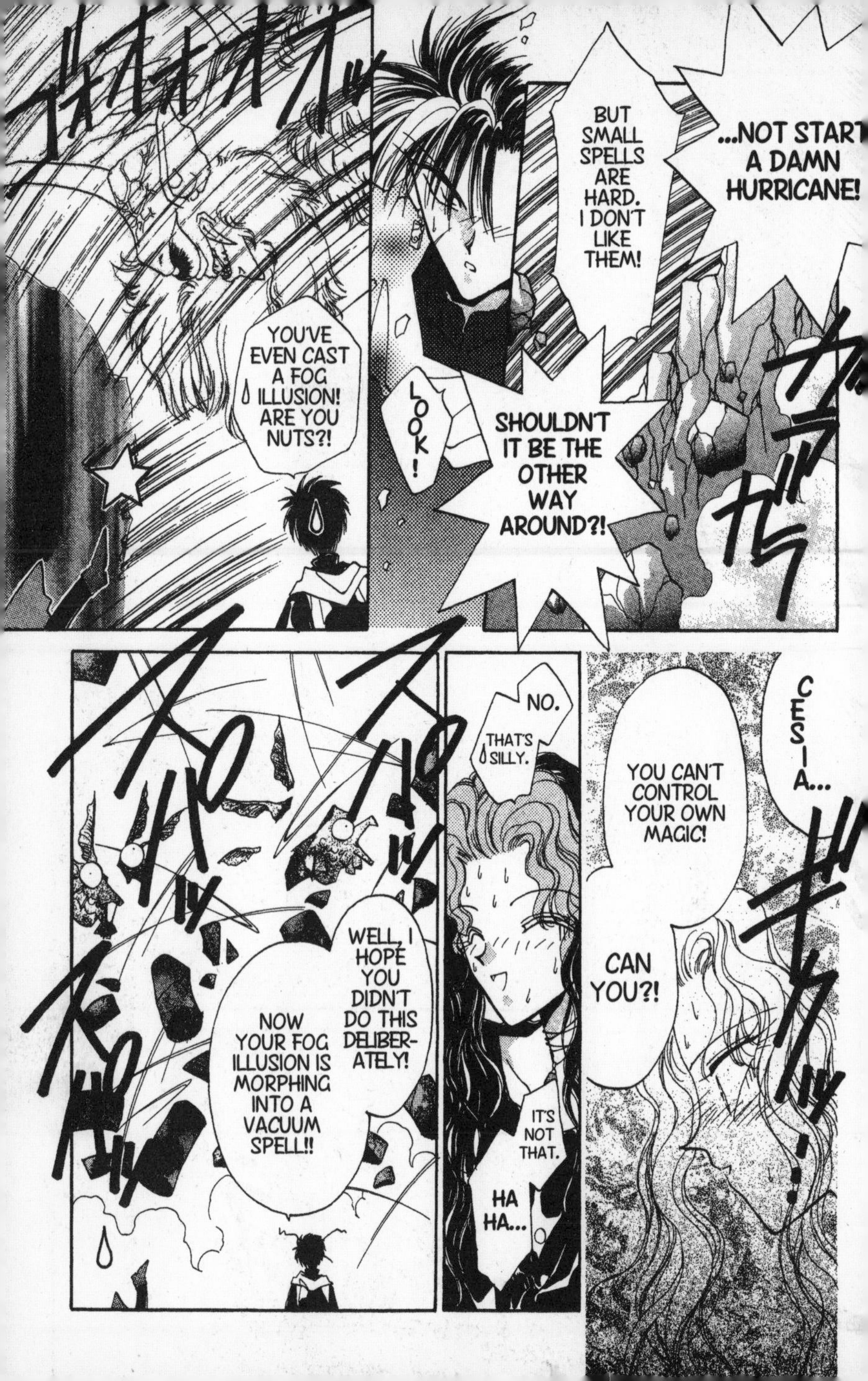
...NOT START A DAMN HURRICANE!
BUT SMALL SPELLS ARE HARD. I DON'T LIKE THEM!
LOOK!
SHOULDN'T IT BE THE OTHER WAY AROUND?!
YOU'VE EVEN CAST A FOG ILLUSION! ARE YOU NUTS?!
CESIA...
YOU CAN'T CONTROL YOUR OWN MAGIC!
CAN YOU?!
NO.
THAT'S SILLY.
IT'S NOT THAT.
HA HA...
WELL, I HOPE YOU DIDN'T DO THIS DELIBER-ATELY!
NOW YOUR FOG ILLUSION IS MORPHING INTO A VACUUM SPELL!!

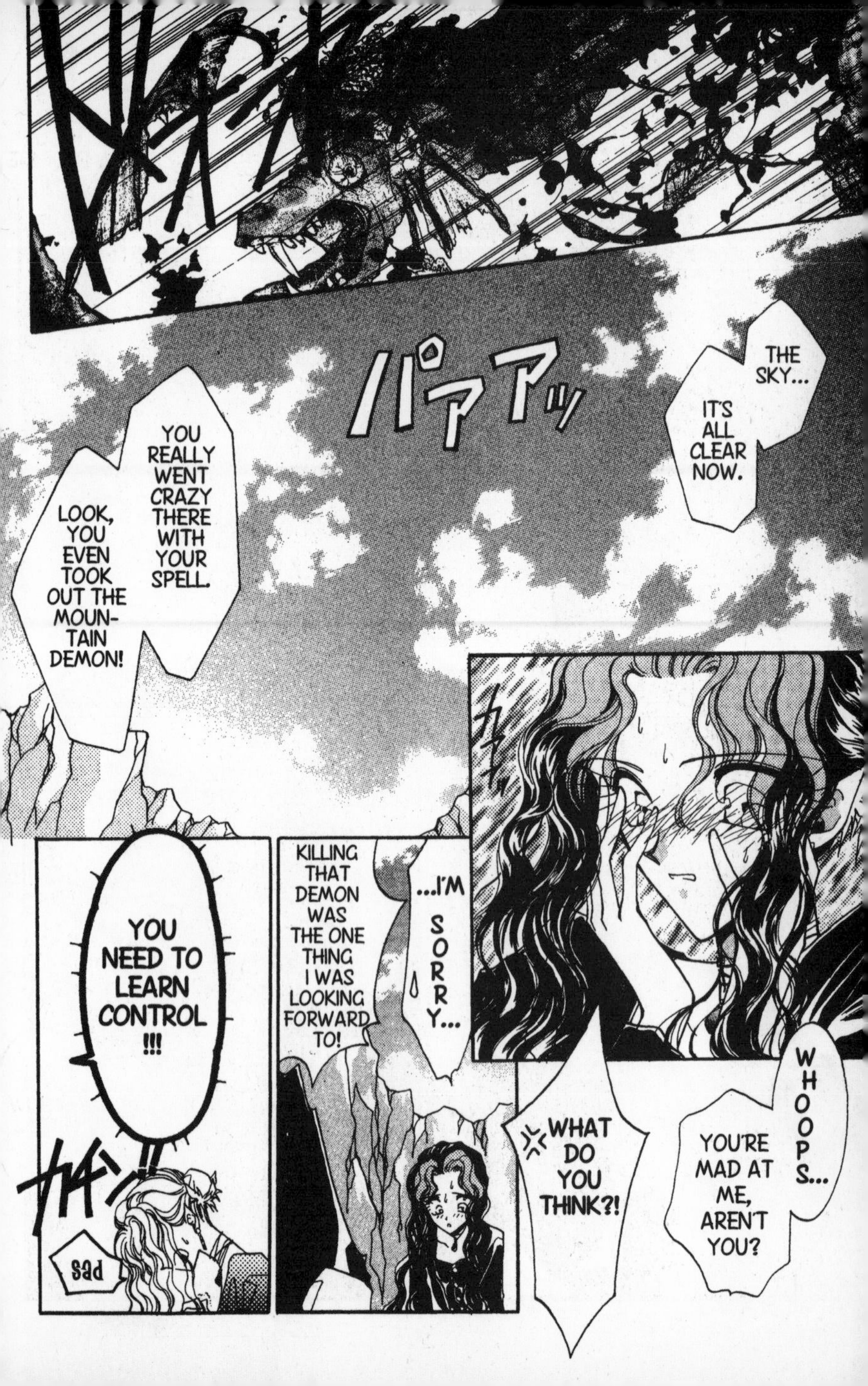
パアアッ
THE SKY... IT'S ALL CLEAR NOW.
YOU REALLY WENT CRAZY THERE WITH YOUR SPELL.
LOOK, YOU EVEN TOOK OUT THE MOUN-TAIN DEMON!
WHOOPS...
YOU'RE MAD AT ME, AREN'T YOU?
WHAT DO YOU THINK?!
...I'M SORRY...
KILLING THAT DEMON WAS THE ONE THING I WAS LOOKING FORWARD TO!
YOU NEED TO LEARN CONTROL!!!
sad

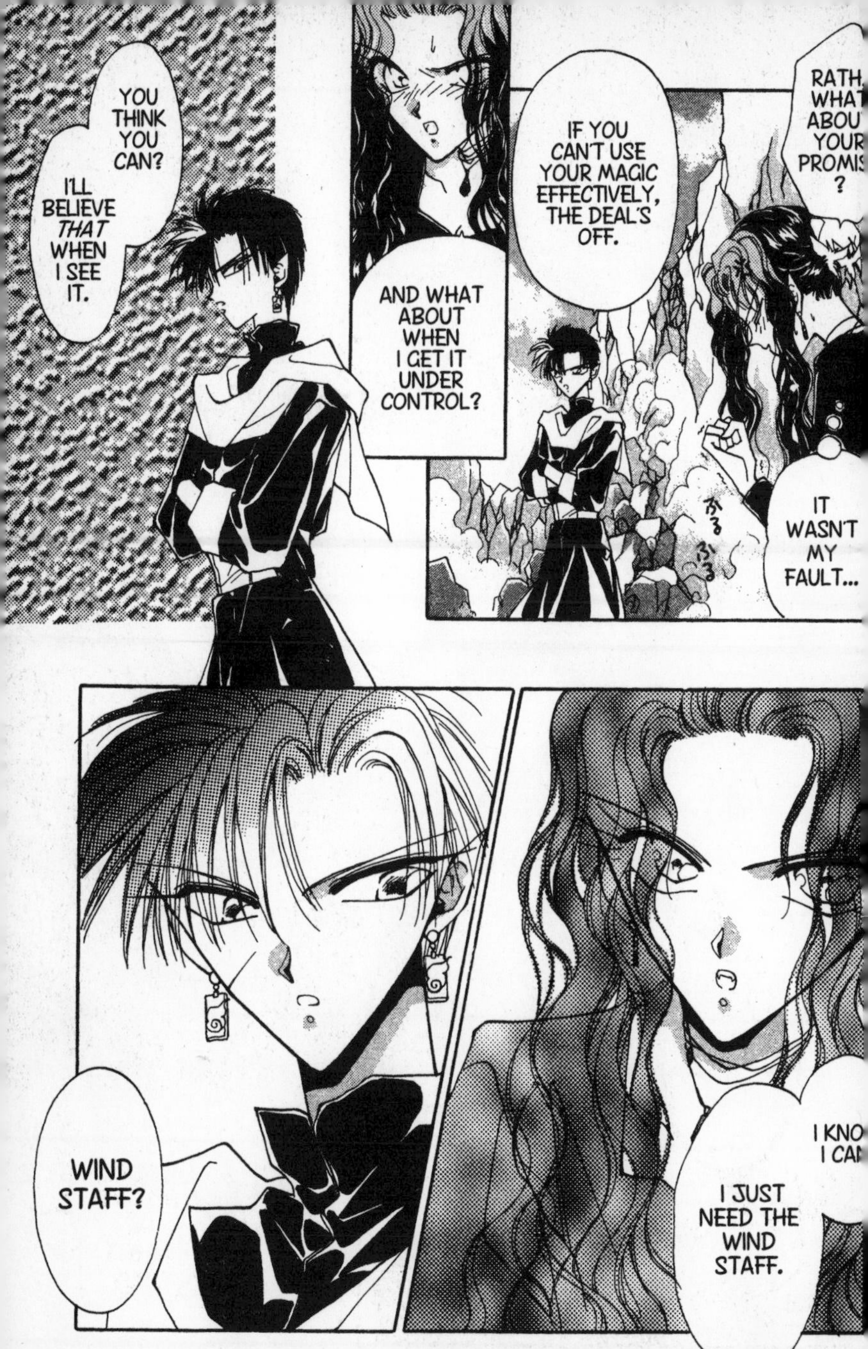
RATH, WHAT ABOU YOUR PROMIS ?
IT WASN'T MY FAULT...
ぷる ぷる
IF YOU CAN'T USE YOUR MAGIC EFFECTIVELY, THE DEAL'S OFF.
AND WHAT ABOUT WHEN I GET IT UNDER CONTROL?
YOU THINK YOU CAN?
I'LL BELIEVE *THAT* WHEN I SEE IT.
I KNO I CA
I JUST NEED THE WIND STAFF.
WIND STAFF?

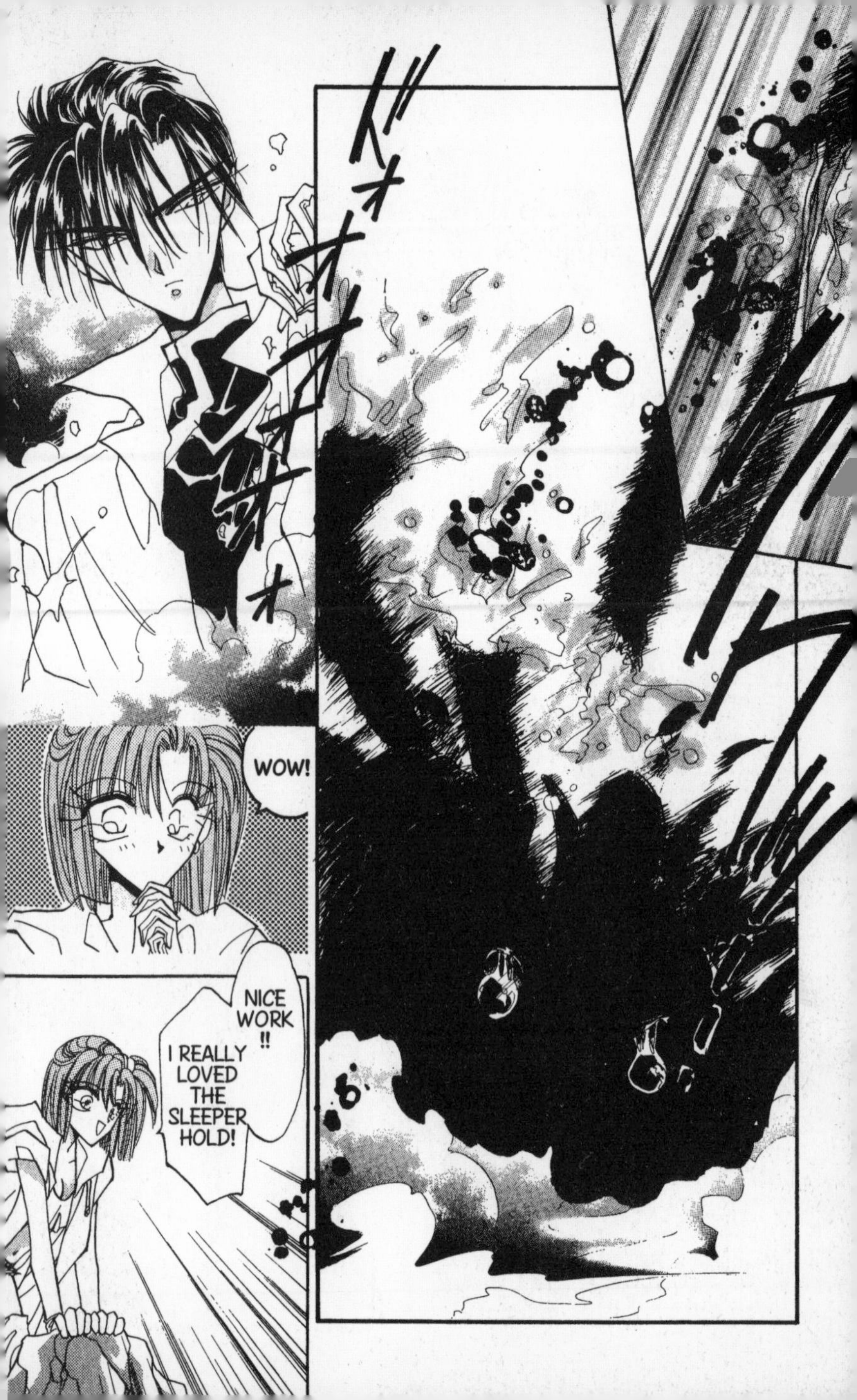
WOW!
NICE WORK!!
I REALLY LOVED THE SLEEPER HOLD!

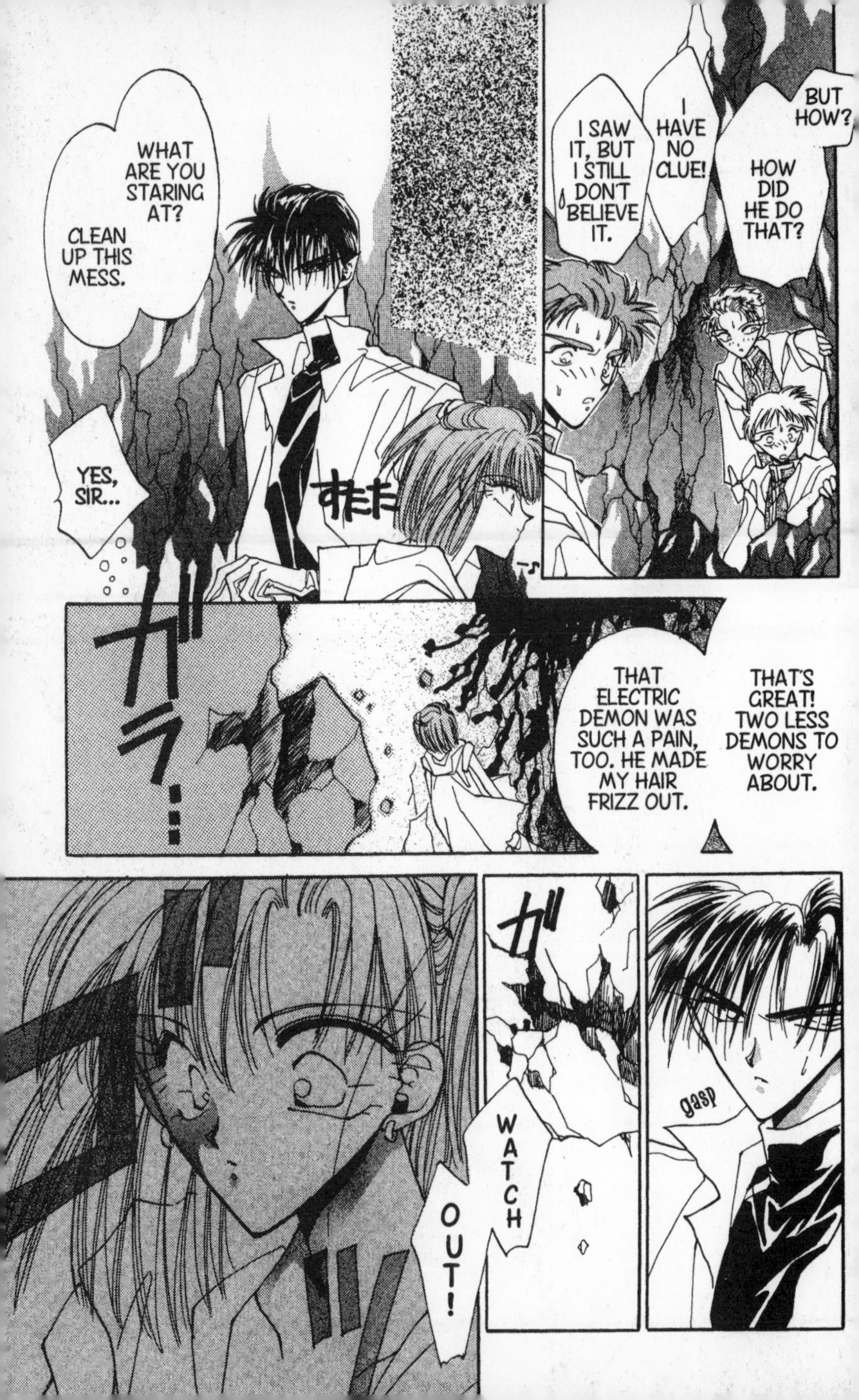
BUT HOW?
HOW DID HE DO THAT?
I HAVE NO CLUE!
I SAW IT, BUT I STILL DON'T BELIEVE IT.
WHAT ARE YOU STARING AT?
CLEAN UP THIS MESS.
YES, SIR...
THAT'S GREAT! TWO LESS DEMONS TO WORRY ABOUT.
THAT ELECTRIC DEMON WAS SUCH A PAIN, TOO. HE MADE MY HAIR FRIZZ OUT.
ガラ…
gasp
ガ
WATCH OUT!

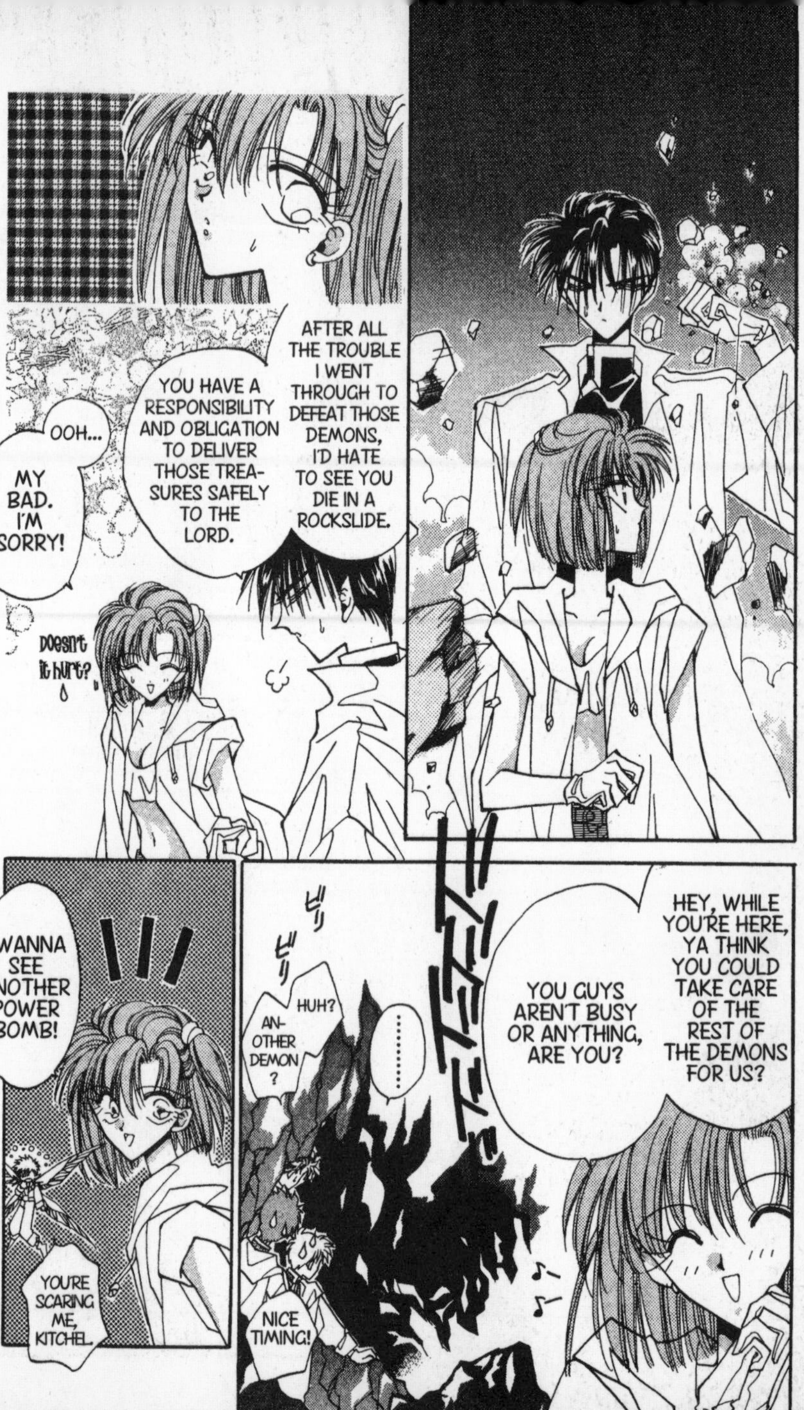
AFTER ALL THE TROUBLE I WENT THROUGH TO DEFEAT THOSE DEMONS, I'D HATE TO SEE YOU DIE IN A ROCKSLIDE.
YOU HAVE A RESPONSIBILITY AND OBLIGATION TO DELIVER THOSE TREASURES SAFELY TO THE LORD.
OOH...
MY BAD. I'M SORRY!
Doesn't it hurt?
HEY, WHILE YOU'RE HERE, YA THINK YOU COULD TAKE CARE OF THE REST OF THE DEMONS FOR US?
YOU GUYS AREN'T BUSY OR ANYTHING, ARE YOU?
ビリ
ビリ
....
HUH?
ANOTHER DEMON?
NICE TIMING!
I WANNA SEE ANOTHER POWER BOMB!
YOU'RE SCARING ME, KITCHEL.

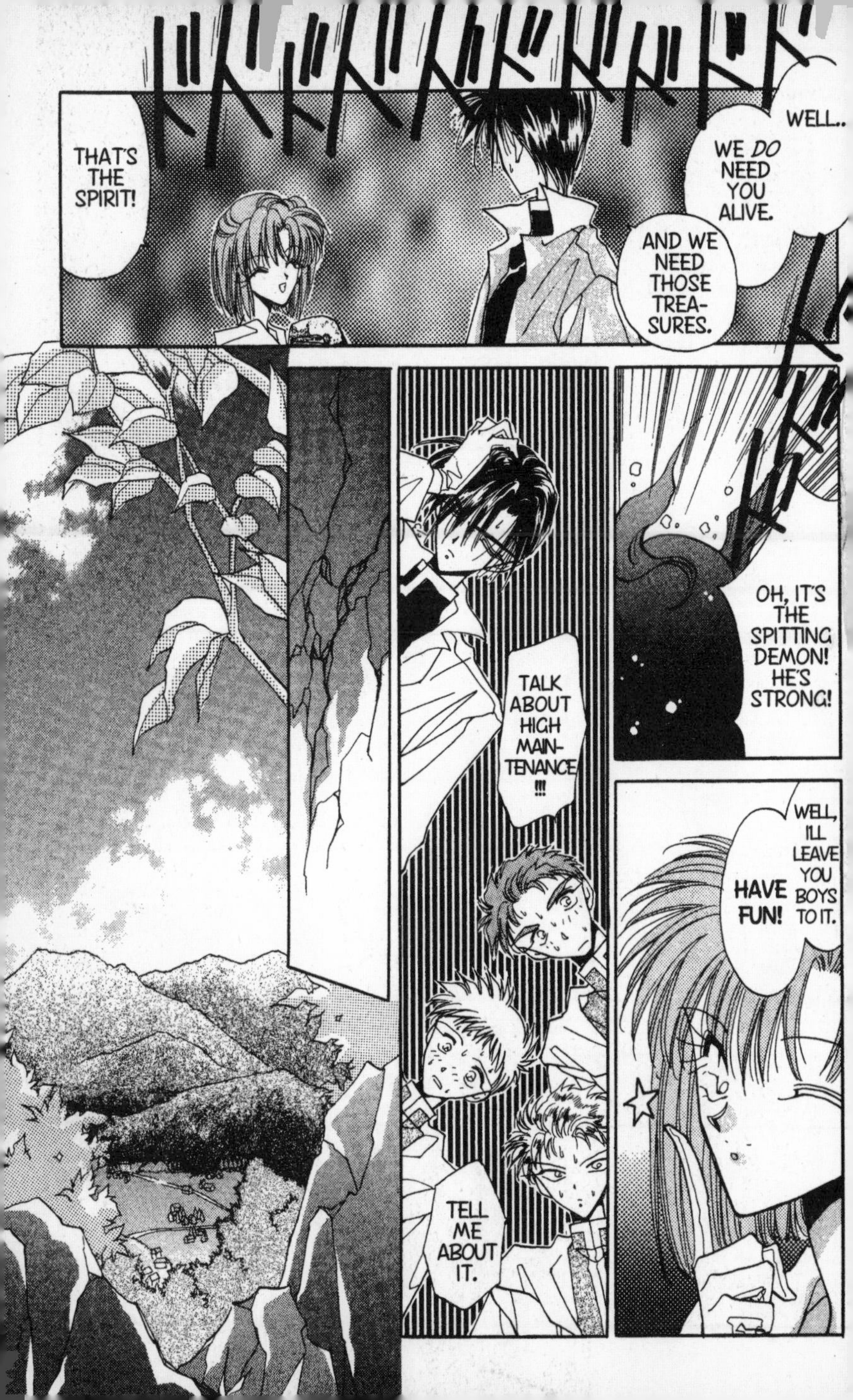
WELL..
WE *DO* NEED YOU ALIVE.
AND WE NEED THOSE TREA-SURES.
THAT'S THE SPIRIT!
OH, IT'S THE SPITTING DEMON! HE'S STRONG!
WELL, I'LL LEAVE YOU BOYS TO IT.
HAVE FUN!
TALK ABOUT HIGH MAIN-TENANCE!!!
TELL ME ABOUT IT.

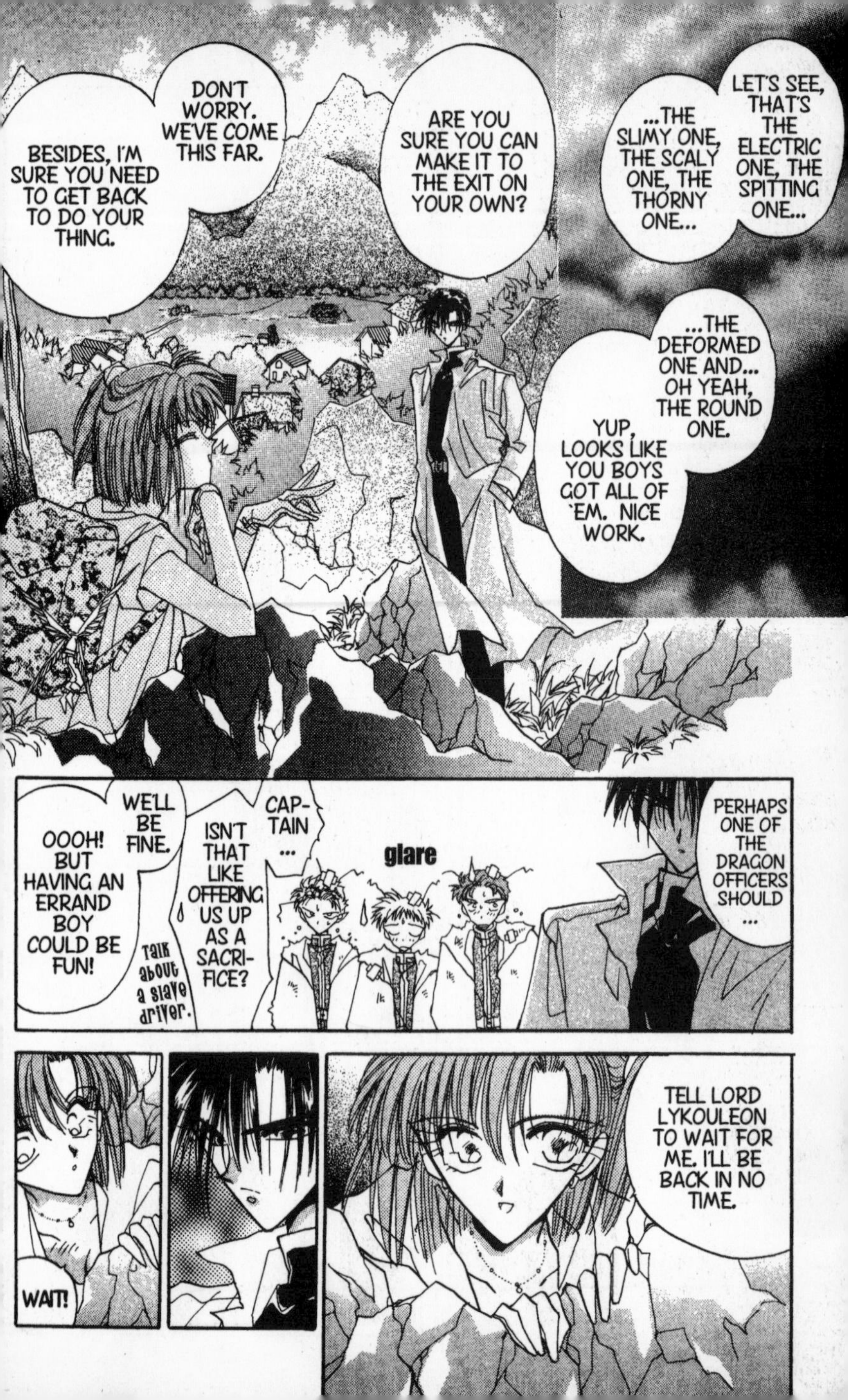
LET'S SEE, THAT'S THE ELECTRIC ONE, THE SPITTING ONE...
...THE SLIMY ONE, THE SCALY ONE, THE THORNY ONE...
...THE DEFORMED ONE AND... OH YEAH, THE ROUND ONE.
YUP, LOOKS LIKE YOU BOYS GOT ALL OF 'EM. NICE WORK.
ARE YOU SURE YOU CAN MAKE IT TO THE EXIT ON YOUR OWN?
DON'T WORRY. WE'VE COME THIS FAR.
BESIDES, I'M SURE YOU NEED TO GET BACK TO DO YOUR THING.
PERHAPS ONE OF THE DRAGON OFFICERS SHOULD ...
glare
CAP-TAIN ...
ISN'T THAT LIKE OFFERING US UP AS A SACRI-FICE?
Talk about a slave driver.
WE'LL BE FINE.
OOOH! BUT HAVING AN ERRAND BOY COULD BE FUN!
TELL LORD LYKOULEON TO WAIT FOR ME. I'LL BE BACK IN NO TIME.
WAIT!

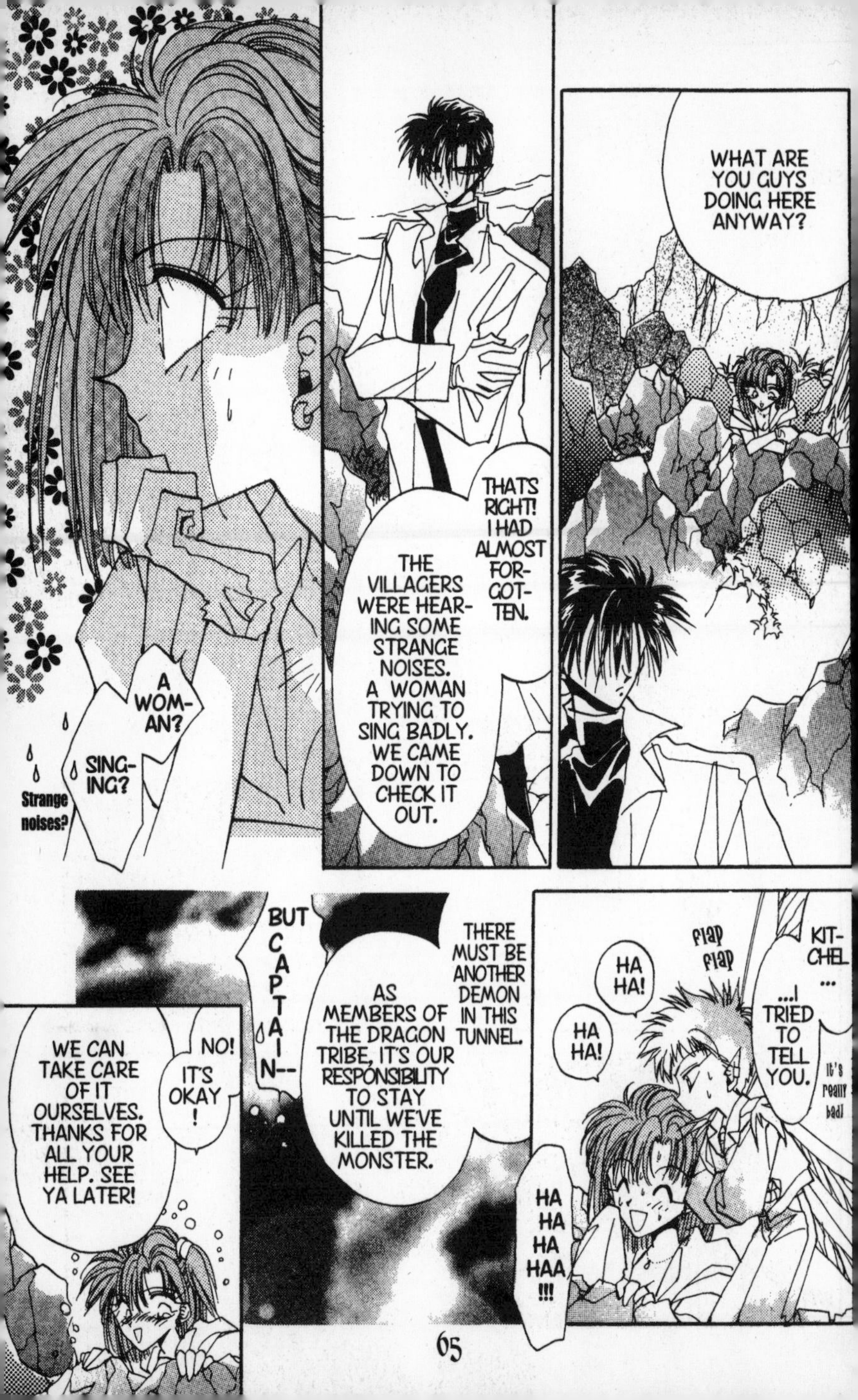
WHAT ARE YOU GUYS DOING HERE ANYWAY?
THATS RIGHT! I HAD ALMOST FOR-GOT-TEN.
THE VILLAGERS WERE HEAR-ING SOME STRANGE NOISES. A WOMAN TRYING TO SING BADLY. WE CAME DOWN TO CHECK IT OUT.
A WOM-AN?
SING-ING?
Strange noises?
KIT-CHEL ...
...I TRIED TO TELL YOU.
It's really bad!
flap flap
HA HA!
HA HA!
HA HA HA HAA !!!
THERE MUST BE ANOTHER DEMON IN THIS TUNNEL.
AS MEMBERS OF THE DRAGON TRIBE, IT'S OUR RESPONSIBILITY TO STAY UNTIL WE'VE KILLED THE MONSTER.
BUT CAPTAIN--
NO! IT'S OKAY!
WE CAN TAKE CARE OF IT OURSELVES. THANKS FOR ALL YOUR HELP. SEE YA LATER!

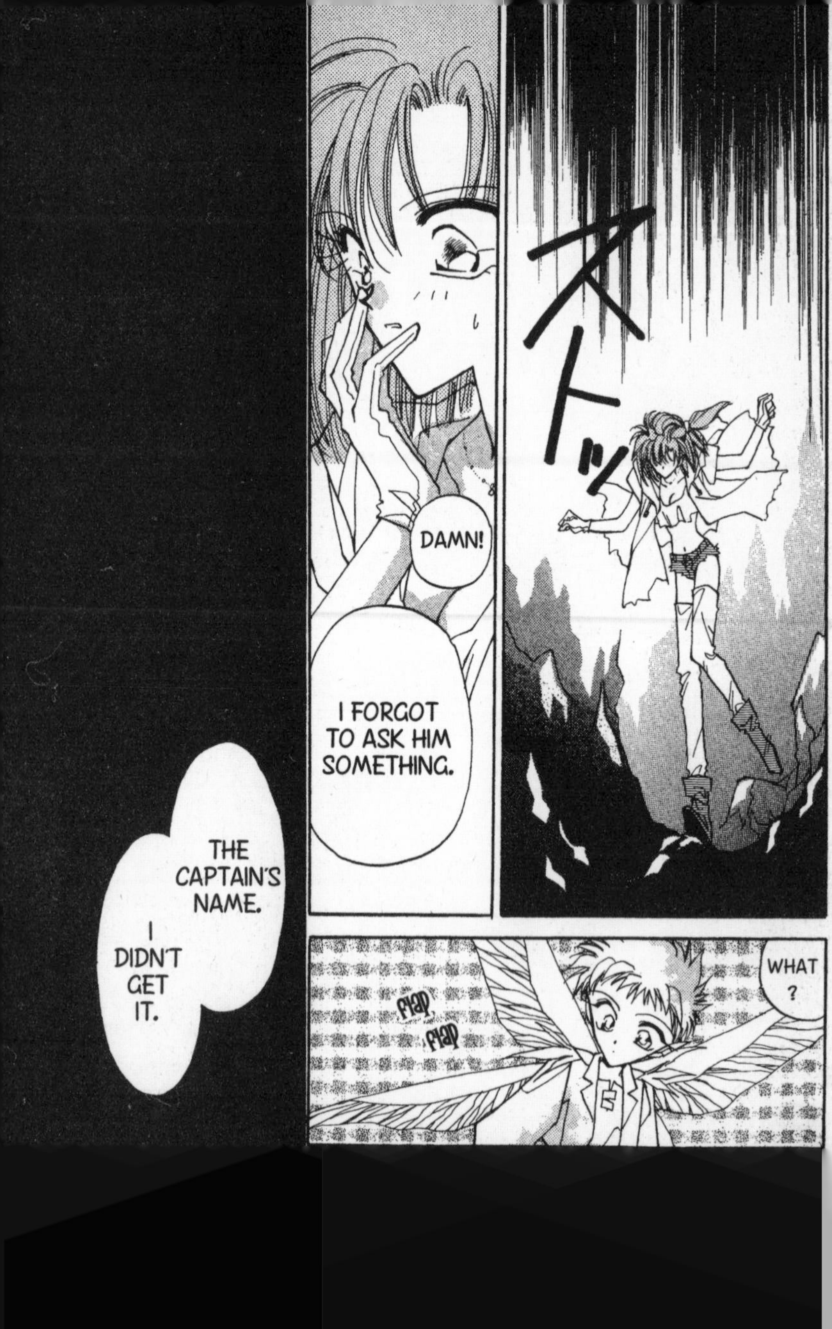
ストッ
DAMN!
I FORGOT TO ASK HIM SOMETHING.
flap flap
WHAT?
THE CAPTAIN'S NAME.
I DIDN'T GET IT.

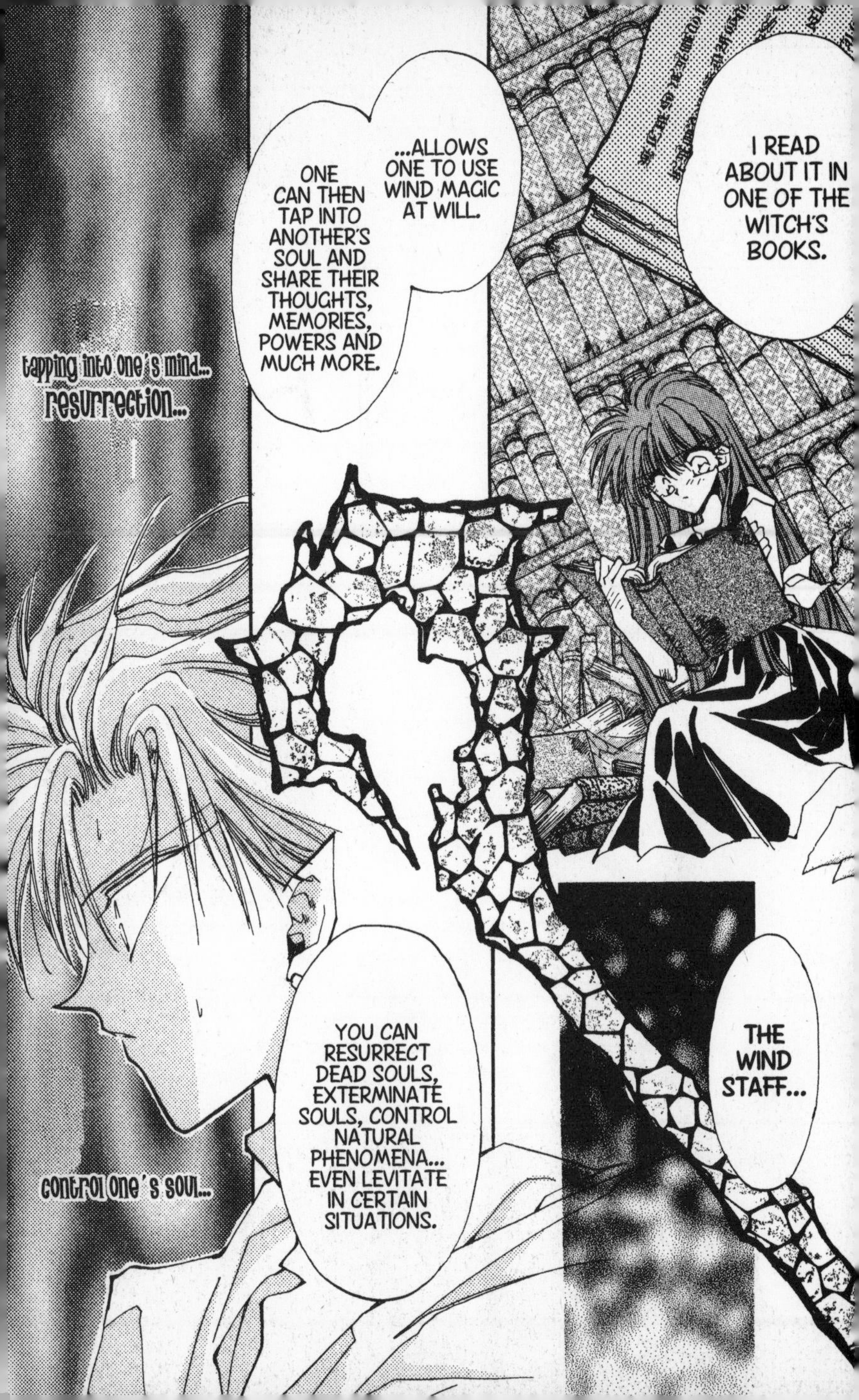
I READ ABOUT IT IN ONE OF THE WITCH'S BOOKS.
THE WIND STAFF...
...ALLOWS ONE TO USE WIND MAGIC AT WILL.
ONE CAN THEN TAP INTO ANOTHER'S SOUL AND SHARE THEIR THOUGHTS, MEMORIES, POWERS AND MUCH MORE.
YOU CAN RESURRECT DEAD SOULS, EXTERMINATE SOULS, CONTROL NATURAL PHENOMENA... EVEN LEVITATE IN CERTAIN SITUATIONS.
tapping into one's mind...
resurrection...
control one's soul...

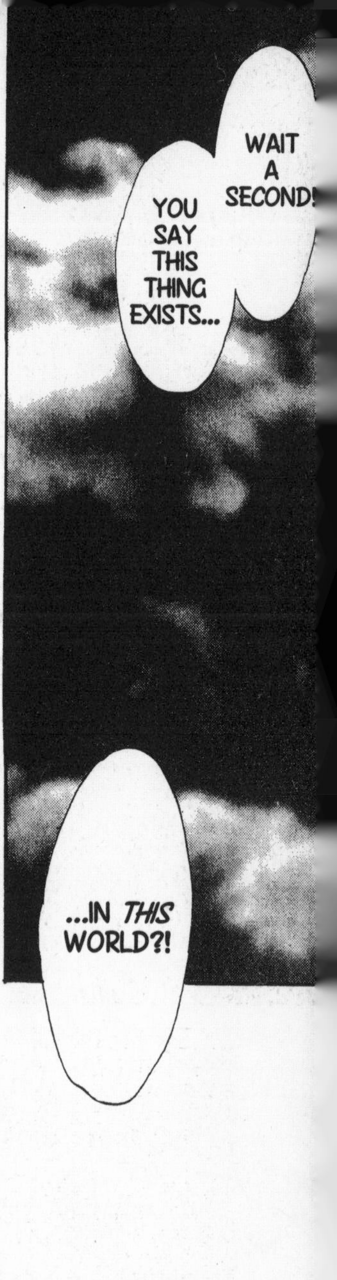
WAIT A SECOND!
YOU SAY THIS THING EXISTS...
...IN *THIS* WORLD?!
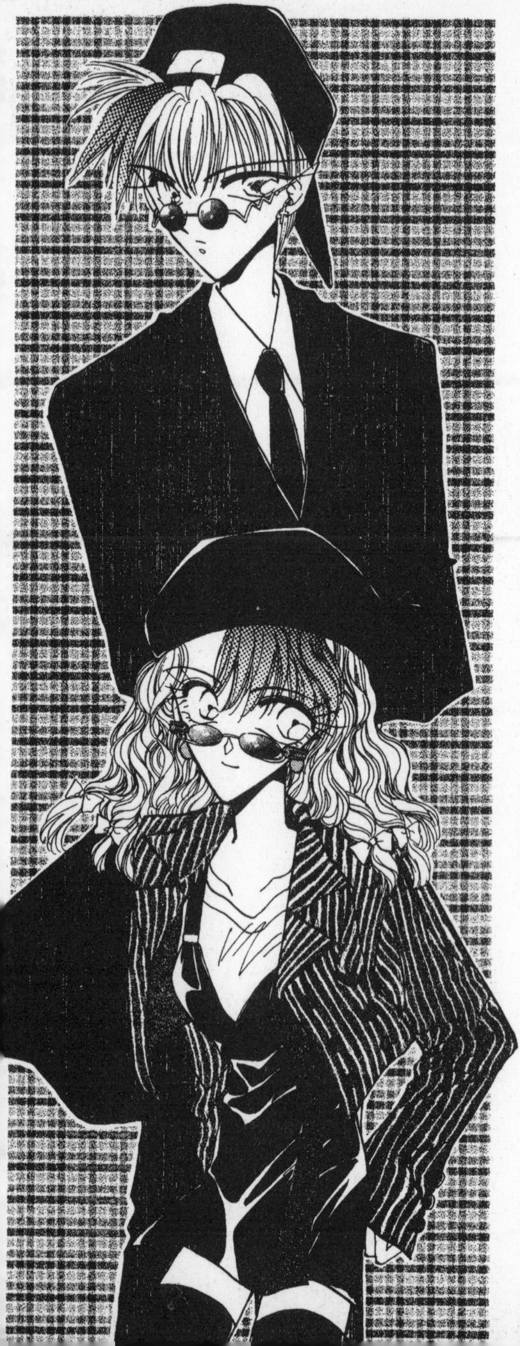

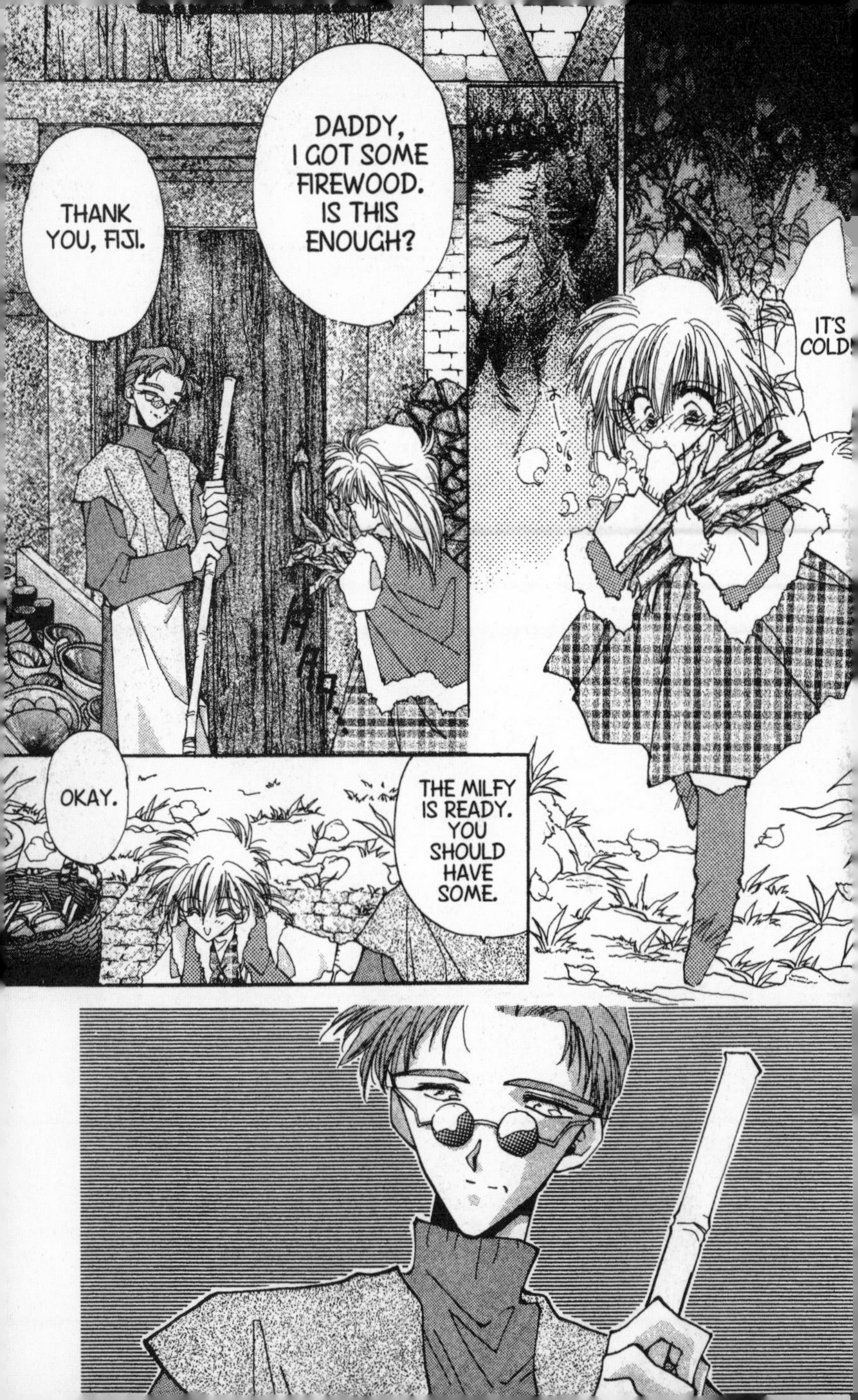
IT'S COLD!
DADDY, I GOT SOME FIREWOOD. IS THIS ENOUGH?
THANK YOU, FIJI.
THE MILFY IS READY. YOU SHOULD HAVE SOME.
OKAY.

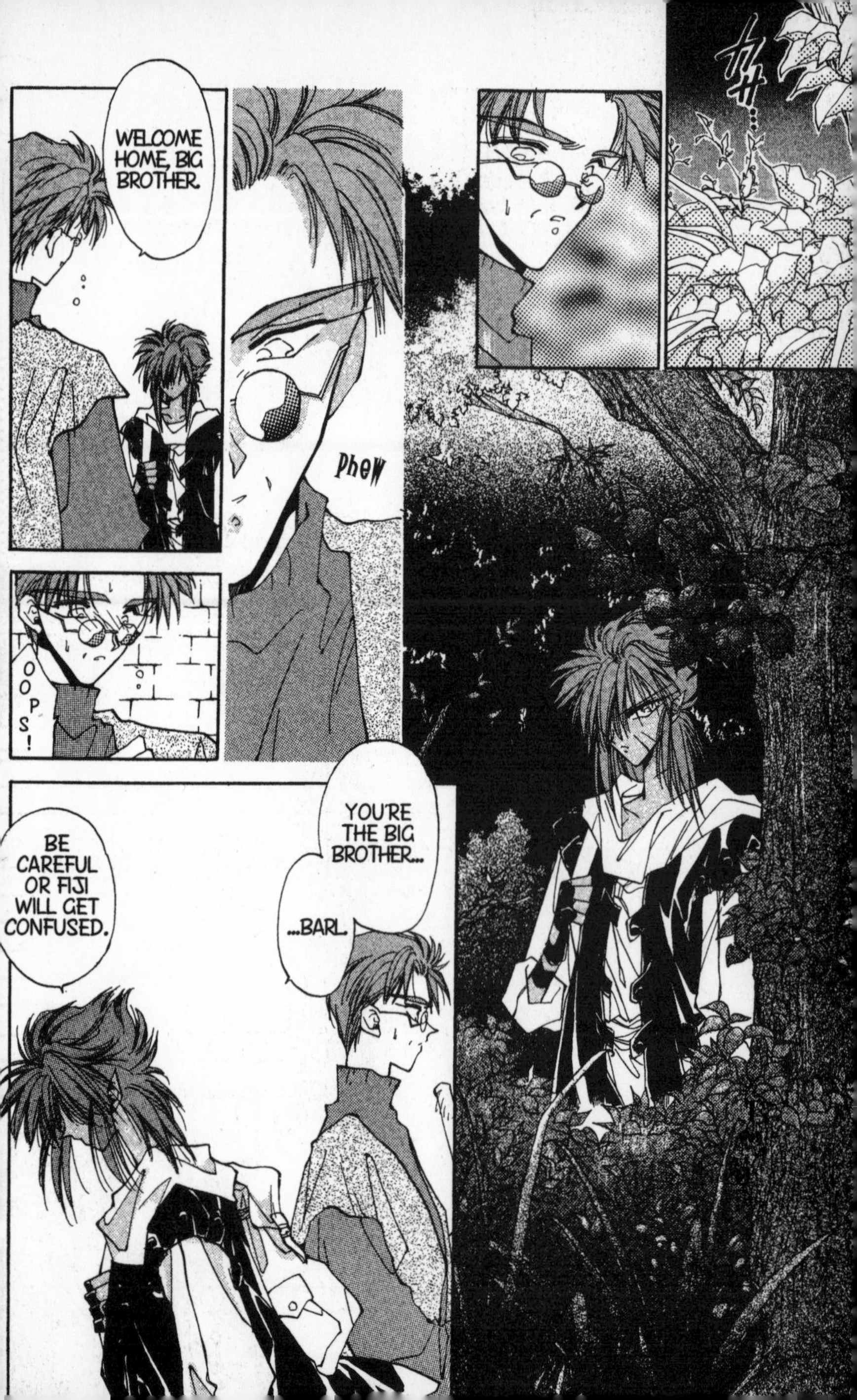
PheW
WELCOME HOME, BIG BROTHER.
OOPS!
YOU'RE THE BIG BROTHER...
...BARL.
BE CAREFUL OR FIJI WILL GET CONFUSED.

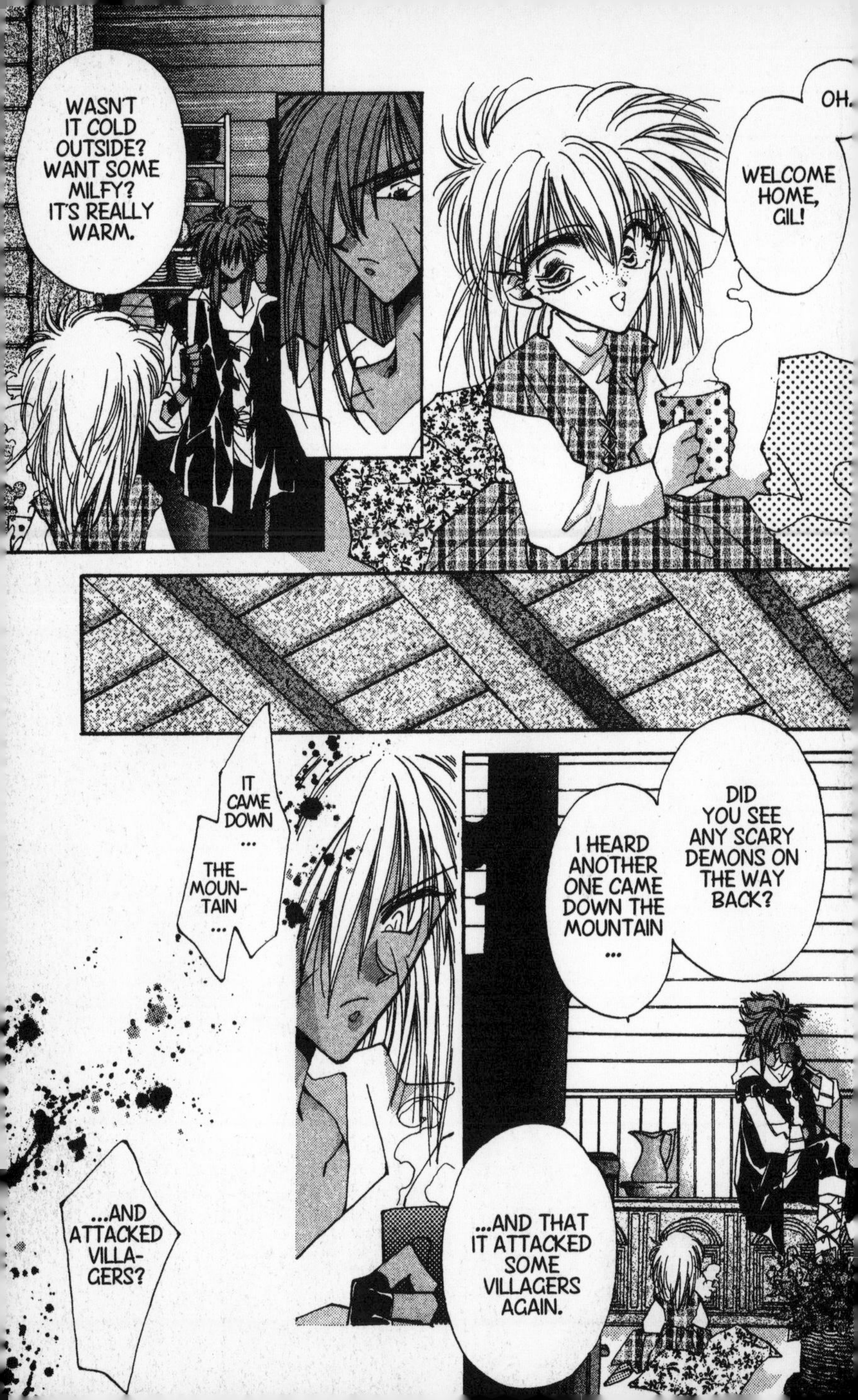
OH.
WELCOME HOME, GIL!
WASN'T IT COLD OUTSIDE? WANT SOME MILFY? IT'S REALLY WARM.
DID YOU SEE ANY SCARY DEMONS ON THE WAY BACK?
I HEARD ANOTHER ONE CAME DOWN THE MOUNTAIN ...
IT CAME DOWN ... THE MOUN-TAIN ...
...AND THAT IT ATTACKED SOME VILLAGERS AGAIN.
...AND ATTACKED VILLA-GERS?

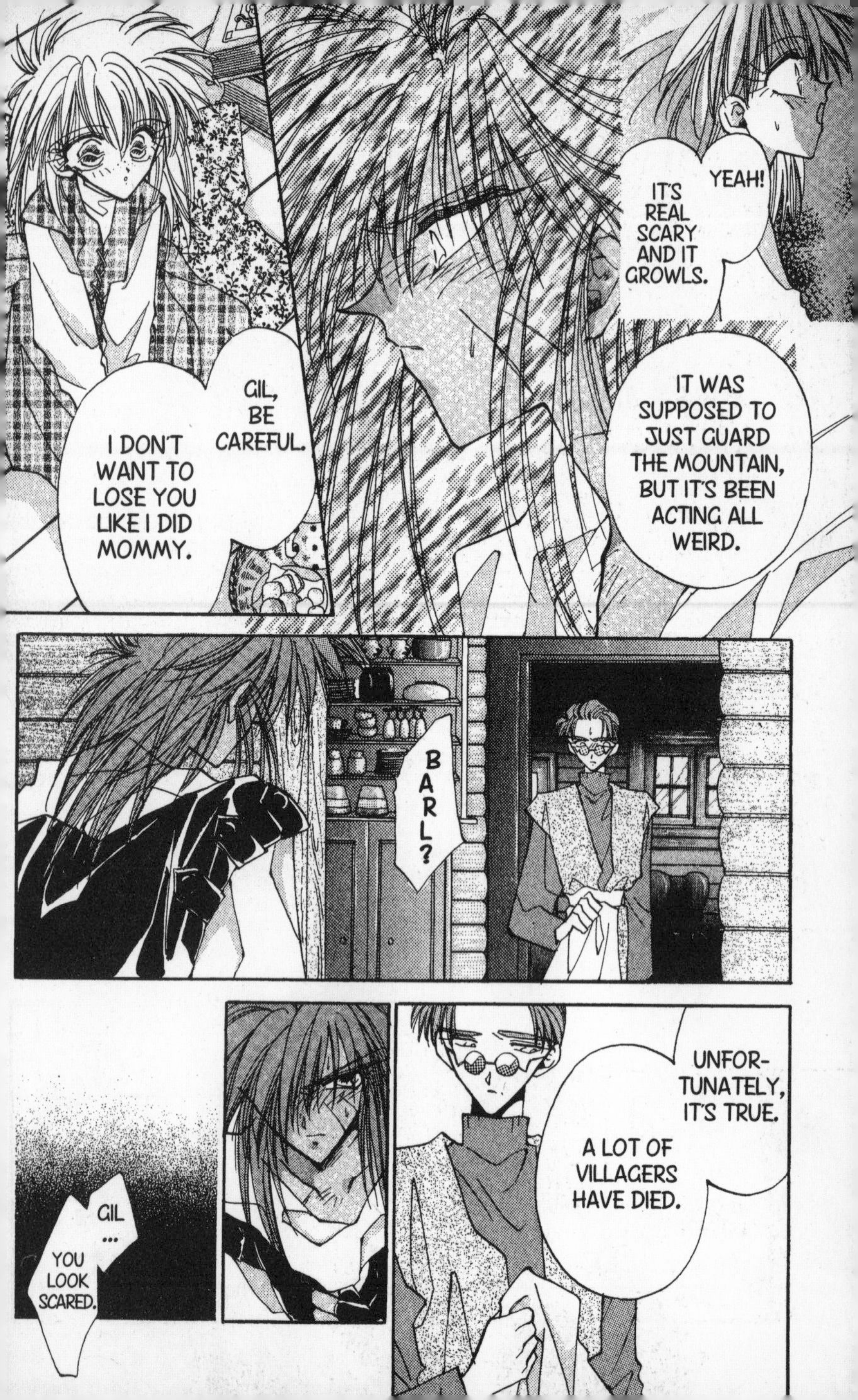
YEAH! IT'S REAL SCARY AND IT GROWLS.
IT WAS SUPPOSED TO JUST GUARD THE MOUNTAIN, BUT IT'S BEEN ACTING ALL WEIRD.
GIL, BE CAREFUL.
I DON'T WANT TO LOSE YOU LIKE I DID MOMMY.
BARL?
UNFOR-TUNATELY, IT'S TRUE.
A LOT OF VILLAGERS HAVE DIED.
GIL ... YOU LOOK SCARED.

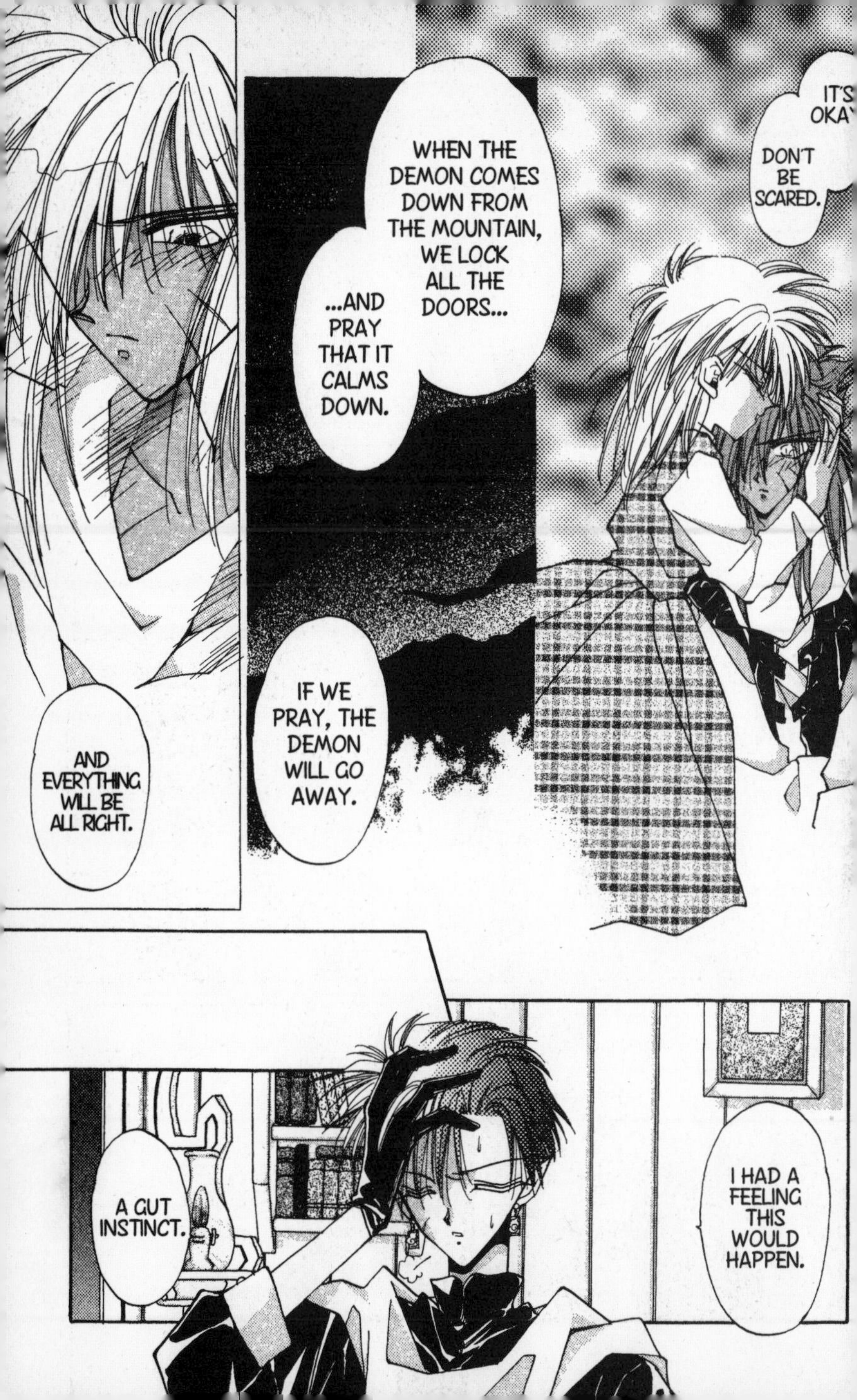
IT'S OKA
DON'T BE SCARED.
WHEN THE DEMON COMES DOWN FROM THE MOUNTAIN, WE LOCK ALL THE DOORS...
...AND PRAY THAT IT CALMS DOWN.
IF WE PRAY, THE DEMON WILL GO AWAY.
AND EVERYTHING WILL BE ALL RIGHT.
I HAD A FEELING THIS WOULD HAPPEN.
A GUT INSTINCT.

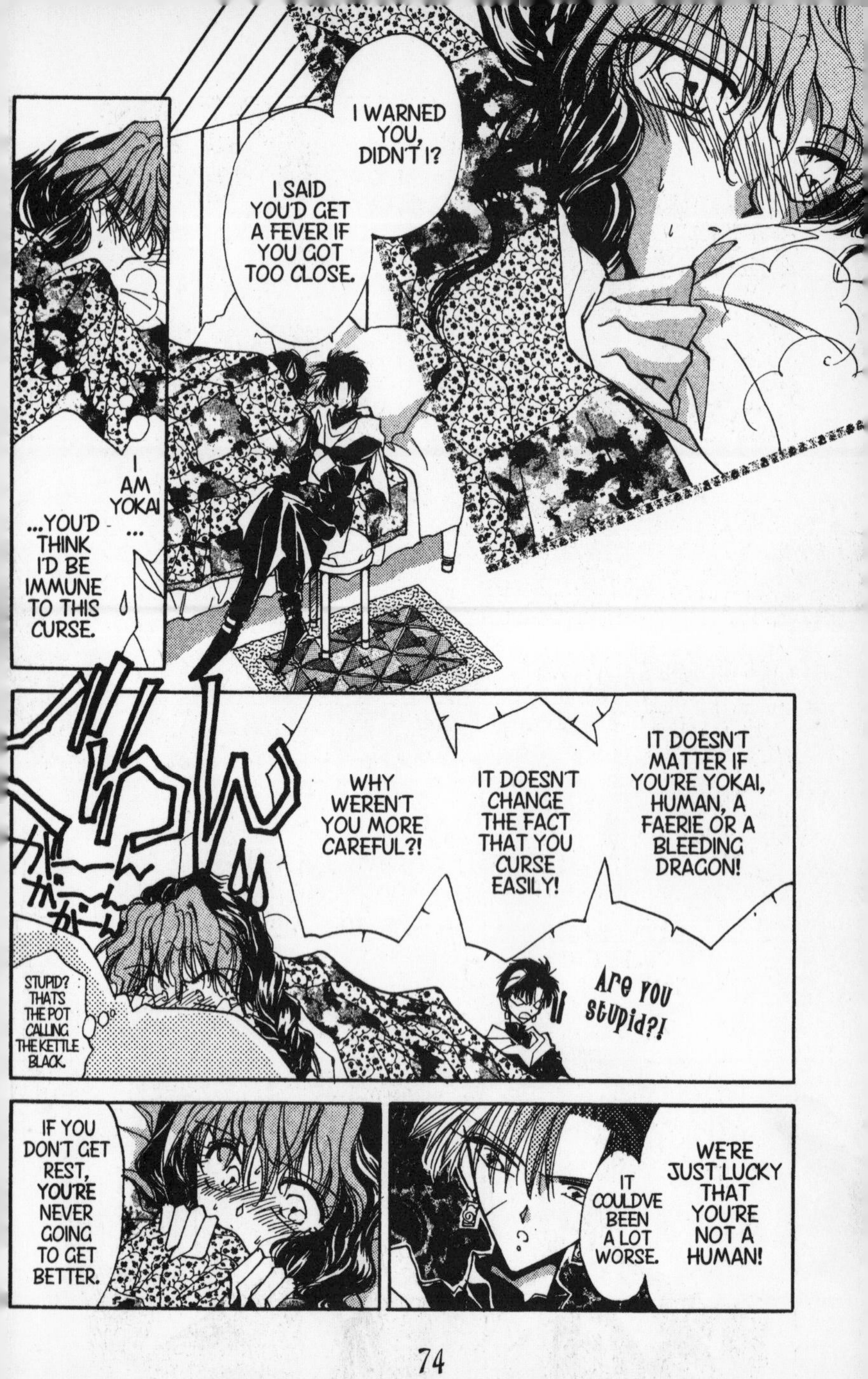
I WARNED YOU, DIDN'T I?
I SAID YOU'D GET A FEVER IF YOU GOT TOO CLOSE.
I AM YOKAI...
...YOU'D THINK I'D BE IMMUNE TO THIS CURSE.
IT DOESN'T MATTER IF YOU'RE YOKAI, HUMAN, A FAERIE OR A BLEEDING DRAGON!
IT DOESN'T CHANGE THE FACT THAT YOU CURSE EASILY!
WHY WEREN'T YOU MORE CAREFUL?!
Are you stupid?!
STUPID? THATS THE POT CALLING THE KETTLE BLACK.
WE'RE JUST LUCKY THAT YOU'RE NOT A HUMAN!
IT COULDVE BEEN A LOT WORSE.
IF YOU DON'T GET REST, YOU'RE NEVER GOING TO GET BETTER.

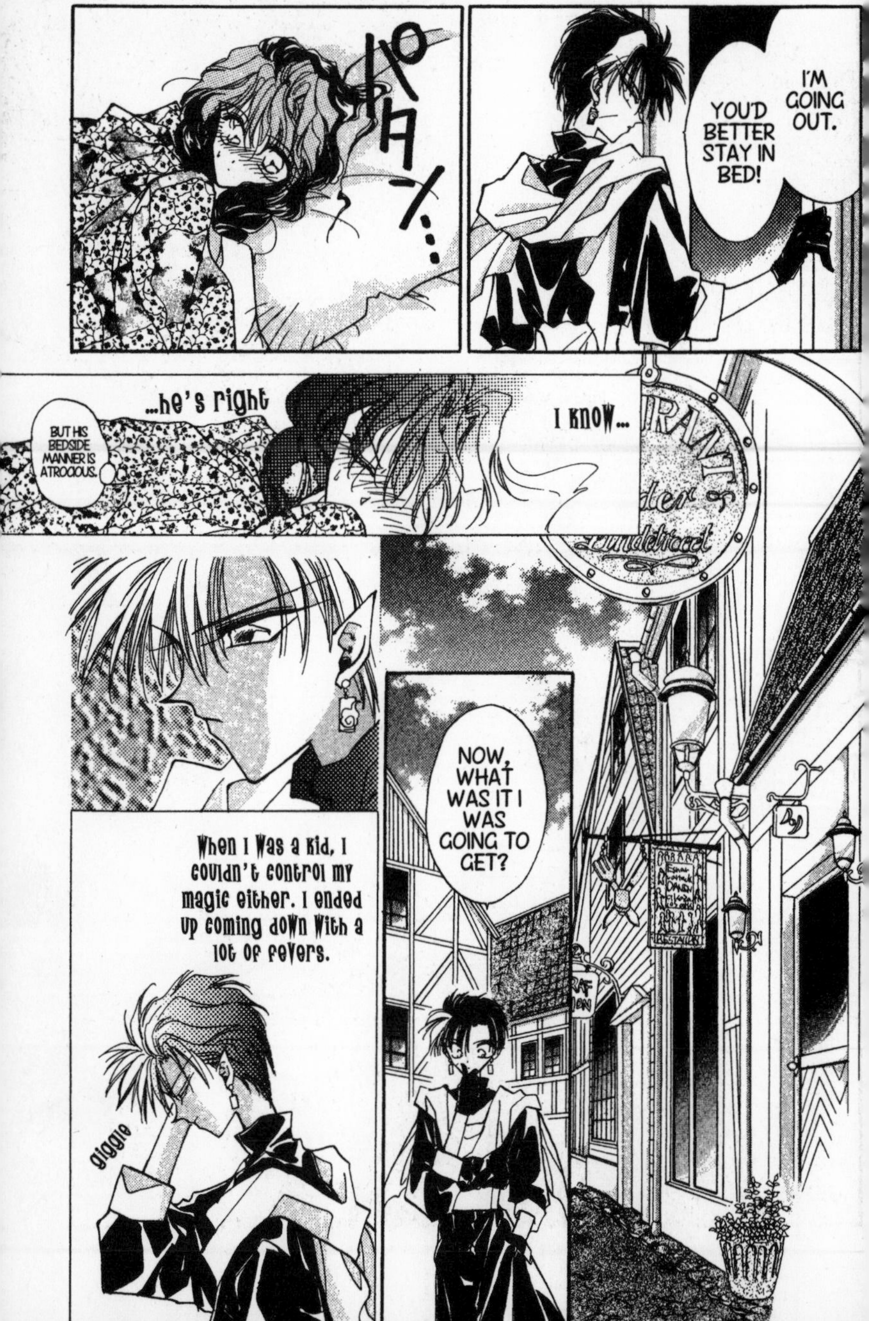
I'M GOING OUT.
YOU'D BETTER STAY IN BED!
パターン…
I KNOW...
...he's right
BUT HIS BEDSIDE MANNER IS ATROCIOUS.
NOW, WHAT WAS IT I WAS GOING TO GET?
When I was a kid, I couldn't control my magic either. I ended up coming down with a lot of fevers.
giggle

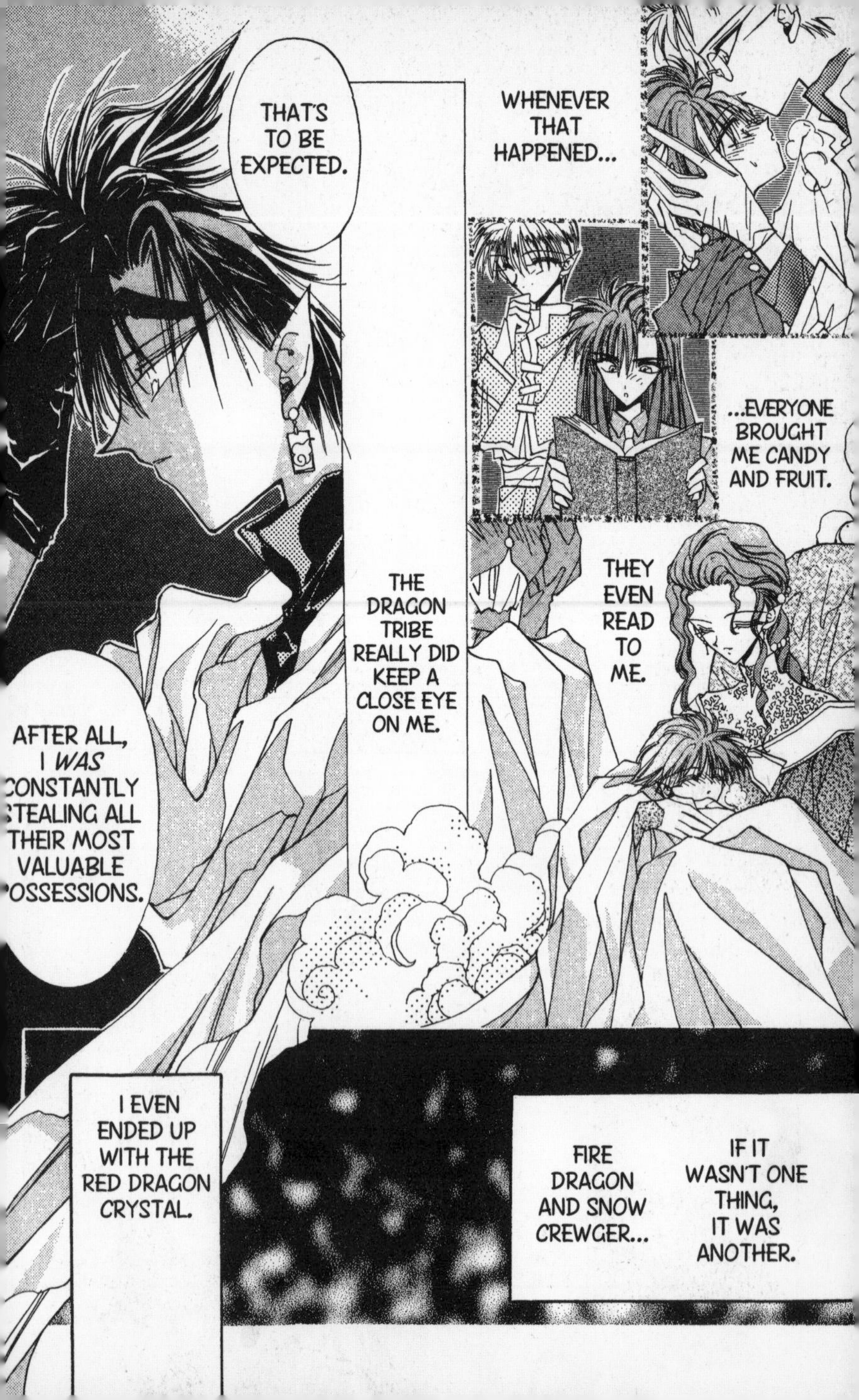

WHENEVER THAT HAPPENED...
...EVERYONE BROUGHT ME CANDY AND FRUIT.
THEY EVEN READ TO ME.
THE DRAGON TRIBE REALLY DID KEEP A CLOSE EYE ON ME.
THAT'S TO BE EXPECTED.
AFTER ALL, I *WAS* CONSTANTLY STEALING ALL THEIR MOST VALUABLE POSSESSIONS.
IF IT WASN'T ONE THING, IT WAS ANOTHER.
FIRE DRAGON AND SNOW CREWGER...
I EVEN ENDED UP WITH THE RED DRAGON CRYSTAL.

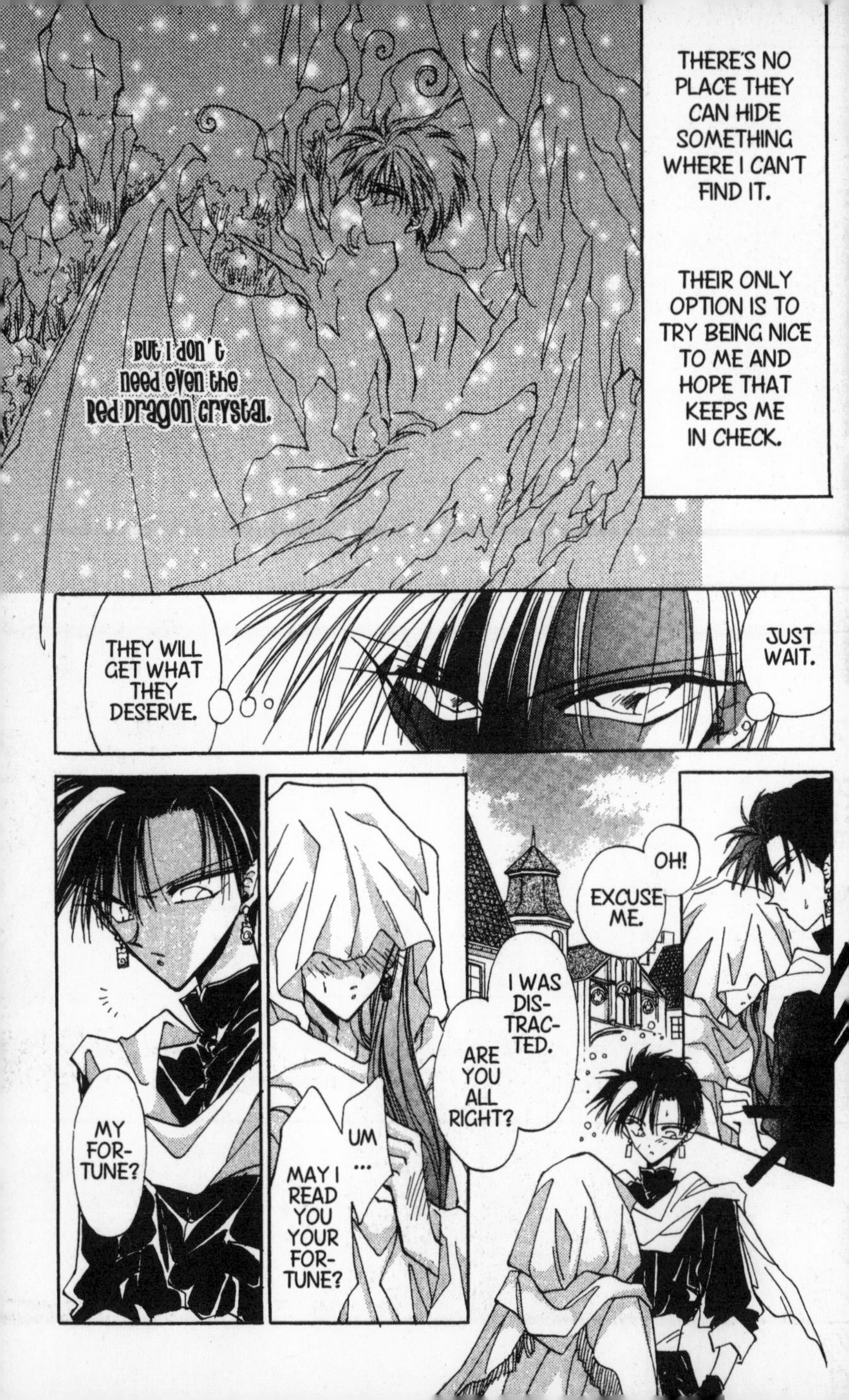
THERE'S NO PLACE THEY CAN HIDE SOMETHING WHERE I CAN'T FIND IT.
THEIR ONLY OPTION IS TO TRY BEING NICE TO ME AND HOPE THAT KEEPS ME IN CHECK.
But I don't need even the Red Dragon Crystal.
JUST WAIT.
THEY WILL GET WHAT THEY DESERVE.
OH!
EXCUSE ME.
I WAS DIS-TRAC-TED.
ARE YOU ALL RIGHT?
UM ...
MAY I READ YOU YOUR FOR-TUNE?
MY FOR-TUNE?

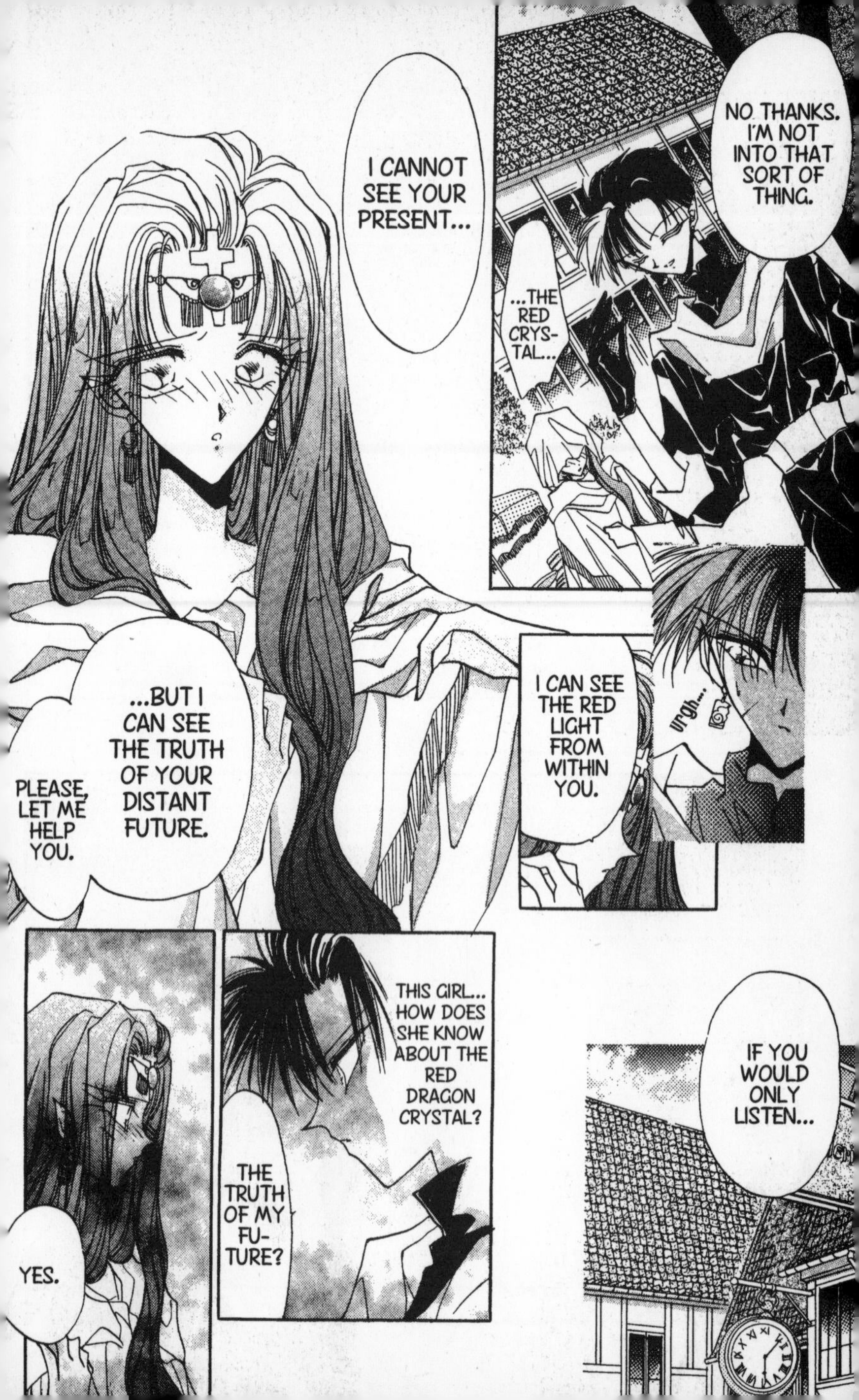
NO THANKS. I'M NOT INTO THAT SORT OF THING.
...THE RED CRYS-TAL...
Urgh...
I CAN SEE THE RED LIGHT FROM WITHIN YOU.
I CANNOT SEE YOUR PRESENT...
...BUT I CAN SEE THE TRUTH OF YOUR DISTANT FUTURE.
PLEASE, LET ME HELP YOU.
IF YOU WOULD ONLY LISTEN...
THIS GIRL... HOW DOES SHE KNOW ABOUT THE RED DRAGON CRYSTAL?
THE TRUTH OF MY FU-TURE?
YES.

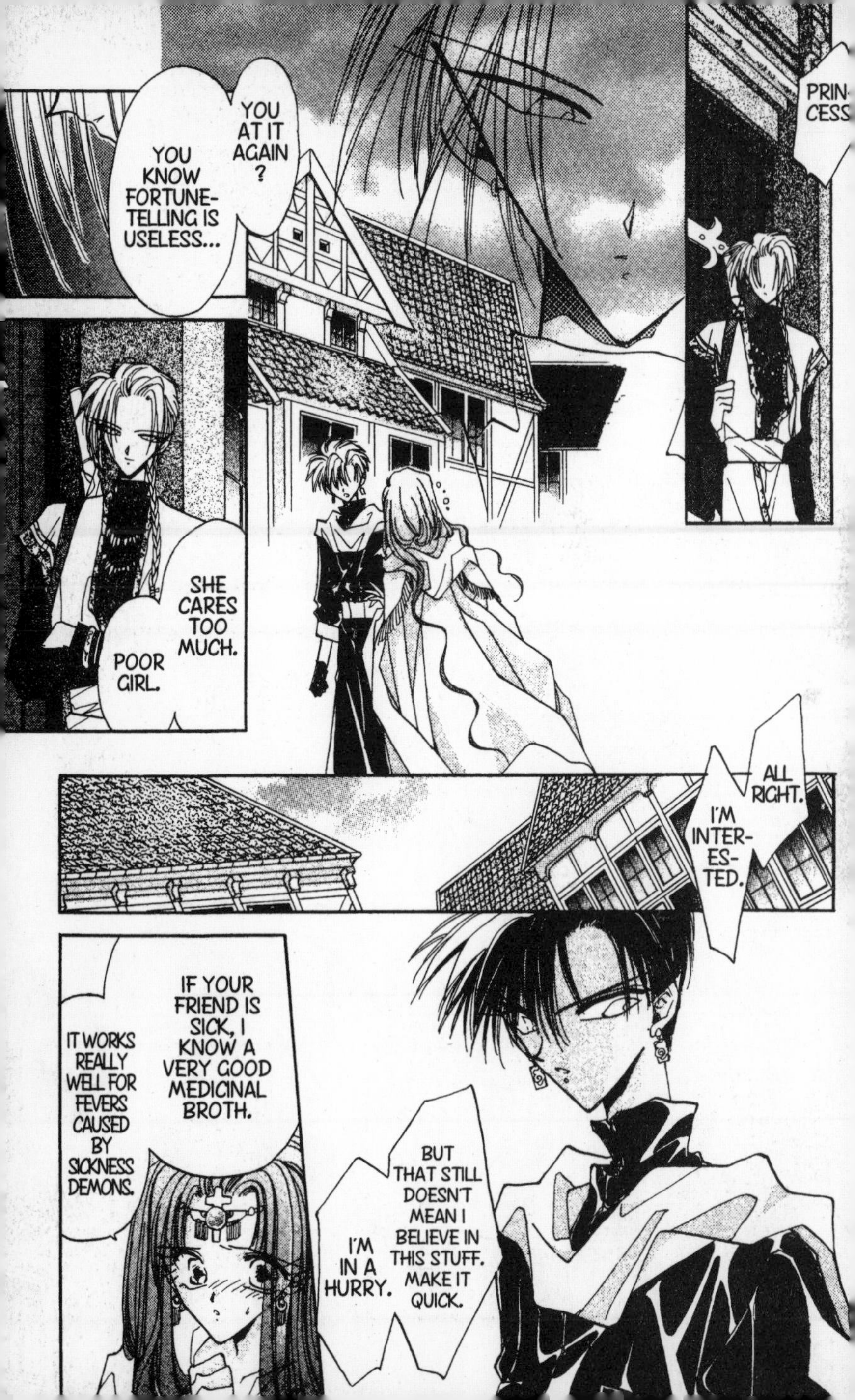
PRINCESS
YOU AT IT AGAIN?
YOU KNOW FORTUNE-TELLING IS USELESS...
SHE CARES TOO MUCH.
POOR GIRL.
ALL RIGHT.
I'M INTERESTED.
IF YOUR FRIEND IS SICK, I KNOW A VERY GOOD MEDICINAL BROTH.
IT WORKS REALLY WELL FOR FEVERS CAUSED BY SICKNESS DEMONS.
BUT THAT STILL DOESN'T MEAN I BELIEVE IN THIS STUFF. MAKE IT QUICK.
I'M IN A HURRY.

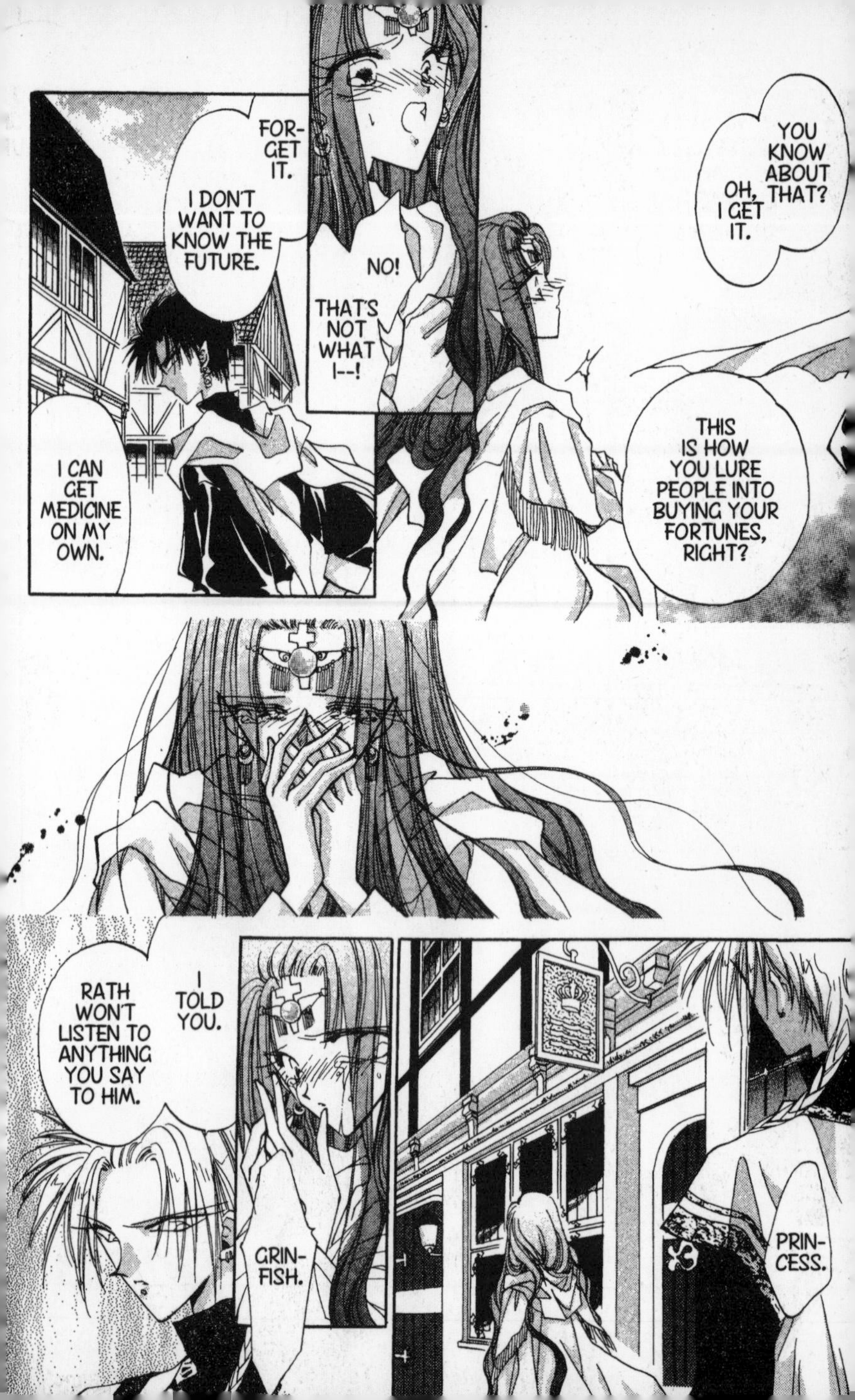
YOU KNOW ABOUT THAT?
OH, I GET IT.
THIS IS HOW YOU LURE PEOPLE INTO BUYING YOUR FORTUNES, RIGHT?
NO!
THAT'S NOT WHAT I--!
FOR-GET IT.
I DON'T WANT TO KNOW THE FUTURE.
I CAN GET MEDICINE ON MY OWN.
PRIN-CESS.
GRIN-FISH.
I TOLD YOU.
RATH WON'T LISTEN TO ANYTHING YOU SAY TO HIM.

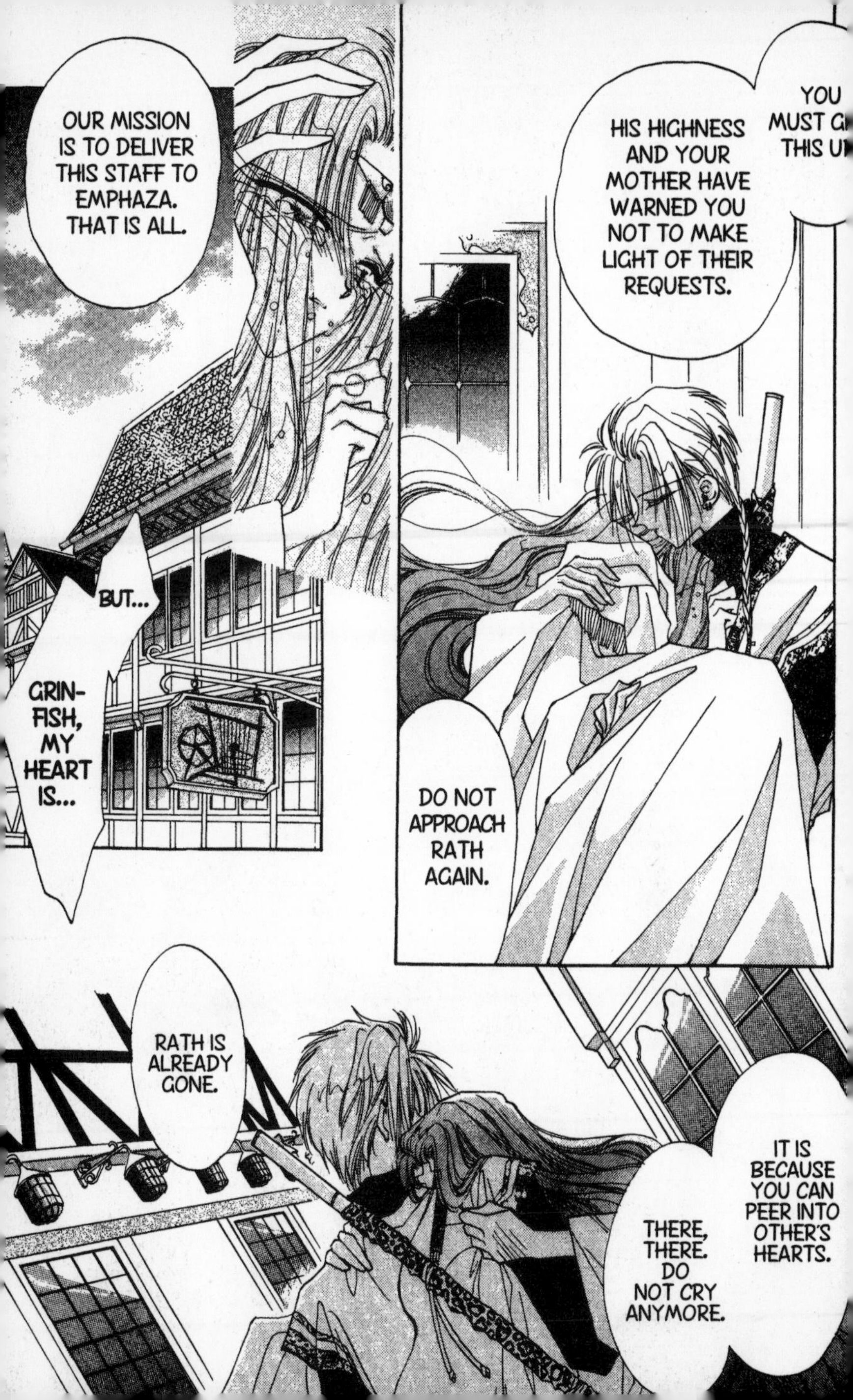

YOU MUST G
THIS U
HIS HIGHNESS AND YOUR MOTHER HAVE WARNED YOU NOT TO MAKE LIGHT OF THEIR REQUESTS.
DO NOT APPROACH RATH AGAIN.
OUR MISSION IS TO DELIVER THIS STAFF TO EMPHAZA. THAT IS ALL.
BUT...
GRIN-FISH, MY HEART IS...
IT IS BECAUSE YOU CAN PEER INTO OTHER'S HEARTS.
THERE, THERE. DO NOT CRY ANYMORE.
RATH IS ALREADY GONE.

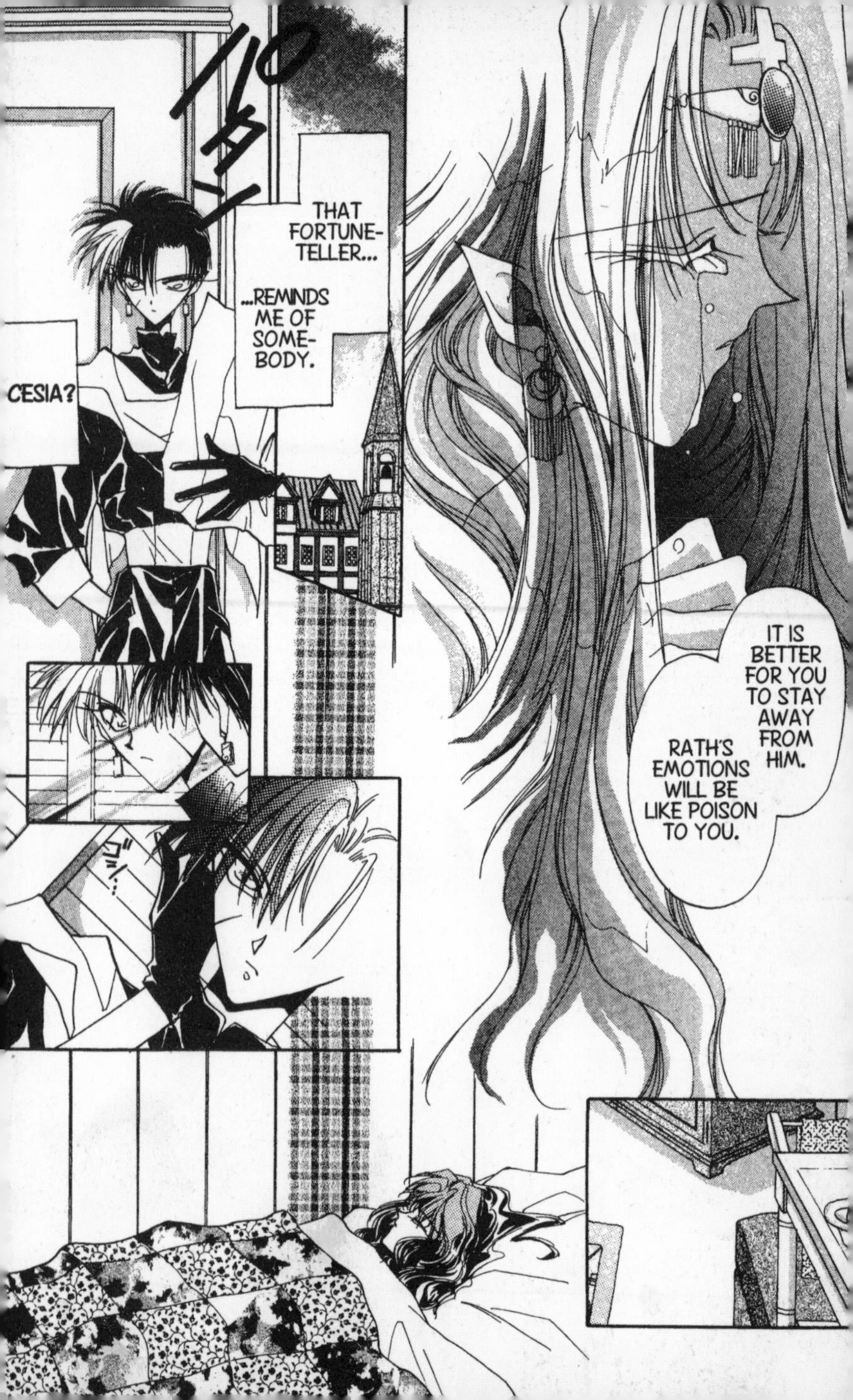
IT IS BETTER FOR YOU TO STAY AWAY FROM HIM.
RATH'S EMOTIONS WILL BE LIKE POISON TO YOU.
THAT FORTUNE-TELLER...
...REMINDS ME OF SOME-BODY.
CESIA?

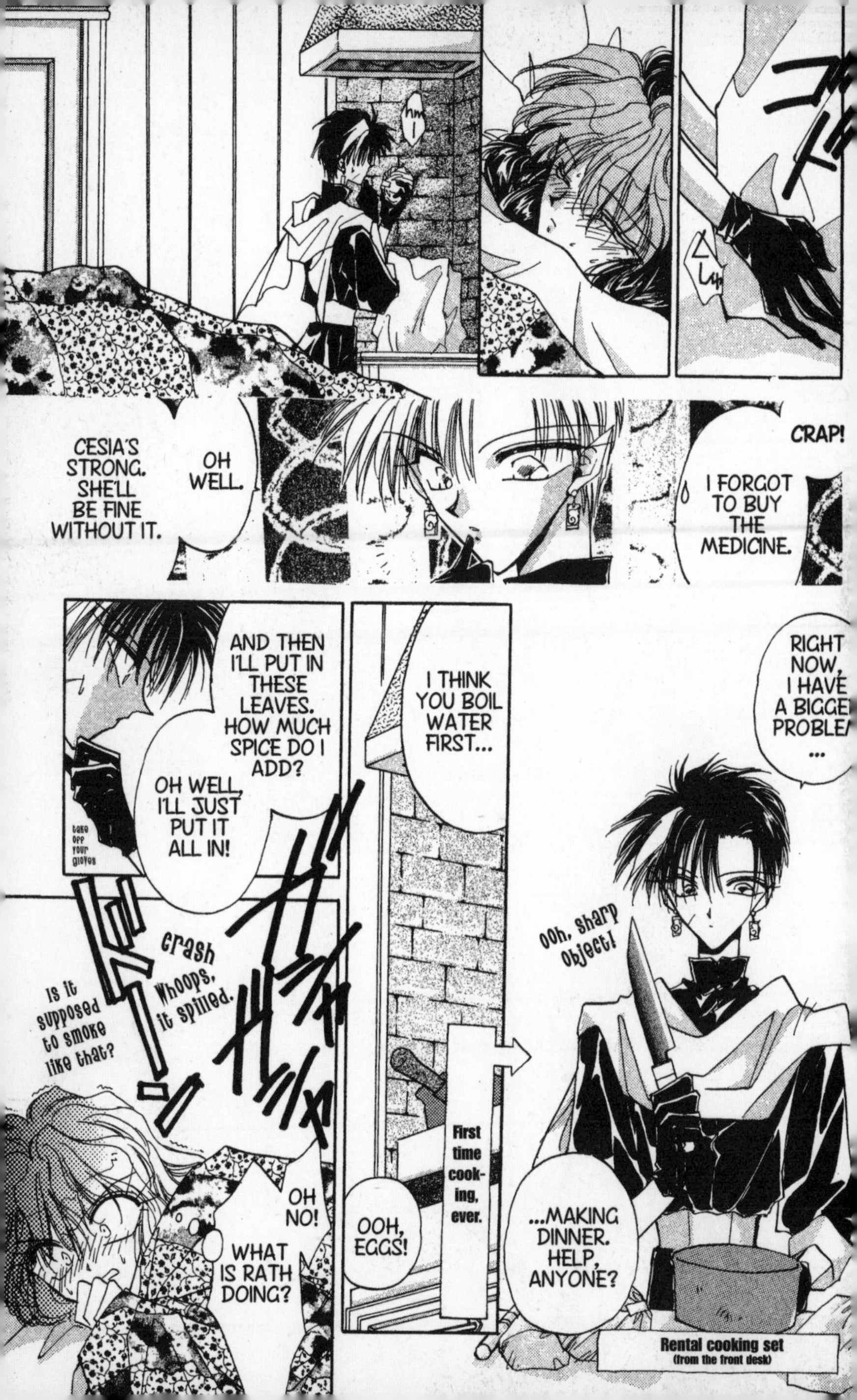

hm
CRAP!
I FORGOT TO BUY THE MEDICINE.
OH WELL.
CESIA'S STRONG. SHE'LL BE FINE WITHOUT IT.
RIGHT NOW, I HAVE A BIGGER PROBLEM...
Ooh, sharp object!
...MAKING DINNER. HELP, ANYONE?
Rental cooking set
(from the front desk)
I THINK YOU BOIL WATER FIRST...
First time cooking, ever.
OOH, EGGS!
AND THEN I'LL PUT IN THESE LEAVES. HOW MUCH SPICE DO I ADD?
OH WELL, I'LL JUST PUT IT ALL IN!
take off your gloves
Crash
Whoops, it spilled.
Is it supposed to smoke like that?
OH NO!
WHAT IS RATH DOING?

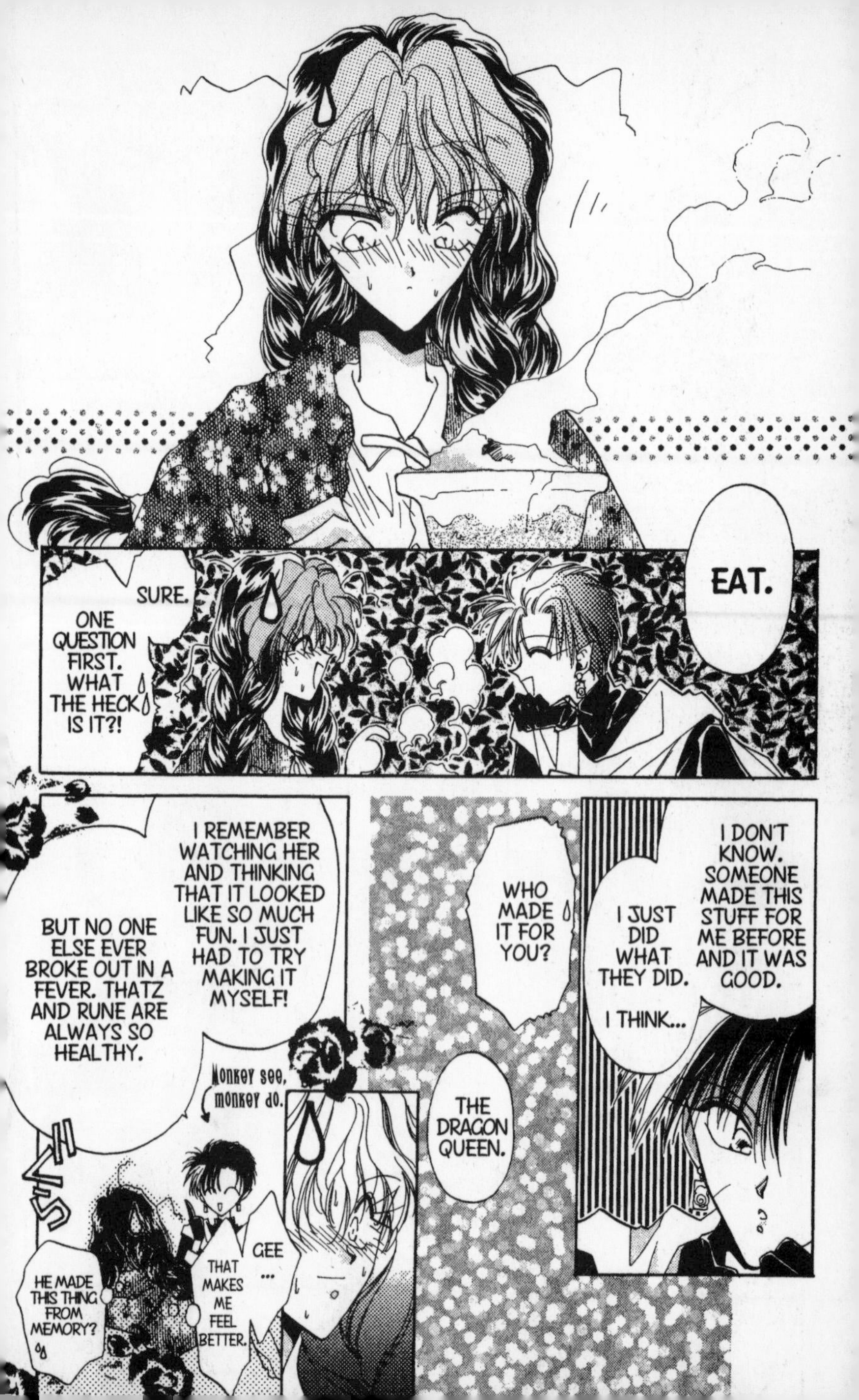
EAT.
SURE.
ONE QUESTION FIRST. WHAT THE HECK IS IT?!
I DON'T KNOW. SOMEONE MADE THIS STUFF FOR ME BEFORE AND IT WAS GOOD.
I JUST DID WHAT THEY DID.
I THINK...
WHO MADE IT FOR YOU?
THE DRAGON QUEEN.
I REMEMBER WATCHING HER AND THINKING THAT IT LOOKED LIKE SO MUCH FUN. I JUST HAD TO TRY MAKING IT MYSELF!
BUT NO ONE ELSE EVER BROKE OUT IN A FEVER. THATZ AND RUNE ARE ALWAYS SO HEALTHY.
Monkey see, monkey do.
GEE...
THAT MAKES ME FEEL BETTER.
HE MADE THIS THING FROM MEMORY?

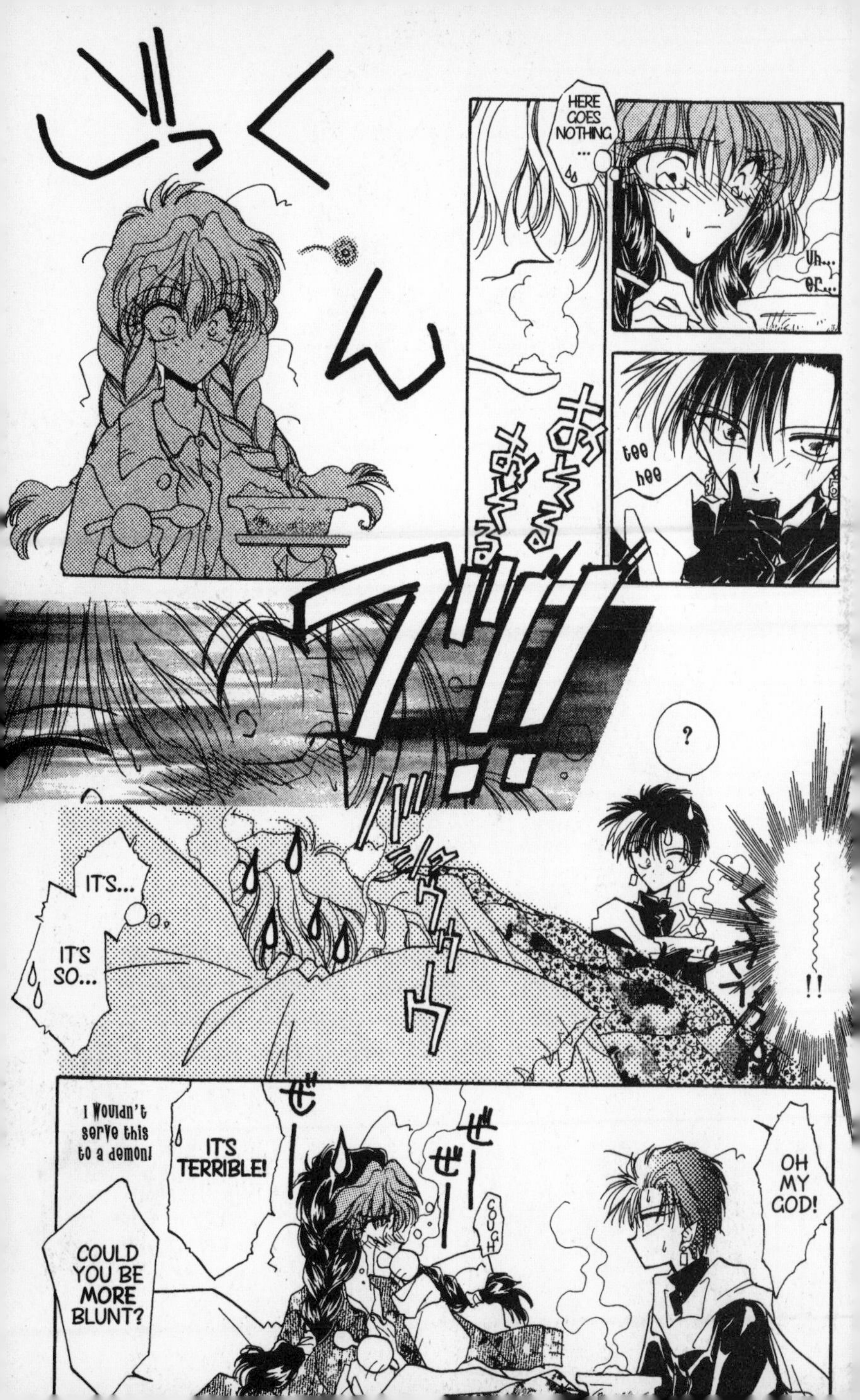

HERE GOES NOTHING ...
Uh... er...
tee hee
?
!!
IT'S...
IT'S SO...
OH MY GOD!
COUGH
IT'S TERRIBLE!
I wouldn't serve this to a demon!
COULD YOU BE MORE BLUNT?

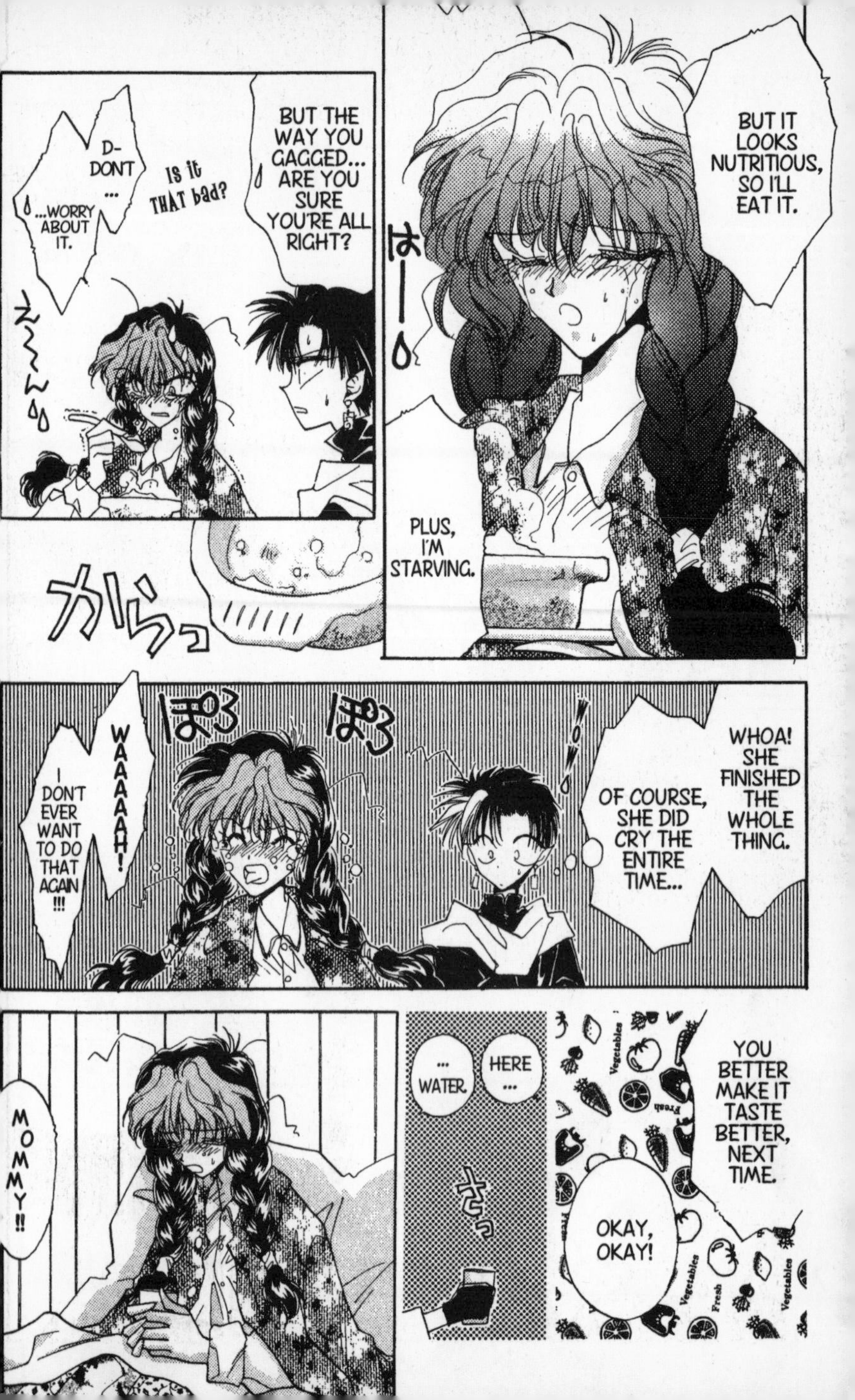
BUT IT LOOKS NUTRITIOUS, SO I'LL EAT IT.
PLUS, I'M STARVING.
BUT THE WAY YOU GAGGED... ARE YOU SURE YOU'RE ALL RIGHT?
Is it THAT bad?
D-DONT ... ...WORRY ABOUT IT.
からっ
WHOA! SHE FINISHED THE WHOLE THING.
OF COURSE, SHE DID CRY THE ENTIRE TIME...
ぽろ ぽろ
WAAAAAAH!
I DON'T EVER WANT TO DO THAT AGAIN!!!
YOU BETTER MAKE IT TASTE BETTER, NEXT TIME.
OKAY, OKAY!
HERE...
...WATER.
さっ
MOMMY!!

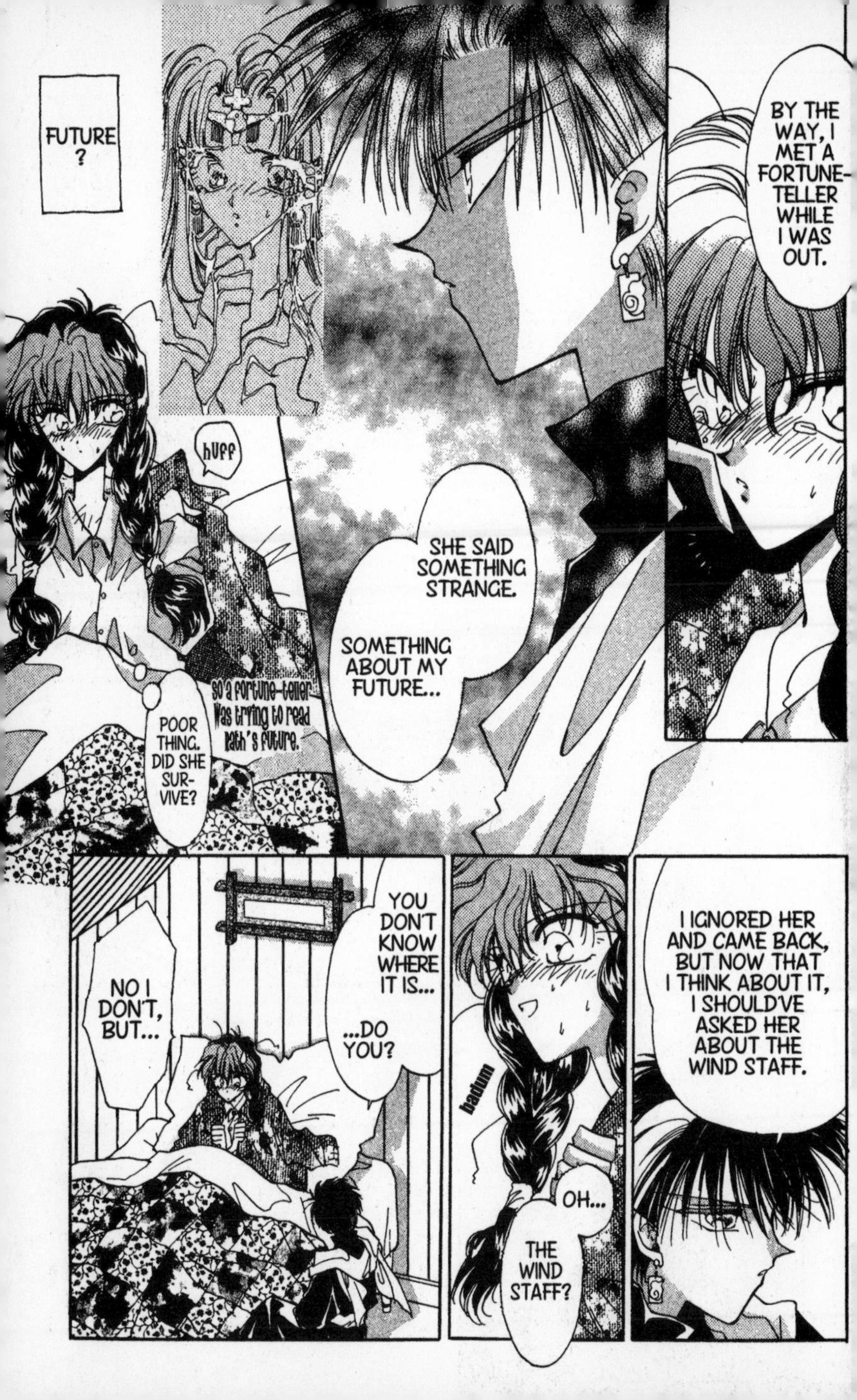
BY THE WAY, I MET A FORTUNE-TELLER WHILE I WAS OUT.
SHE SAID SOMETHING STRANGE.
SOMETHING ABOUT MY FUTURE...
FUTURE ?
huff
So a fortune-teller Was trying to read Bath's future.
POOR THING. DID SHE SUR-VIVE?
I IGNORED HER AND CAME BACK, BUT NOW THAT I THINK ABOUT IT, I SHOULD'VE ASKED HER ABOUT THE WIND STAFF.
badum
OH...
THE WIND STAFF?
YOU DON'T KNOW WHERE IT IS...
...DO YOU?
NO I DON'T, BUT...

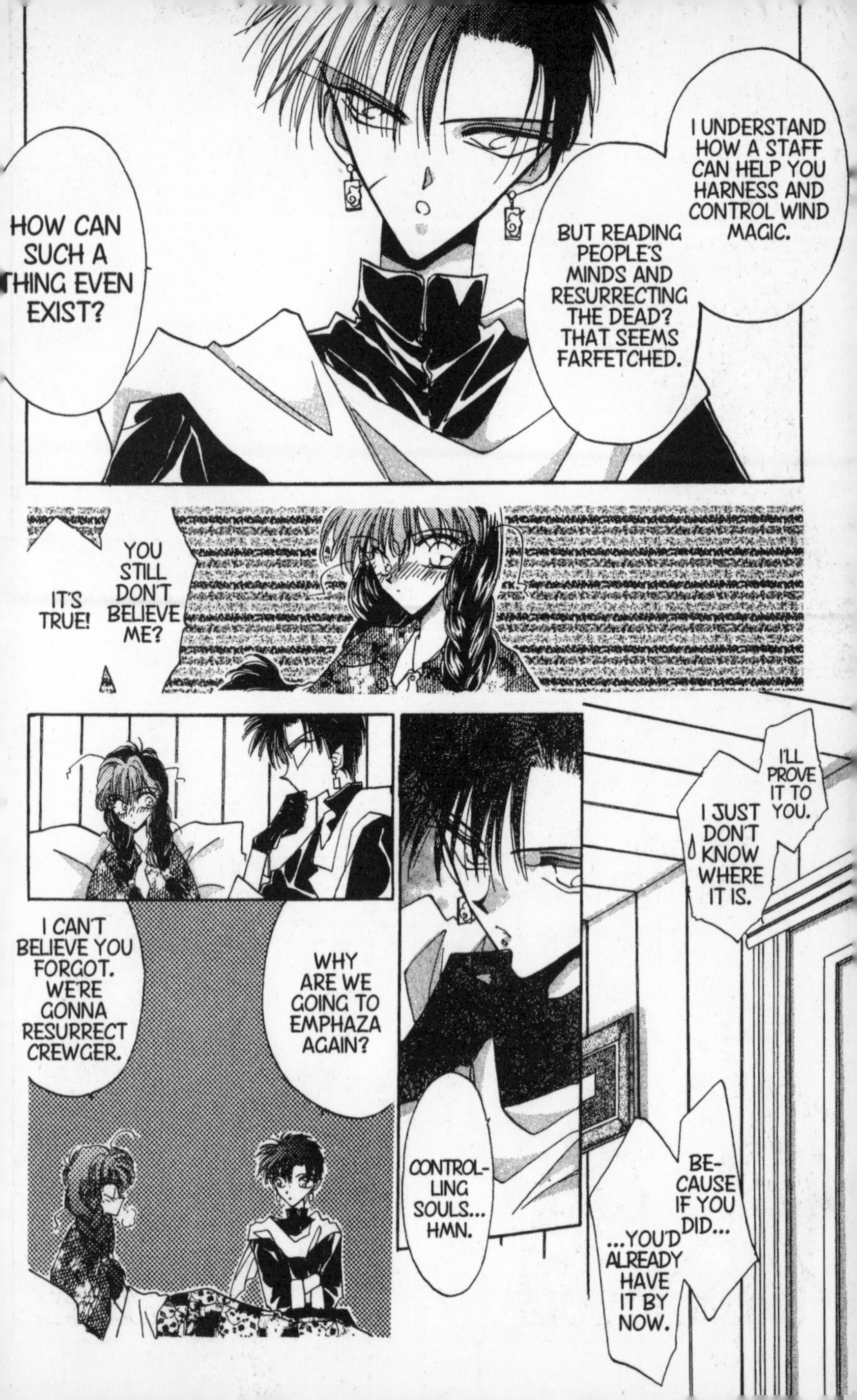
I UNDERSTAND HOW A STAFF CAN HELP YOU HARNESS AND CONTROL WIND MAGIC.
BUT READING PEOPLE'S MINDS AND RESURRECTING THE DEAD? THAT SEEMS FARFETCHED.
HOW CAN SUCH A THING EVEN EXIST?
YOU STILL DON'T BELIEVE ME?
IT'S TRUE!
I'LL PROVE IT TO YOU.
I JUST DON'T KNOW WHERE IT IS.
BE-CAUSE IF YOU DID...
...YOU'D ALREADY HAVE IT BY NOW.
CONTROL-LING SOULS... HMN.
WHY ARE WE GOING TO EMPHAZA AGAIN?
I CAN'T BELIEVE YOU FORGOT. WE'RE GONNA RESURRECT CREWGER.

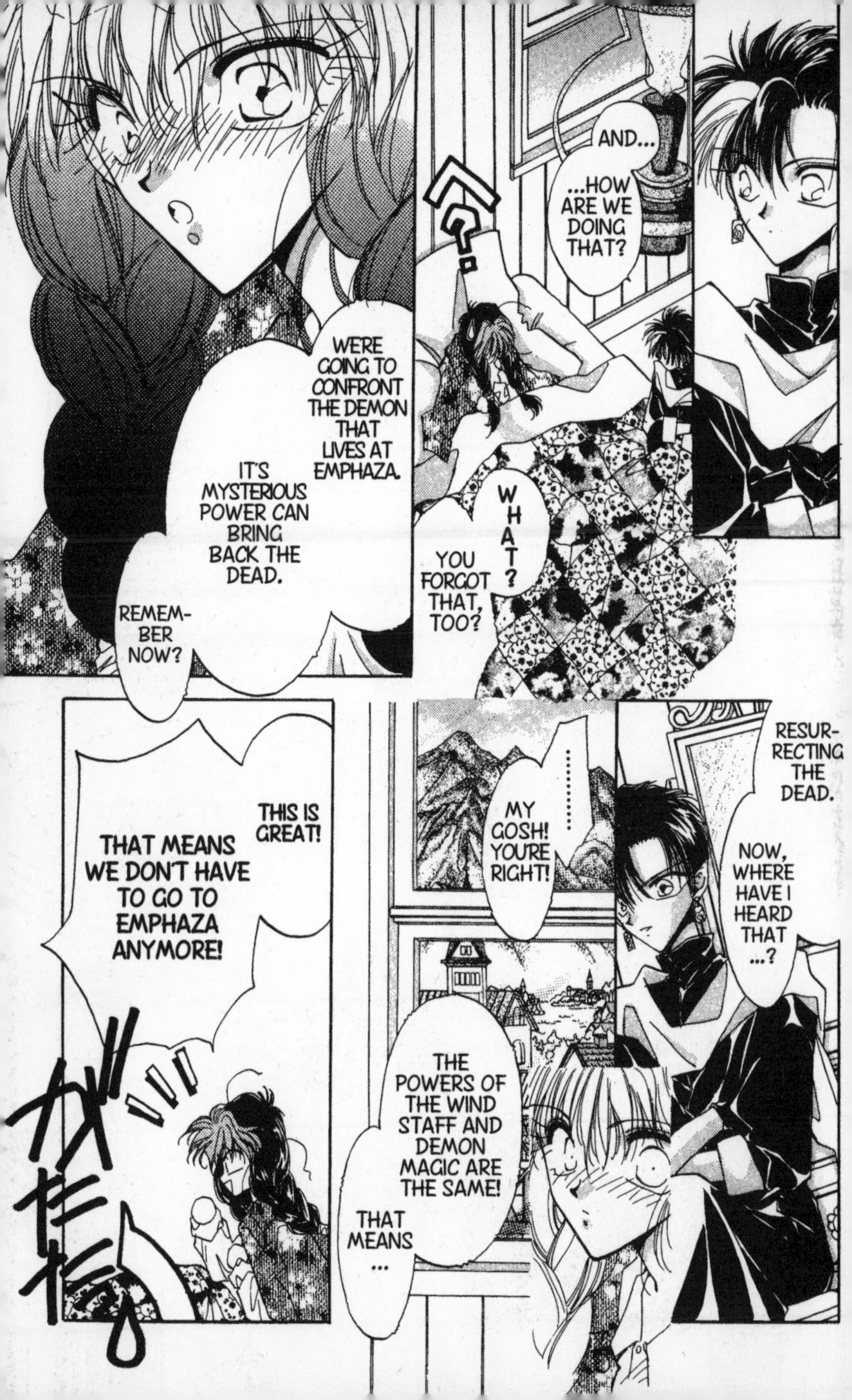
AND...
...HOW ARE WE DOING THAT?
?
WHAT?
YOU FORGOT THAT, TOO?
WERE GOING TO CONFRONT THE DEMON THAT LIVES AT EMPHAZA.
IT'S MYSTERIOUS POWER CAN BRING BACK THE DEAD.
REMEM-BER NOW?
RESUR-RECTING THE DEAD.
NOW, WHERE HAVE I HEARD THAT ...?
......
MY GOSH! YOURE RIGHT!
THE POWERS OF THE WIND STAFF AND DEMON MAGIC ARE THE SAME!
THAT MEANS ...
THIS IS GREAT!
THAT MEANS WE DON'T HAVE TO GO TO EMPHAZA ANYMORE!

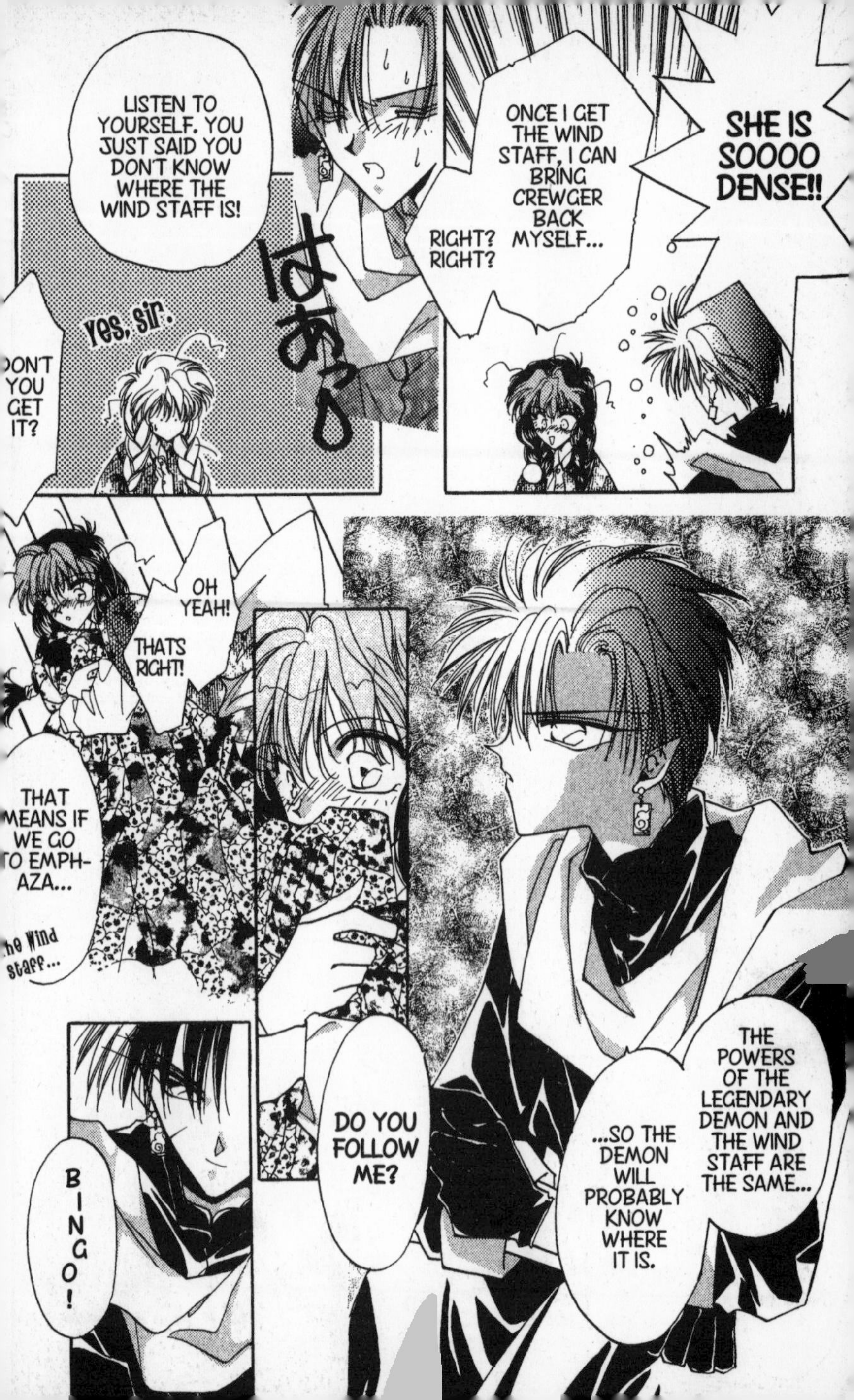
ONCE I GET THE WIND STAFF, I CAN BRING CREWGER BACK MYSELF...
RIGHT? RIGHT?
SHE IS SOOOO DENSE!!
LISTEN TO YOURSELF. YOU JUST SAID YOU DON'T KNOW WHERE THE WIND STAFF IS!
はあっ
yes, sir.
DON'T YOU GET IT?
THE POWERS OF THE LEGENDARY DEMON AND THE WIND STAFF ARE THE SAME...
...SO THE DEMON WILL PROBABLY KNOW WHERE IT IS.
DO YOU FOLLOW ME?
OH YEAH!
THATS RIGHT!
THAT MEANS IF WE GO O EMPH-AZA...
he Wind staff...
BINGO!

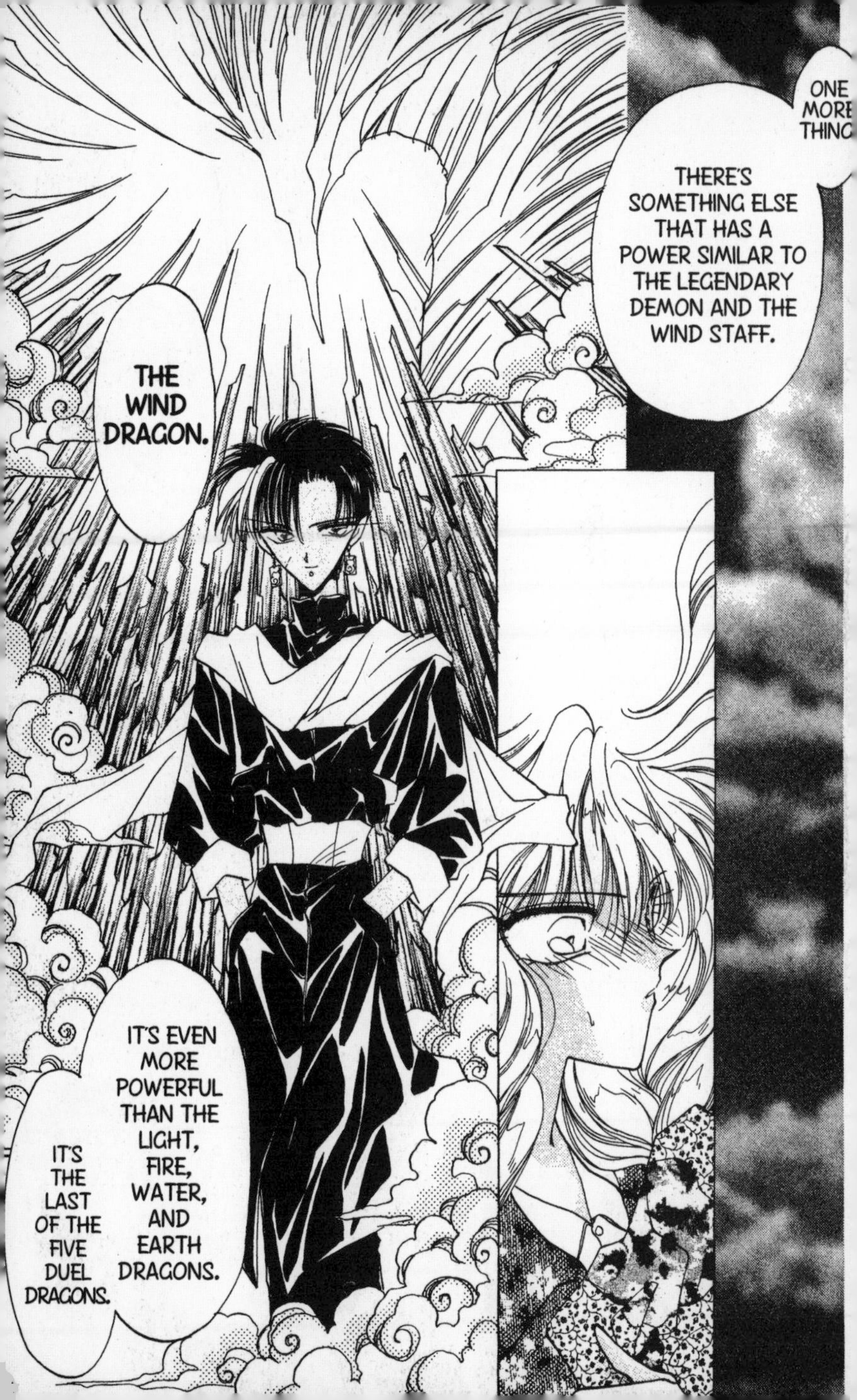
ONE MORE THING
THERE'S SOMETHING ELSE THAT HAS A POWER SIMILAR TO THE LEGENDARY DEMON AND THE WIND STAFF.
THE WIND DRAGON.
IT'S EVEN MORE POWERFUL THAN THE LIGHT, FIRE, WATER, AND EARTH DRAGONS.
IT'S THE LAST OF THE FIVE DUEL DRAGONS.

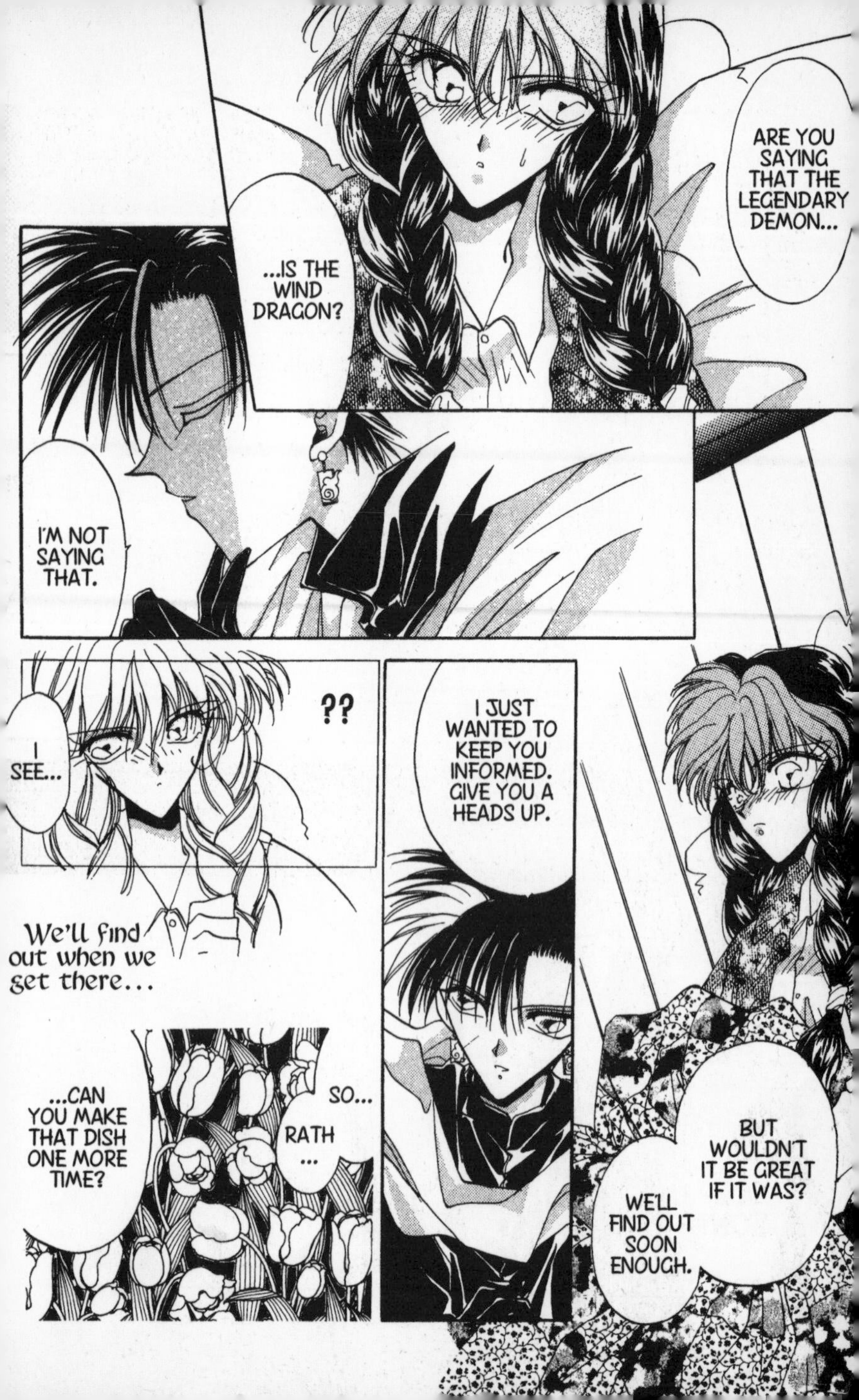
ARE YOU SAYING THAT THE LEGENDARY DEMON...
...IS THE WIND DRAGON?
I'M NOT SAYING THAT.
I JUST WANTED TO KEEP YOU INFORMED. GIVE YOU A HEADS UP.
??
I SEE...
We'll find out when we get there...
BUT WOULDN'T IT BE GREAT IF IT WAS?
WE'LL FIND OUT SOON ENOUGH.
SO... RATH ...
...CAN YOU MAKE THAT DISH ONE MORE TIME?

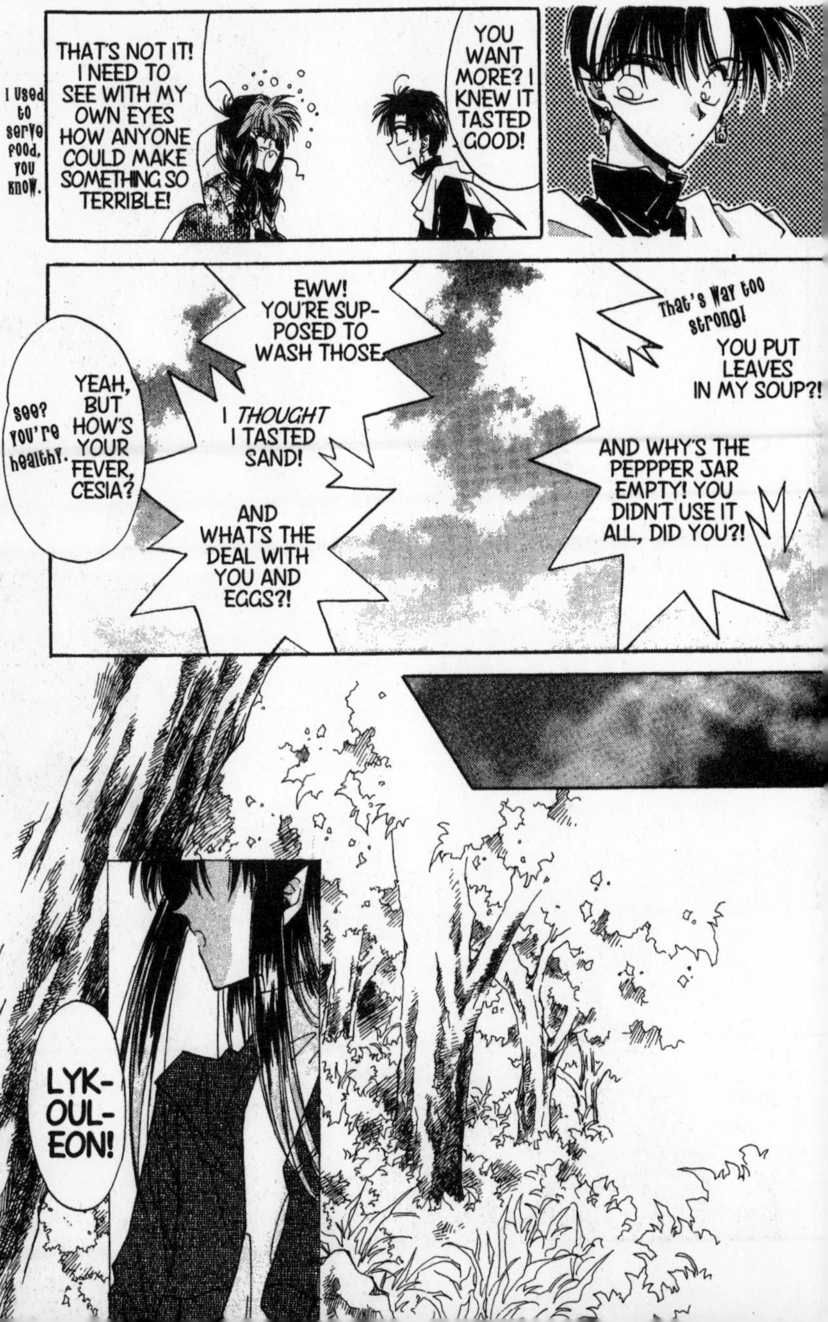
YOU WANT MORE? I KNEW IT TASTED GOOD!
THAT'S NOT IT! I NEED TO SEE WITH MY OWN EYES HOW ANYONE COULD MAKE SOMETHING SO TERRIBLE!
I used to serve food, you know.
That's way too strong!
YOU PUT LEAVES IN MY SOUP?!
EWW! YOU'RE SUP-POSED TO WASH THOSE.
AND WHY'S THE PEPPPER JAR EMPTY! YOU DIDN'T USE IT ALL, DID YOU?!
I *THOUGHT* I TASTED SAND!
AND WHAT'S THE DEAL WITH YOU AND EGGS?!
YEAH, BUT HOW'S YOUR FEVER, CESIA?
See? You're healthy.
LYK-OUL-EON!

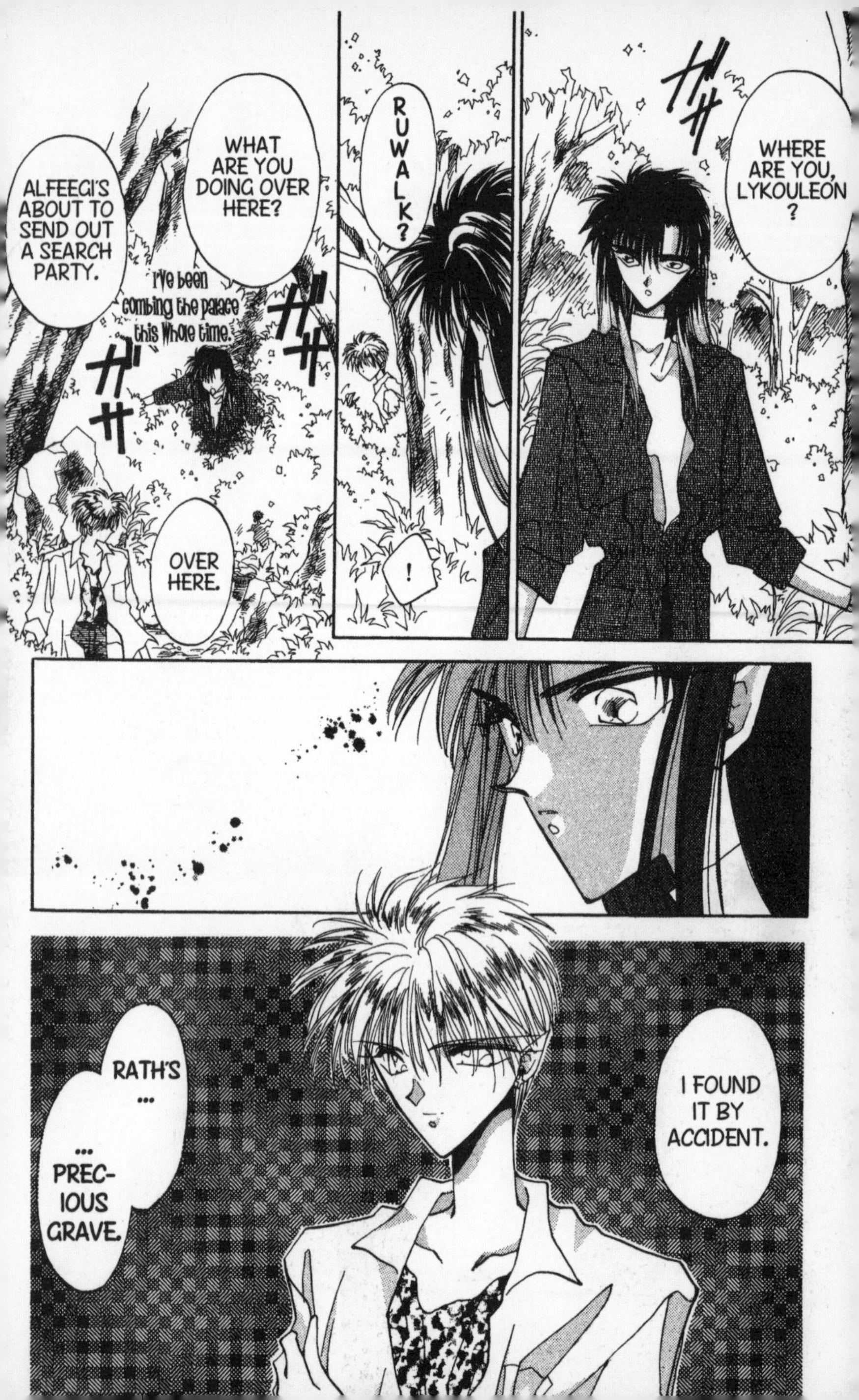

ガサ
WHERE ARE YOU, LYKOULEON?
RUWALK?
!
WHAT ARE YOU DOING OVER HERE?
ALFEEGI'S ABOUT TO SEND OUT A SEARCH PARTY.
I've been combing the palace this whole time.
ガサ
ガサ
OVER HERE.
I FOUND IT BY ACCIDENT.
RATH'S ...
... PRECIOUS GRAVE.

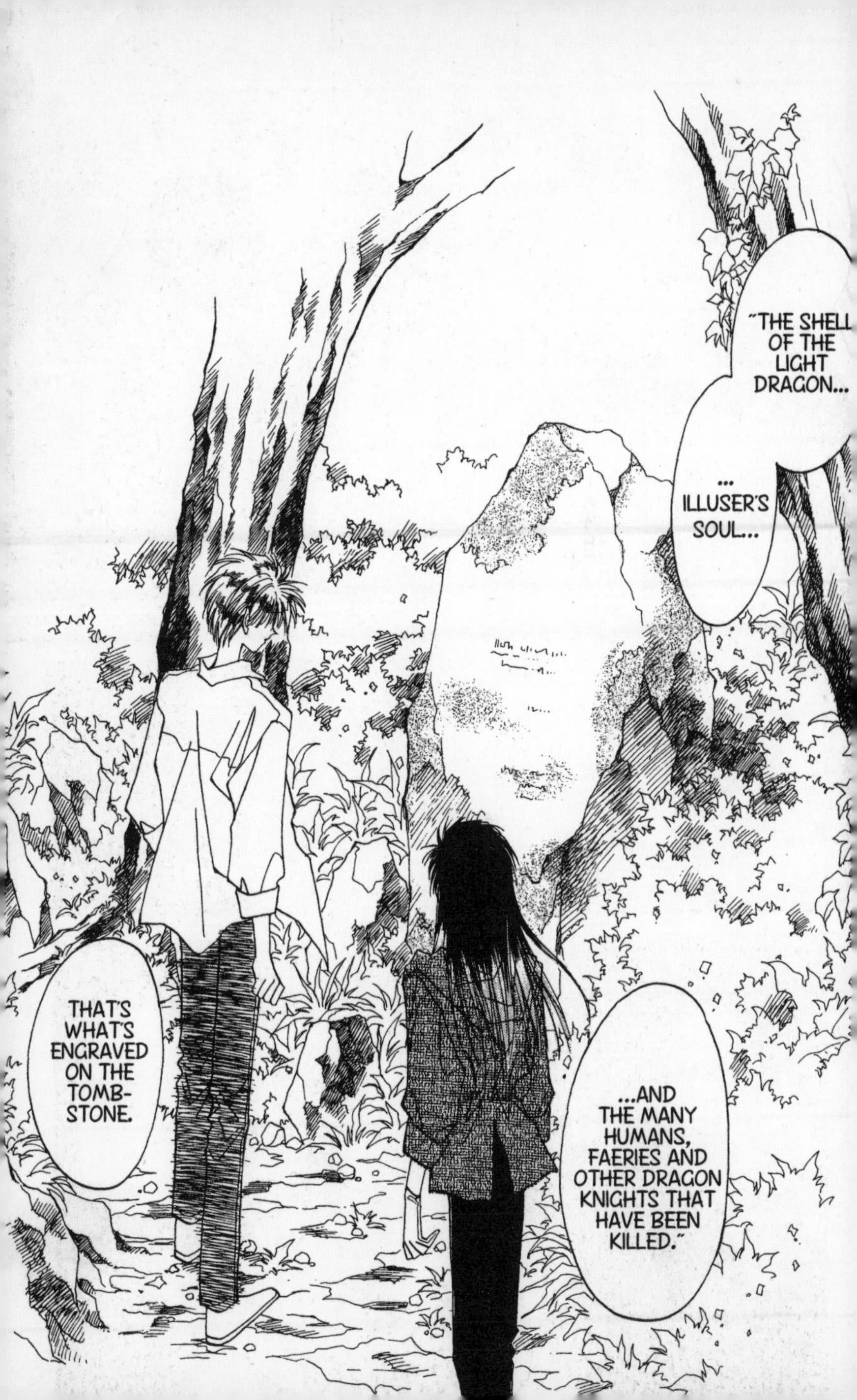
"THE SHELL OF THE LIGHT DRAGON...
... ILLUSER'S SOUL...
...AND THE MANY HUMANS, FAERIES AND OTHER DRAGON KNIGHTS THAT HAVE BEEN KILLED."
THAT'S WHAT'S ENGRAVED ON THE TOMB-STONE.

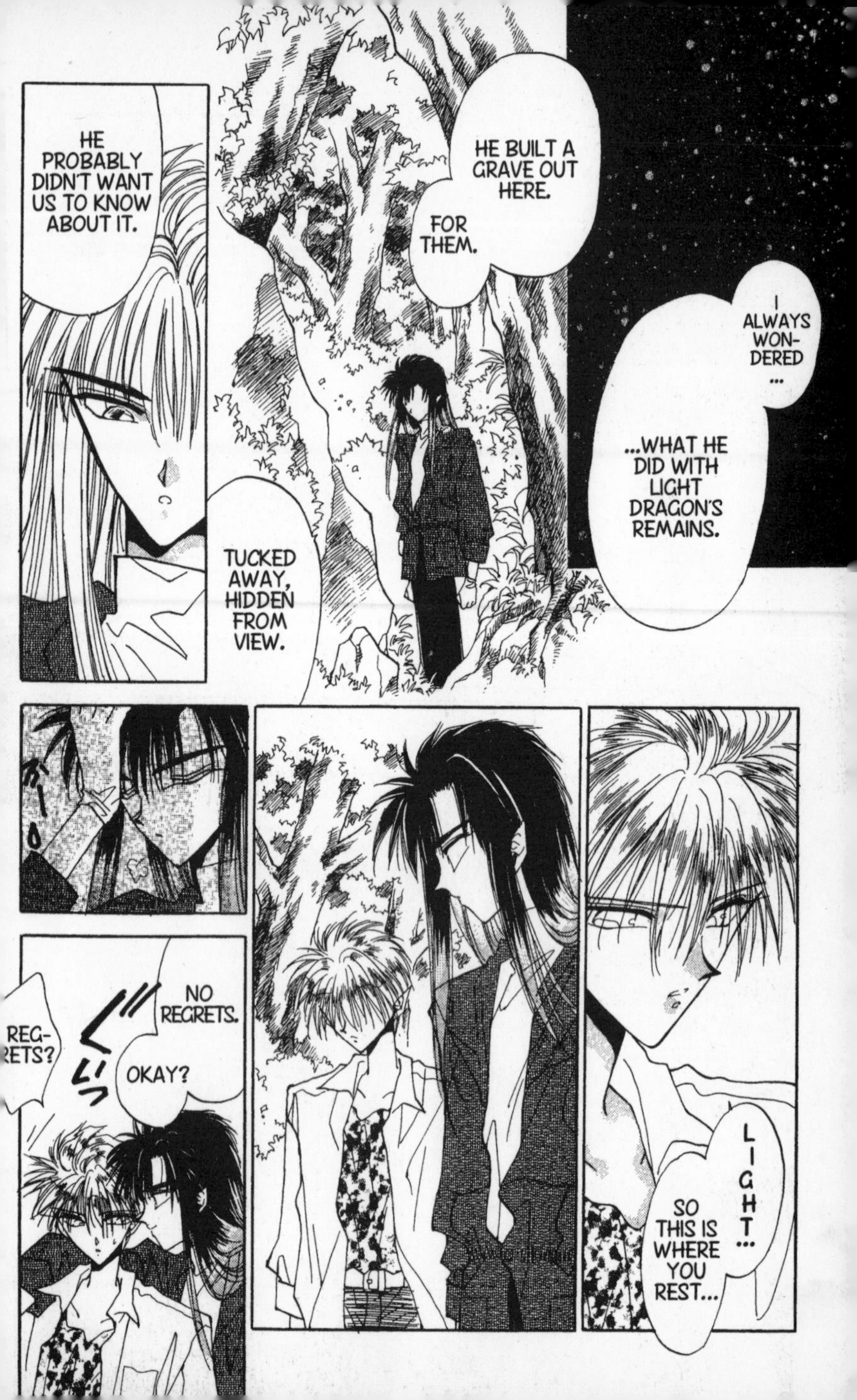
I ALWAYS WON-DERED ...
...WHAT HE DID WITH LIGHT DRAGON'S REMAINS.
HE BUILT A GRAVE OUT HERE.
FOR THEM.
TUCKED AWAY, HIDDEN FROM VIEW.
HE PROBABLY DIDN'T WANT US TO KNOW ABOUT IT.
LIGHT...
SO THIS IS WHERE YOU REST...
NO REGRETS.
OKAY?
REG-RETS?

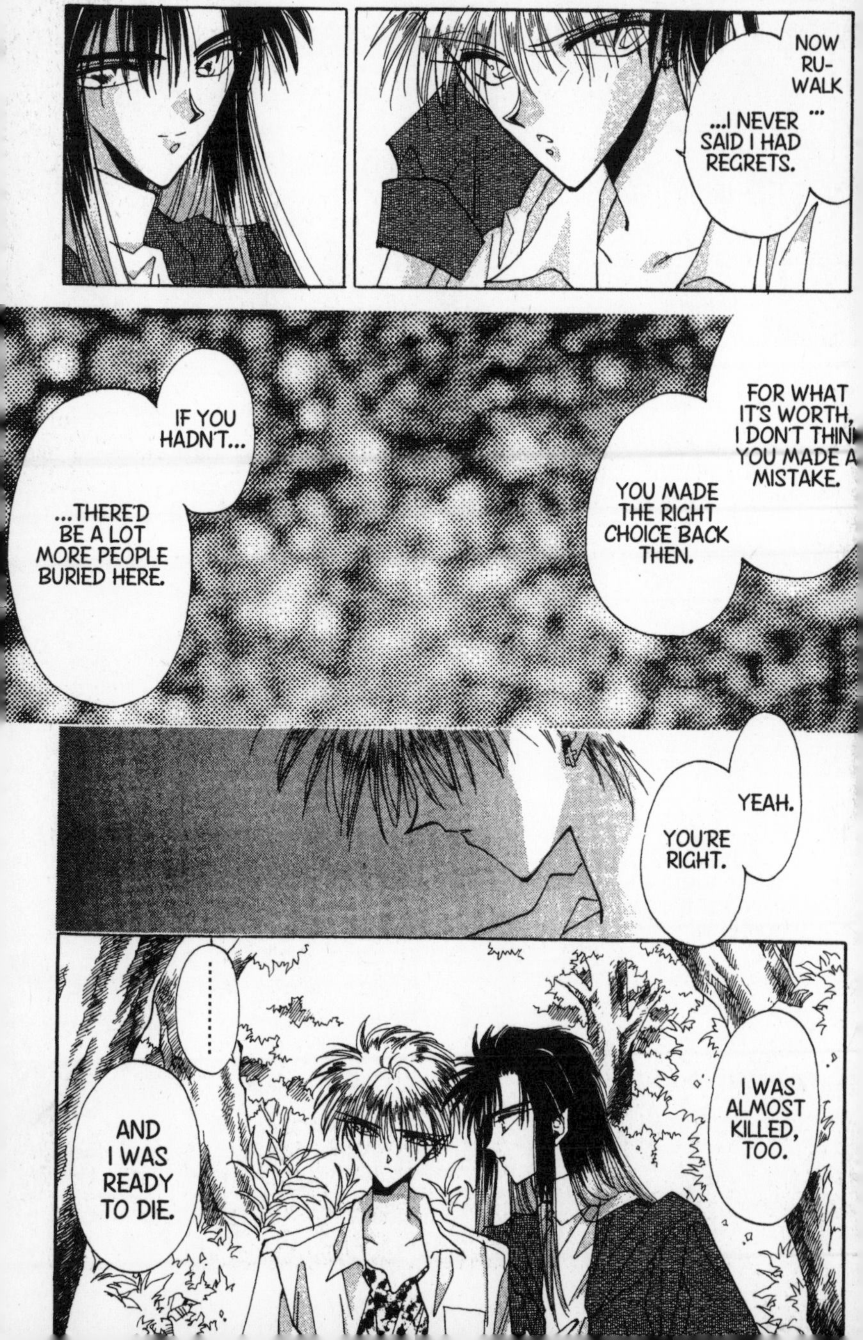
NOW RU-WALK ...
...I NEVER SAID I HAD REGRETS.
FOR WHAT IT'S WORTH, I DON'T THIN YOU MADE A MISTAKE.
YOU MADE THE RIGHT CHOICE BACK THEN.
IF YOU HADN'T...
...THERE'D BE A LOT MORE PEOPLE BURIED HERE.
YEAH.
YOU'RE RIGHT.
I WAS ALMOST KILLED, TOO.
......
AND I WAS READY TO DIE.

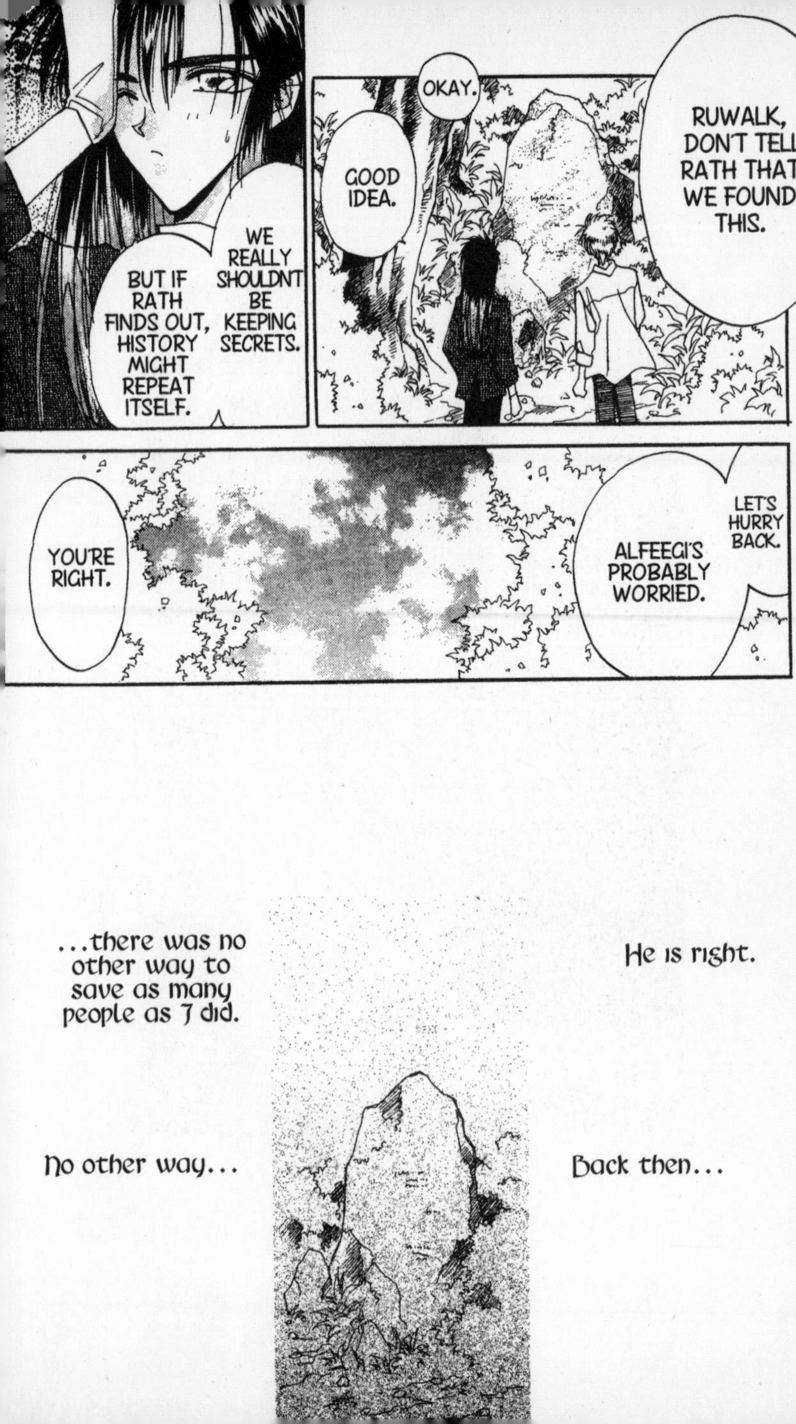

RUWALK, DON'T TELL RATH THAT WE FOUND THIS.
OKAY.
GOOD IDEA.
WE REALLY SHOULDNT BE KEEPING SECRETS.
BUT IF RATH FINDS OUT, HISTORY MIGHT REPEAT ITSELF.
LET'S HURRY BACK.
ALFEEGI'S PROBABLY WORRIED.
YOU'RE RIGHT.
He is right.
Back then...
...there was no other way to save as many people as I did.
No other way...

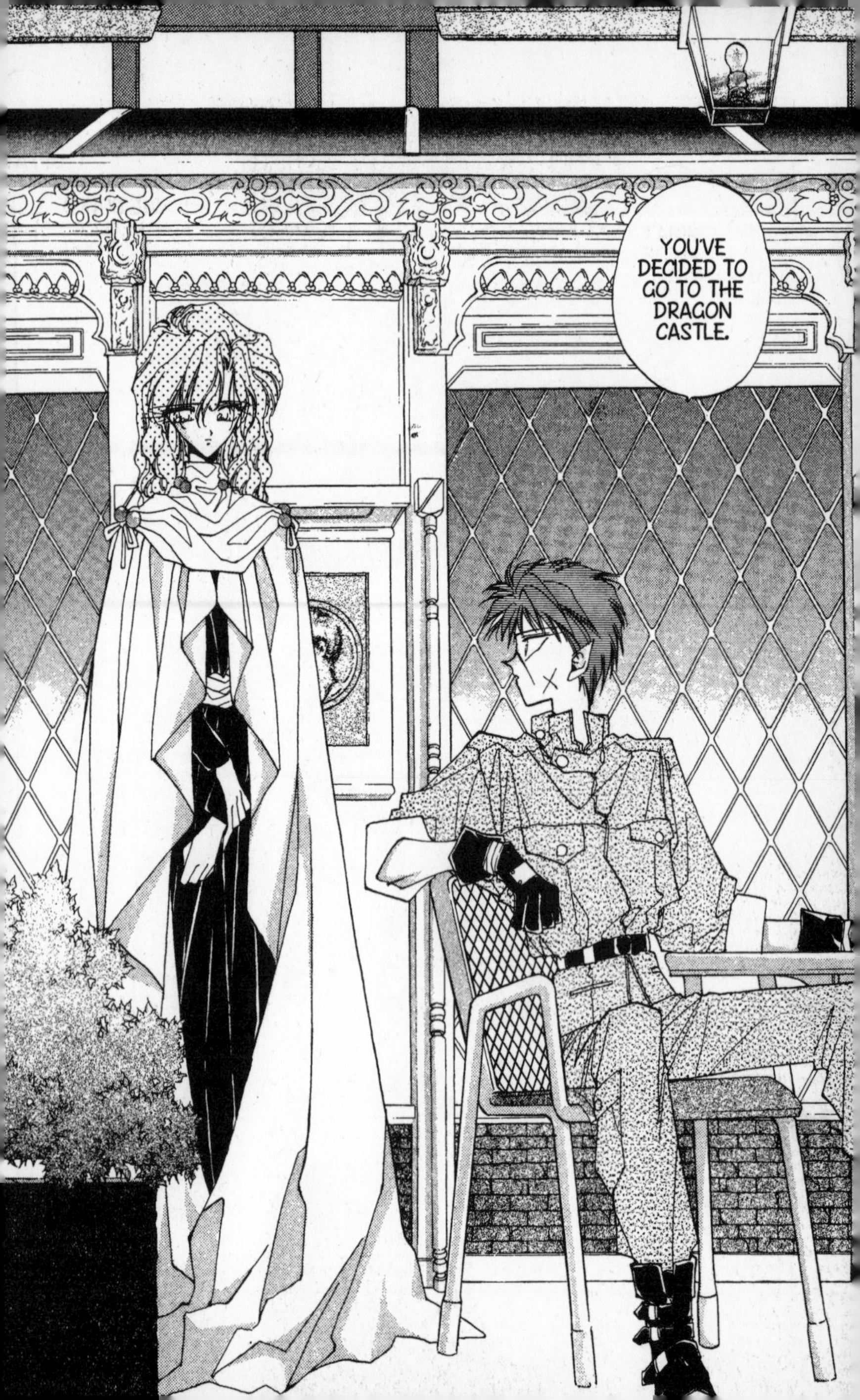
YOU'VE DECIDED TO GO TO THE DRAGON CASTLE.

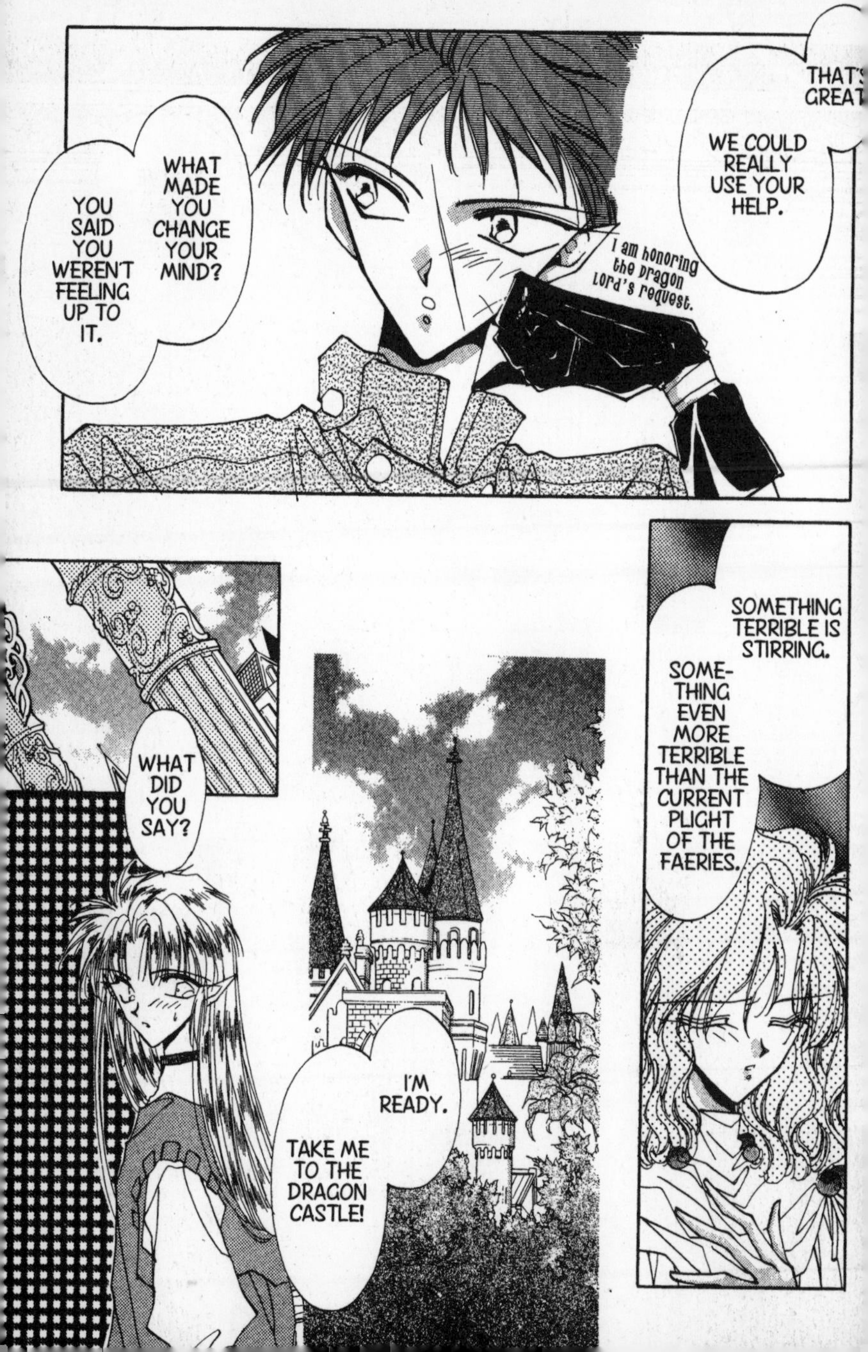
THAT'S GREAT.
WE COULD REALLY USE YOUR HELP.
I am honoring the Dragon Lord's request.
WHAT MADE YOU CHANGE YOUR MIND?
YOU SAID YOU WEREN'T FEELING UP TO IT.
SOMETHING TERRIBLE IS STIRRING.
SOMETHING EVEN MORE TERRIBLE THAN THE CURRENT PLIGHT OF THE FAERIES.
I'M READY.
TAKE ME TO THE DRAGON CASTLE!
WHAT DID YOU SAY?

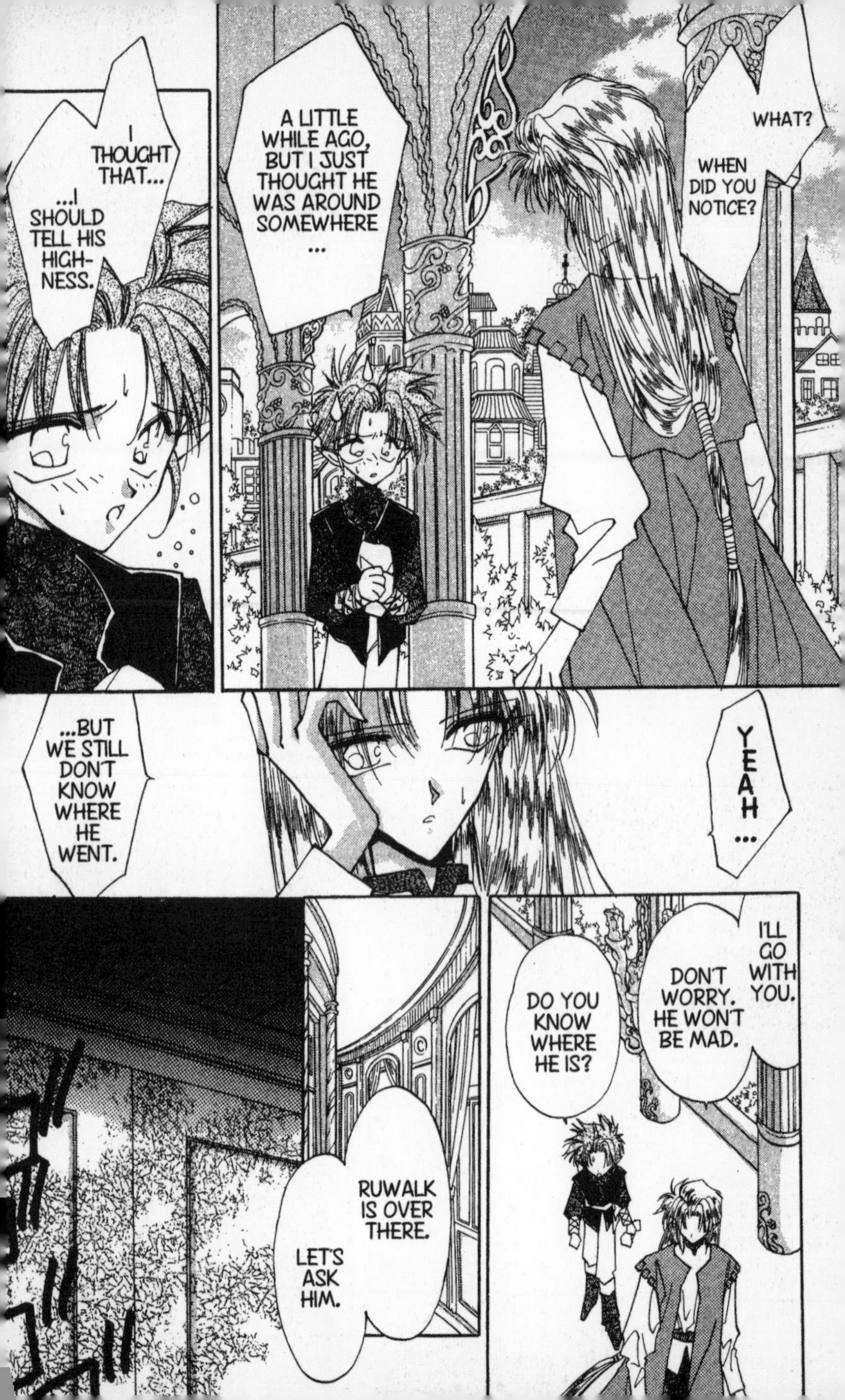
WHAT?
WHEN DID YOU NOTICE?
A LITTLE WHILE AGO, BUT I JUST THOUGHT HE WAS AROUND SOMEWHERE...
I THOUGHT THAT...
...I SHOULD TELL HIS HIGH-NESS.
YEAH...
...BUT WE STILL DON'T KNOW WHERE HE WENT.
I'LL GO WITH YOU.
DON'T WORRY. HE WON'T BE MAD.
DO YOU KNOW WHERE HE IS?
RUWALK IS OVER THERE.
LET'S ASK HIM.

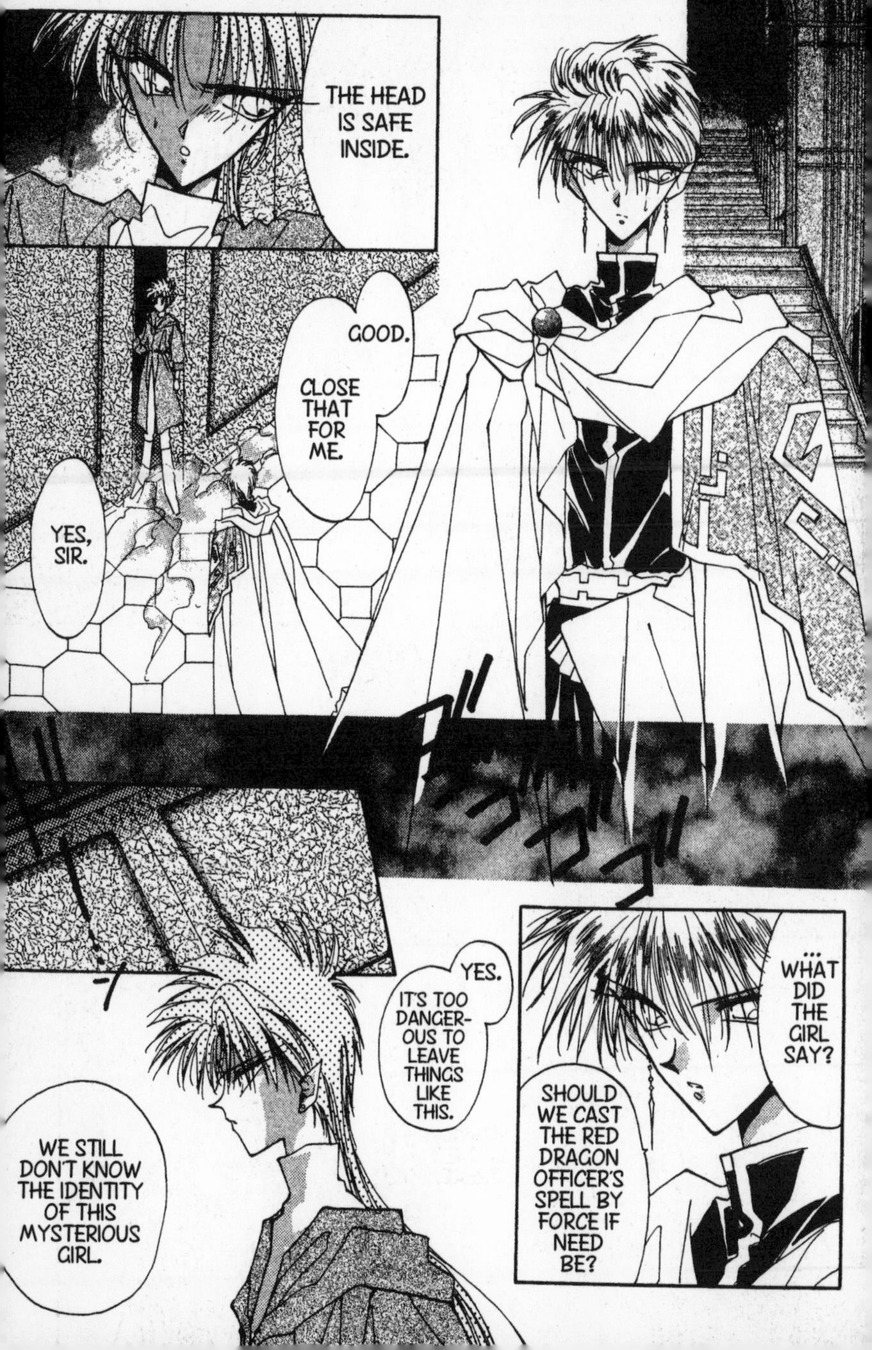
THE HEAD IS SAFE INSIDE.
GOOD.
CLOSE THAT FOR ME.
YES, SIR.
...WHAT DID THE GIRL SAY?
SHOULD WE CAST THE RED DRAGON OFFICER'S SPELL BY FORCE IF NEED BE?
YES.
IT'S TOO DANGER-OUS TO LEAVE THINGS LIKE THIS.
WE STILL DON'T KNOW THE IDENTITY OF THIS MYSTERIOUS GIRL.

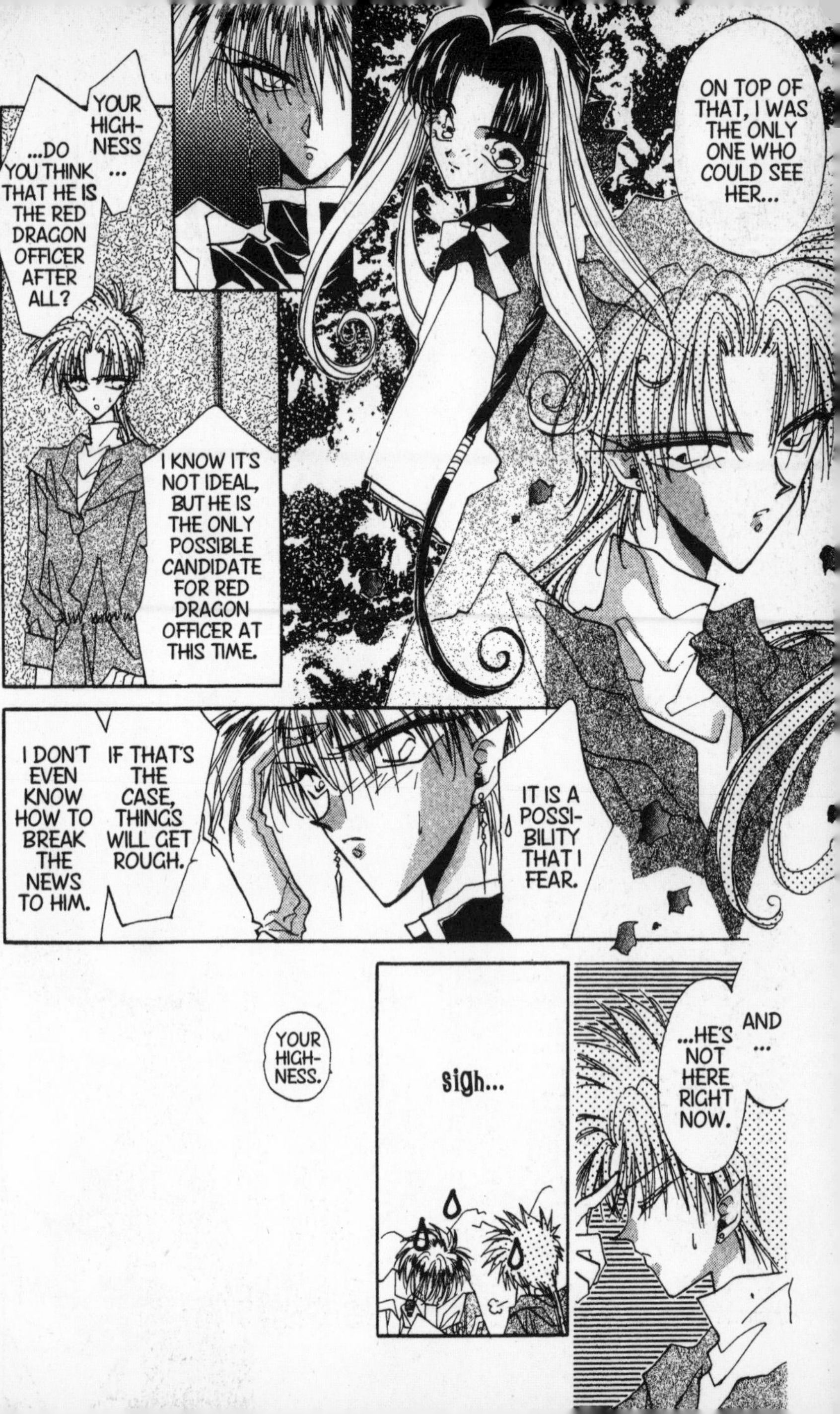
ON TOP OF THAT, I WAS THE ONLY ONE WHO COULD SEE HER...
YOUR HIGHNESS...
...DO YOU THINK THAT HE IS THE RED DRAGON OFFICER AFTER ALL?
I KNOW IT'S NOT IDEAL, BUT HE IS THE ONLY POSSIBLE CANDIDATE FOR RED DRAGON OFFICER AT THIS TIME.
IT IS A POSSIBILITY THAT I FEAR.
IF THAT'S THE CASE, THINGS WILL GET ROUGH.
I DON'T EVEN KNOW HOW TO BREAK THE NEWS TO HIM.
AND...
...HE'S NOT HERE RIGHT NOW.
sigh...
YOUR HIGHNESS.

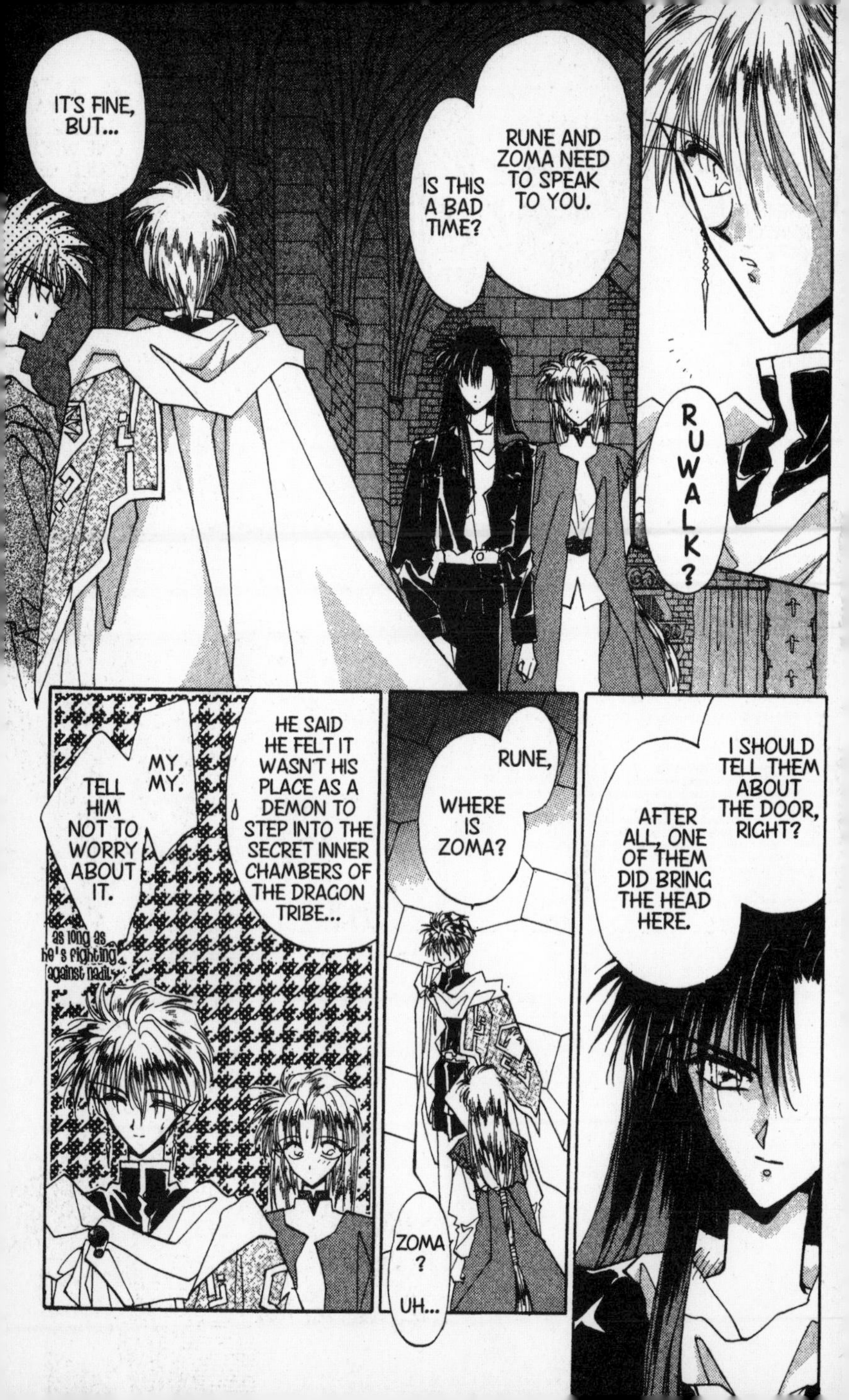
RUWALK?
RUNE AND ZOMA NEED TO SPEAK TO YOU.
IS THIS A BAD TIME?
IT'S FINE, BUT...
I SHOULD TELL THEM ABOUT THE DOOR, RIGHT?
AFTER ALL, ONE OF THEM DID BRING THE HEAD HERE.
RUNE,
WHERE IS ZOMA?
ZOMA?
UH...
HE SAID HE FELT IT WASN'T HIS PLACE AS A DEMON TO STEP INTO THE SECRET INNER CHAMBERS OF THE DRAGON TRIBE...
MY, MY.
TELL HIM NOT TO WORRY ABOUT IT.
as long as he's fighting against nadil.

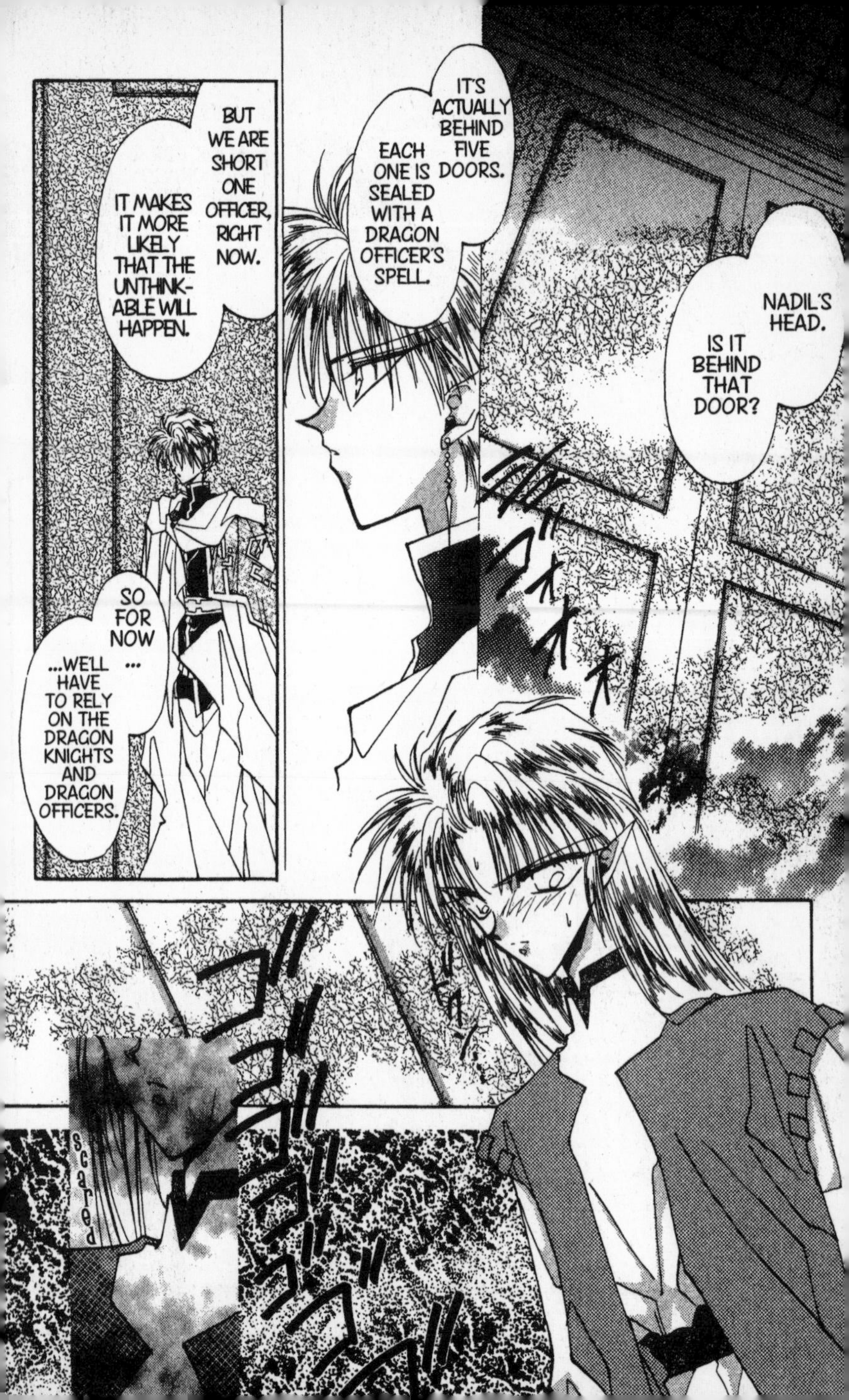
NADIL'S HEAD.
IS IT BEHIND THAT DOOR?
IT'S ACTUALLY BEHIND FIVE DOORS.
EACH ONE IS SEALED WITH A DRAGON OFFICER'S SPELL.
BUT WE ARE SHORT ONE OFFICER, RIGHT NOW.
IT MAKES IT MORE LIKELY THAT THE UNTHINK-ABLE WILL HAPPEN.
SO FOR NOW ...
...WE'LL HAVE TO RELY ON THE DRAGON KNIGHTS AND DRAGON OFFICERS.
scared

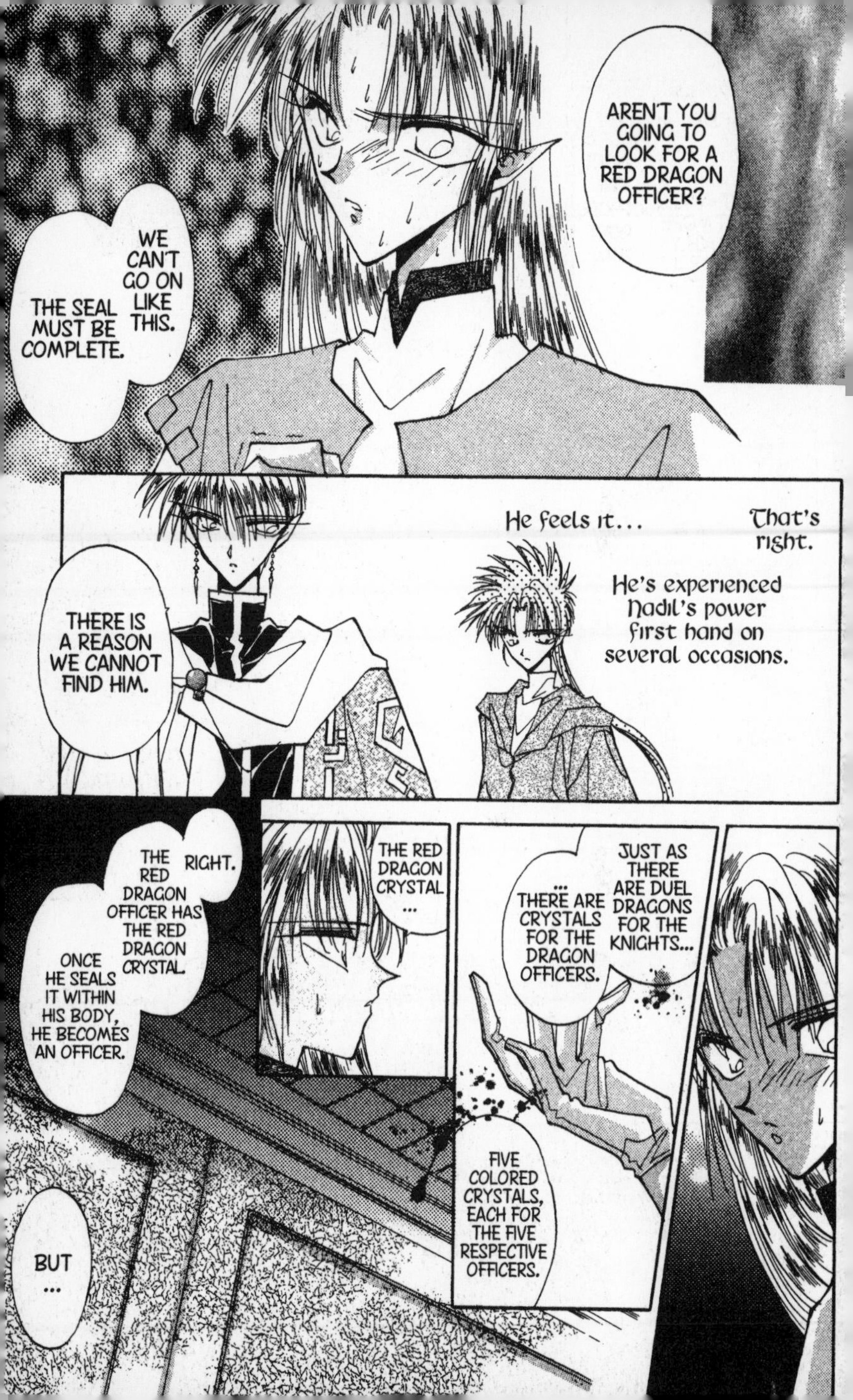
AREN'T YOU GOING TO LOOK FOR A RED DRAGON OFFICER?
WE CAN'T GO ON LIKE THIS.
THE SEAL MUST BE COMPLETE.
That's right.
He feels it...
He's experienced Nadil's power first hand on several occasions.
THERE IS A REASON WE CANNOT FIND HIM.
JUST AS THERE ARE DUEL DRAGONS FOR THE KNIGHTS...
...THERE ARE CRYSTALS FOR THE DRAGON OFFICERS.
FIVE COLORED CRYSTALS, EACH FOR THE FIVE RESPECTIVE OFFICERS.
THE RED DRAGON CRYSTAL ...
RIGHT.
THE RED DRAGON OFFICER HAS THE RED DRAGON CRYSTAL.
ONCE HE SEALS IT WITHIN HIS BODY, HE BECOMES AN OFFICER.
BUT ...

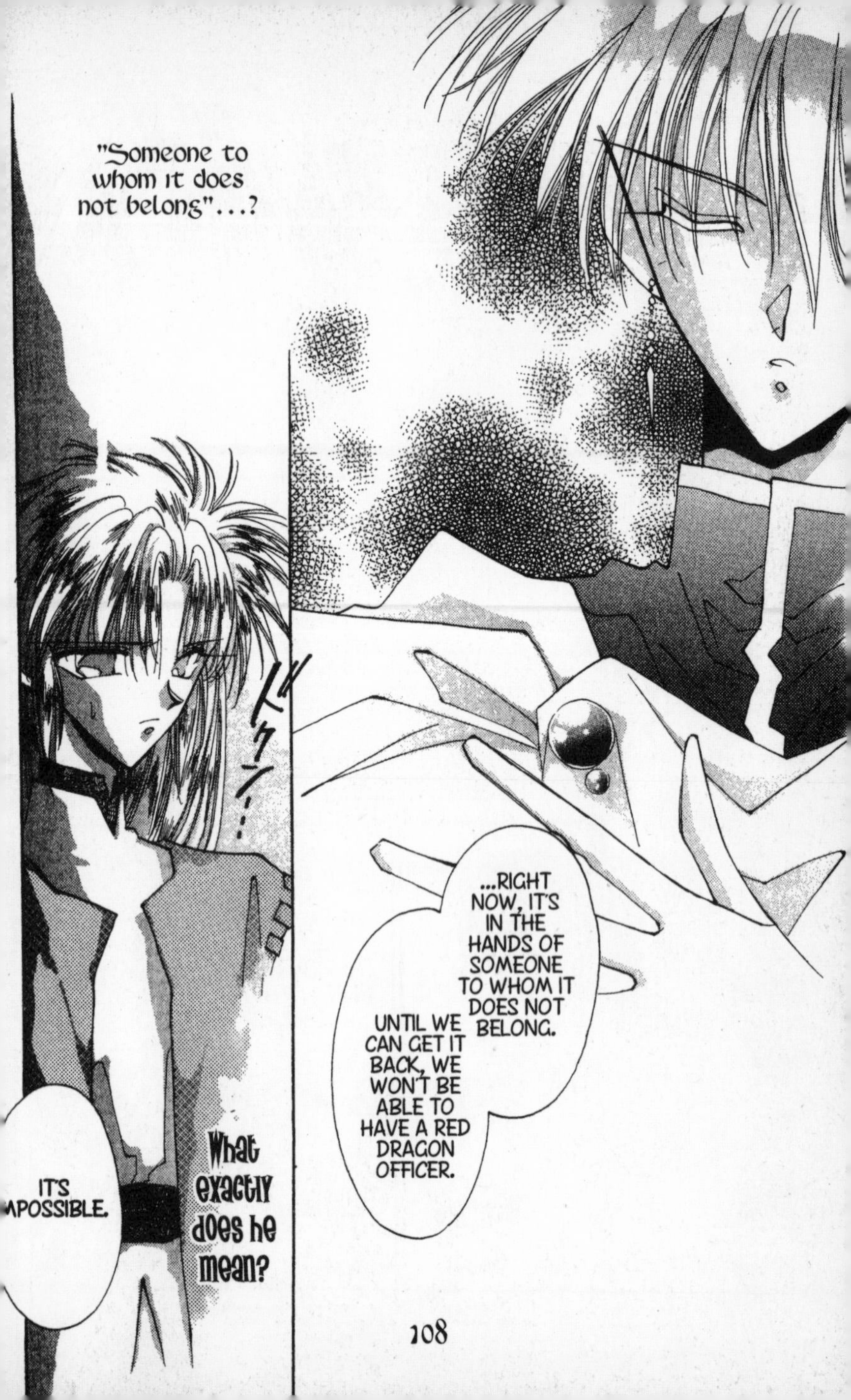
...RIGHT NOW, IT'S IN THE HANDS OF SOMEONE TO WHOM IT DOES NOT BELONG.
UNTIL WE CAN GET IT BACK, WE WON'T BE ABLE TO HAVE A RED DRAGON OFFICER.
"Someone to whom it does not belong"...?
What exactly does he mean?
IT'S MPOSSIBLE.

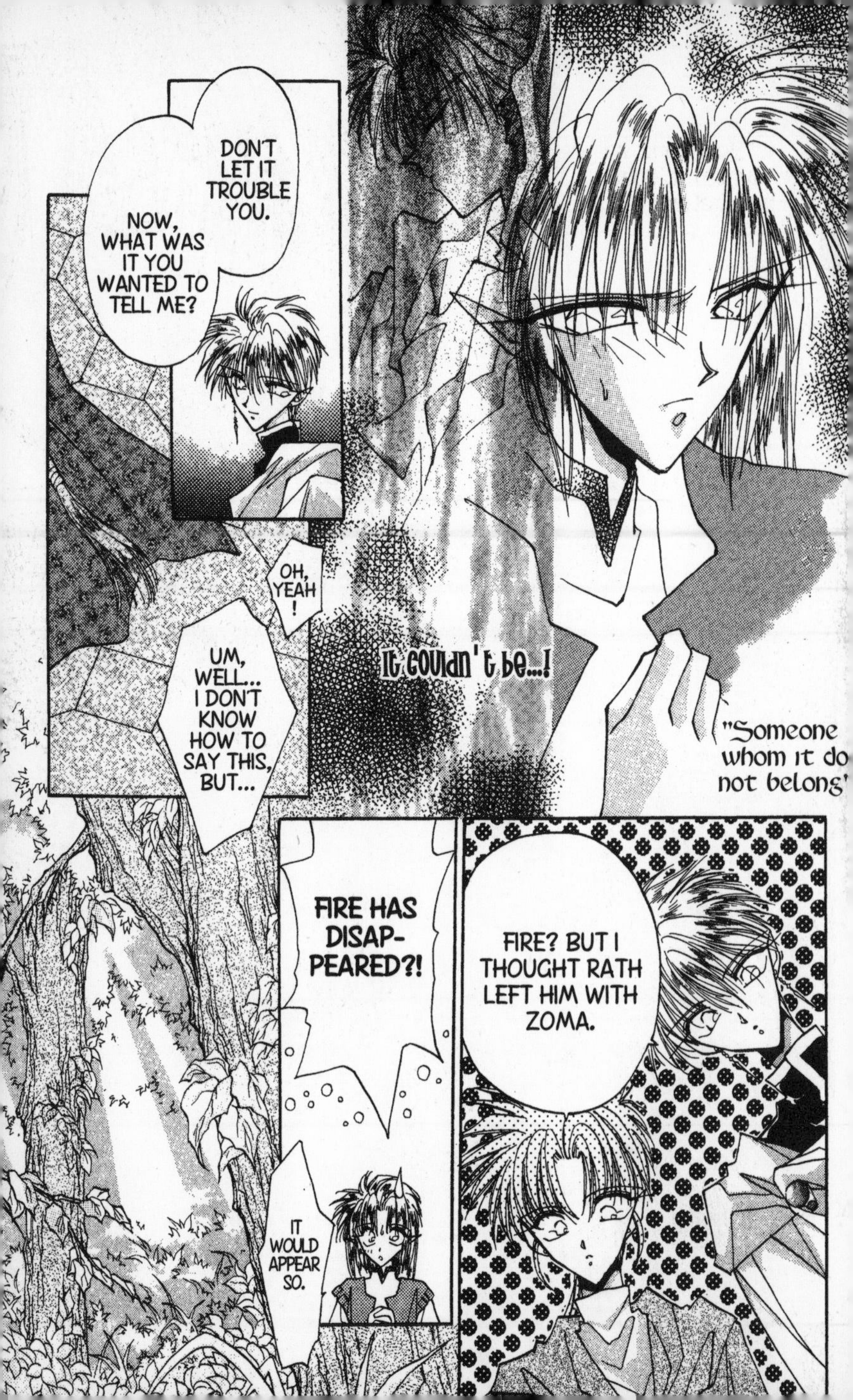
It couldn't be...!
"Someone whom it do not belong'
DON'T LET IT TROUBLE YOU.
NOW, WHAT WAS IT YOU WANTED TO TELL ME?
OH, YEAH!
UM, WELL... I DON'T KNOW HOW TO SAY THIS, BUT...
FIRE? BUT I THOUGHT RATH LEFT HIM WITH ZOMA.
FIRE HAS DISAP-PEARED?!
IT WOULD APPEAR SO.

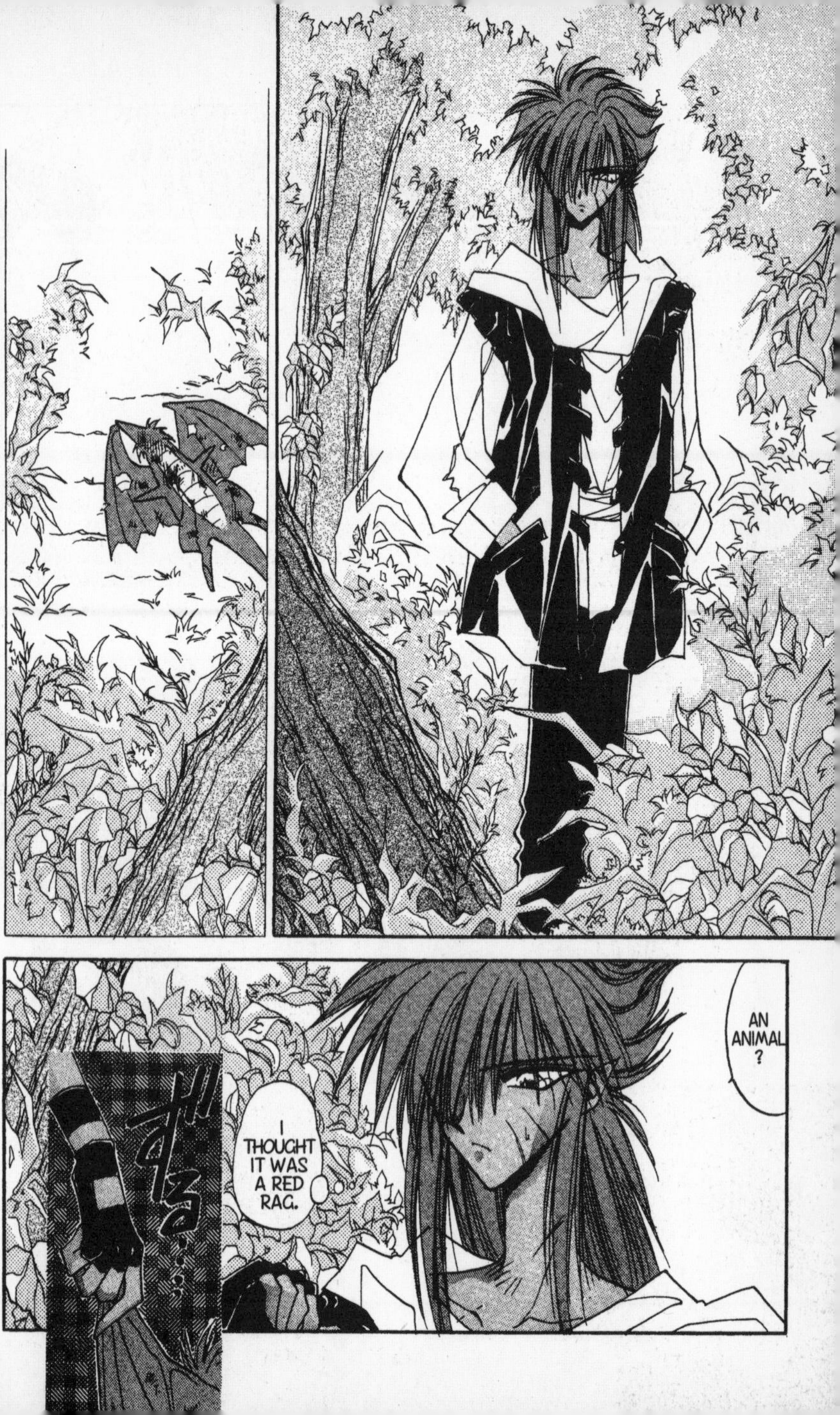
AN ANIMAL ?
I THOUGHT IT WAS A RED RAG.

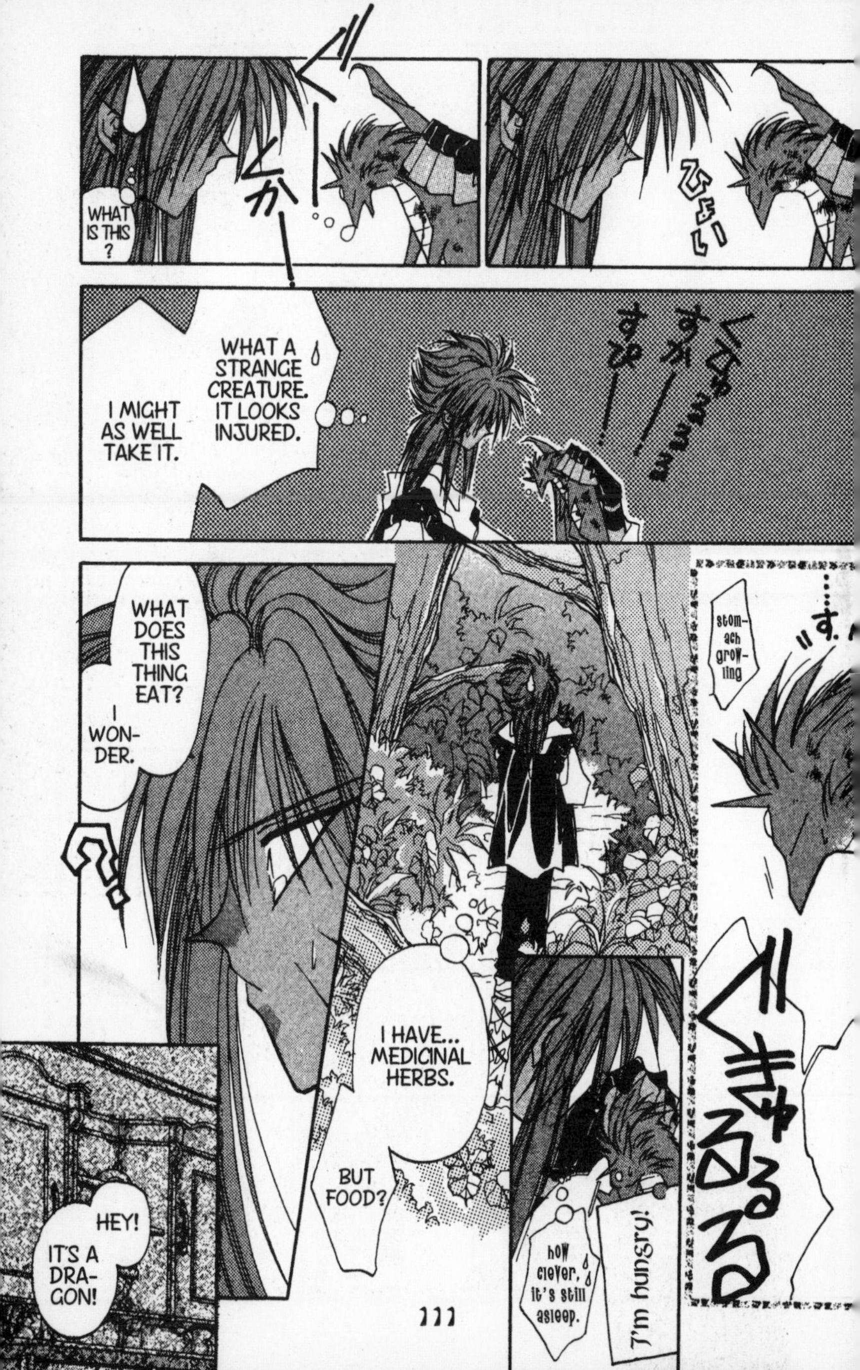
ひょい
WHAT IS THIS?
WHAT A STRANGE CREATURE. IT LOOKS INJURED.
I MIGHT AS WELL TAKE IT.
stomach growling
ぐぎゅるるる
I'm hungry!
how clever, it's still asleep.
I HAVE... MEDICINAL HERBS.
BUT FOOD?
WHAT DOES THIS THING EAT?
I WONDER.
HEY!
IT'S A DRAGON!

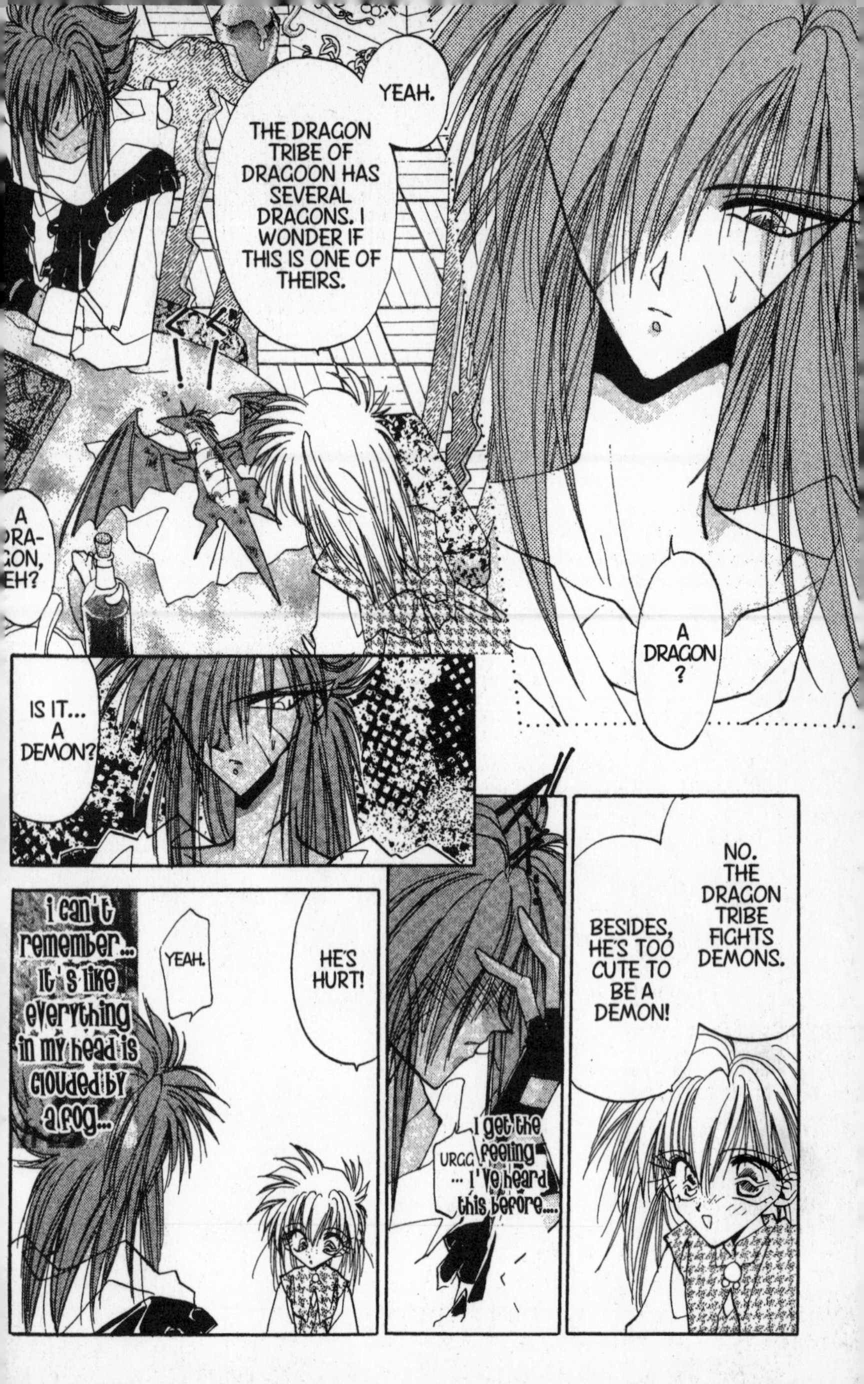
A DRAGON ?
YEAH.
THE DRAGON TRIBE OF DRAGOON HAS SEVERAL DRAGONS. I WONDER IF THIS IS ONE OF THEIRS.
A DRA-GON, EH?
IS IT... A DEMON?
NO. THE DRAGON TRIBE FIGHTS DEMONS.
BESIDES, HE'S TOO CUTE TO BE A DEMON!
I get the feeling ... I've heard this before....
URGG
HE'S HURT!
YEAH.
i can't remember... it's like everything in my head is clouded by a fog...

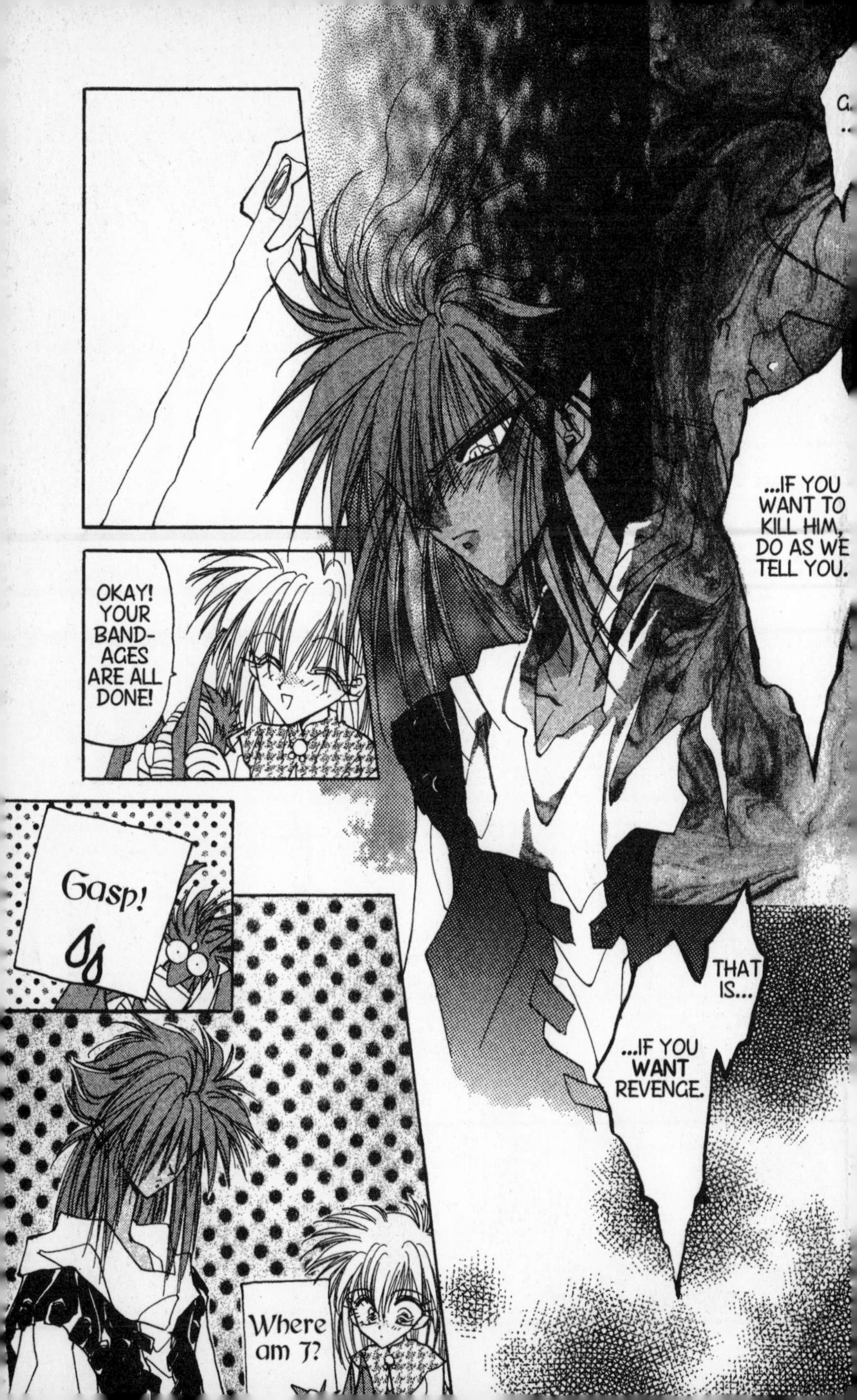
...IF YOU WANT TO KILL HIM, DO AS WE TELL YOU.
THAT IS...
...IF YOU WANT REVENGE.
OKAY! YOUR BAND-AGES ARE ALL DONE!
Gasp!
Where am I?

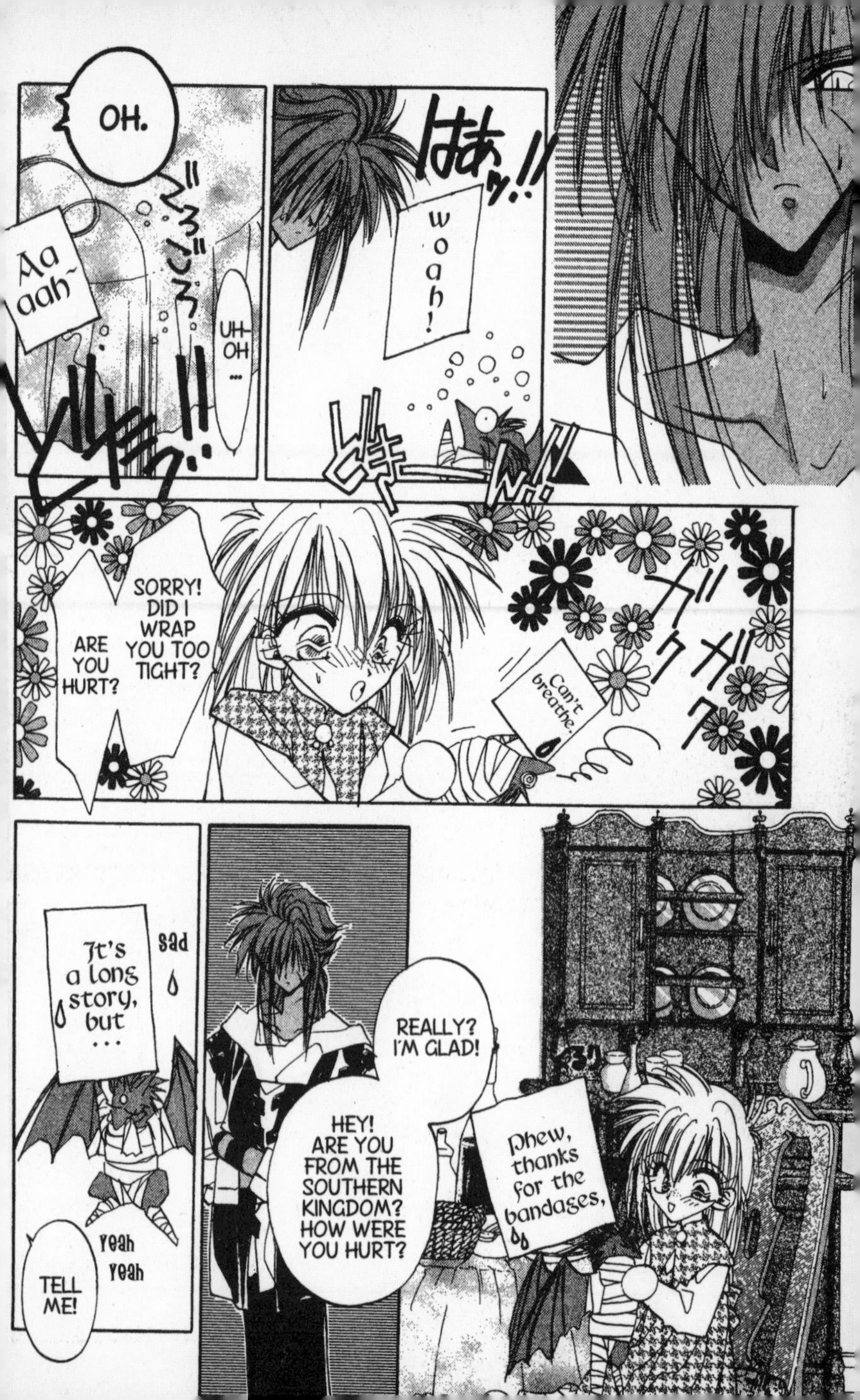

はあッ!!
woah!
OH.
Aa aah~
UH-OH ...
Can't breathe.
SORRY! DID I WRAP YOU TOO TIGHT?
ARE YOU HURT?
Phew, thanks for the bandages,
REALLY? I'M GLAD!
HEY! ARE YOU FROM THE SOUTHERN KINGDOM? HOW WERE YOU HURT?
It's a long story, but . . .
sad
yeah yeah
TELL ME!

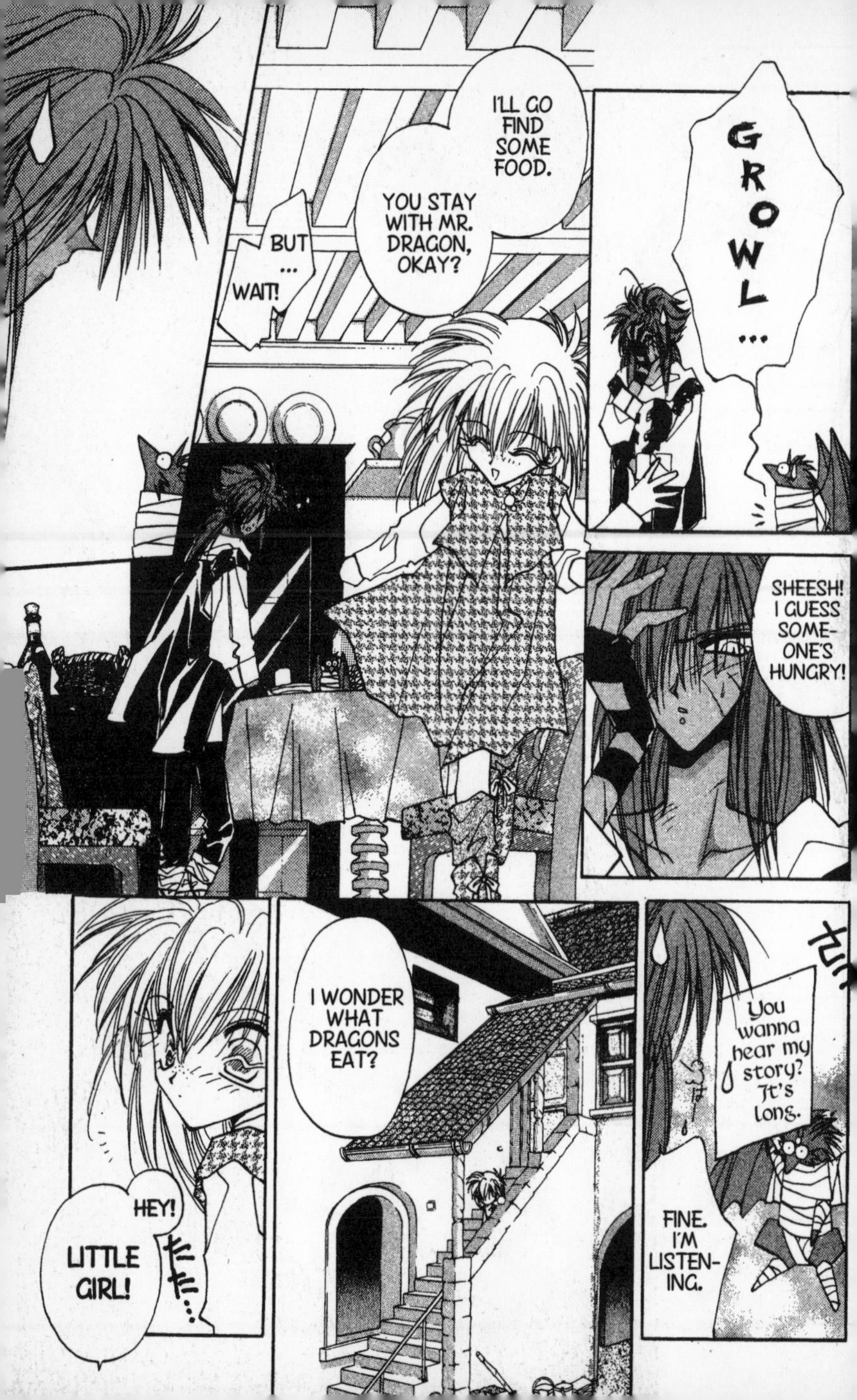
GROWL ...
SHEESH! I GUESS SOME-ONE'S HUNGRY!
I'LL GO FIND SOME FOOD.
YOU STAY WITH MR. DRAGON, OKAY?
BUT ... WAIT!
You wanna hear my story? It's long.
FINE. I'M LISTEN-ING.
I WONDER WHAT DRAGONS EAT?
HEY!
LITTLE GIRL!

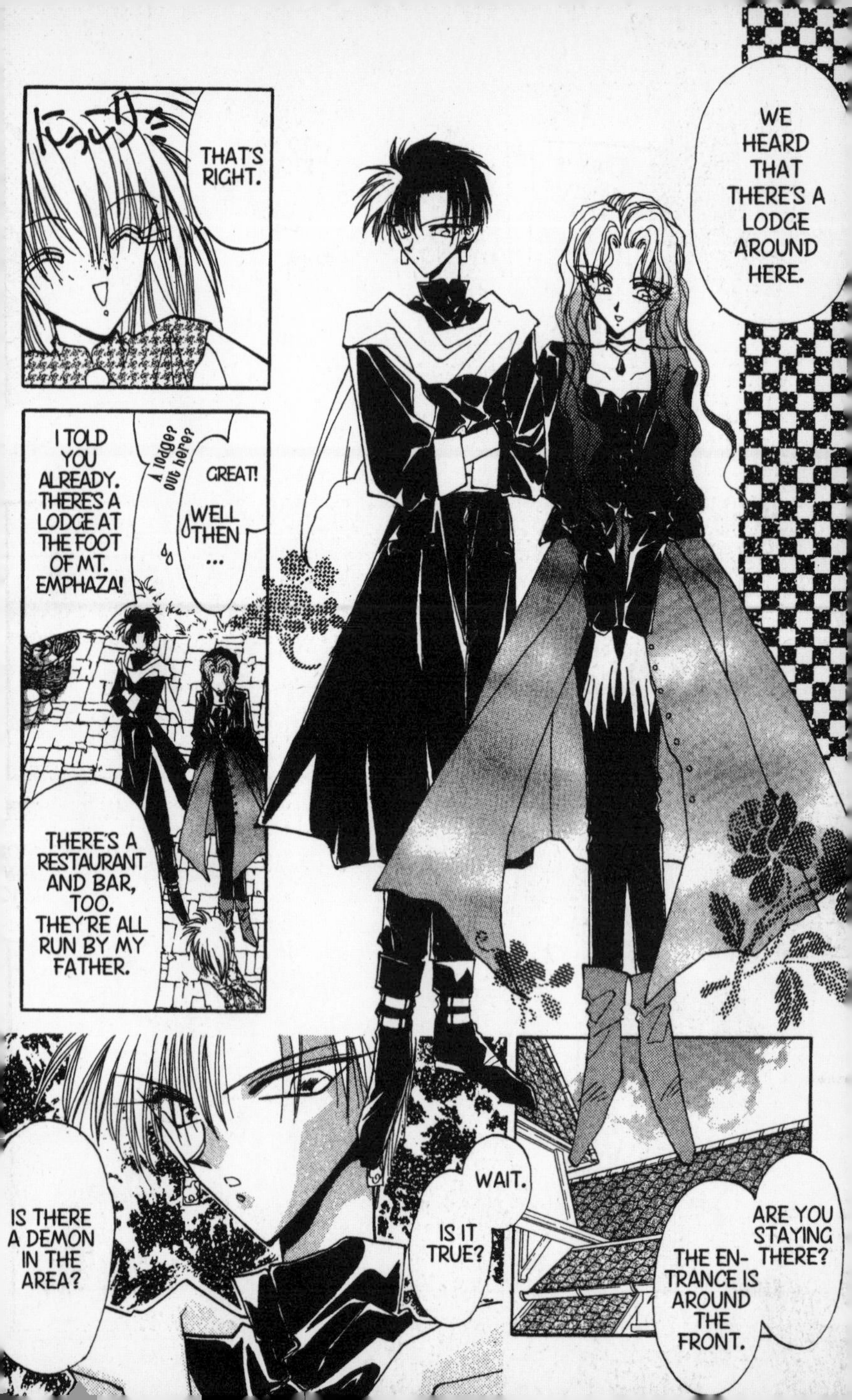
WE HEARD THAT THERE'S A LODGE AROUND HERE.
THAT'S RIGHT.
GREAT!
WELL THEN ...
A lodge? out here?
I TOLD YOU ALREADY. THERE'S A LODGE AT THE FOOT OF MT. EMPHAZA!
THERE'S A RESTAURANT AND BAR, TOO. THEY'RE ALL RUN BY MY FATHER.
ARE YOU STAYING THERE?
THE EN-TRANCE IS AROUND THE FRONT.
WAIT.
IS IT TRUE?
IS THERE A DEMON IN THE AREA?

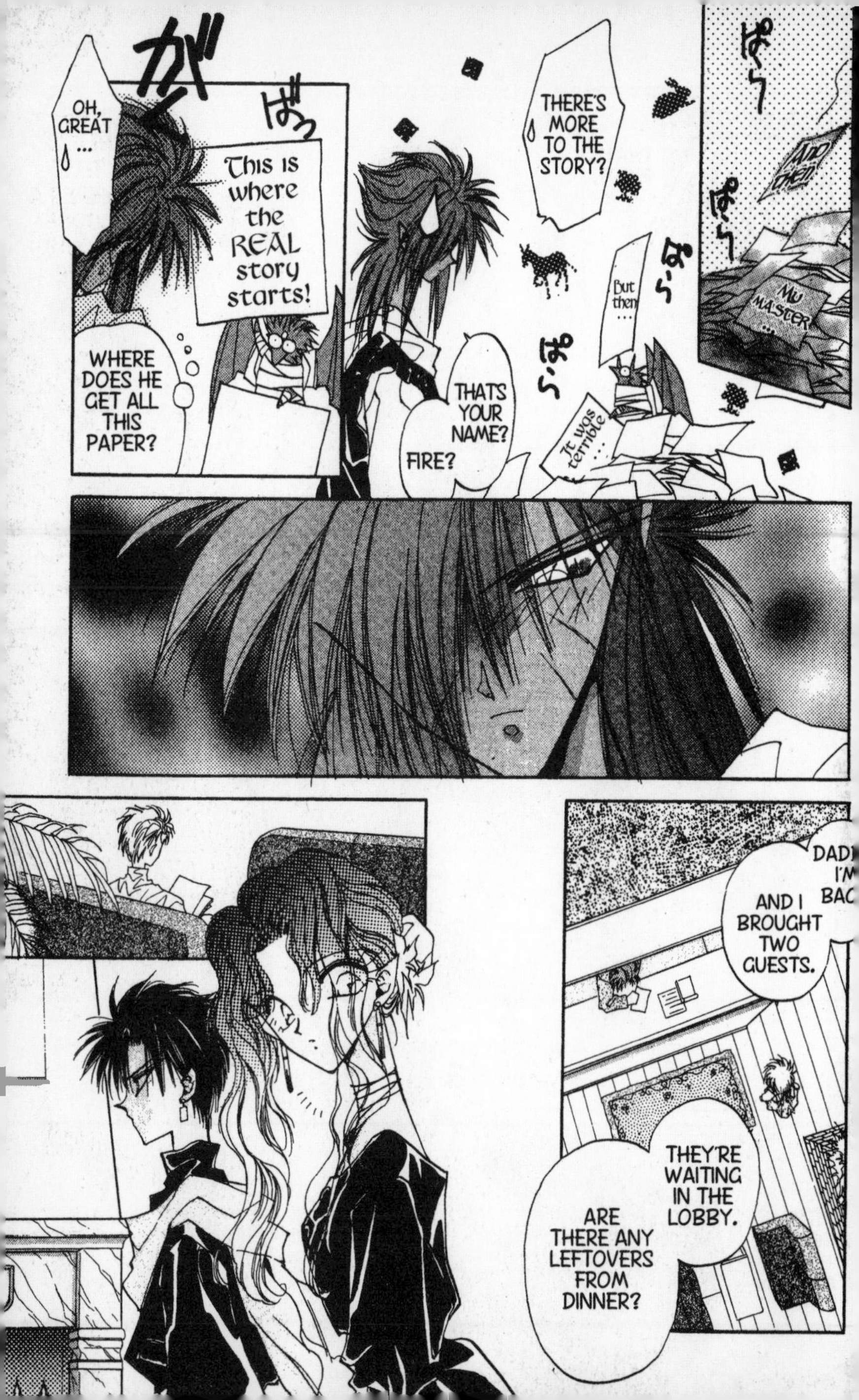
ぱら
ぱら
AND THEN
MY MASTER...
THERE'S MORE TO THE STORY?
ぱら
But then...
ぱら
It was terrible...
THATS YOUR NAME? FIRE?
が
ばっ
OH, GREAT...
This is where the REAL story starts!
WHERE DOES HE GET ALL THIS PAPER?
DAD I'M BAC
AND I BROUGHT TWO GUESTS.
THEY'RE WAITING IN THE LOBBY.
ARE THERE ANY LEFTOVERS FROM DINNER?

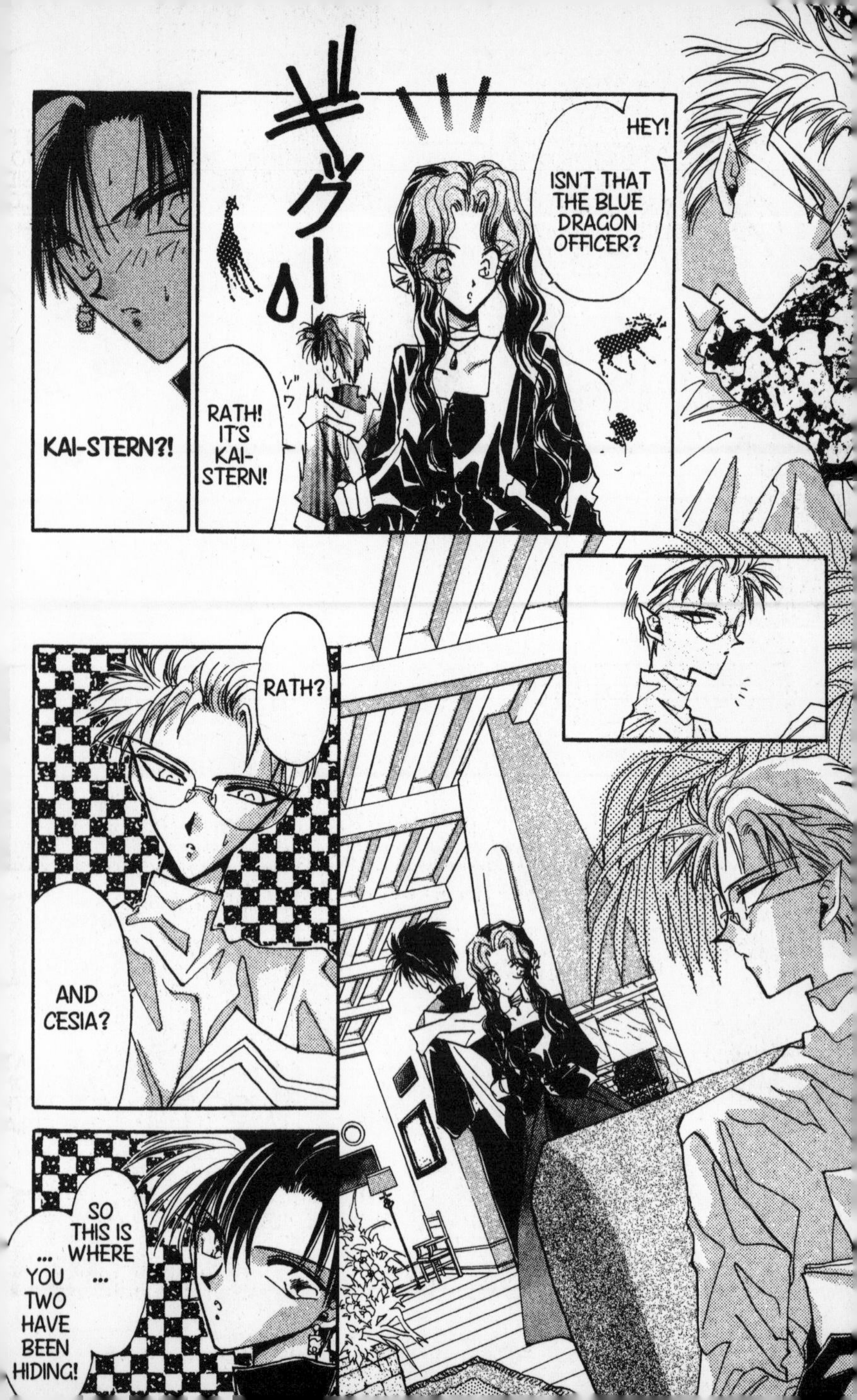

ギクー
HEY!
ISN'T THAT THE BLUE DRAGON OFFICER?
RATH! IT'S KAI-STERN!
KAI-STERN?!
RATH?
AND CESIA?
SO THIS IS WHERE ...
... YOU TWO HAVE BEEN HIDING!

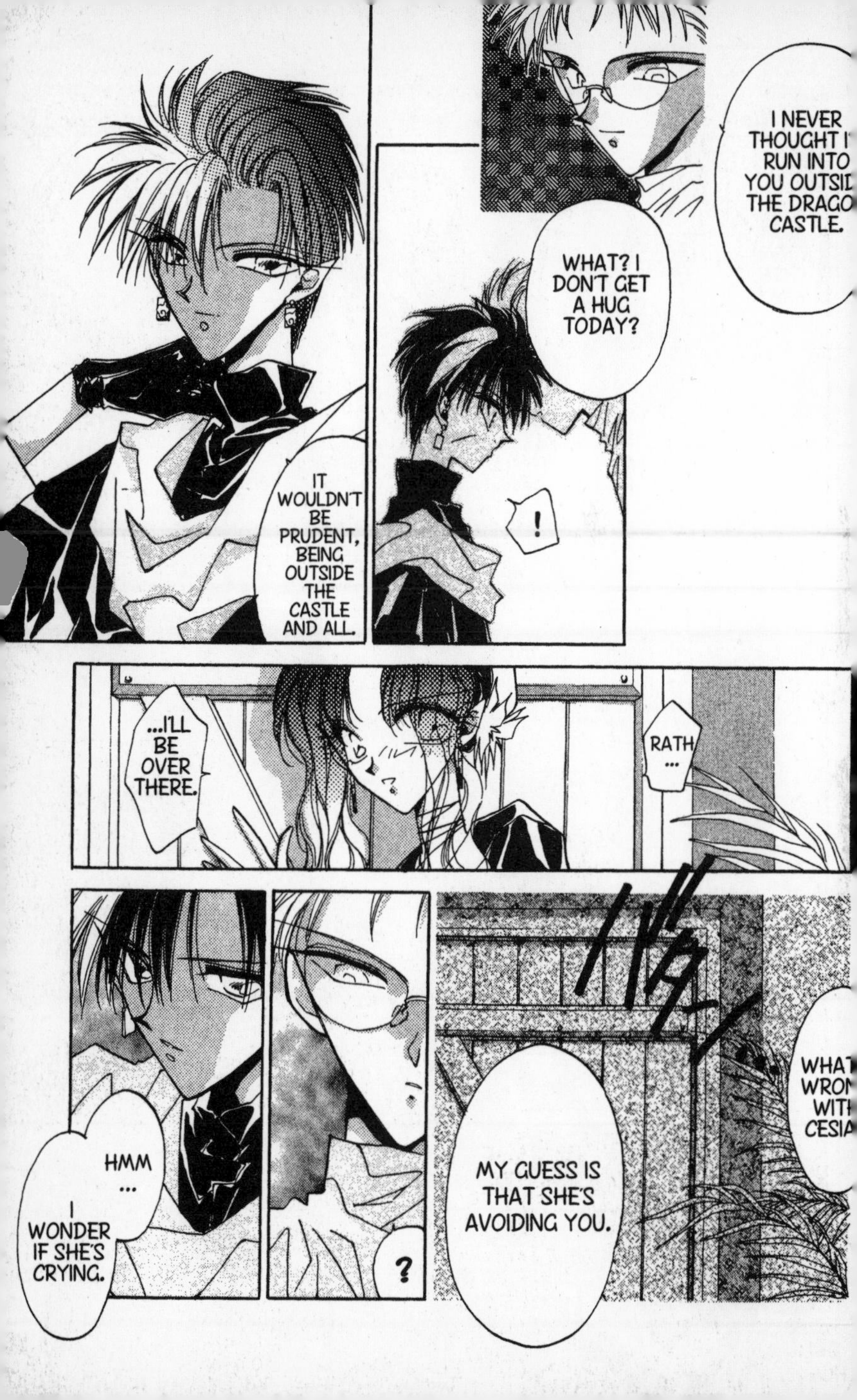
I NEVER THOUGHT I' RUN INTO YOU OUTSID THE DRAGO CASTLE.
WHAT? I DON'T GET A HUG TODAY?
!
IT WOULDN'T BE PRUDENT, BEING OUTSIDE THE CASTLE AND ALL.
RATH ...
...I'LL BE OVER THERE.
WHAT WRON WITH CESIA
MY GUESS IS THAT SHE'S AVOIDING YOU.
?
HMM ...
I WONDER IF SHE'S CRYING.

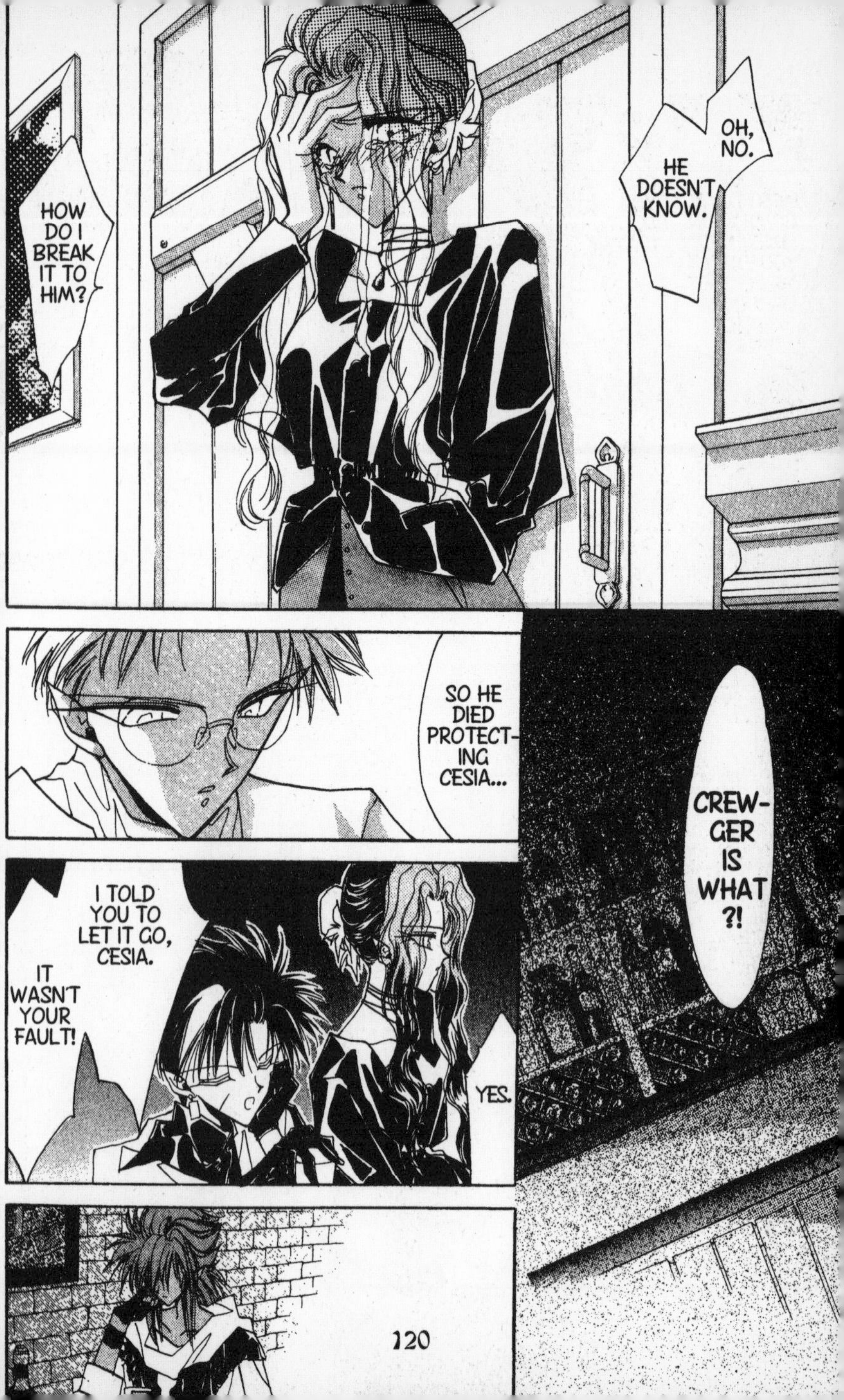
OH, NO. HE DOESN'T KNOW.
HOW DO I BREAK IT TO HIM?
CREW-GER IS WHAT?!
SO HE DIED PROTECT-ING CESIA...
I TOLD YOU TO LET IT GO, CESIA.
IT WASN'T YOUR FAULT!
YES.

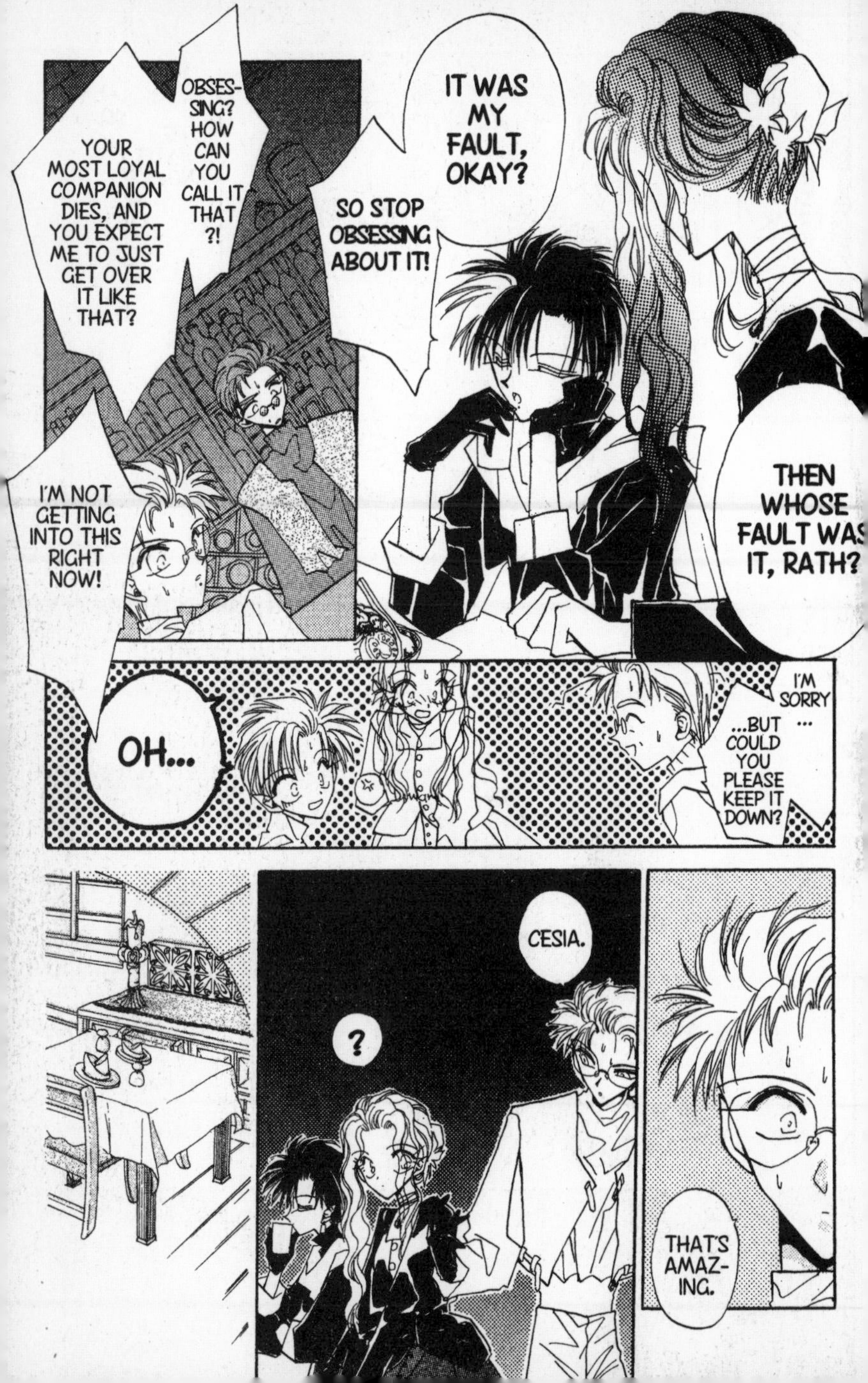
THEN WHOSE FAULT WAS IT, RATH?
IT WAS MY FAULT, OKAY?
SO STOP OBSESSING ABOUT IT!
OBSES-SING? HOW CAN YOU CALL IT THAT?!
YOUR MOST LOYAL COMPANION DIES, AND YOU EXPECT ME TO JUST GET OVER IT LIKE THAT?
I'M NOT GETTING INTO THIS RIGHT NOW!
I'M SORRY ...
...BUT COULD YOU PLEASE KEEP IT DOWN?
OH...
THAT'S AMAZ-ING.
CESIA.
?

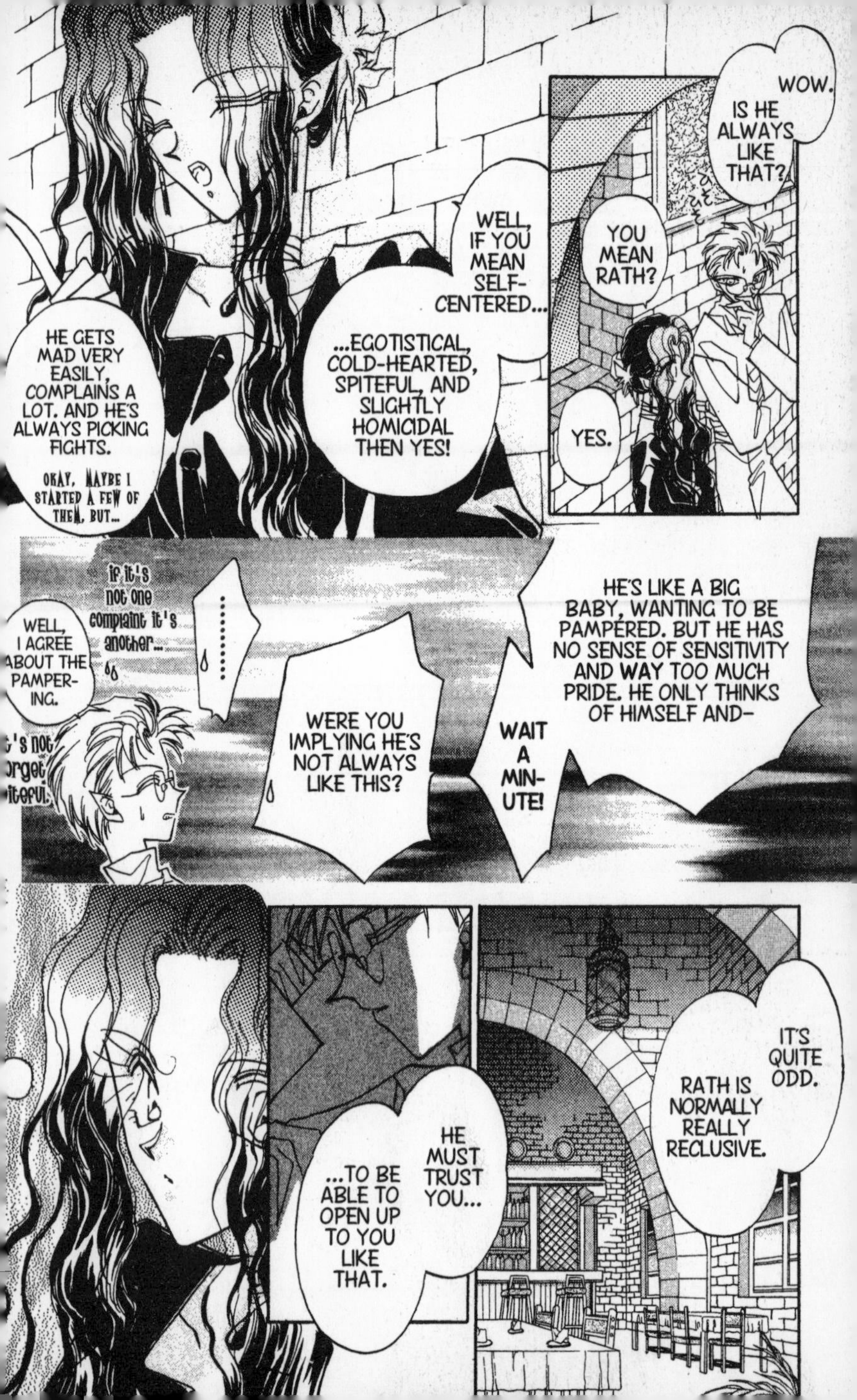
WOW. IS HE ALWAYS LIKE THAT?
YOU MEAN RATH?
YES.
WELL, IF YOU MEAN SELF-CENTERED...
...EGOTISTICAL, COLD-HEARTED, SPITEFUL, AND SLIGHTLY HOMICIDAL THEN YES!
HE GETS MAD VERY EASILY, COMPLAINS A LOT. AND HE'S ALWAYS PICKING FIGHTS.
OKAY, MAYBE I STARTED A FEW OF THEM, BUT...
HE'S LIKE A BIG BABY, WANTING TO BE PAMPERED. BUT HE HAS NO SENSE OF SENSITIVITY AND WAY TOO MUCH PRIDE. HE ONLY THINKS OF HIMSELF AND–
WAIT A MIN-UTE!
WERE YOU IMPLYING HE'S NOT ALWAYS LIKE THIS?
......
if it's not one complaint it's another...
WELL, I AGREE ABOUT THE PAMPER-ING.
IT'S QUITE ODD.
RATH IS NORMALLY REALLY RECLUSIVE.
HE MUST TRUST YOU...
...TO BE ABLE TO OPEN UP TO YOU LIKE THAT.

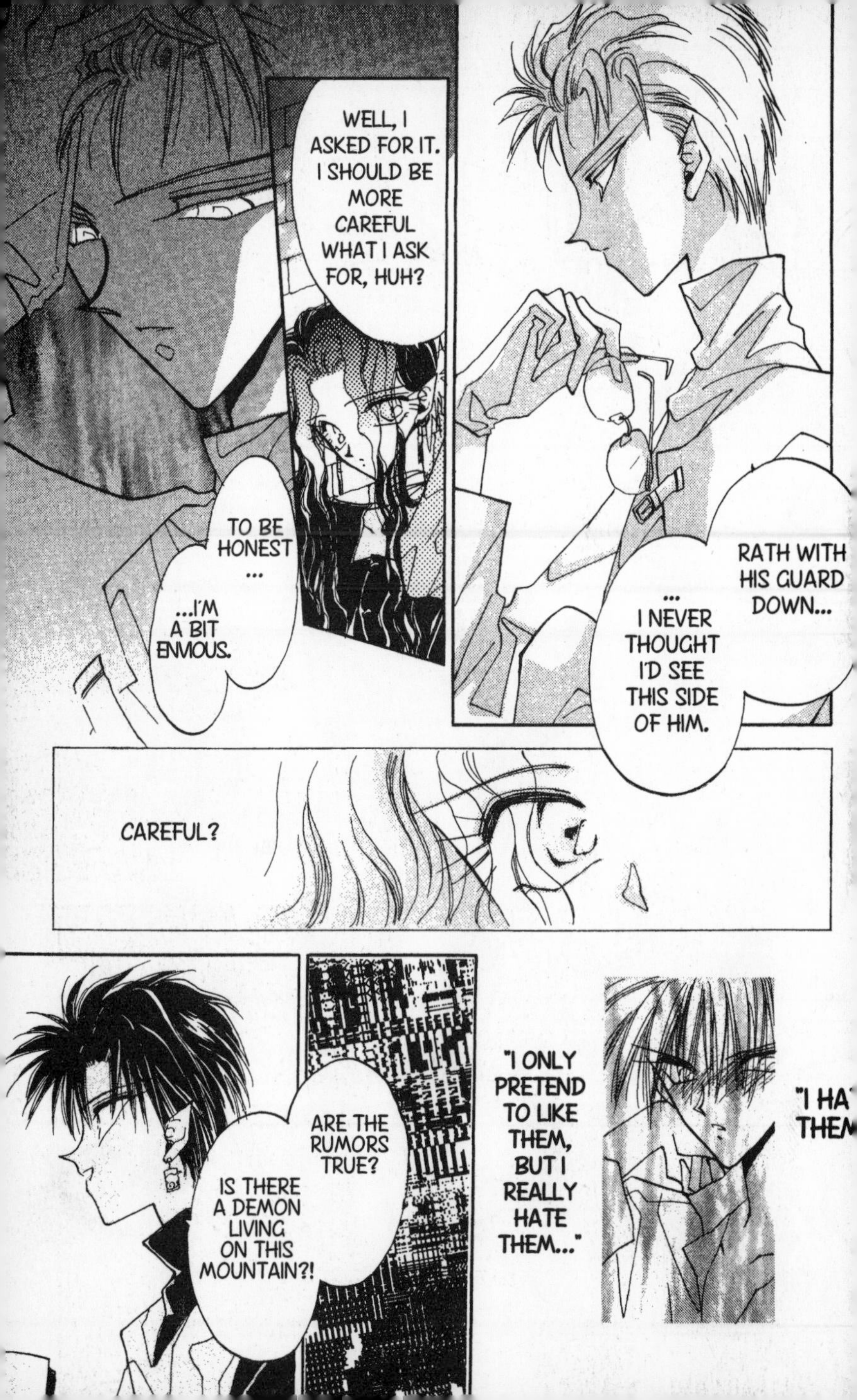
RATH WITH HIS GUARD DOWN...
... I NEVER THOUGHT I'D SEE THIS SIDE OF HIM.
WELL, I ASKED FOR IT. I SHOULD BE MORE CAREFUL WHAT I ASK FOR, HUH?
TO BE HONEST ...
...I'M A BIT ENVIOUS.
CAREFUL?
"I HA
THEM
"I ONLY PRETEND TO LIKE THEM, BUT I REALLY HATE THEM..."
ARE THE RUMORS TRUE?
IS THERE A DEMON LIVING ON THIS MOUNTAIN?!

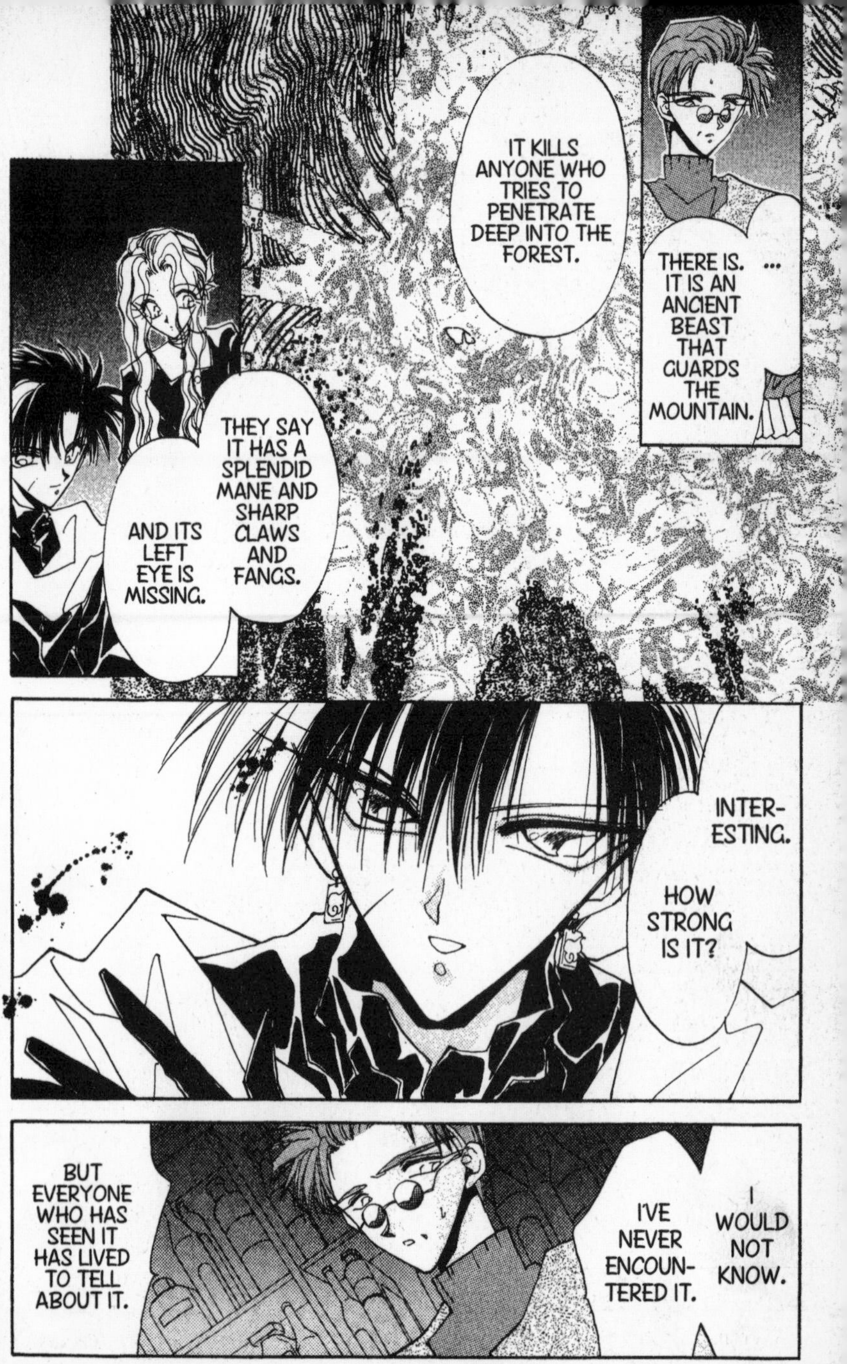

... THERE IS. IT IS AN ANCIENT BEAST THAT GUARDS THE MOUNTAIN.
IT KILLS ANYONE WHO TRIES TO PENETRATE DEEP INTO THE FOREST.
THEY SAY IT HAS A SPLENDID MANE AND SHARP CLAWS AND FANGS.
AND ITS LEFT EYE IS MISSING.
INTER-ESTING.
HOW STRONG IS IT?
I WOULD NOT KNOW.
I'VE NEVER ENCOUN-TERED IT.
BUT EVERYONE WHO HAS SEEN IT HAS LIVED TO TELL ABOUT IT.

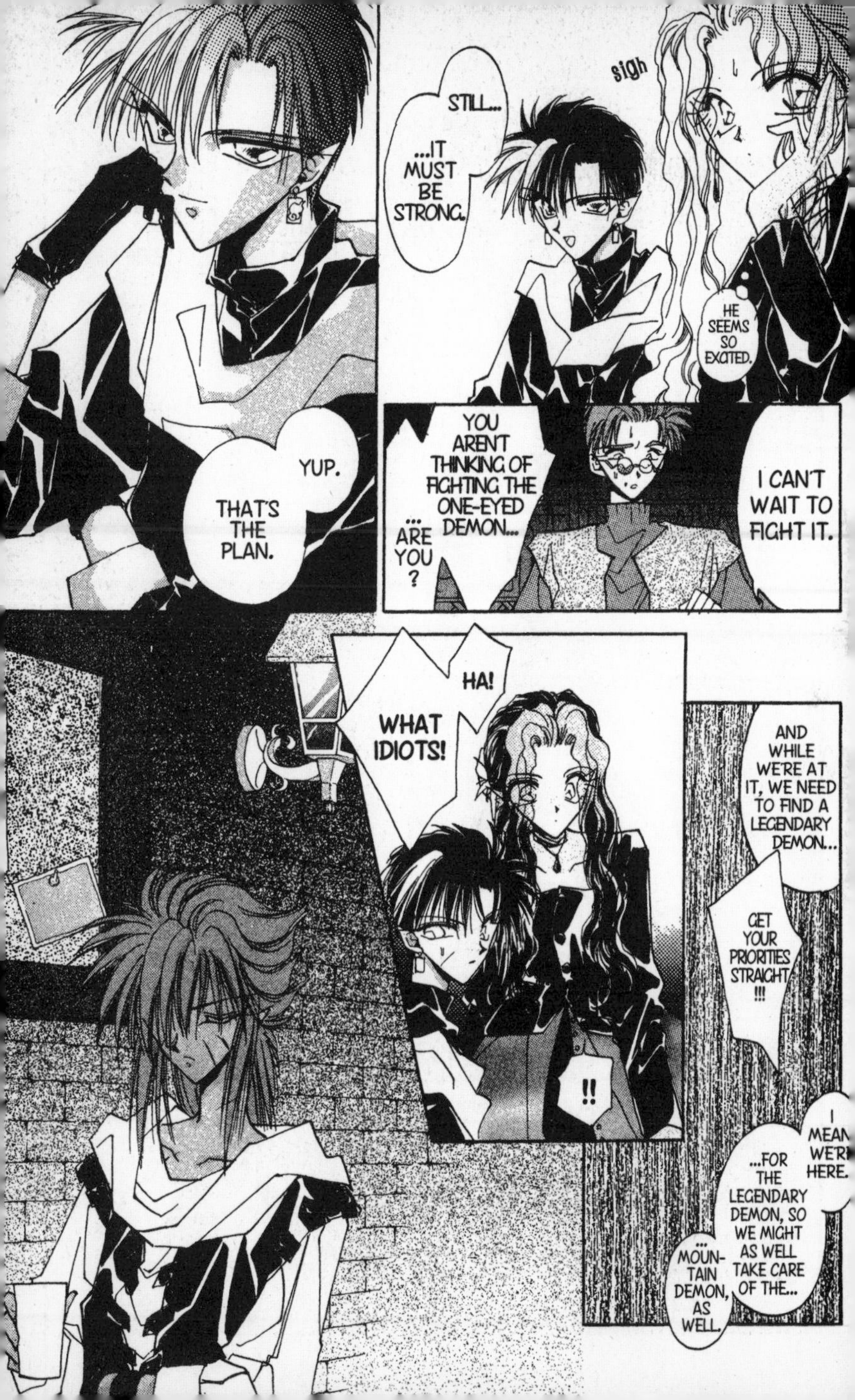
sigh
STILL...
...IT MUST BE STRONG.
HE SEEMS SO EXCITED.
I CAN'T WAIT TO FIGHT IT.
YOU AREN'T THINKING OF FIGHTING THE ONE-EYED DEMON...
...ARE YOU?
YUP.
THAT'S THE PLAN.
AND WHILE WE'RE AT IT, WE NEED TO FIND A LEGENDARY DEMON...
GET YOUR PRIORITIES STRAIGHT!!!
I MEAN WE'RE HERE.
...FOR THE LEGENDARY DEMON, SO WE MIGHT AS WELL TAKE CARE OF THE...
...MOUNTAIN DEMON, AS WELL.
HA!
WHAT IDIOTS!
!!

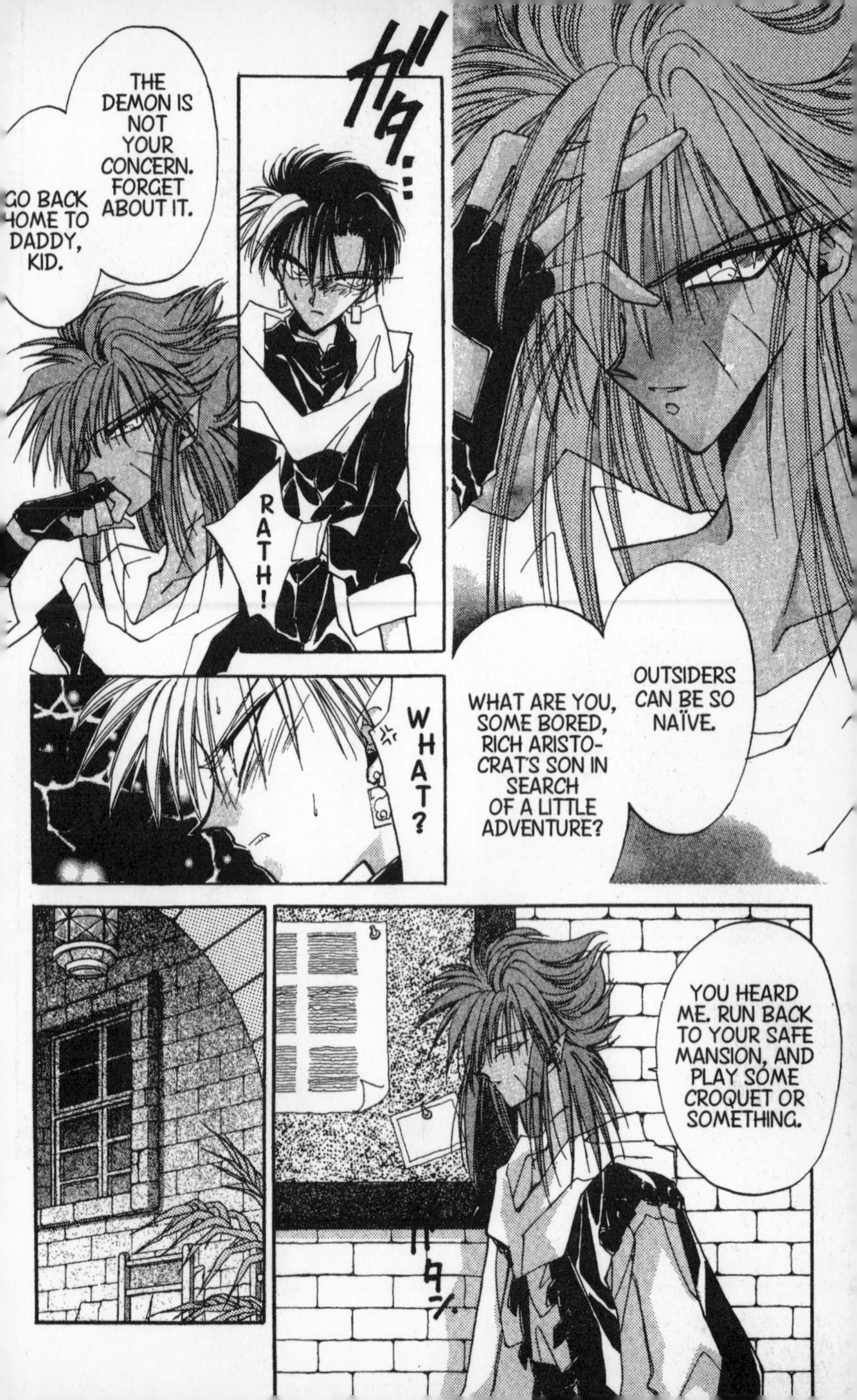
OUTSIDERS CAN BE SO NAÏVE.
WHAT ARE YOU, SOME BORED, RICH ARISTO-CRAT'S SON IN SEARCH OF A LITTLE ADVENTURE?
RATH!
THE DEMON IS NOT YOUR CONCERN. FORGET ABOUT IT.
GO BACK HOME TO DADDY, KID.
WHAT?
YOU HEARD ME. RUN BACK TO YOUR SAFE MANSION, AND PLAY SOME CROQUET OR SOMETHING.

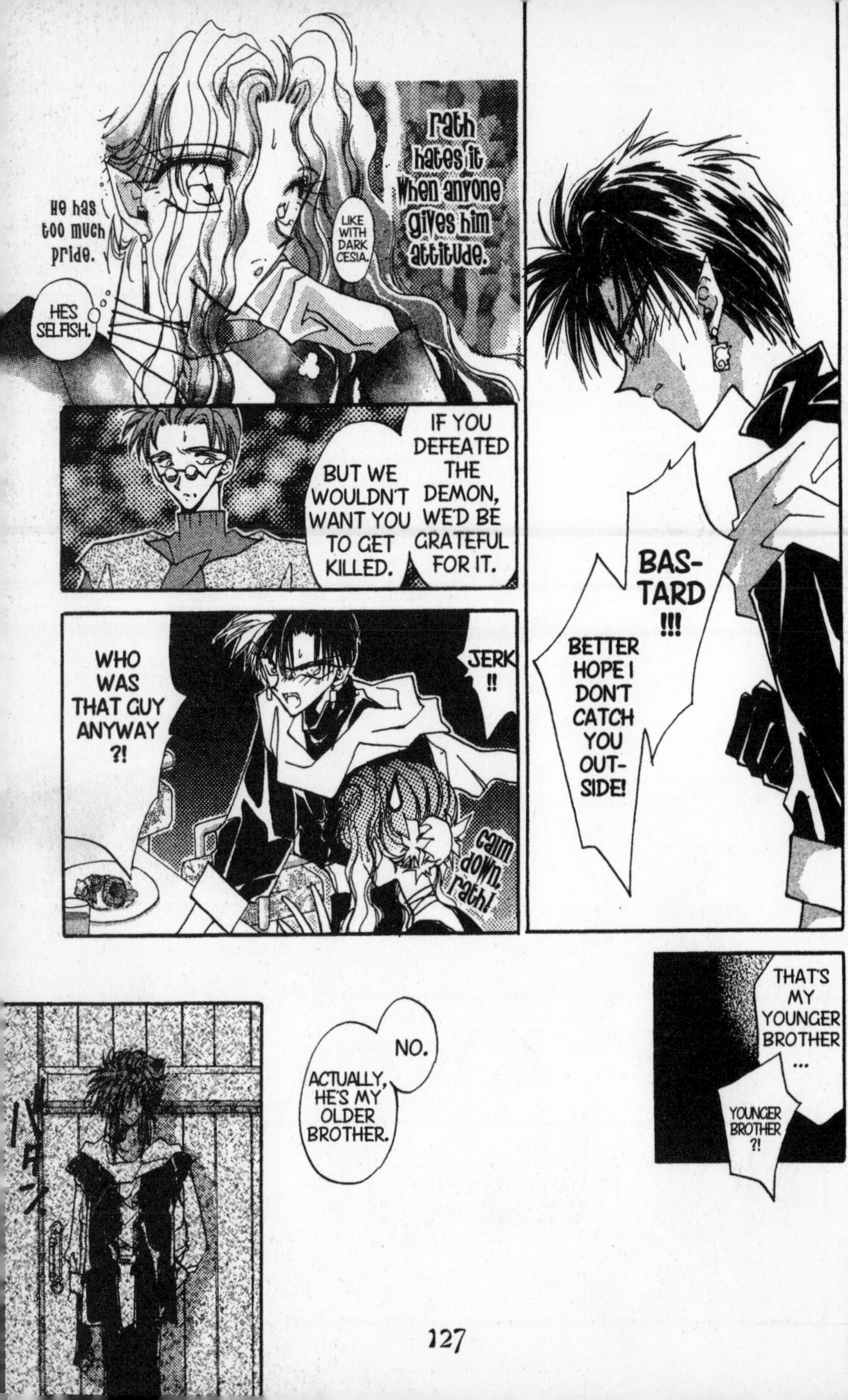
BAS-TARD!!!
BETTER HOPE I DON'T CATCH YOU OUT-SIDE!
rath hates it when anyone gives him attitude.
LIKE WITH DARK CESIA.
He has too much pride.
HES SELFISH.
IF YOU DEFEATED THE DEMON, WE'D BE GRATEFUL FOR IT.
BUT WE WOULDN'T WANT YOU TO GET KILLED.
JERK!!
Calm down, rath!
WHO WAS THAT GUY ANYWAY?!
THAT'S MY YOUNGER BROTHER...
YOUNGER BROTHER?!
NO.
ACTUALLY, HE'S MY OLDER BROTHER.

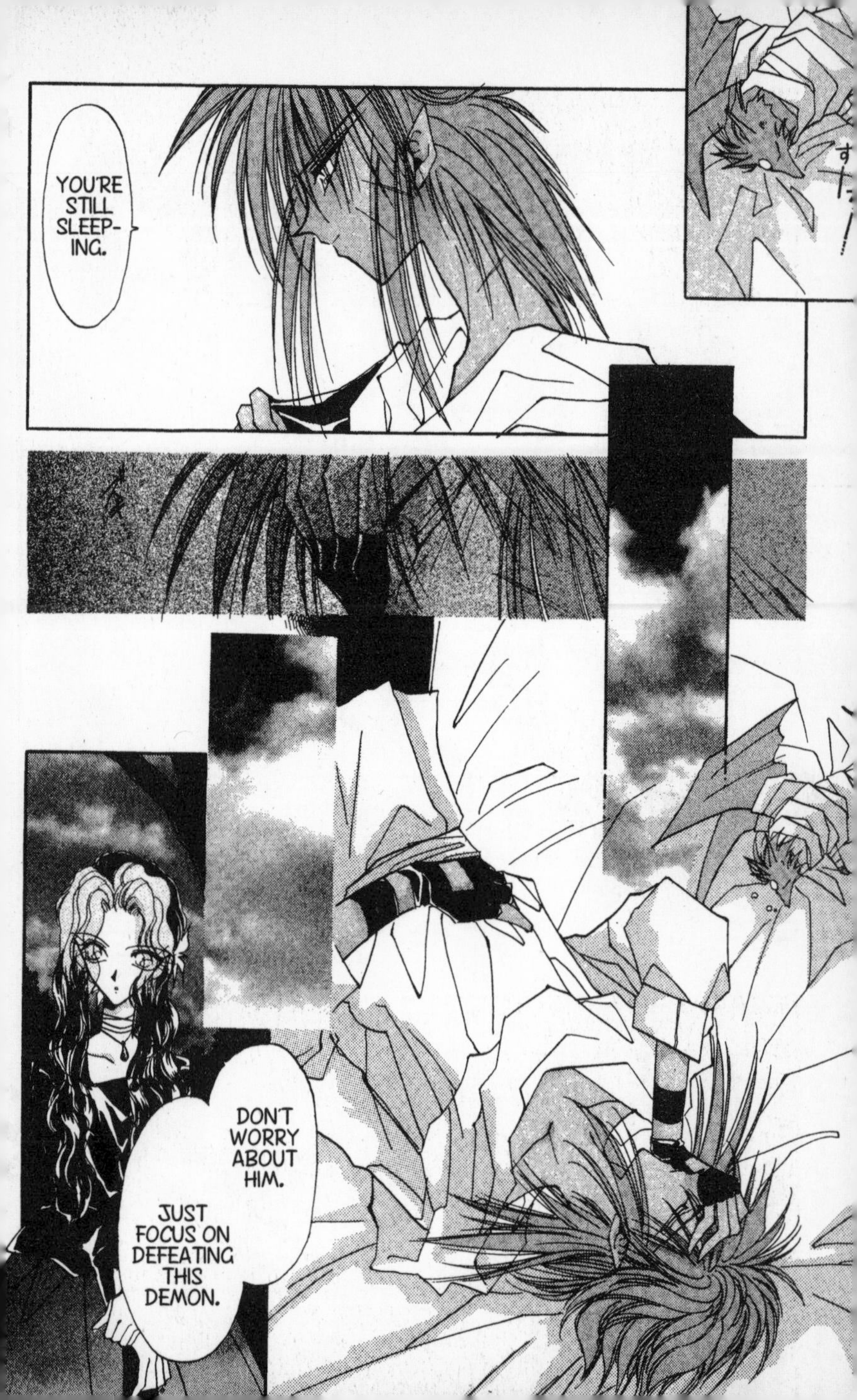
YOU'RE STILL SLEEP-ING.
DON'T WORRY ABOUT HIM.
JUST FOCUS ON DEFEATING THIS DEMON.

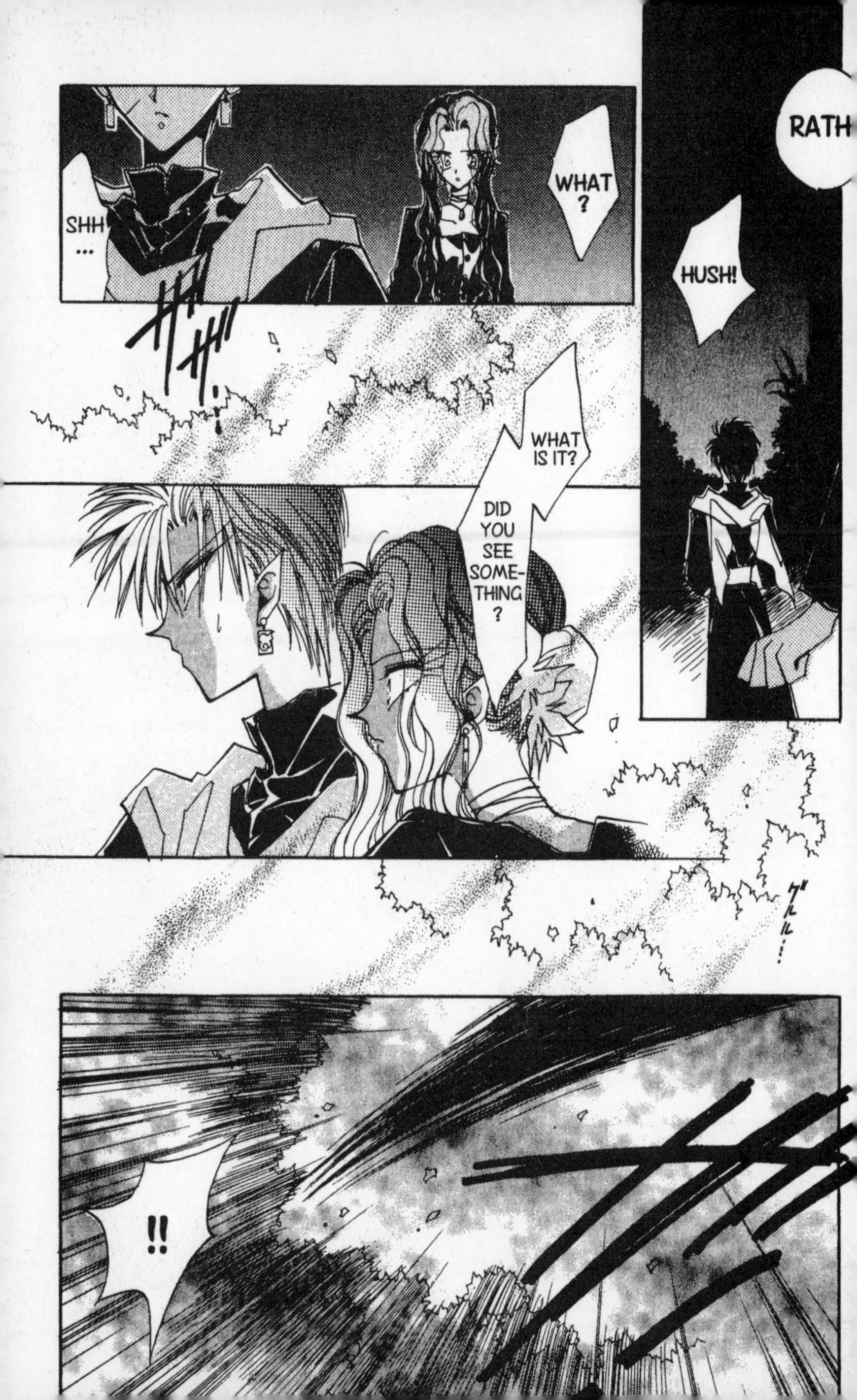
RATH
HUSH!
WHAT ?
SHH ...
WHAT IS IT?
DID YOU SEE SOME-THING ?
グルル…!
!!

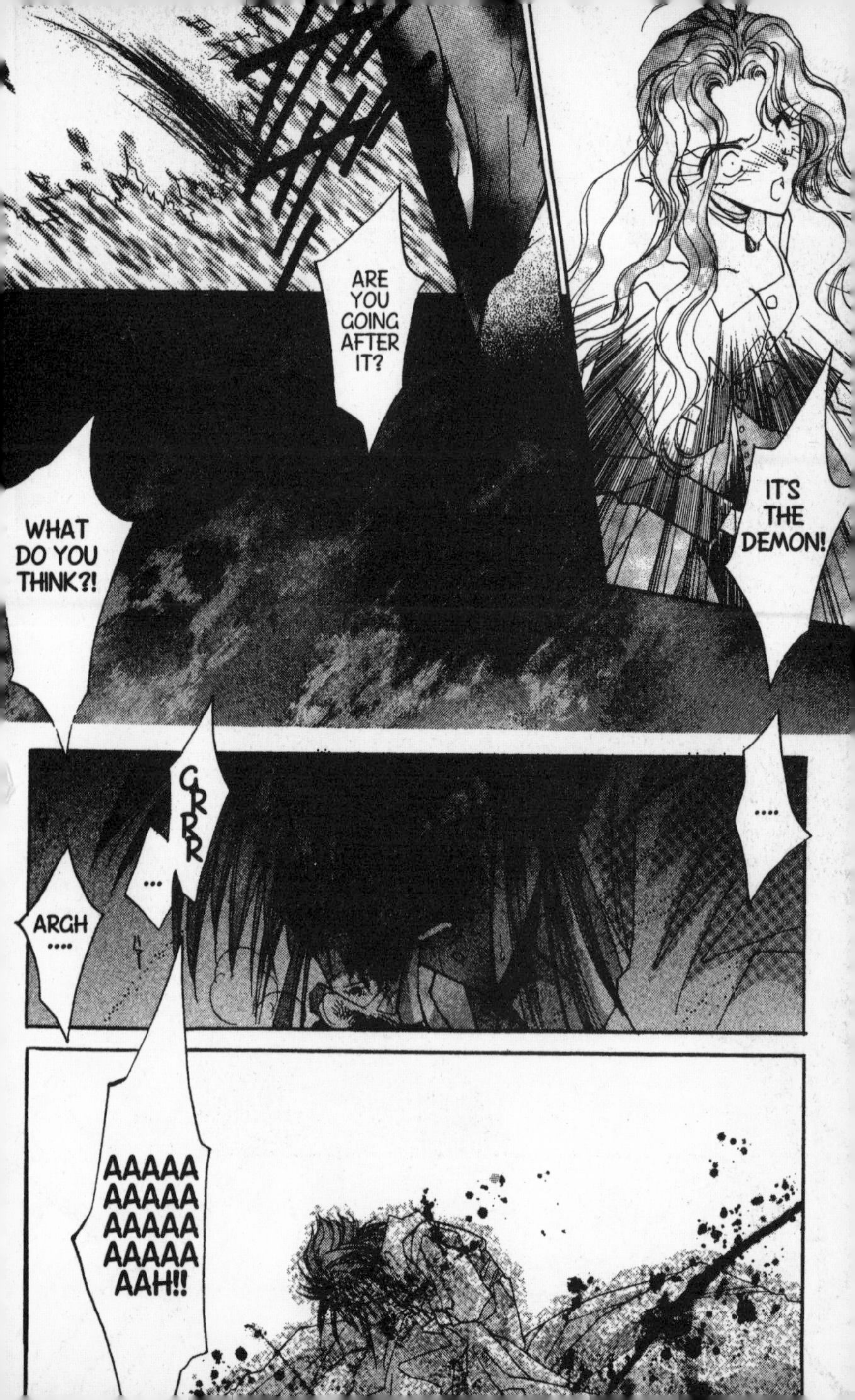
IT'S THE DEMON!
ARE YOU GOING AFTER IT?
WHAT DO YOU THINK?!
....
GRRR
...
ARGH ....
AAAAAAAAAAAAAAAAAAAAAAH!!

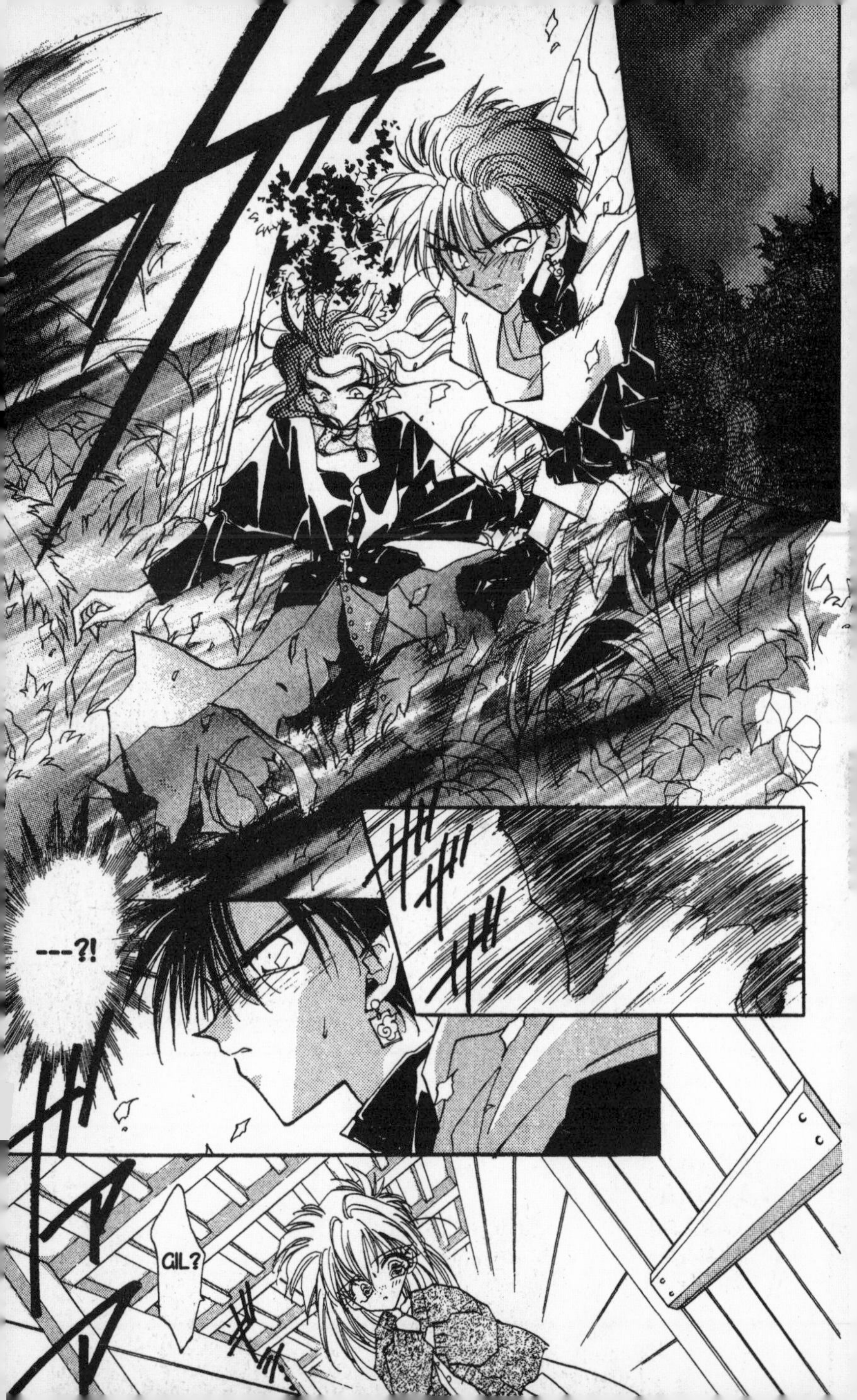
---?!
GIL?

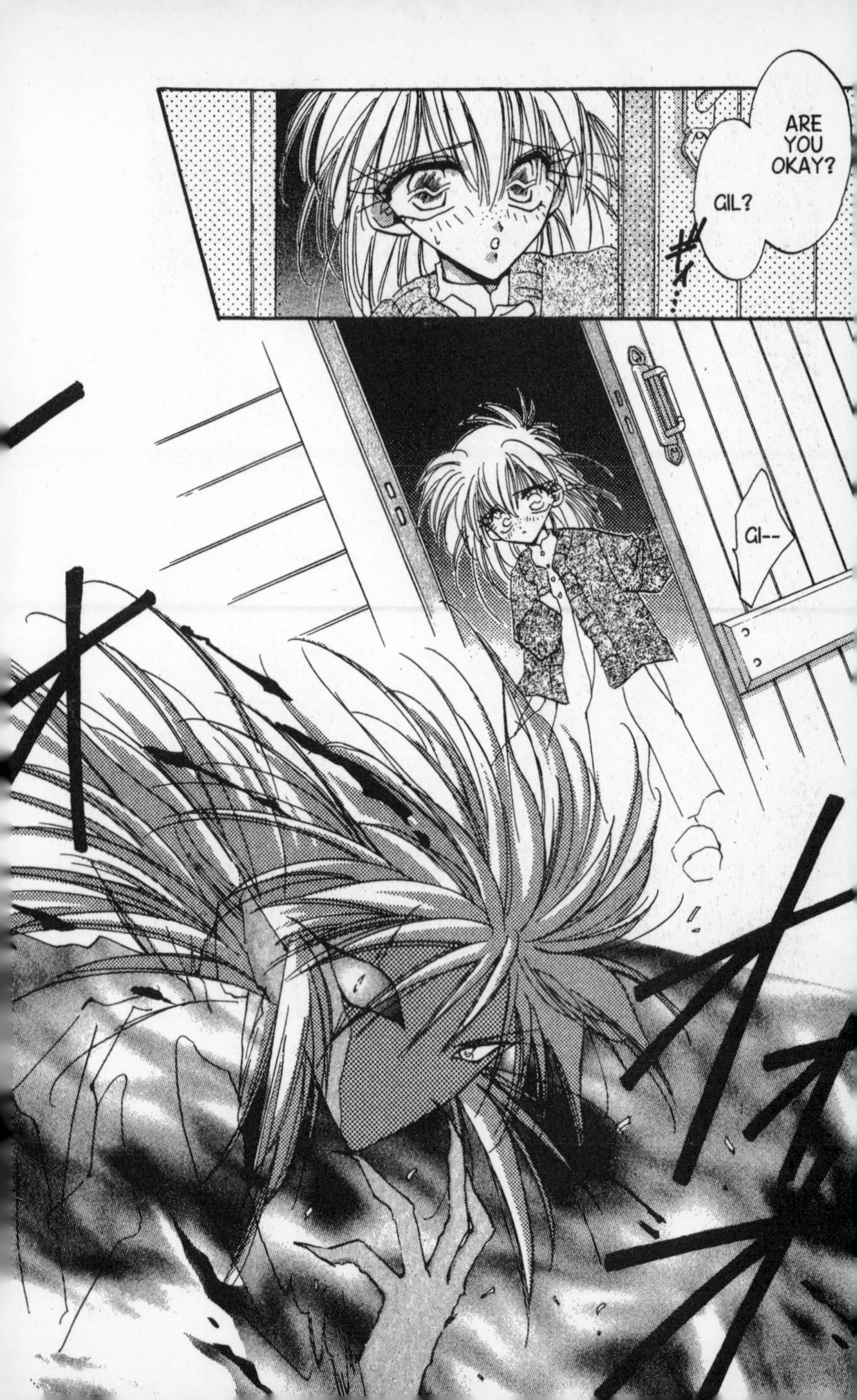

ARE YOU OKAY?
GIL?
GI--

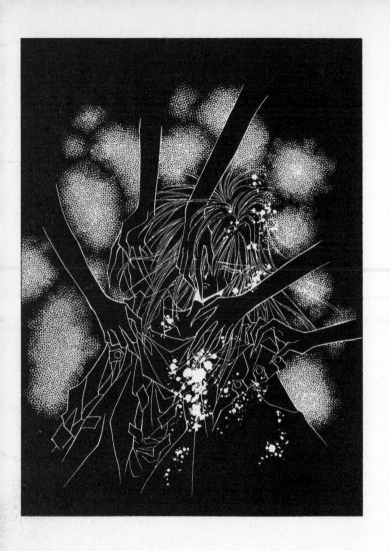

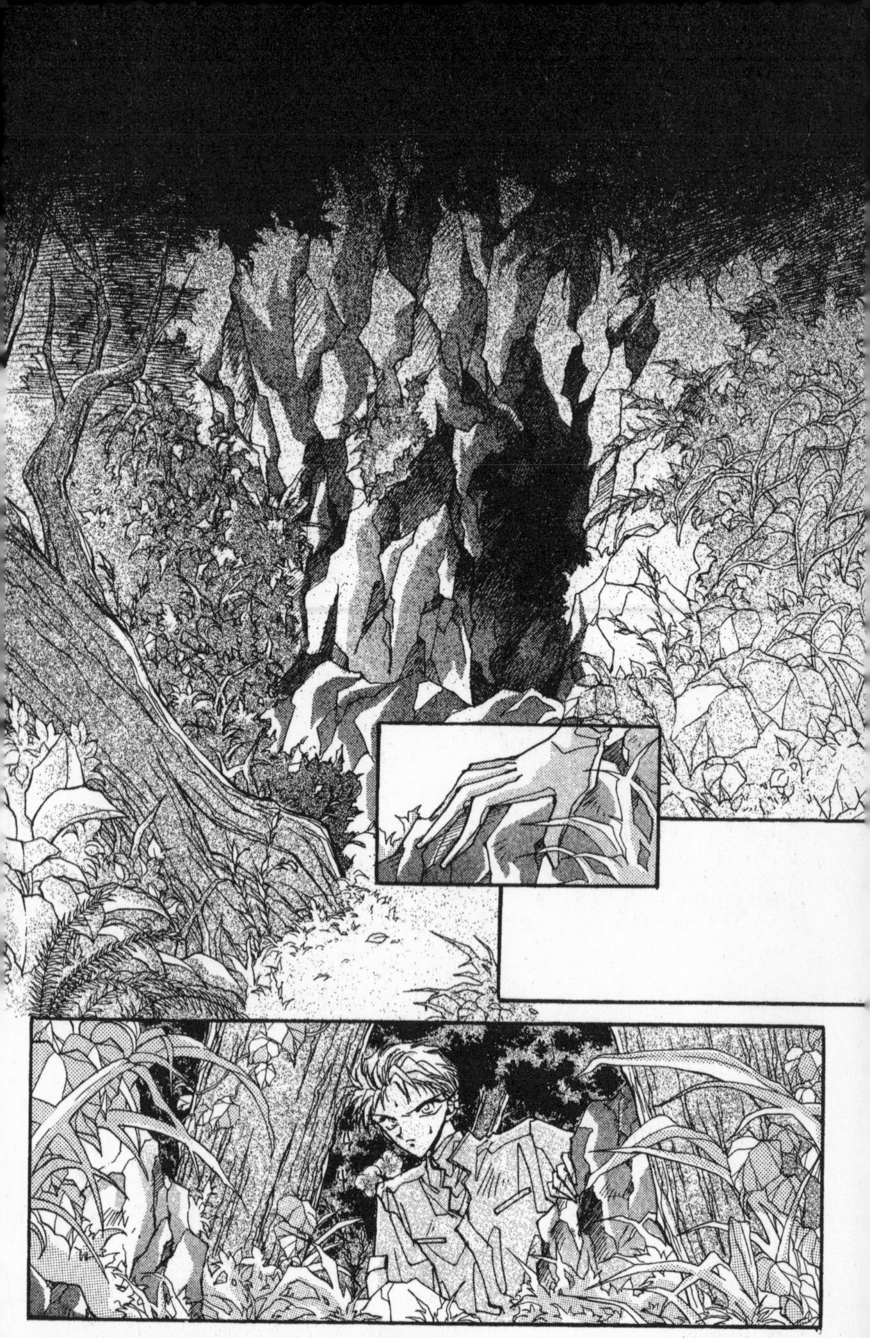

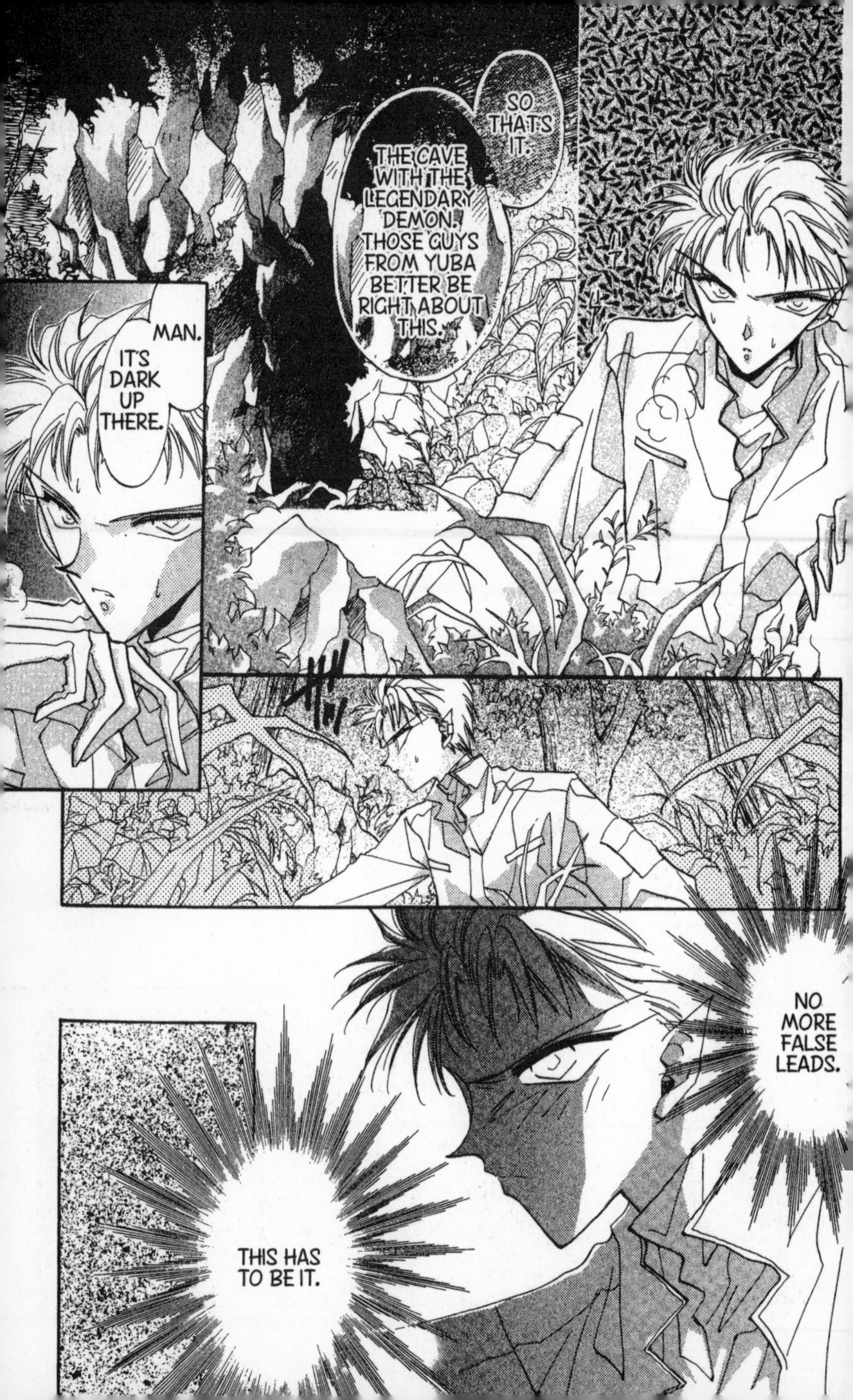
SO THAT'S IT.
THE CAVE WITH THE LEGENDARY DEMON. THOSE GUYS FROM YUBA BETTER BE RIGHT ABOUT THIS.
MAN. IT'S DARK UP THERE.
NO MORE FALSE LEADS.
THIS HAS TO BE IT.

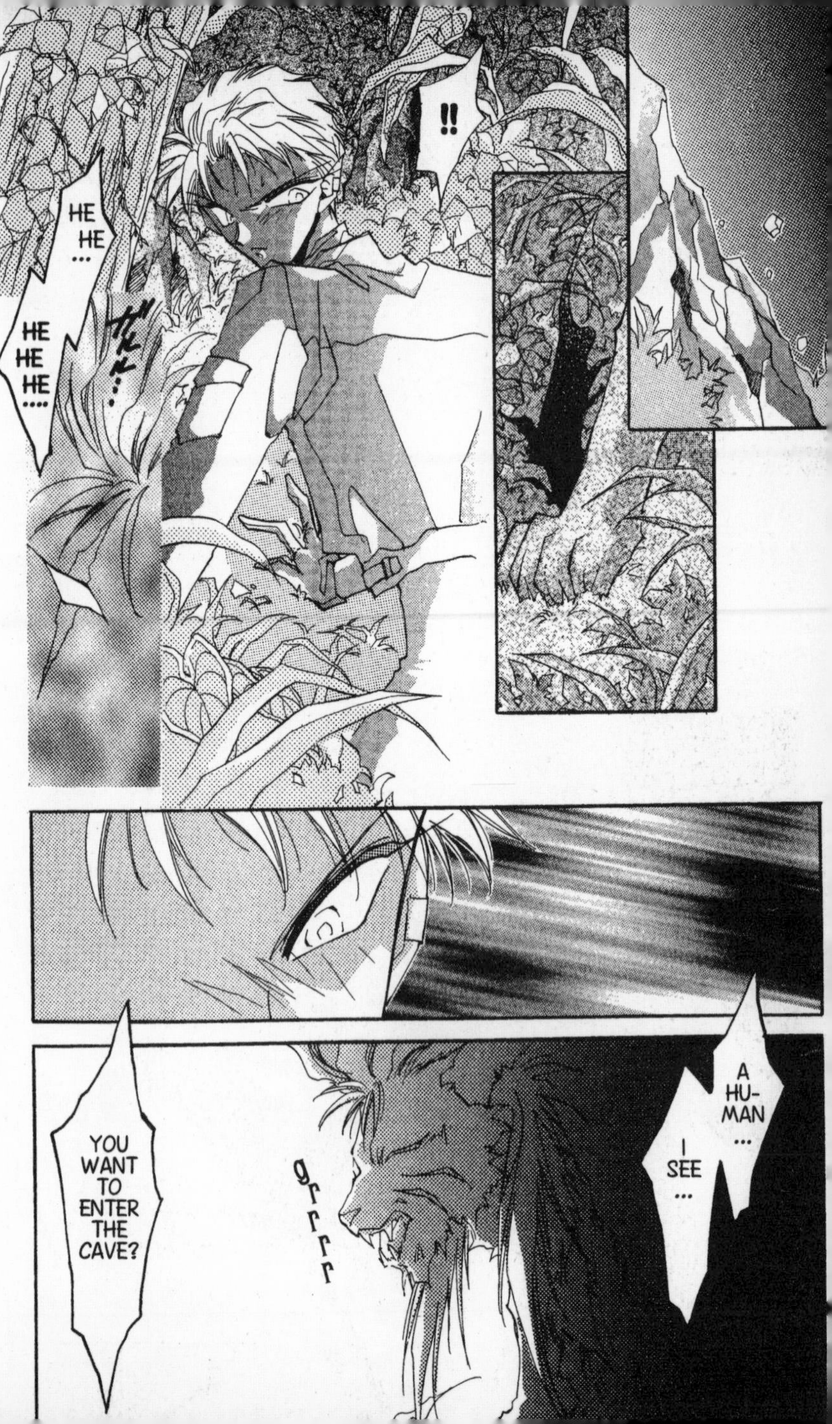
!!
HE HE ...
HE HE HE ....
A HU- MAN ... I SEE ...
grrrr
YOU WANT TO ENTER THE CAVE?

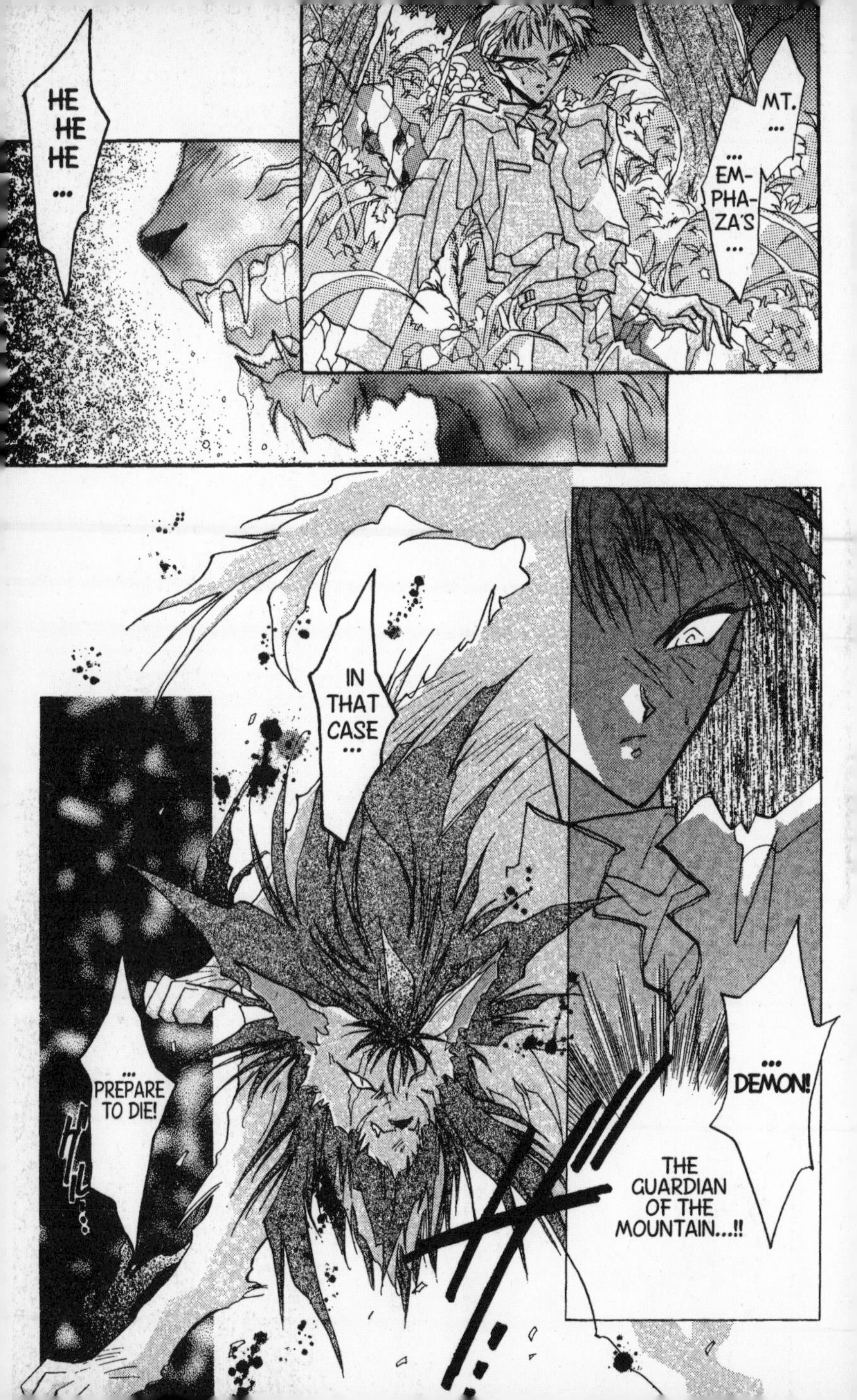
MT. ... ... EMPHAZA'S ...
HE HE HE ...
...DEMON!
THE GUARDIAN OF THE MOUNTAIN...!!
IN THAT CASE ...
...PREPARE TO DIE!

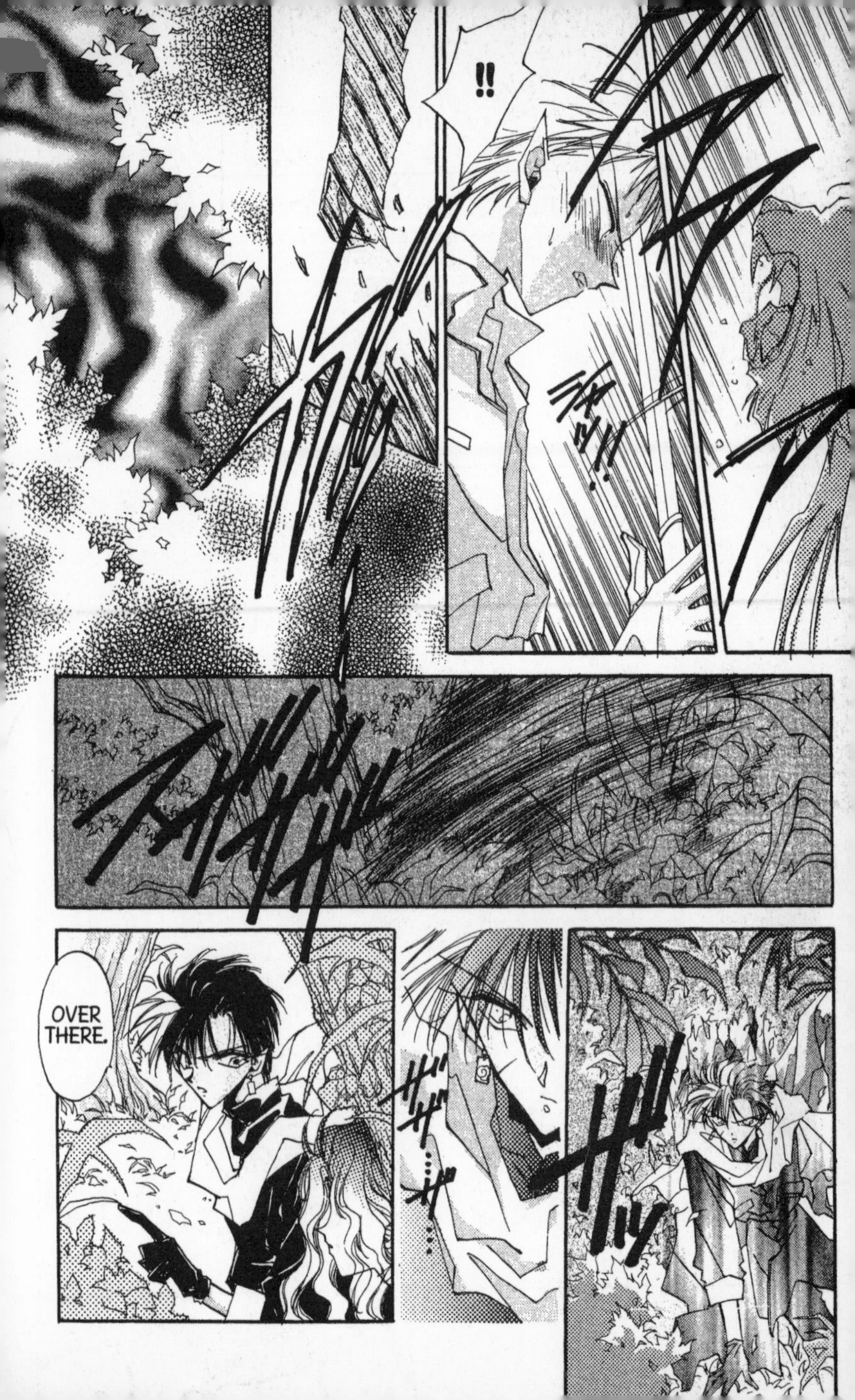
!!
OVER THERE.

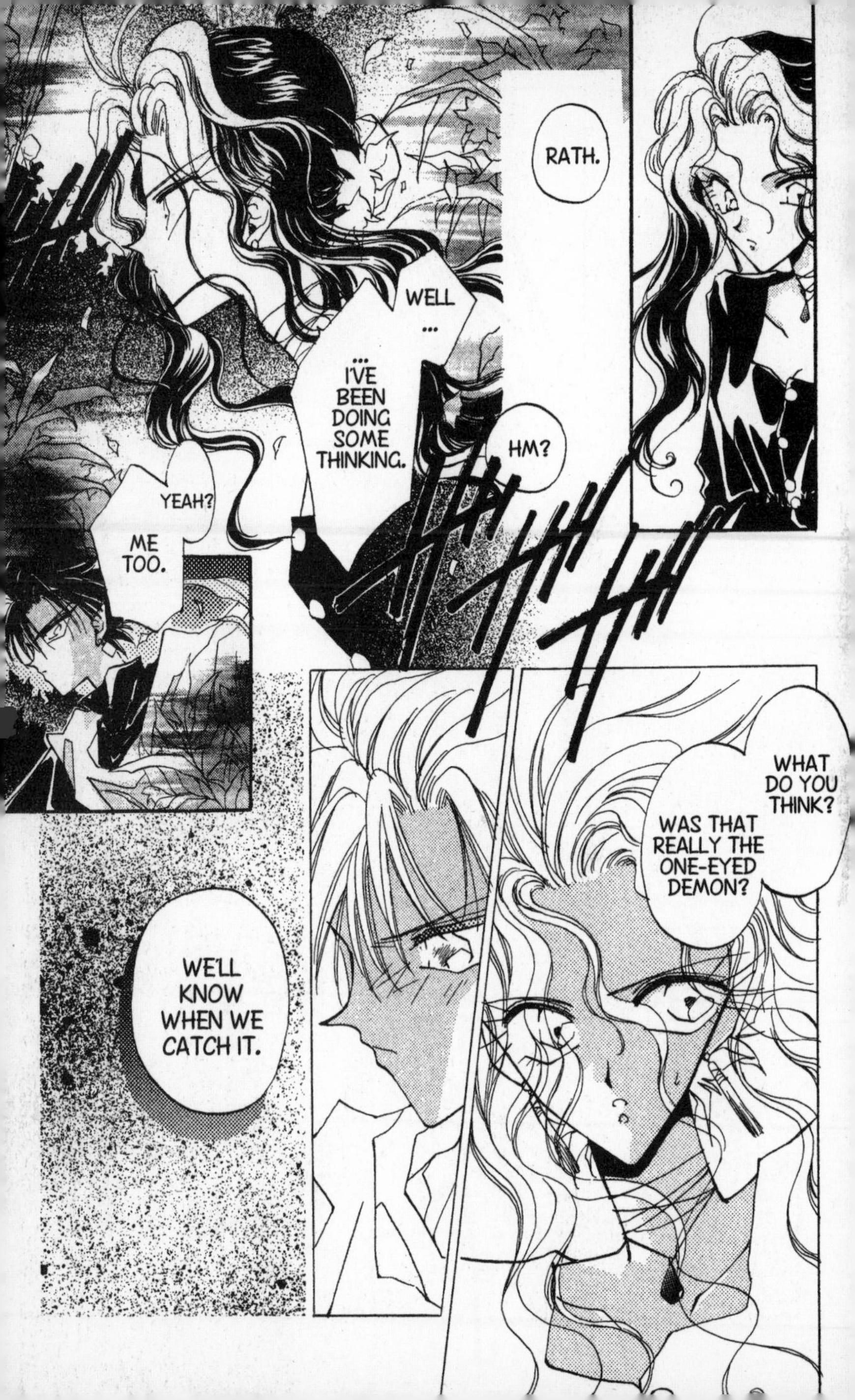
RATH.
HM?
WELL ...
... I'VE BEEN DOING SOME THINKING.
YEAH?
ME TOO.
WHAT DO YOU THINK?
WAS THAT REALLY THE ONE-EYED DEMON?
WE'LL KNOW WHEN WE CATCH IT.

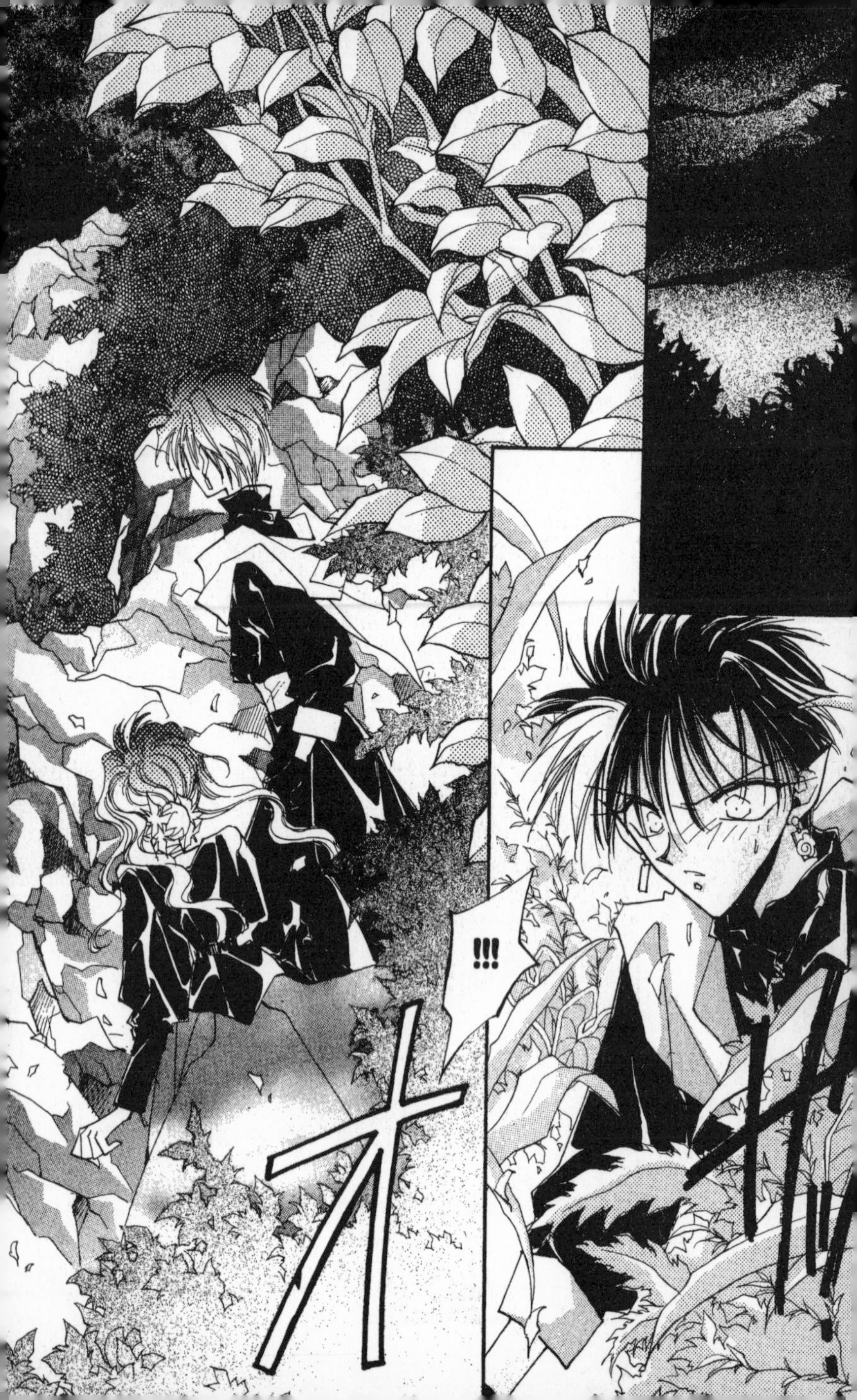
!!!

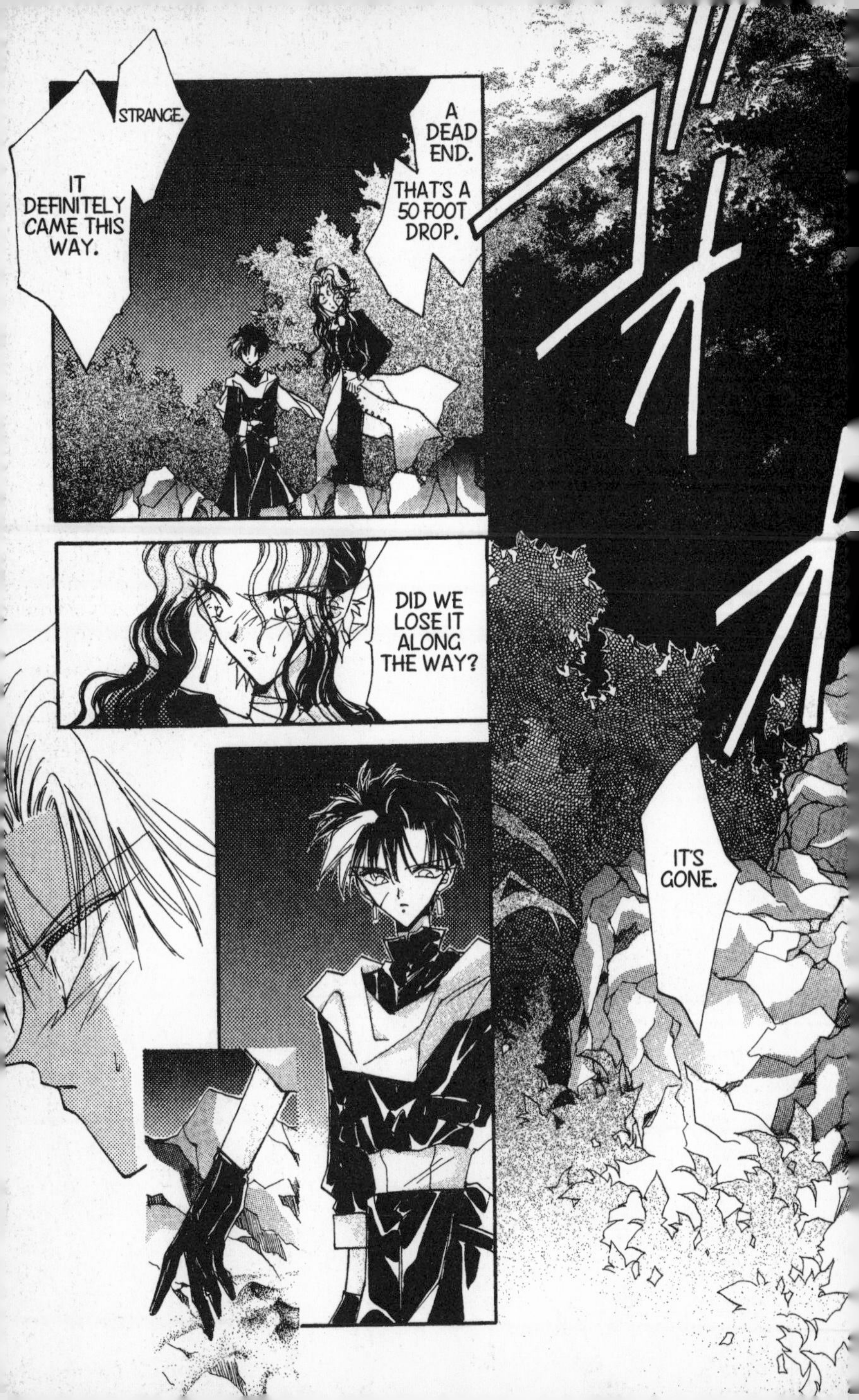
IT'S GONE.
A DEAD END.
THAT'S A 50 FOOT DROP.
STRANGE.
IT DEFINITELY CAME THIS WAY.
DID WE LOSE IT ALONG THE WAY?

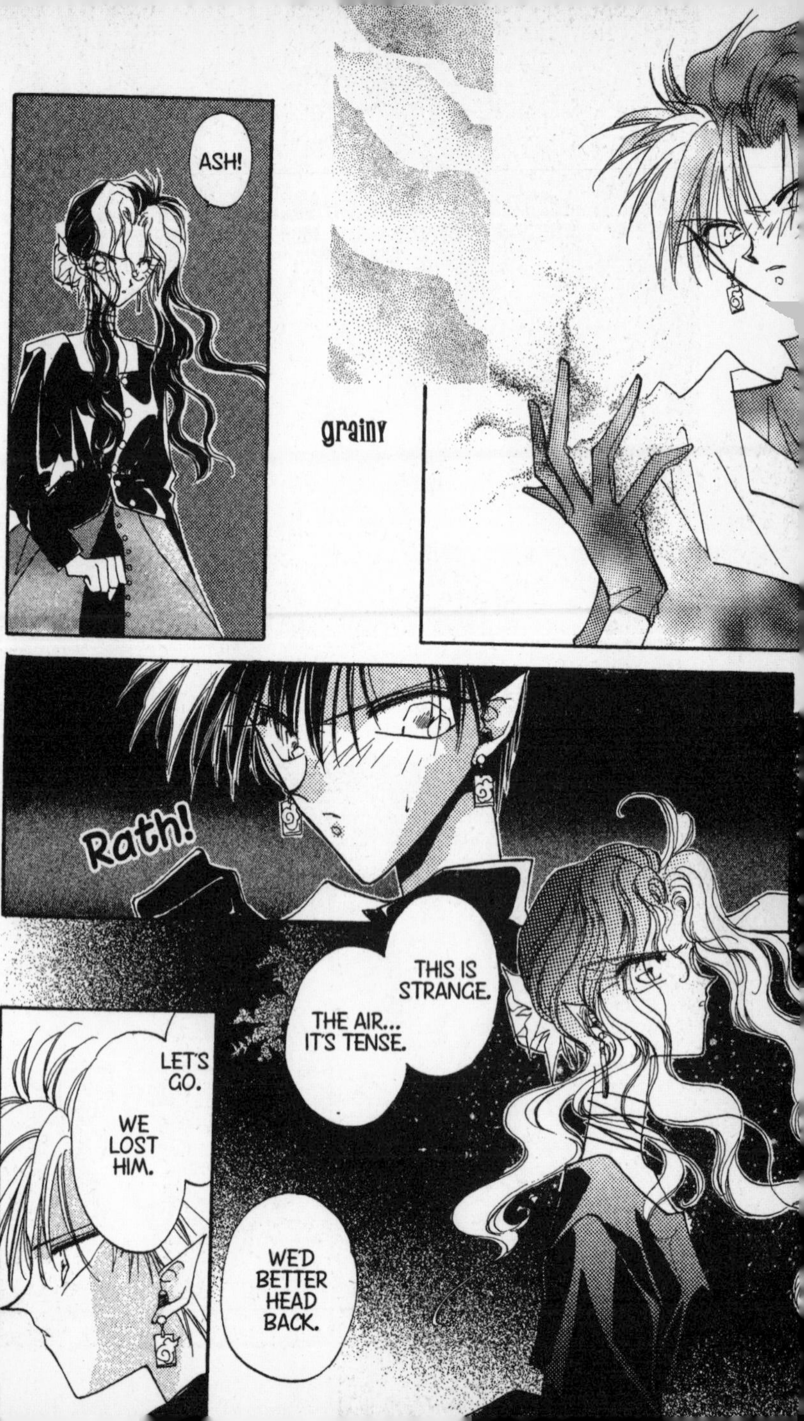
grainy
ASH!
Rath!
THIS IS STRANGE.
THE AIR... IT'S TENSE.
LET'S GO.
WE LOST HIM.
WE'D BETTER HEAD BACK.

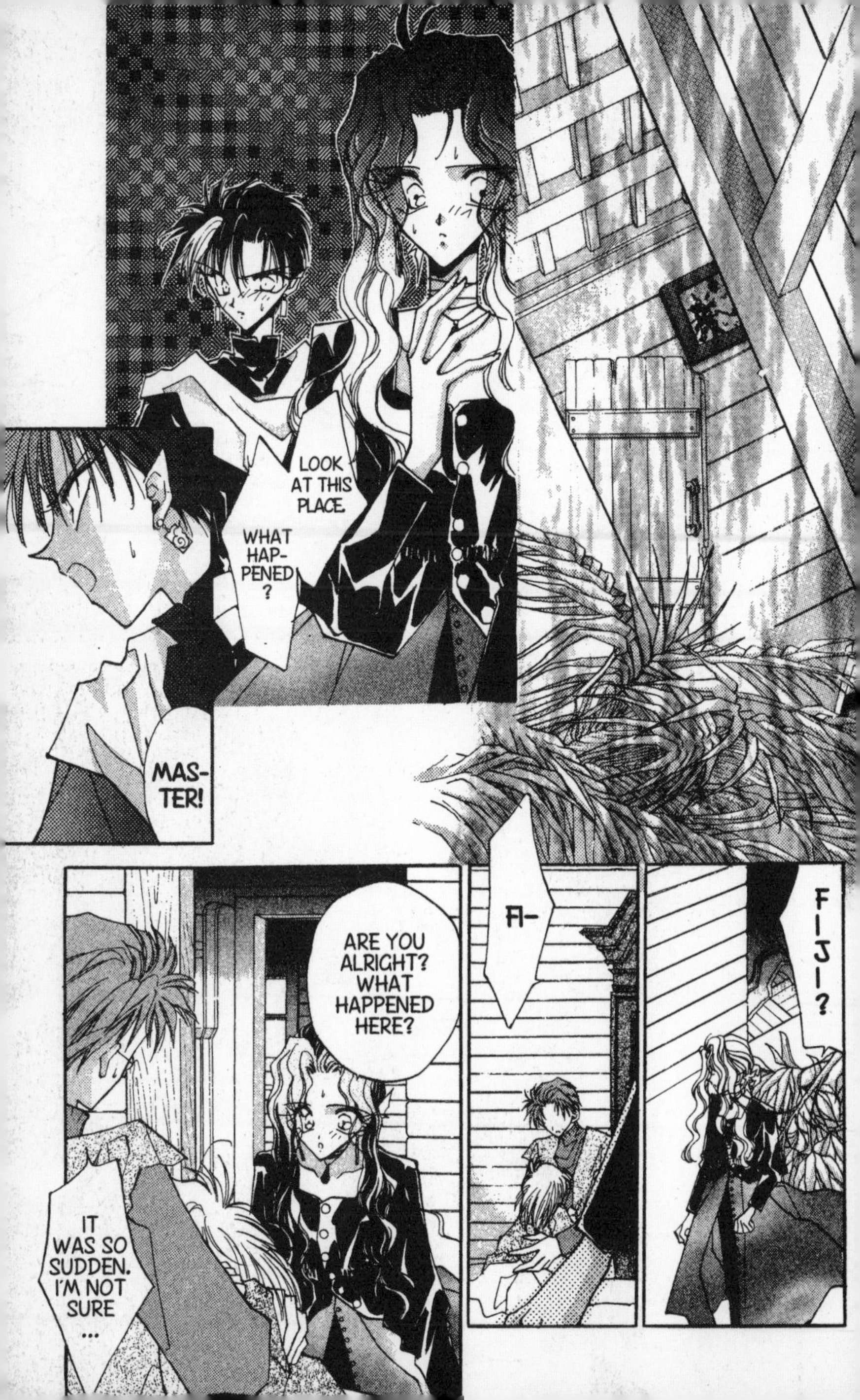
LOOK AT THIS PLACE
WHAT HAP-PENED?
MAS-TER!
FIJI?
FI-
ARE YOU ALRIGHT? WHAT HAPPENED HERE?
IT WAS SO SUDDEN. I'M NOT SURE ...

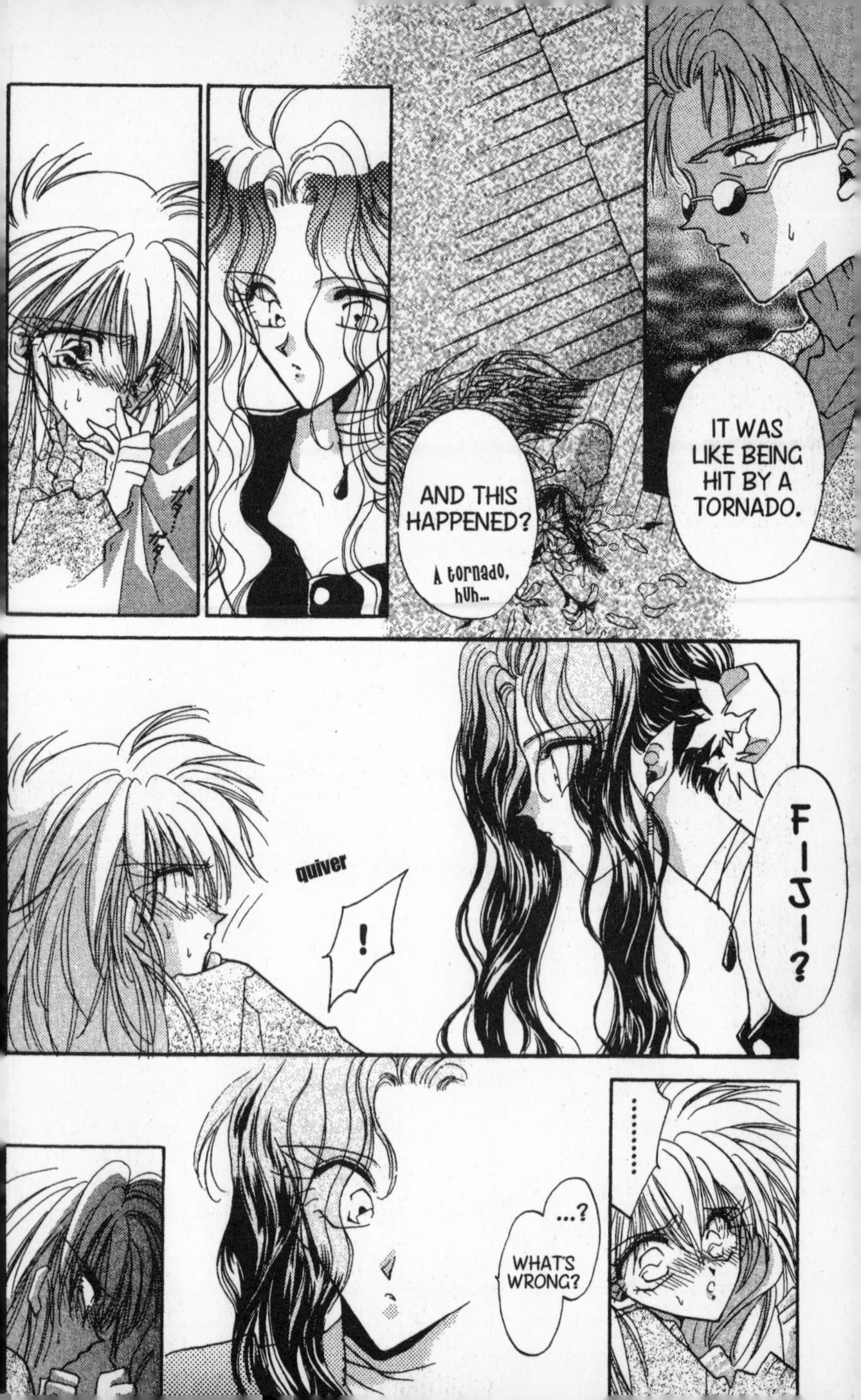
IT WAS LIKE BEING HIT BY A TORNADO.
AND THIS HAPPENED?
A tornado, huh...
FIJI?
!
quiver
......
...?
WHAT'S WRONG?

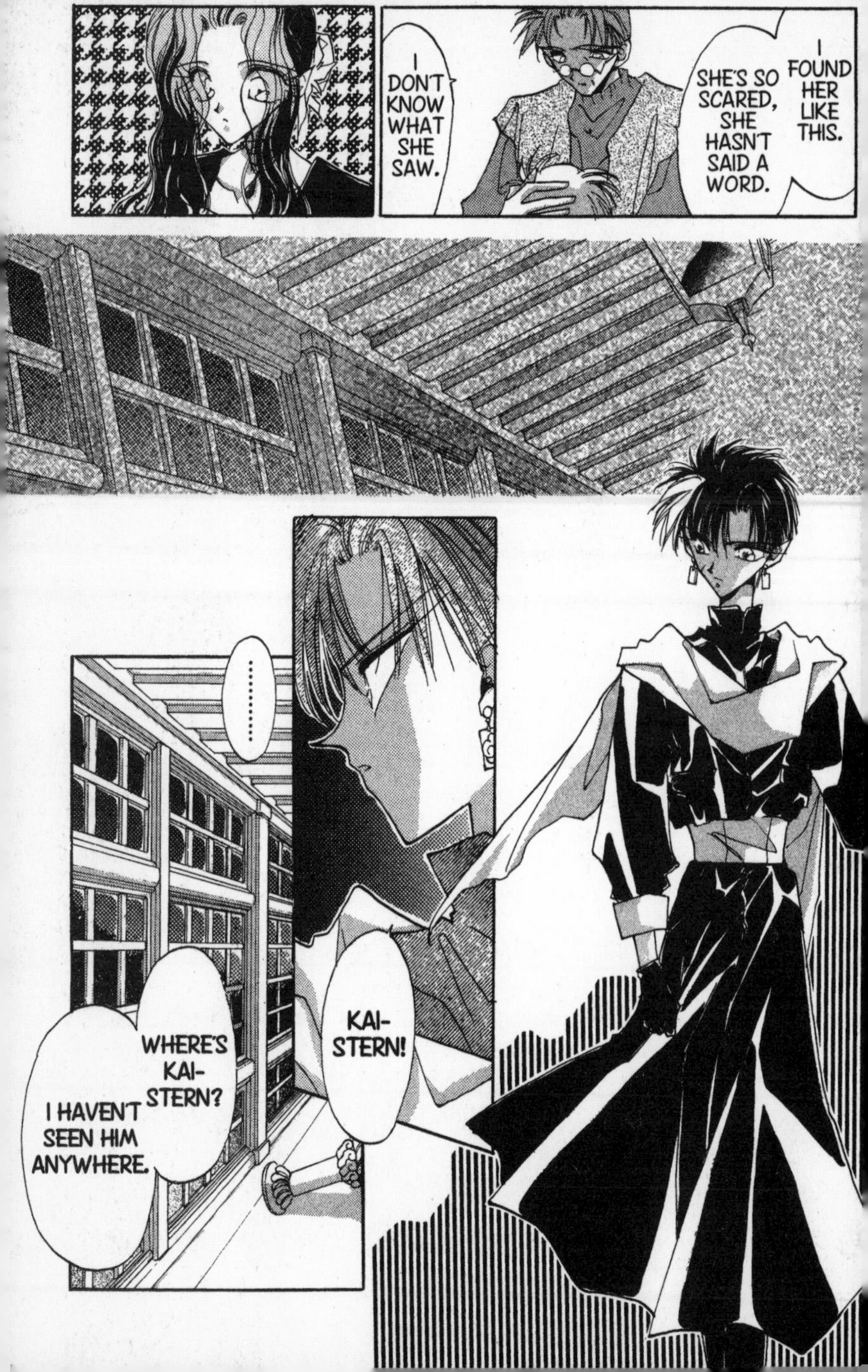
I FOUND HER LIKE THIS.
SHE'S SO SCARED, SHE HASN'T SAID A WORD.
I DON'T KNOW WHAT SHE SAW.
KAI-STERN!
......
WHERE'S KAI-STERN?
I HAVEN'T SEEN HIM ANYWHERE.

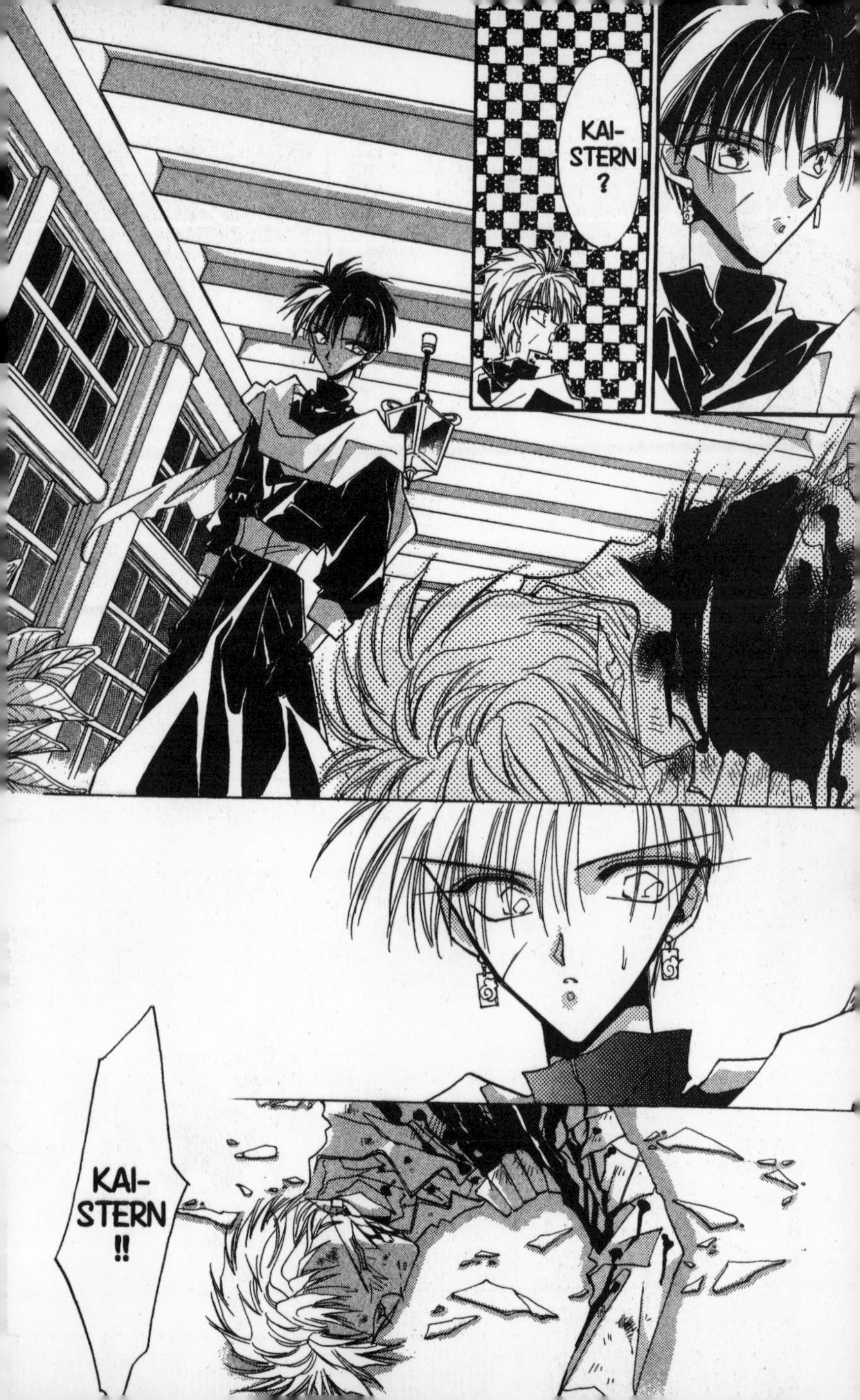
KAI-
STERN
?
KAI-
STERN
!!

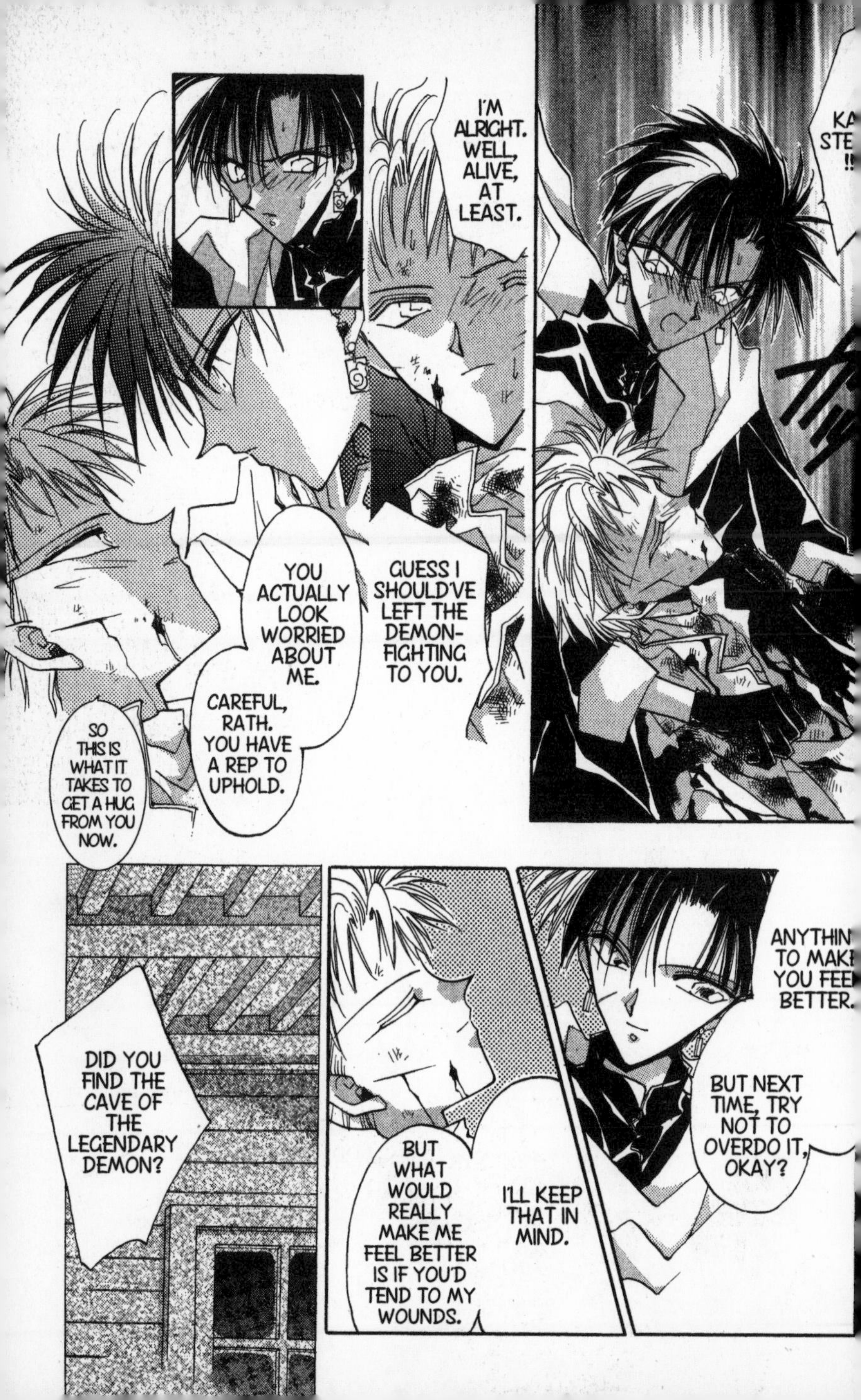

KA STE !!
I'M ALRIGHT. WELL, ALIVE, AT LEAST.
GUESS I SHOULD'VE LEFT THE DEMON-FIGHTING TO YOU.
YOU ACTUALLY LOOK WORRIED ABOUT ME.
CAREFUL, RATH. YOU HAVE A REP TO UPHOLD.
SO THIS IS WHAT IT TAKES TO GET A HUG FROM YOU NOW.
ANYTHIN TO MAK YOU FEE BETTER.
BUT NEXT TIME, TRY NOT TO OVERDO IT, OKAY?
I'LL KEEP THAT IN MIND.
BUT WHAT WOULD REALLY MAKE ME FEEL BETTER IS IF YOU'D TEND TO MY WOUNDS.
DID YOU FIND THE CAVE OF THE LEGENDARY DEMON?

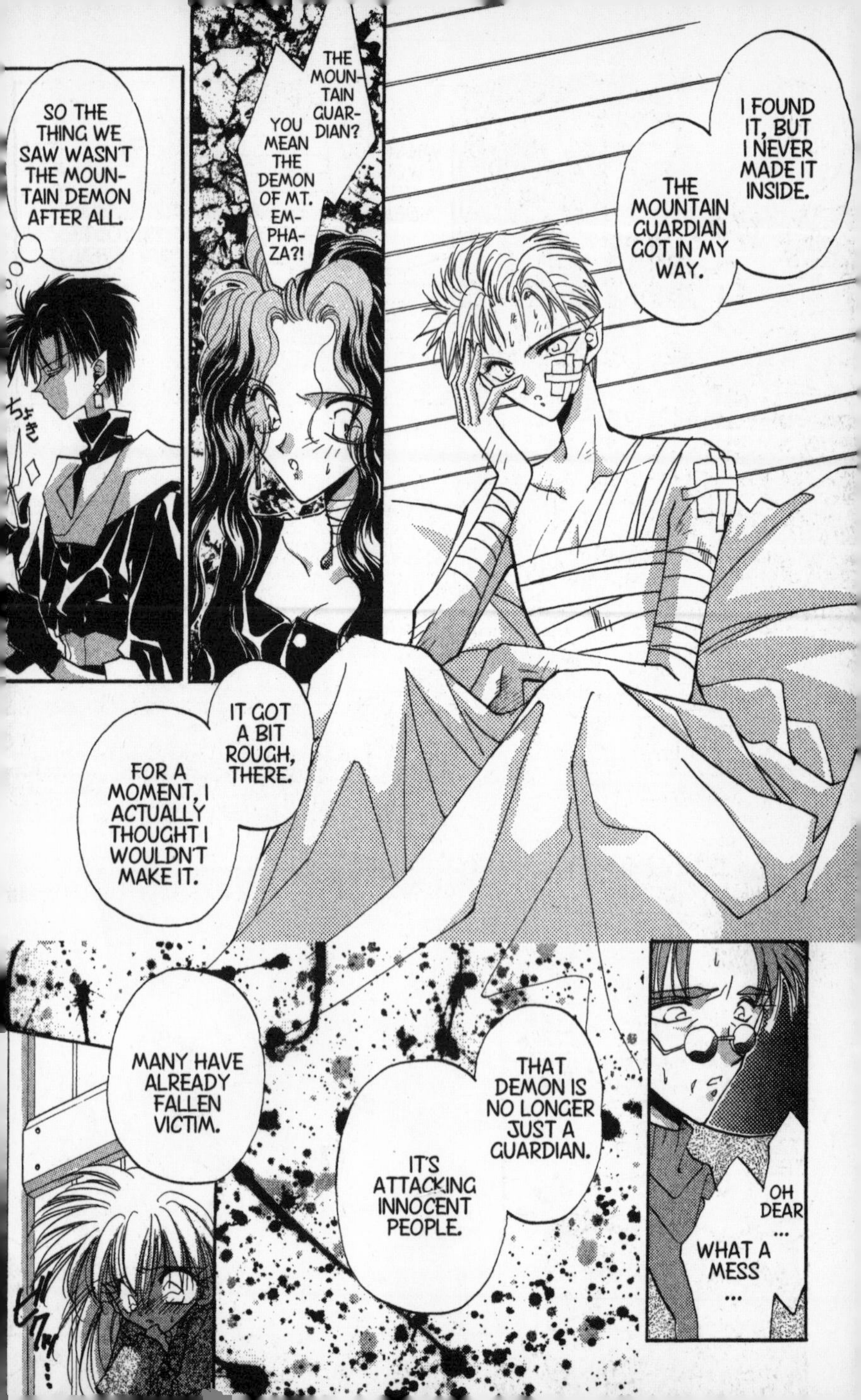
I FOUND IT, BUT I NEVER MADE IT INSIDE.
THE MOUNTAIN GUARDIAN GOT IN MY WAY.
THE MOUN-TAIN GUAR-DIAN?
YOU MEAN THE DEMON OF MT. EM-PHA-ZA?!
SO THE THING WE SAW WASN'T THE MOUN-TAIN DEMON AFTER ALL.
ちょき
IT GOT A BIT ROUGH, THERE.
FOR A MOMENT, I ACTUALLY THOUGHT I WOULDN'T MAKE IT.
OH DEAR...
WHAT A MESS...
THAT DEMON IS NO LONGER JUST A GUARDIAN.
IT'S ATTACKING INNOCENT PEOPLE.
MANY HAVE ALREADY FALLEN VICTIM.

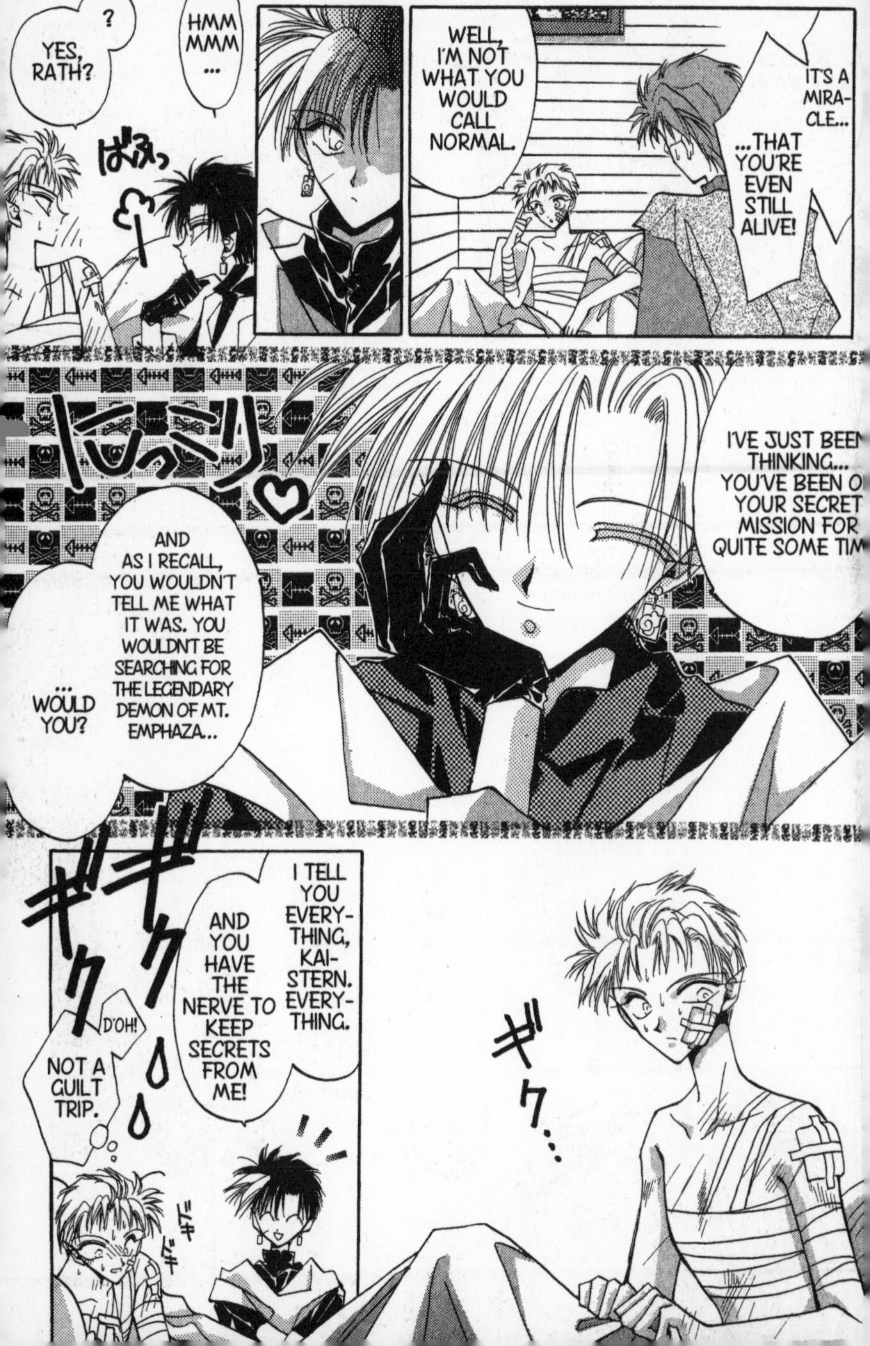
IT'S A MIRACLE...
...THAT YOU'RE EVEN STILL ALIVE!
WELL, I'M NOT WHAT YOU WOULD CALL NORMAL.
HMM MMM ...
?
YES, RATH?
ぱふっ
I'VE JUST BEEN THINKING... YOU'VE BEEN O YOUR SECRET MISSION FOR QUITE SOME TIM
にっこり
AND AS I RECALL, YOU WOULDN'T TELL ME WHAT IT WAS. YOU WOULDN'T BE SEARCHING FOR THE LEGENDARY DEMON OF MT. EMPHAZA...
...WOULD YOU?
ギク...
I TELL YOU EVERY-THING, KAI-STERN. EVERY-THING.
AND YOU HAVE THE NERVE TO KEEP SECRETS FROM ME!
ギクギク
D'OH!
NOT A GUILT TRIP.
ドキドキ

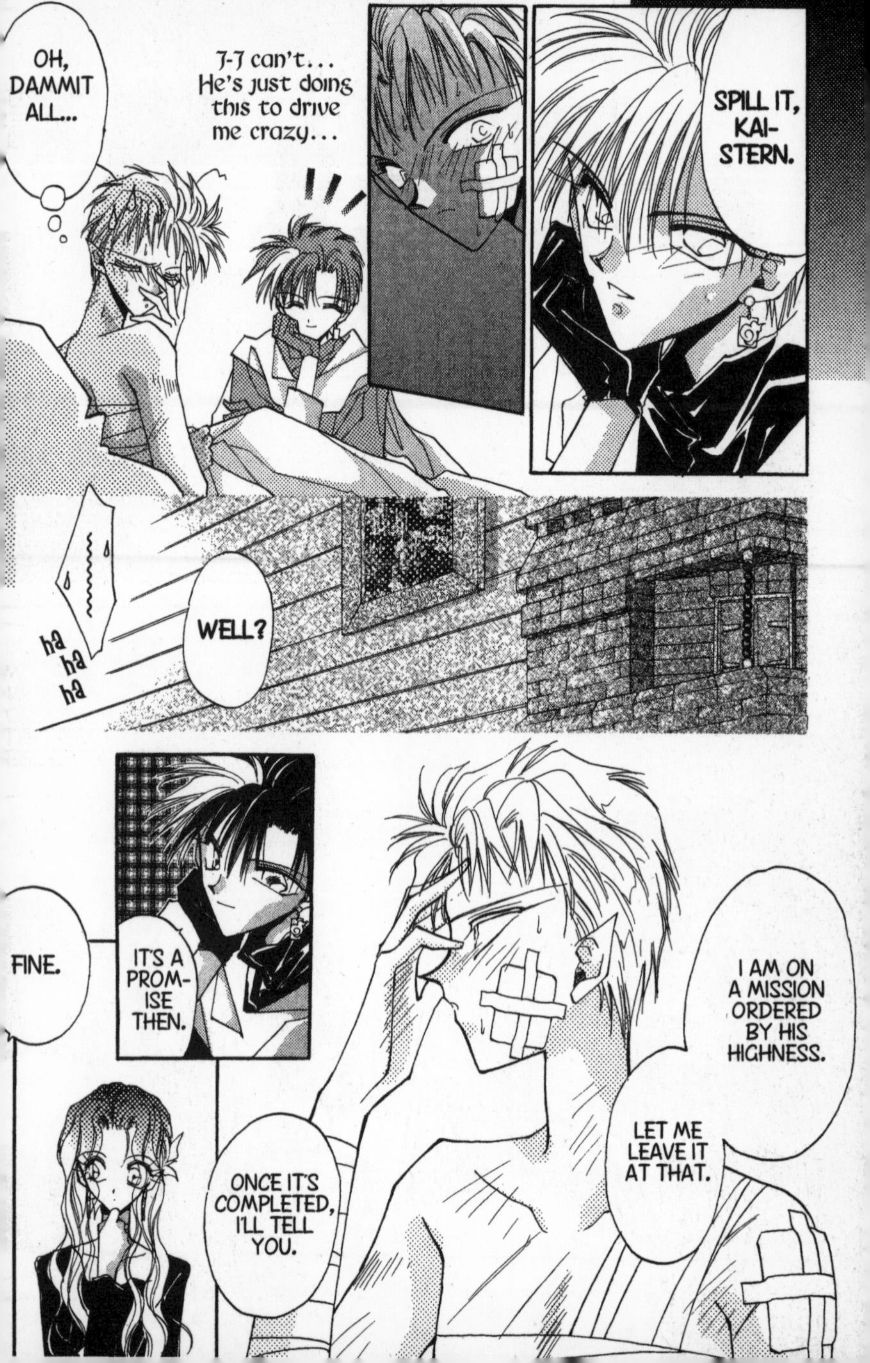
SPILL IT, KAI-STERN.
J-J can't... He's just doing this to drive me crazy...
OH, DAMMIT ALL...
WELL?
ha ha ha
I AM ON A MISSION ORDERED BY HIS HIGHNESS.
LET ME LEAVE IT AT THAT.
ONCE IT'S COMPLETED, I'LL TELL YOU.
IT'S A PROMISE THEN.
FINE.

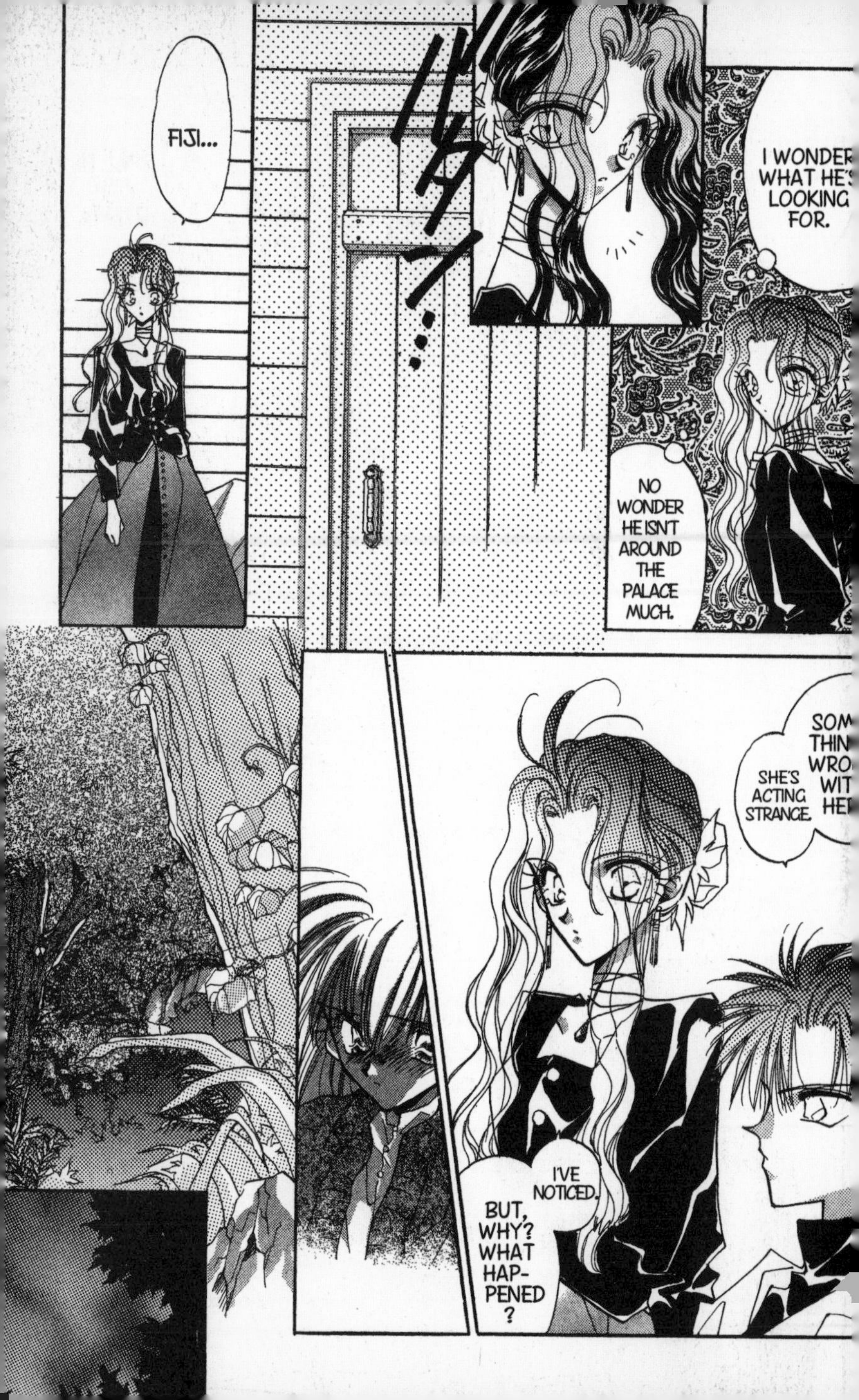
I WONDER WHAT HE'S LOOKING FOR.
NO WONDER HE ISN'T AROUND THE PALACE MUCH.
FIJI...
SOM THIN WRO WIT HE
SHE'S ACTING STRANGE.
I'VE NOTICED.
BUT, WHY? WHAT HAP-PENED?

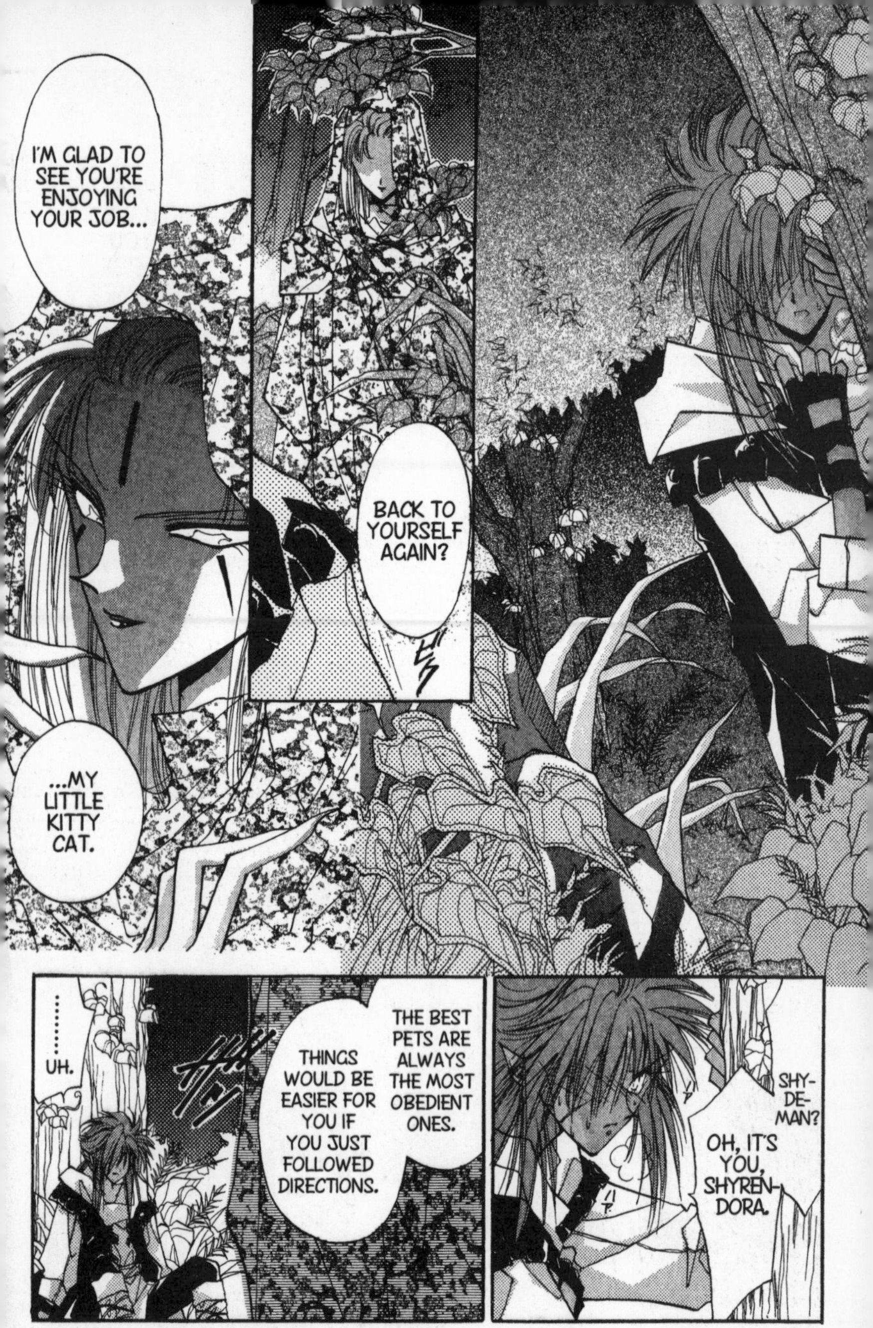
BACK TO YOURSELF AGAIN?
I'M GLAD TO SEE YOU'RE ENJOYING YOUR JOB...
...MY LITTLE KITTY CAT.
SHY-DE-MAN?
OH, IT'S YOU, SHYREN-DORA.
THE BEST PETS ARE ALWAYS THE MOST OBEDIENT ONES.
THINGS WOULD BE EASIER FOR YOU IF YOU JUST FOLLOWED DIRECTIONS.
......UH.

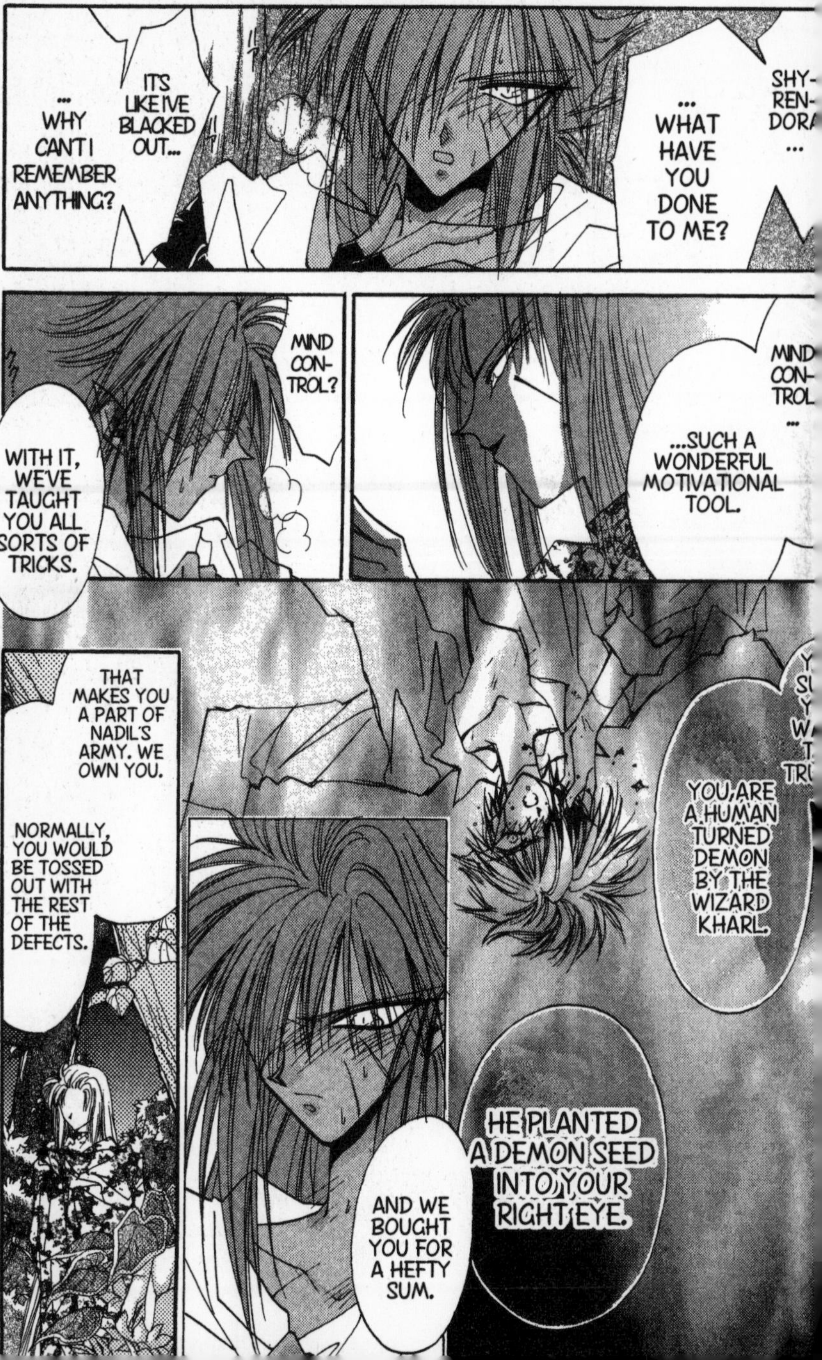
SHY- REN- DORA ...
... WHAT HAVE YOU DONE TO ME?
ITS LIKE IVE BLACKED OUT...
... WHY CANT I REMEMBER ANYTHING?
MIND CON- TROL ...
...SUCH A WONDERFUL MOTIVATIONAL TOOL.
MIND CON- TROL?
WITH IT, WE'VE TAUGHT YOU ALL SORTS OF TRICKS.
YOU ARE A HUMAN TURNED DEMON BY THE WIZARD KHARL.
HE PLANTED A DEMON SEED INTO YOUR RIGHT EYE.
AND WE BOUGHT YOU FOR A HEFTY SUM.
THAT MAKES YOU A PART OF NADIL'S ARMY. WE OWN YOU.
NORMALLY, YOU WOULD BE TOSSED OUT WITH THE REST OF THE DEFECTS.

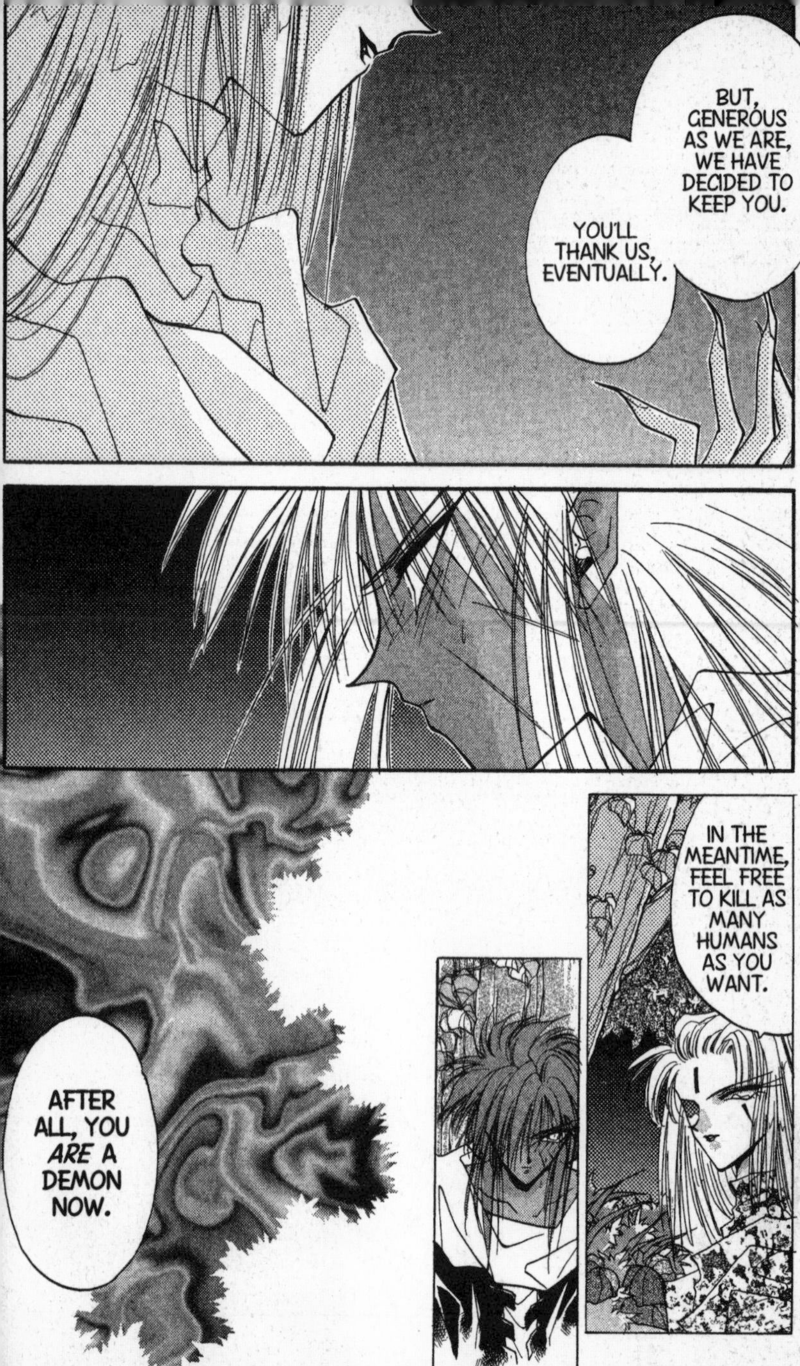
BUT, GENEROUS AS WE ARE, WE HAVE DECIDED TO KEEP YOU.
YOU'LL THANK US, EVENTUALLY.
IN THE MEANTIME, FEEL FREE TO KILL AS MANY HUMANS AS YOU WANT.
AFTER ALL, YOU *ARE* A DEMON NOW.

ALL OF MY HOPES AND DREAMS...
...ARE STEEPED IN DARKNESS.
THE ONE I WISH TO KILL...
...IS NOT IN FRONT OF ME.
WHAT SHOULD I DO? HOW DO I FULFILL MY DREAMS?

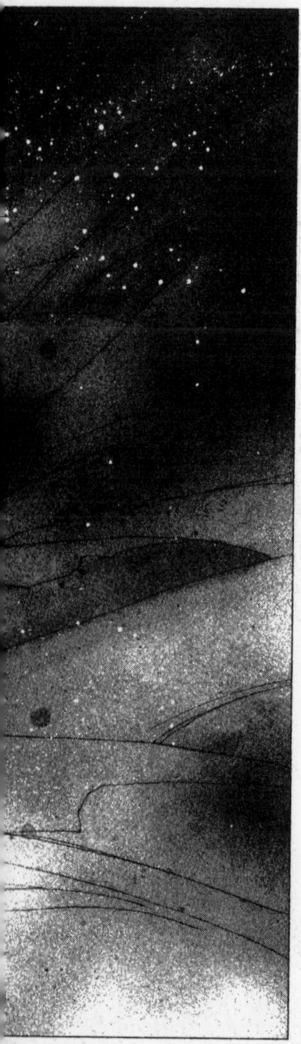

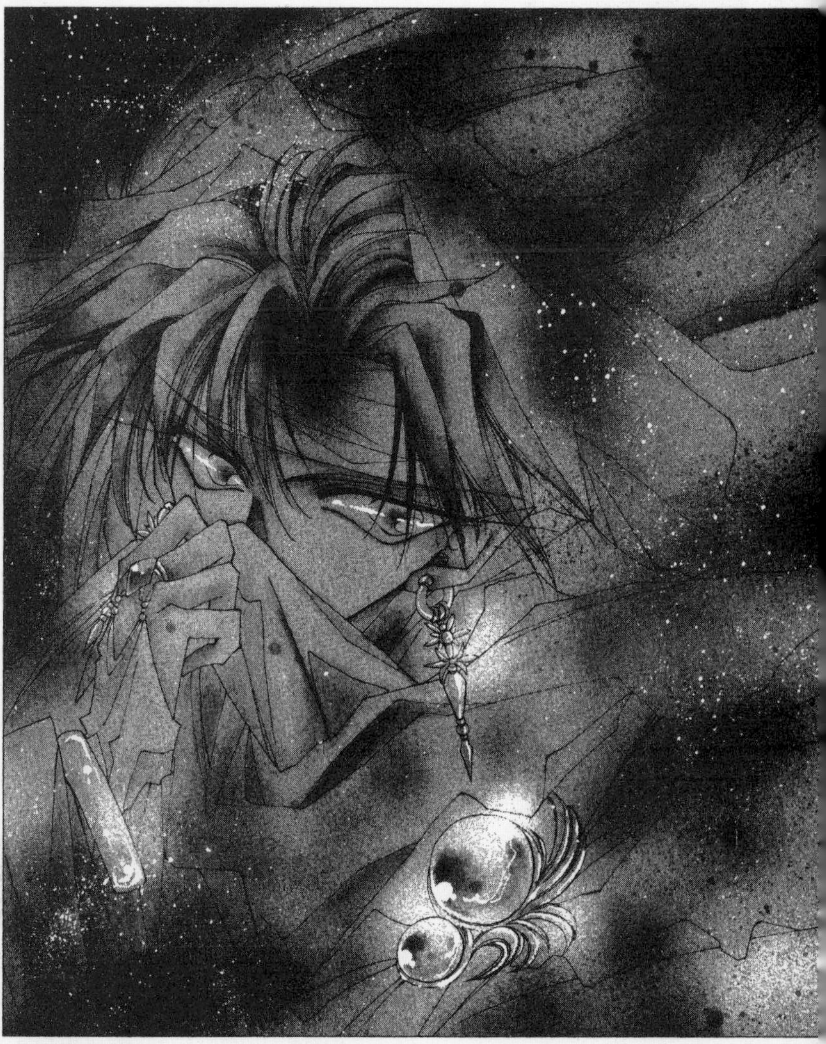

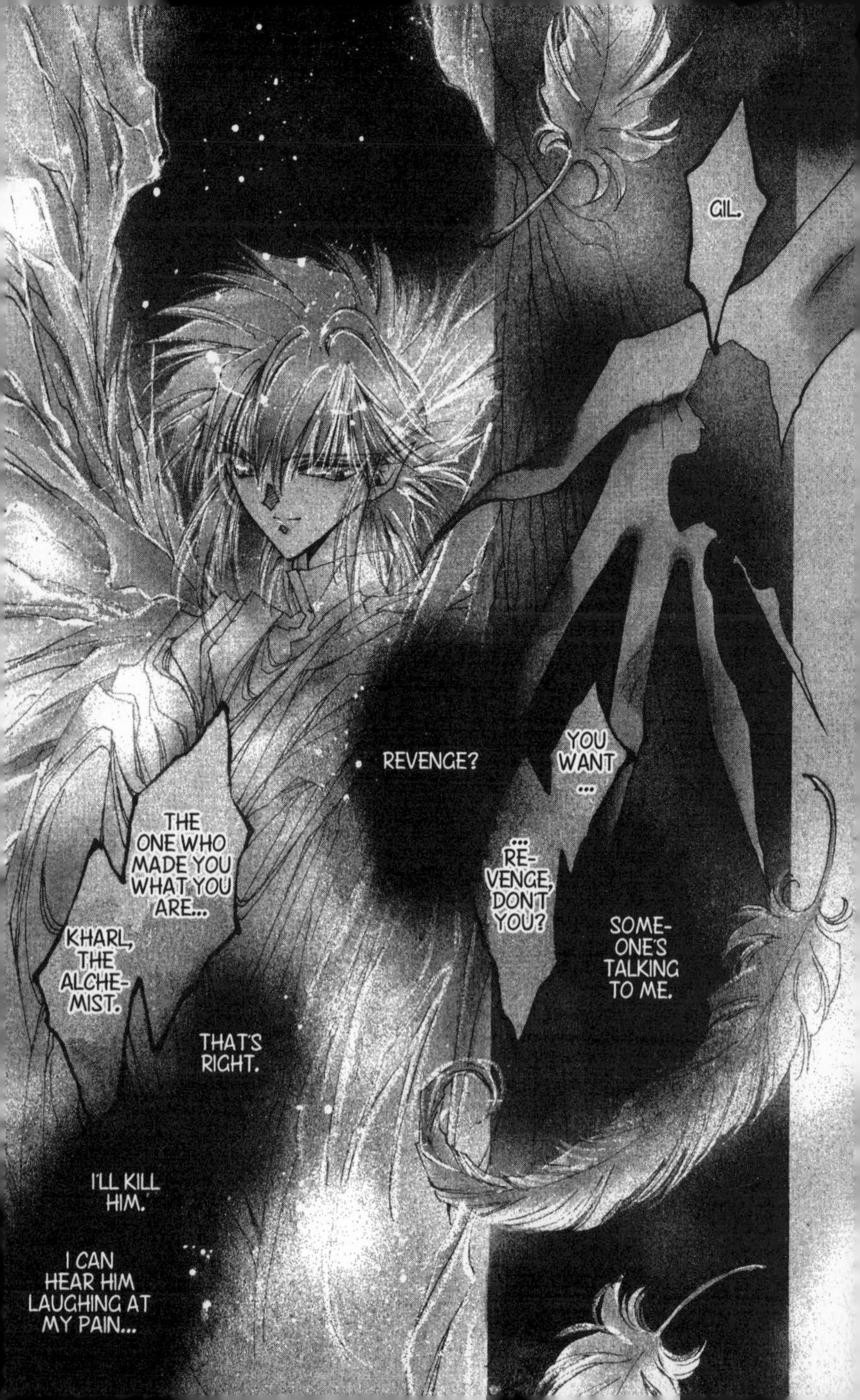
GIL.
YOU WANT ...
... RE-VENGE, DONT YOU?
SOME-ONE'S TALKING TO ME.
REVENGE?
THE ONE WHO MADE YOU WHAT YOU ARE...
KHARL, THE ALCHE-MIST.
THAT'S RIGHT.
I'LL KILL HIM.
I CAN HEAR HIM LAUGHING AT MY PAIN...

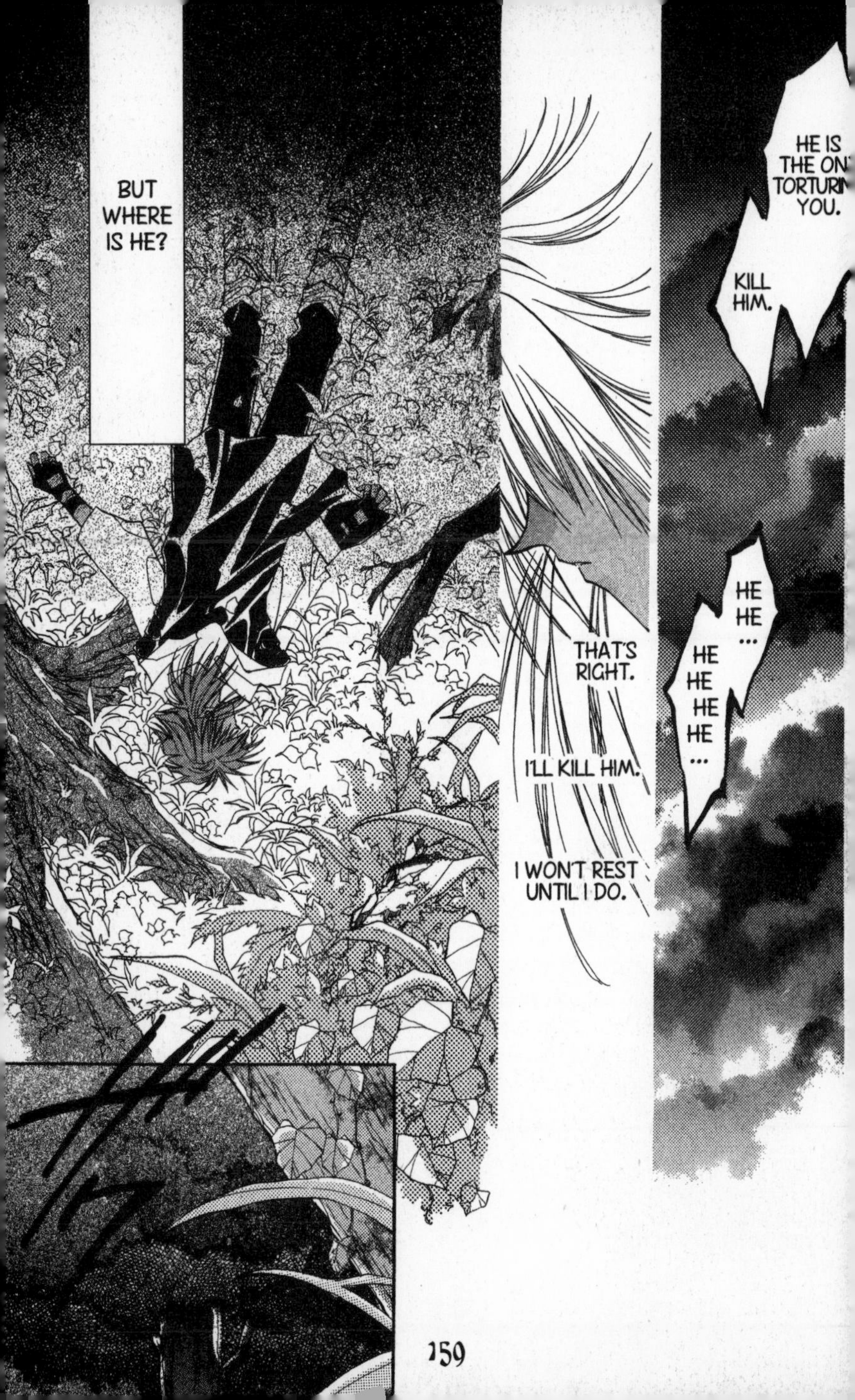
HE IS THE ON TORTURIN YOU.
KILL HIM.
HE HE ...
HE HE HE HE ...
THAT'S RIGHT.
I'LL KILL HIM.
I WON'T REST UNTIL I DO.
BUT WHERE IS HE?

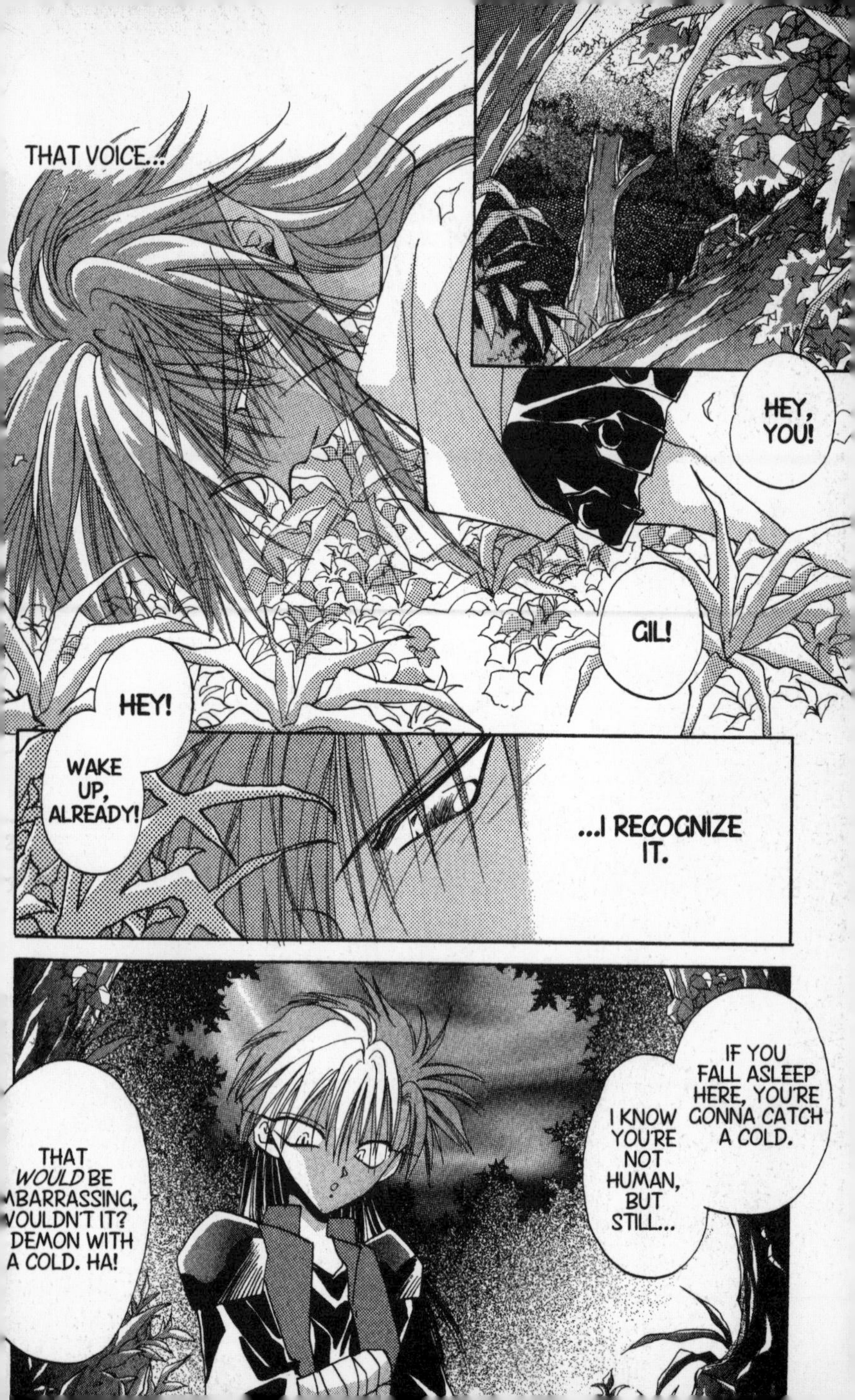
THAT VOICE...
HEY, YOU!
GIL!
HEY!
WAKE UP, ALREADY!
...I RECOGNIZE IT.
IF YOU FALL ASLEEP HERE, YOU'RE GONNA CATCH A COLD.
I KNOW YOU'RE NOT HUMAN, BUT STILL...
THAT *WOULD* BE MBARRASSING, VOULDN'T IT? DEMON WITH A COLD. HA!

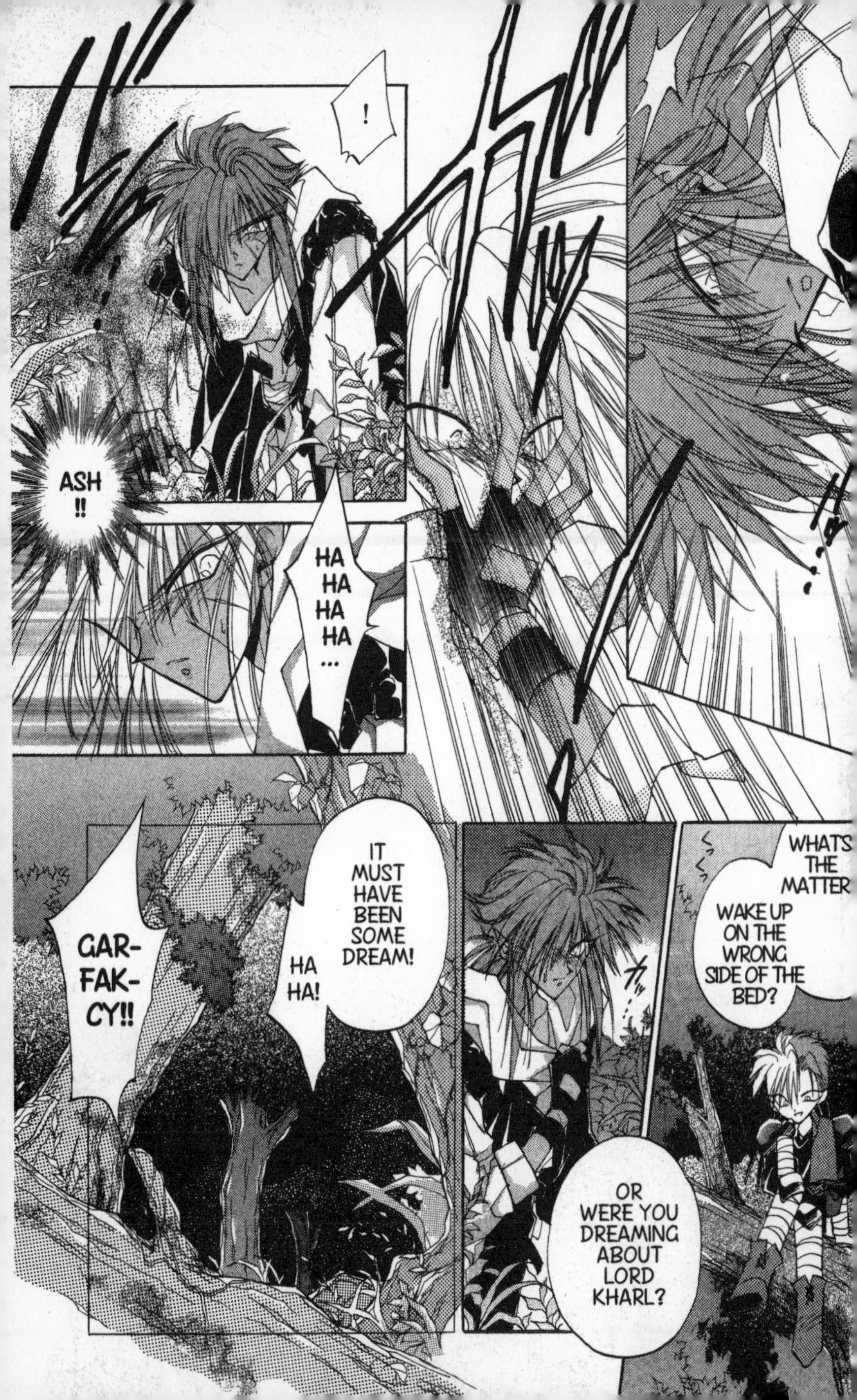
!
ASH !!
HA HA HA HA ...
WHATS THE MATTER
WAKE UP ON THE WRONG SIDE OF THE BED?
OR WERE YOU DREAMING ABOUT LORD KHARL?
IT MUST HAVE BEEN SOME DREAM!
HA HA!
GAR-FAK-CY!!

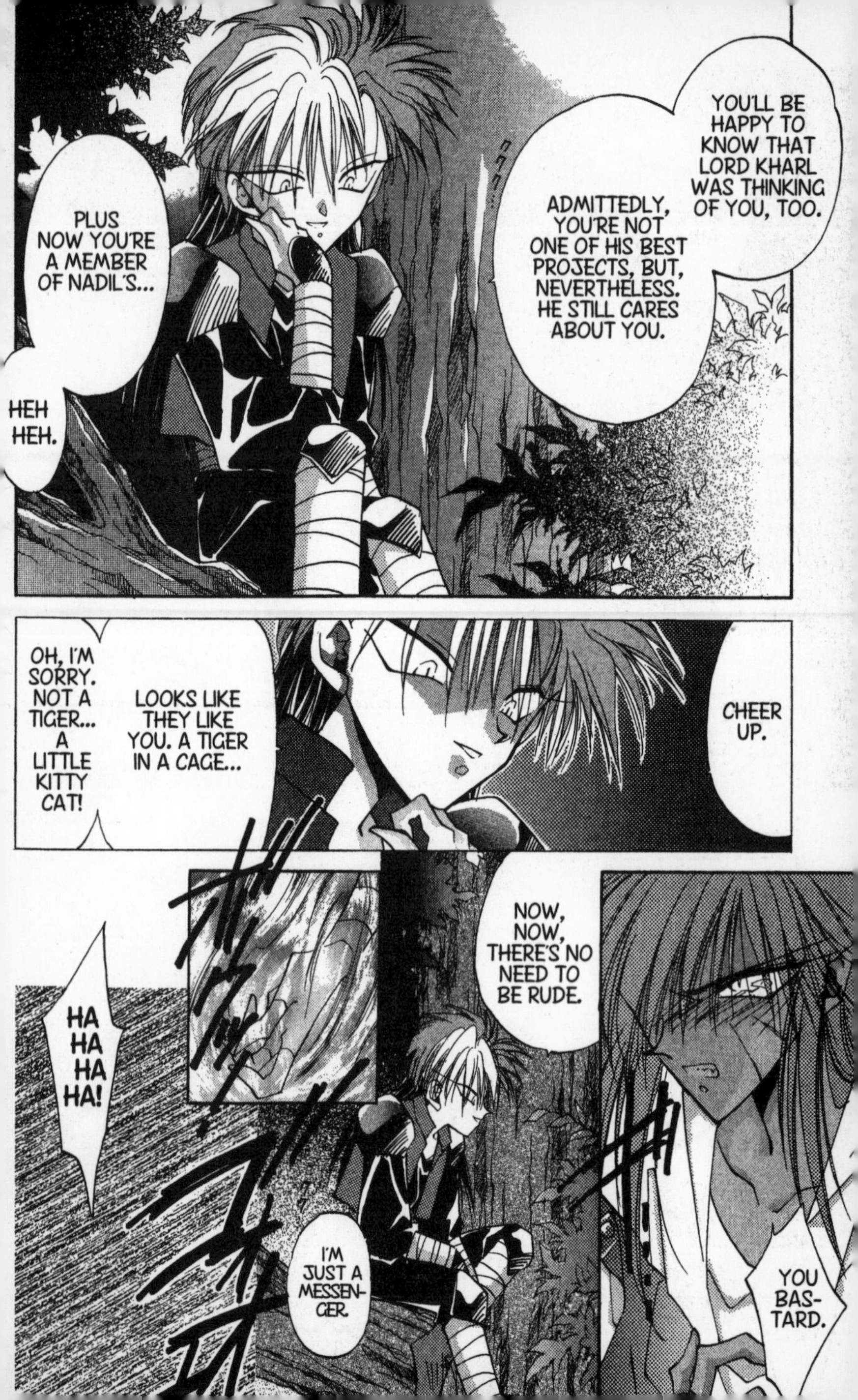
YOU'LL BE HAPPY TO KNOW THAT LORD KHARL WAS THINKING OF YOU, TOO.
ADMITTEDLY, YOU'RE NOT ONE OF HIS BEST PROJECTS, BUT, NEVERTHELESS. HE STILL CARES ABOUT YOU.
PLUS NOW YOU'RE A MEMBER OF NADIL'S...
HEH HEH.
CHEER UP.
LOOKS LIKE THEY LIKE YOU. A TIGER IN A CAGE...
OH, I'M SORRY. NOT A TIGER... A LITTLE KITTY CAT!
YOU BASTARD.
NOW, NOW, THERE'S NO NEED TO BE RUDE.
I'M JUST A MESSENGER.
HA HA HA HA!

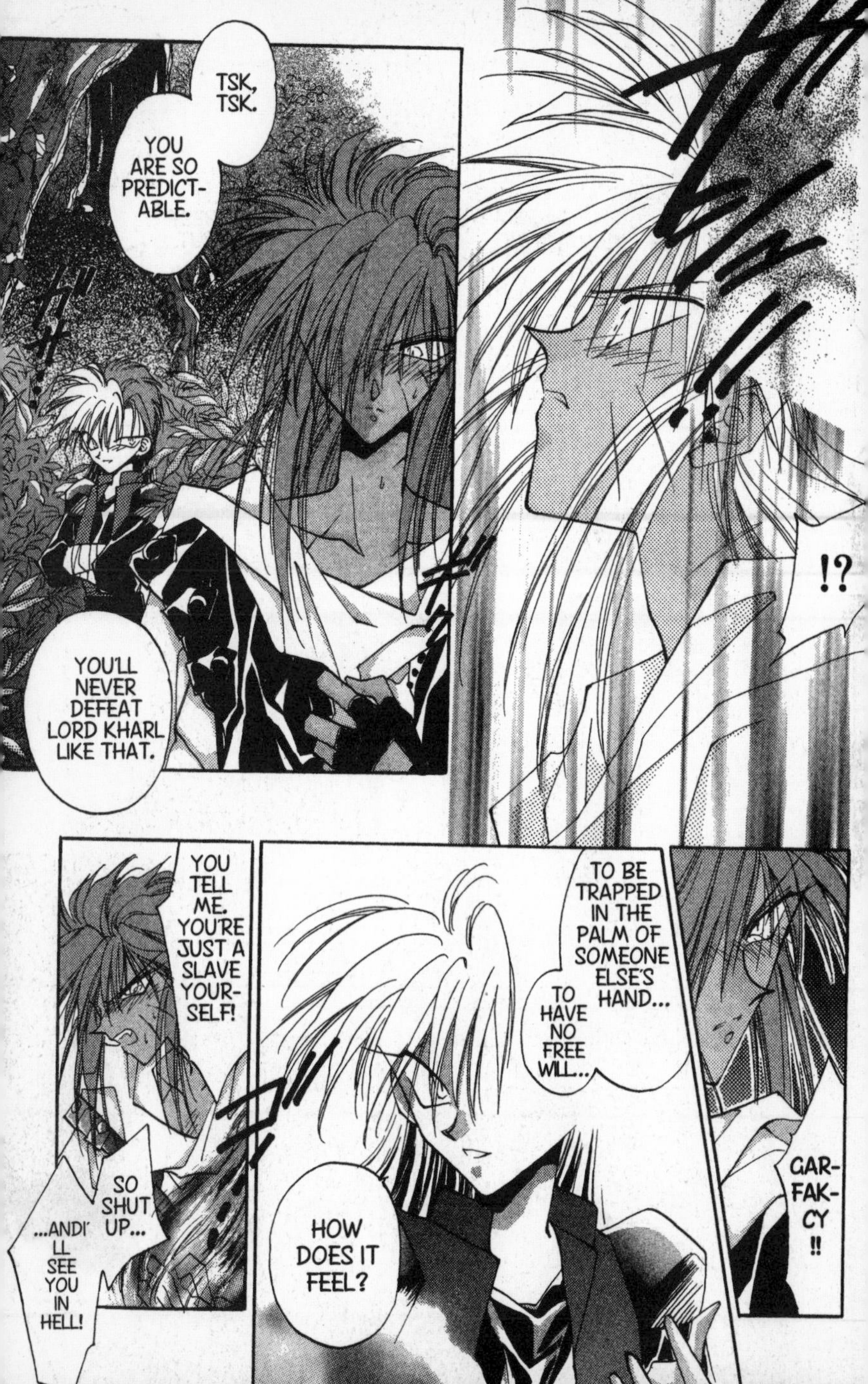
!?
TSK, TSK.
YOU ARE SO PREDICTABLE.
YOU'LL NEVER DEFEAT LORD KHARL LIKE THAT.
GAR-FAK-CY!!
TO BE TRAPPED IN THE PALM OF SOMEONE ELSE'S HAND...
TO HAVE NO FREE WILL...
HOW DOES IT FEEL?
YOU TELL ME. YOU'RE JUST A SLAVE YOURSELF!
SO SHUT UP...
...AND I'LL SEE YOU IN HELL!

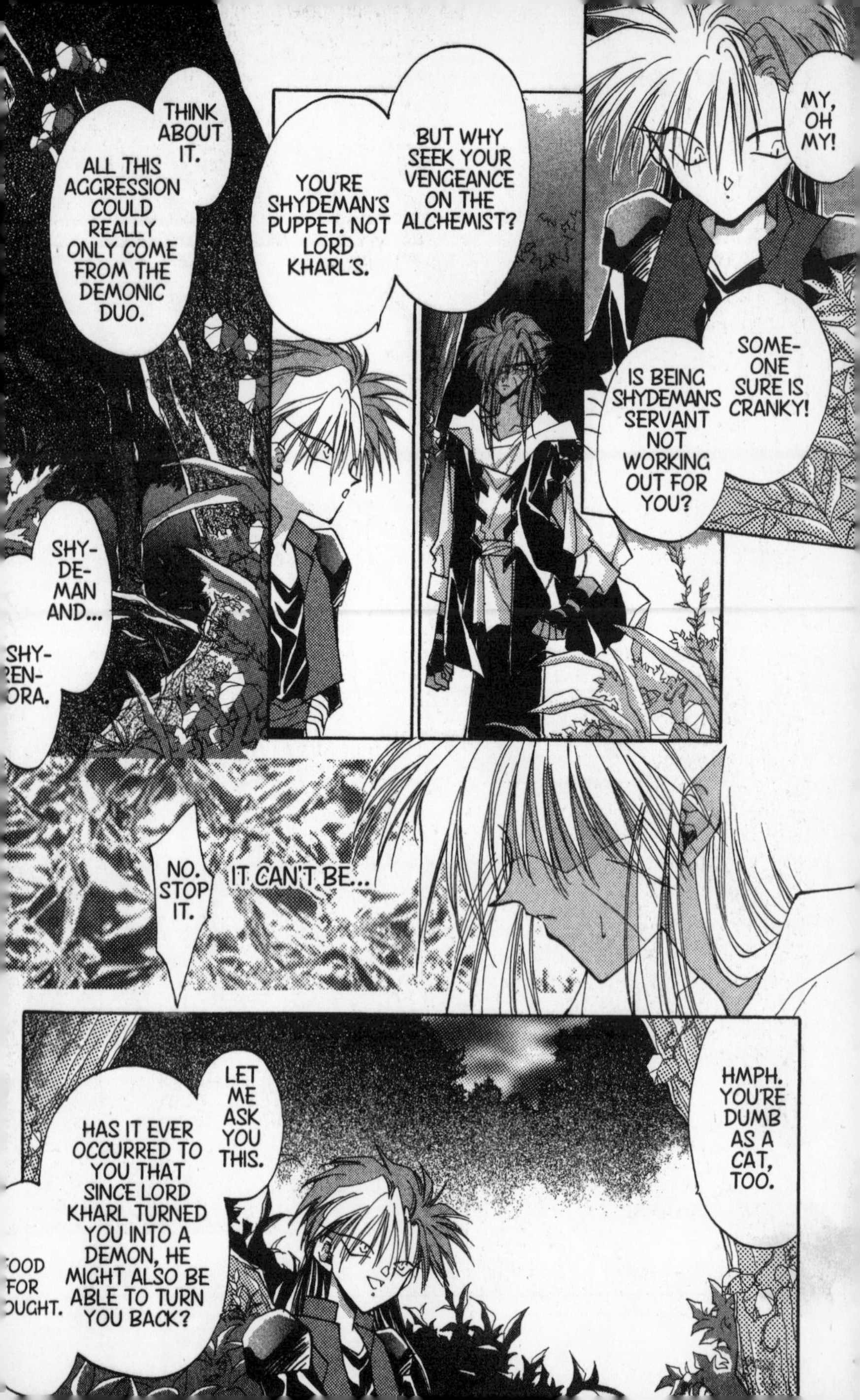
MY, OH MY!
SOME-ONE SURE IS CRANKY!
IS BEING SHYDEMAN'S SERVANT NOT WORKING OUT FOR YOU?
BUT WHY SEEK YOUR VENGEANCE ON THE ALCHEMIST?
YOU'RE SHYDEMAN'S PUPPET. NOT LORD KHARL'S.
THINK ABOUT IT.
ALL THIS AGGRESSION COULD REALLY ONLY COME FROM THE DEMONIC DUO.
SHY-DE-MAN AND...
SHY- REN- ORA.
IT CAN'T BE...
NO. STOP IT.
HMPH. YOU'RE DUMB AS A CAT, TOO.
LET ME ASK YOU THIS.
HAS IT EVER OCCURRED TO YOU THAT SINCE LORD KHARL TURNED YOU INTO A DEMON, HE MIGHT ALSO BE ABLE TO TURN YOU BACK?
OOD FOR OUGHT.

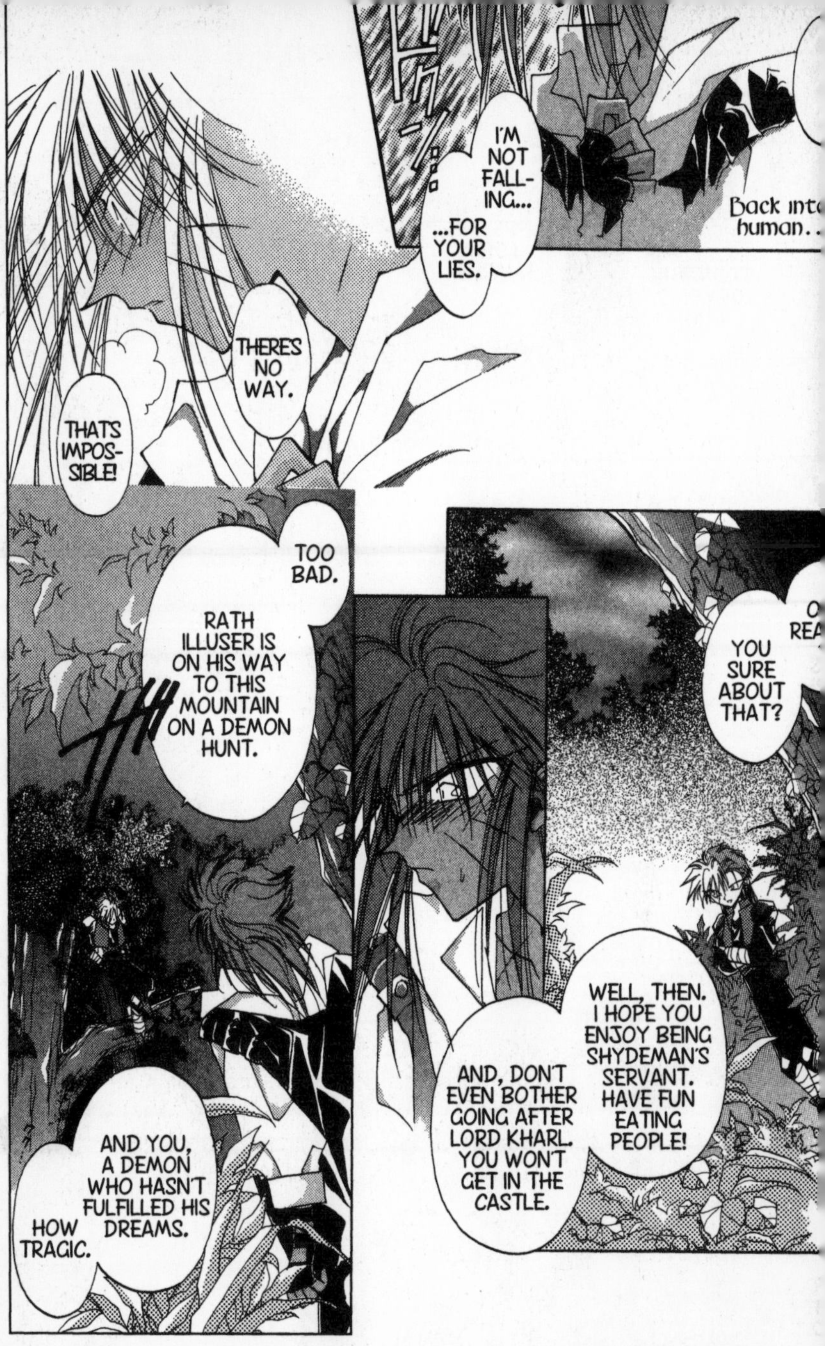
Back int
human..
I'M NOT FALLING...
...FOR YOUR LIES.
THERES NO WAY.
THATS IMPOSSIBLE!
YOU SURE ABOUT THAT?
WELL, THEN. I HOPE YOU ENJOY BEING SHYDEMAN'S SERVANT. HAVE FUN EATING PEOPLE!
AND, DON'T EVEN BOTHER GOING AFTER LORD KHARL. YOU WON'T GET IN THE CASTLE.
TOO BAD.
RATH ILLUSER IS ON HIS WAY TO THIS MOUNTAIN ON A DEMON HUNT.
AND YOU, A DEMON WHO HASN'T FULFILLED HIS DREAMS. HOW TRAGIC.

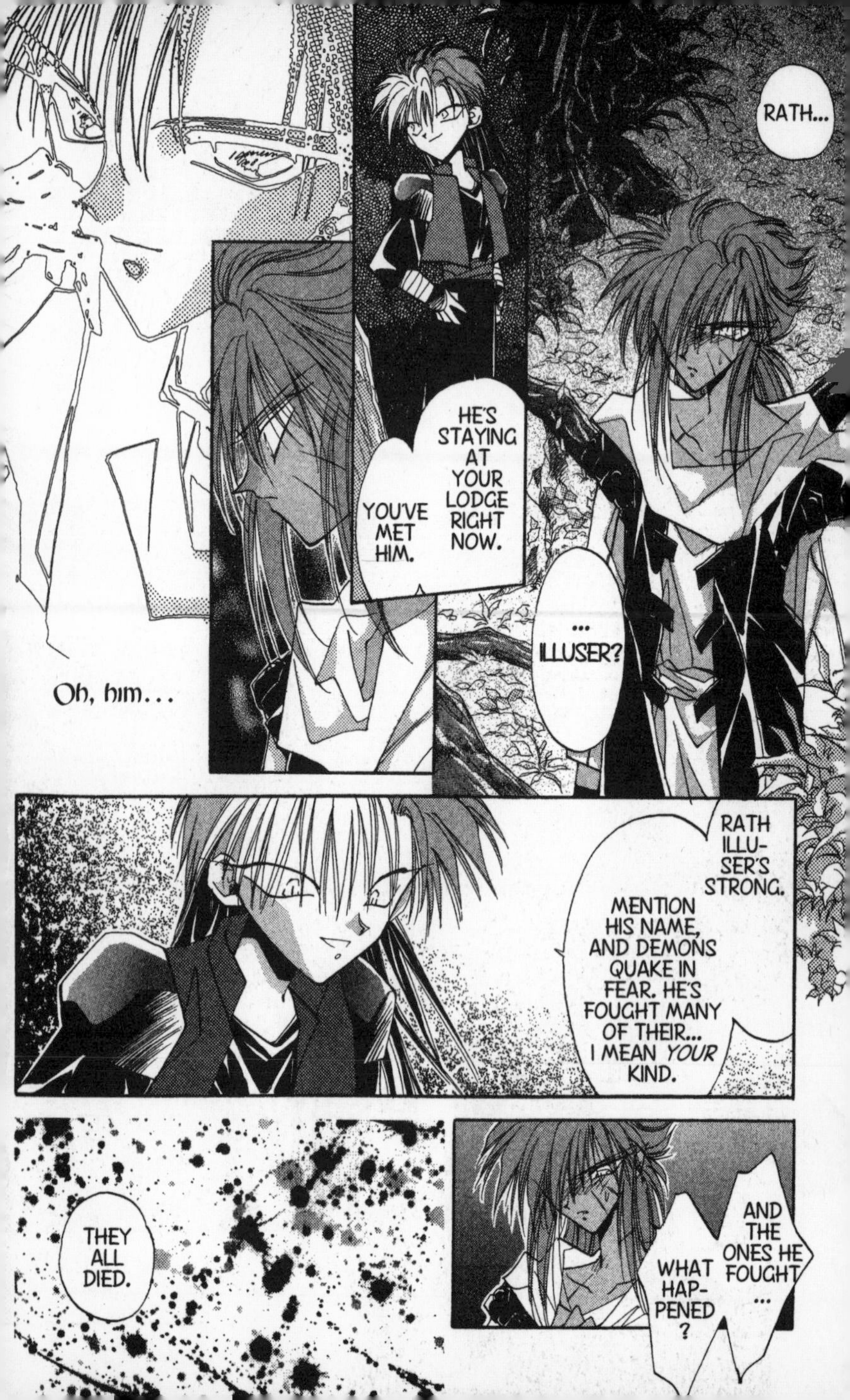
RATH...
... ILLUSER?
HE'S STAYING AT YOUR LODGE RIGHT NOW.
YOU'VE MET HIM.
Oh, him...
RATH ILLU-SER'S STRONG.
MENTION HIS NAME, AND DEMONS QUAKE IN FEAR. HE'S FOUGHT MANY OF THEIR... I MEAN *YOUR* KIND.
AND THE ONES HE FOUGHT...
WHAT HAP-PENED?
THEY ALL DIED.

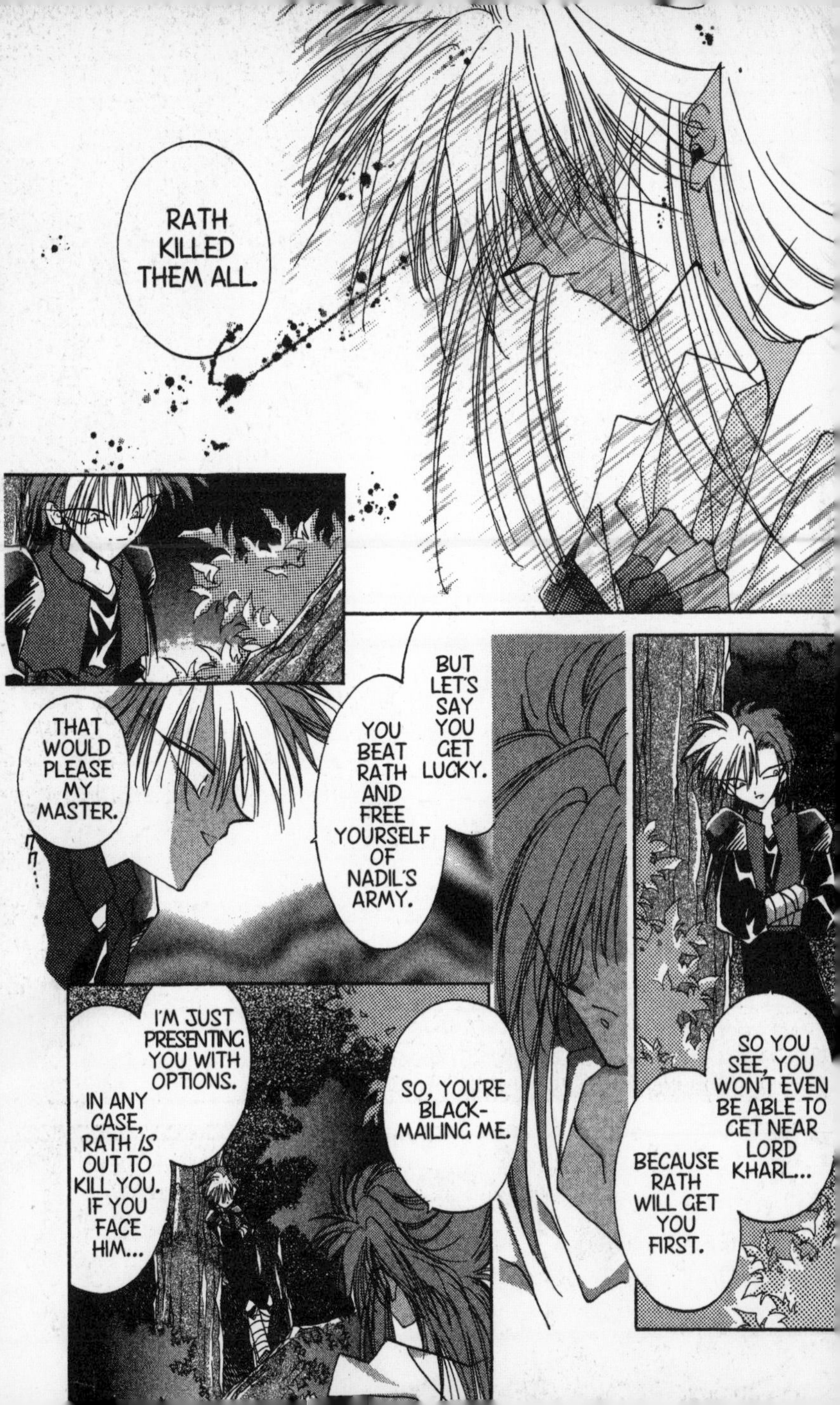
RATH KILLED THEM ALL.
SO YOU SEE, YOU WON'T EVEN BE ABLE TO GET NEAR LORD KHARL...
BECAUSE RATH WILL GET YOU FIRST.
BUT LET'S SAY YOU GET LUCKY.
YOU BEAT RATH AND FREE YOURSELF OF NADIL'S ARMY.
THAT WOULD PLEASE MY MASTER.
SO, YOU'RE BLACK-MAILING ME.
I'M JUST PRESENTING YOU WITH OPTIONS.
IN ANY CASE, RATH *IS* OUT TO KILL YOU. IF YOU FACE HIM...

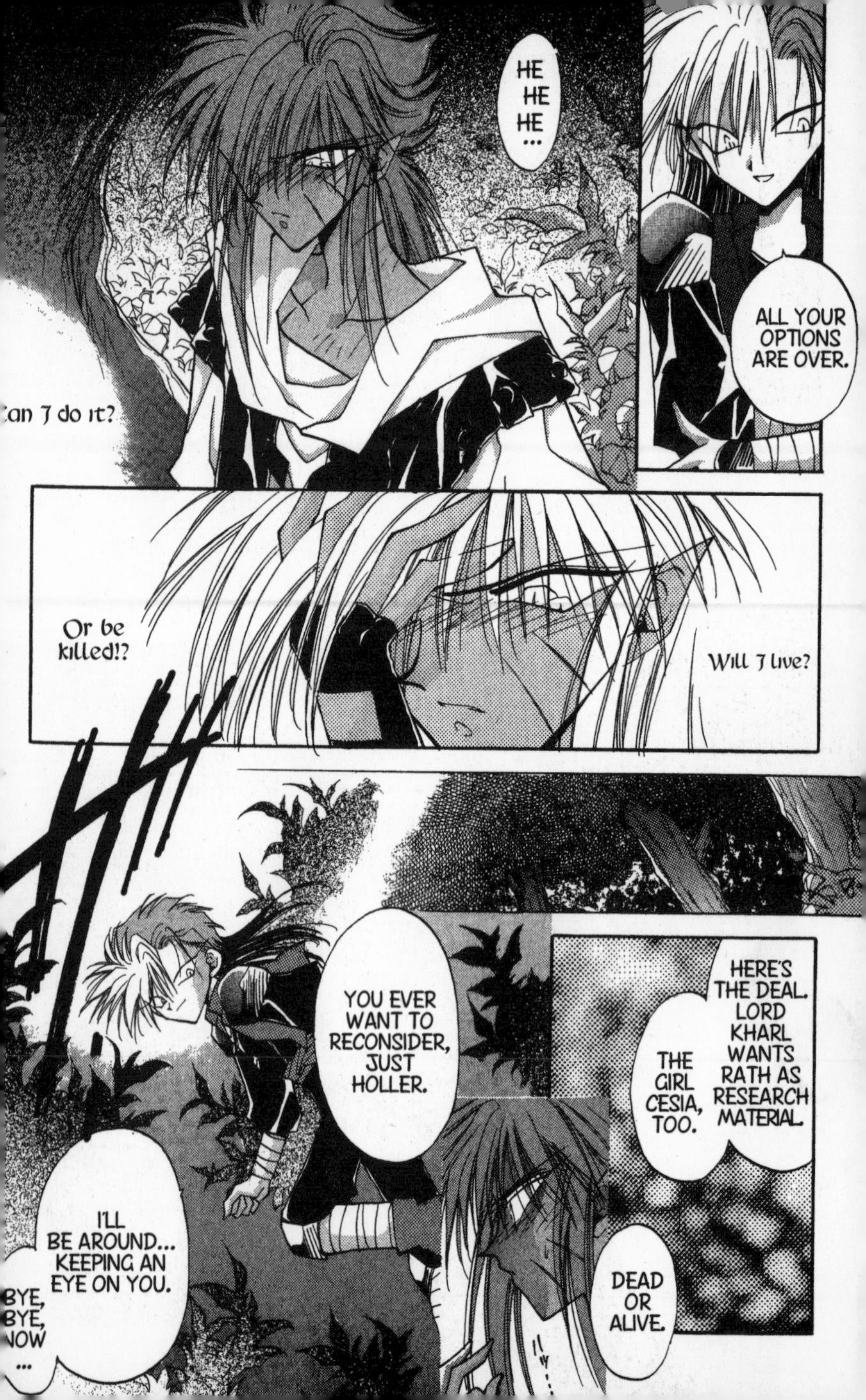

ALL YOUR OPTIONS ARE OVER.
HE HE HE ...
an I do it?
Will I live?
Or be killed!?
HERE'S THE DEAL. LORD KHARL WANTS RATH AS RESEARCH MATERIAL.
THE GIRL CESIA, TOO.
DEAD OR ALIVE.
YOU EVER WANT TO RECONSIDER, JUST HOLLER.
I'LL BE AROUND... KEEPING AN EYE ON YOU.
BYE, BYE, NOW ...

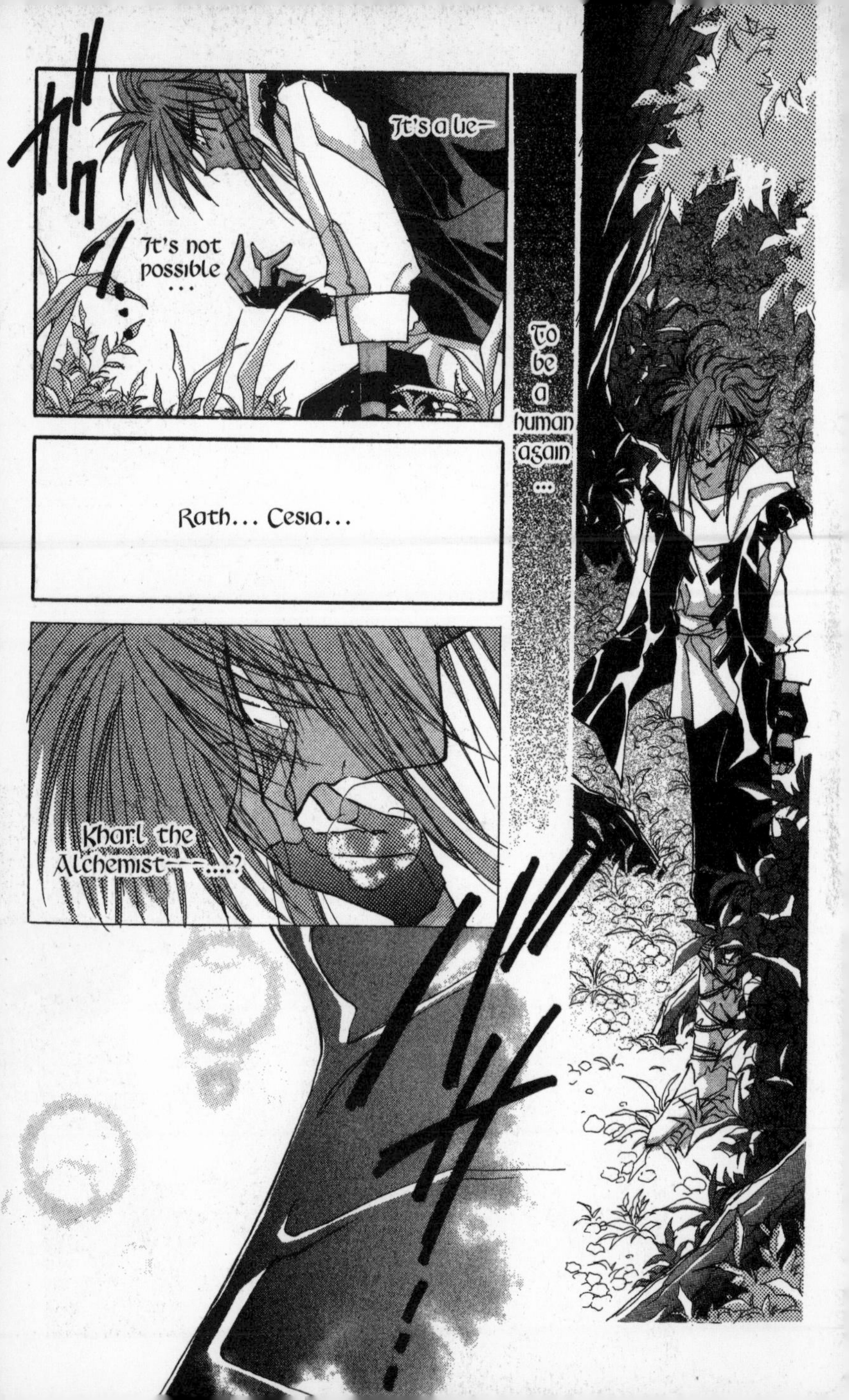

To be a human again...
It's a lie—
It's not possible...
Rath... Cesia...
Kharl the Alchemist——....?

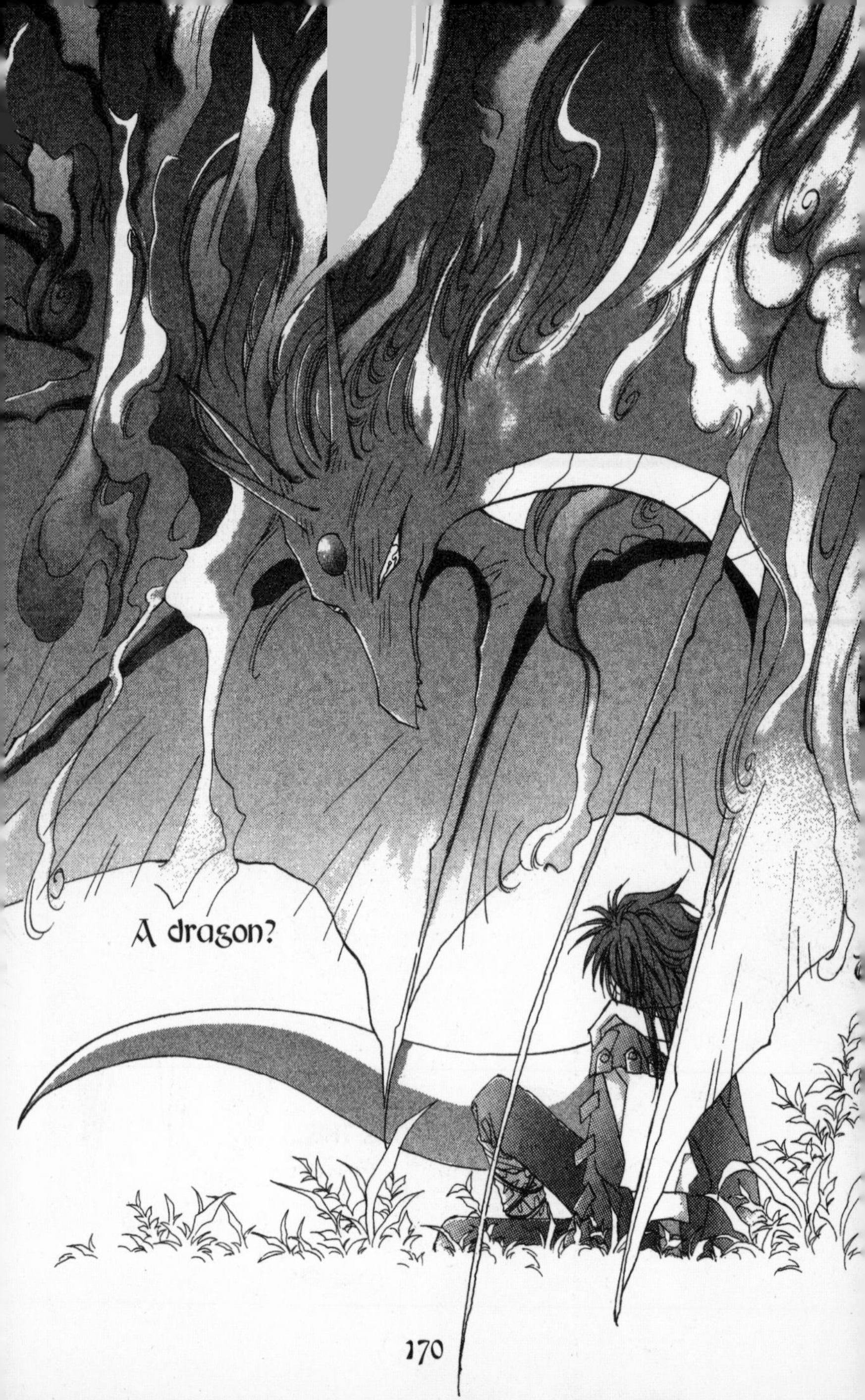
A dragon?

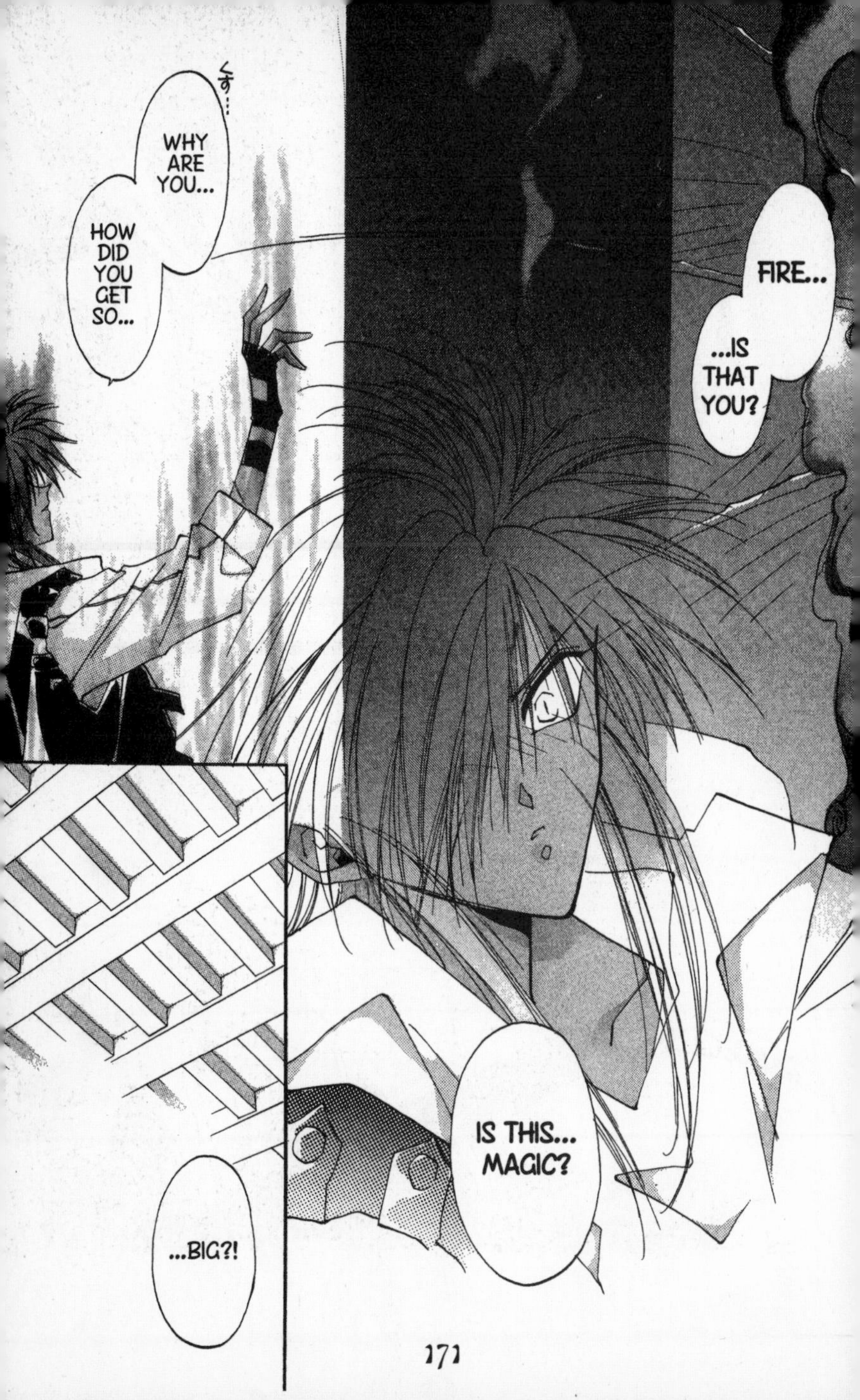
FIRE...
...IS THAT YOU?
IS THIS... MAGIC?
くす…
WHY ARE YOU...
HOW DID YOU GET SO...
...BIG?!

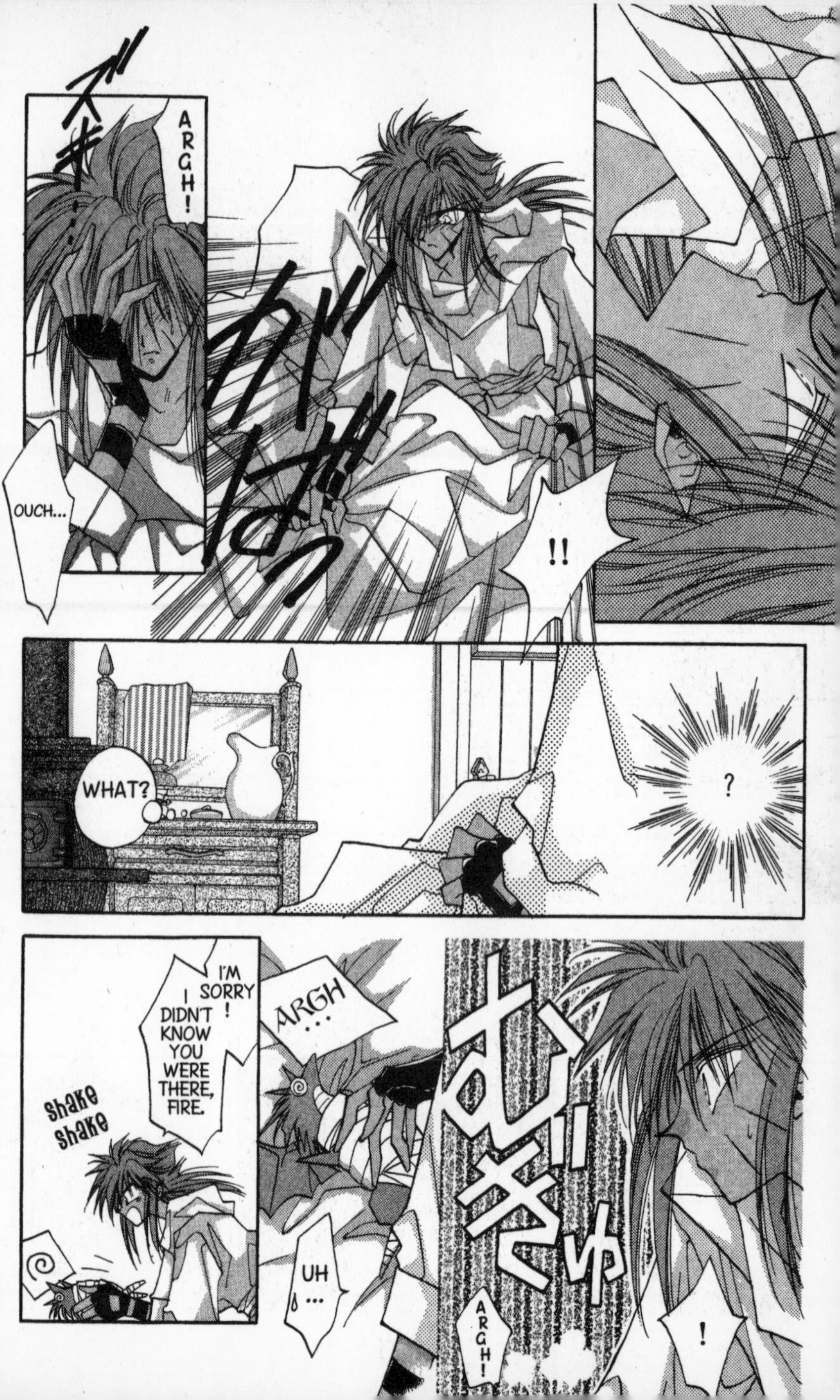
!!
ARGH!
OUCH...
?
WHAT?
!
ARGH!
UH ...
ARGH ...
I'M SORRY!
I DIDN'T KNOW YOU WERE THERE, FIRE.
shake shake

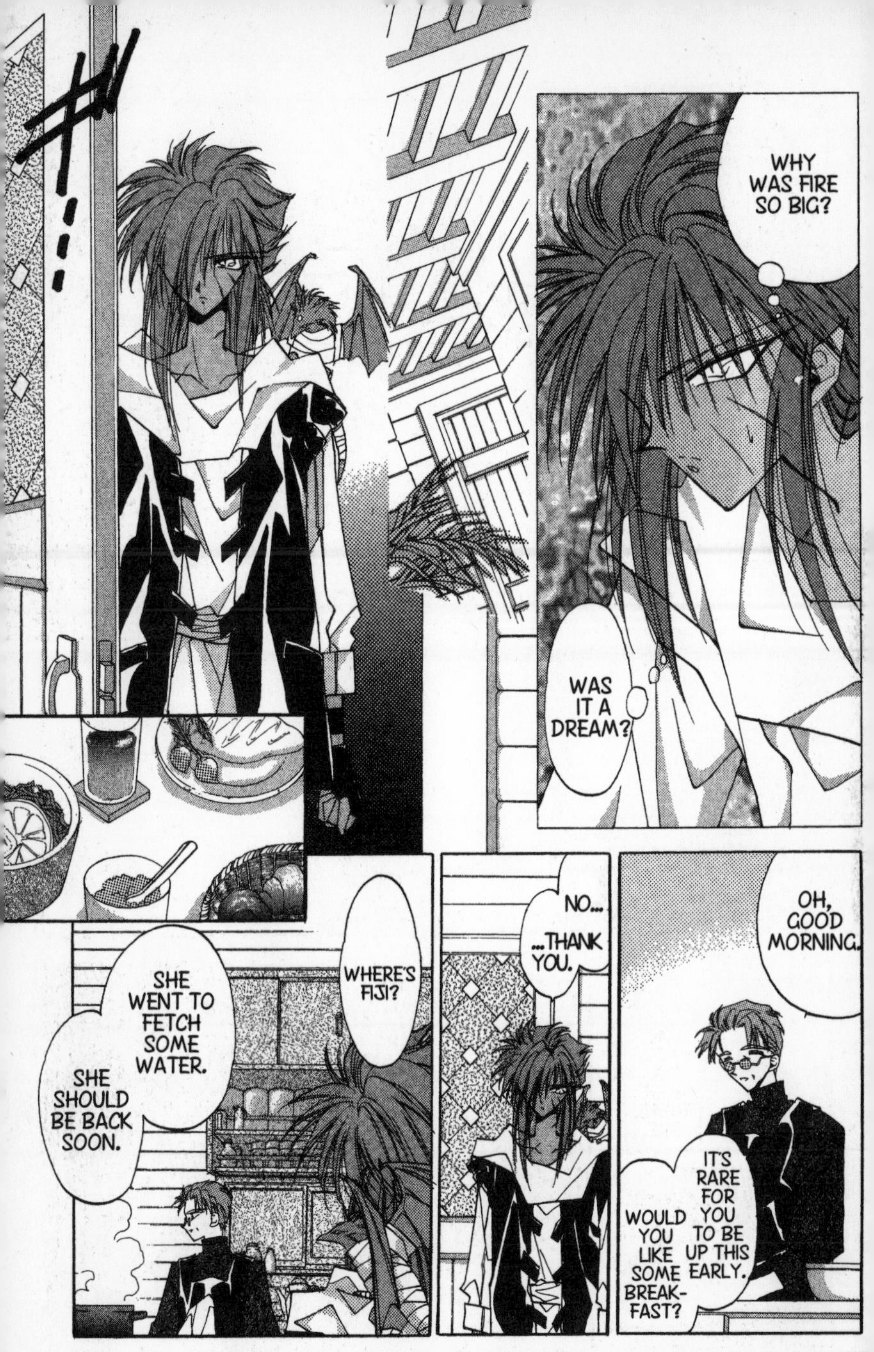
WHY WAS FIRE SO BIG?
WAS IT A DREAM?
OH, GOOD MORNING.
IT'S RARE FOR YOU TO BE UP THIS EARLY.
WOULD YOU LIKE SOME BREAK-FAST?
NO...
...THANK YOU.
WHERE'S FIJI?
SHE WENT TO FETCH SOME WATER.
SHE SHOULD BE BACK SOON.

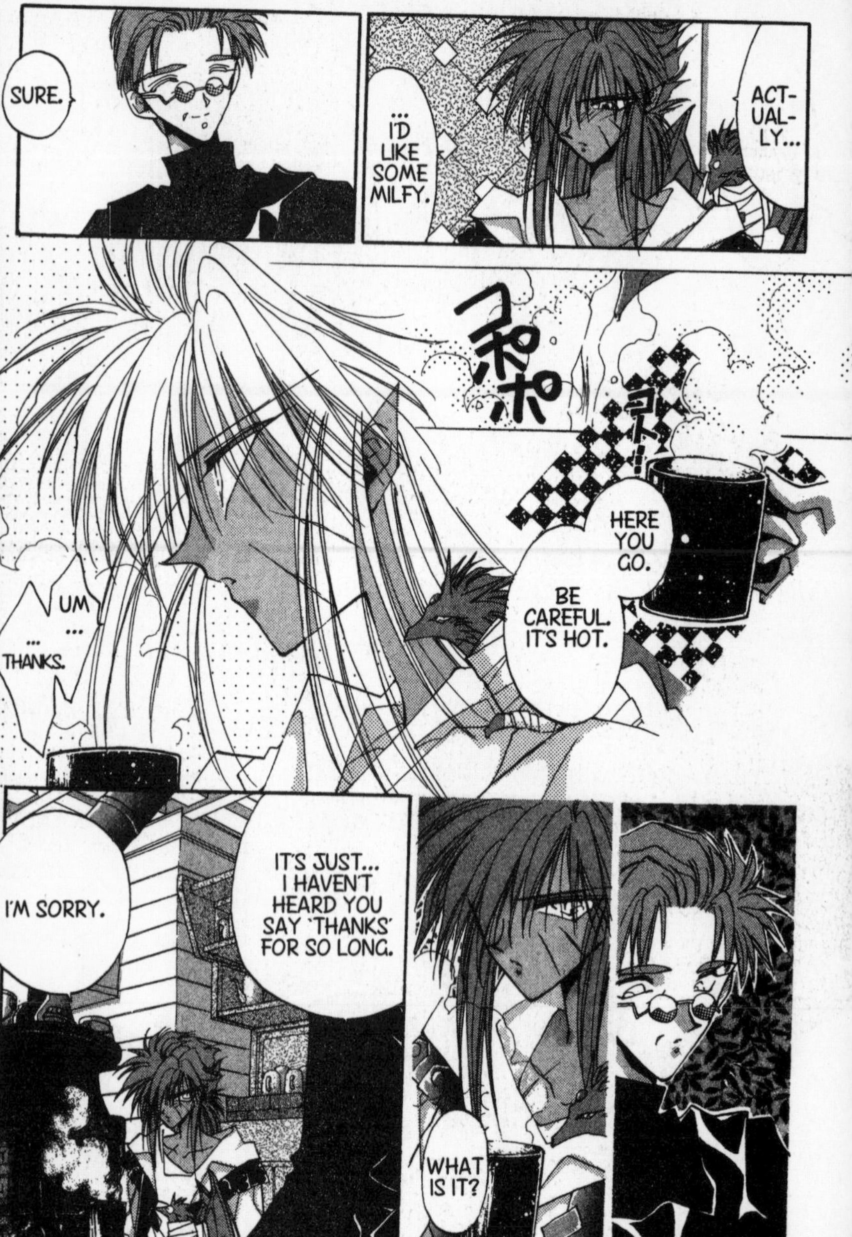
ACT-UAL-LY...
...I'D LIKE SOME MILFY.
SURE.
コポポ
HERE YOU GO.
BE CAREFUL. IT'S HOT.
UM... ...THANKS.
WHAT IS IT?
IT'S JUST... I HAVEN'T HEARD YOU SAY 'THANKS' FOR SO LONG.
I'M SORRY.

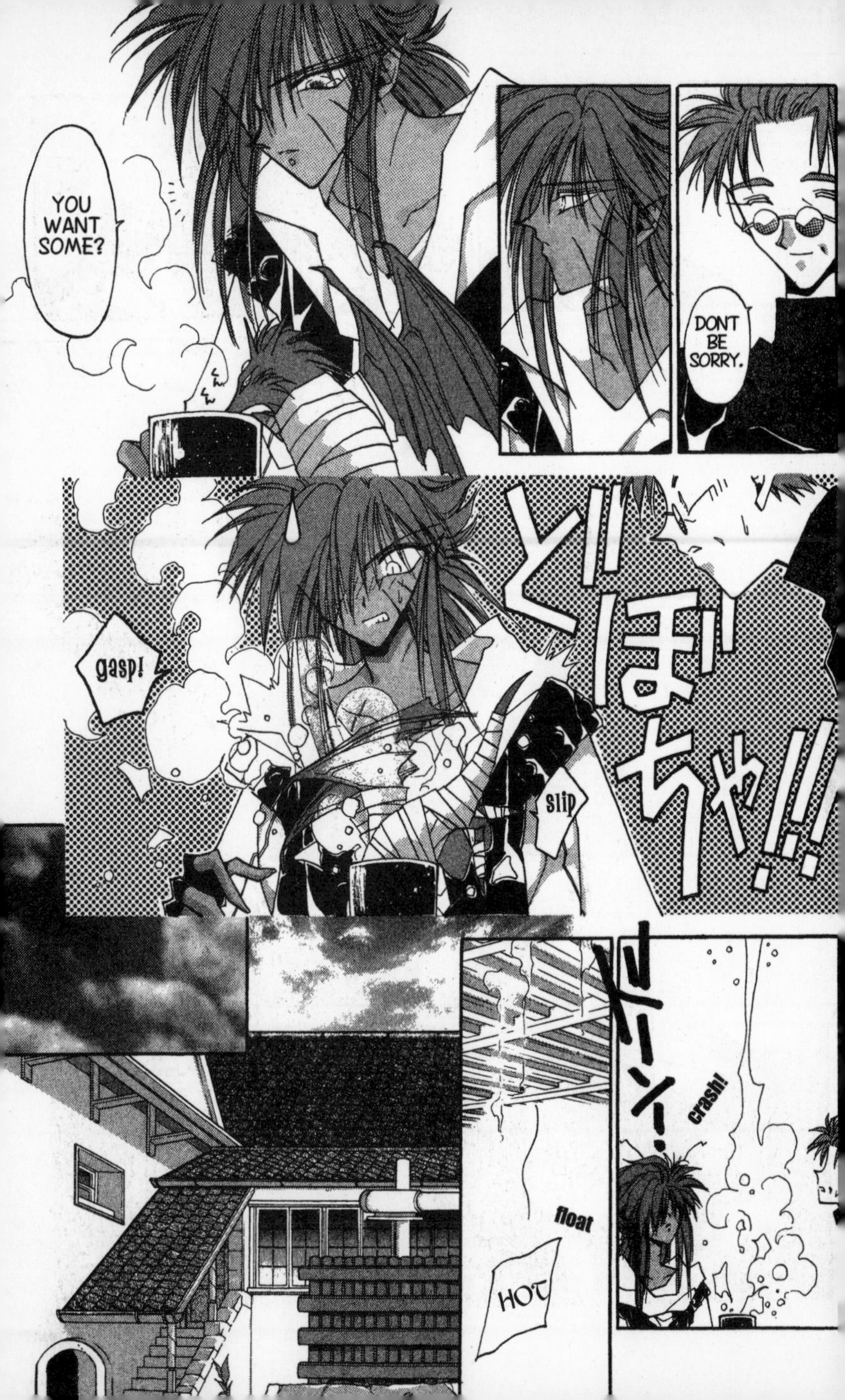
DONT BE SORRY.
YOU WANT SOME?
どぼちゃ!!!
slip
gasp!
ドーン!
crash!
float
HOT

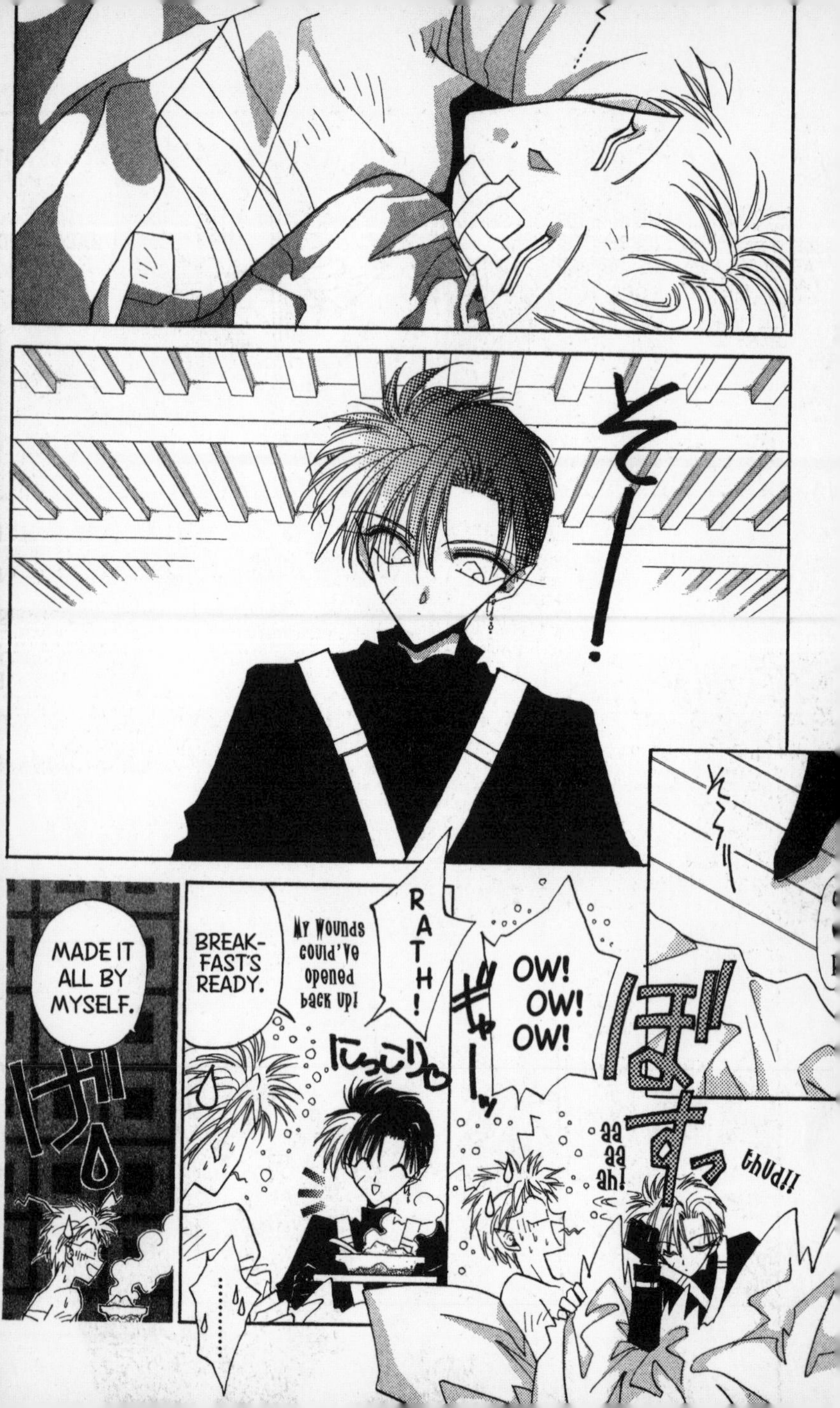
そー！
ぽすっ
THUD!!
aa aa ah!
OW! OW! OW!
ギャーッ
RATH!
My wounds could've opened back up!
BREAK-FAST'S READY.
にっこり
MADE IT ALL BY MYSELF.
げ

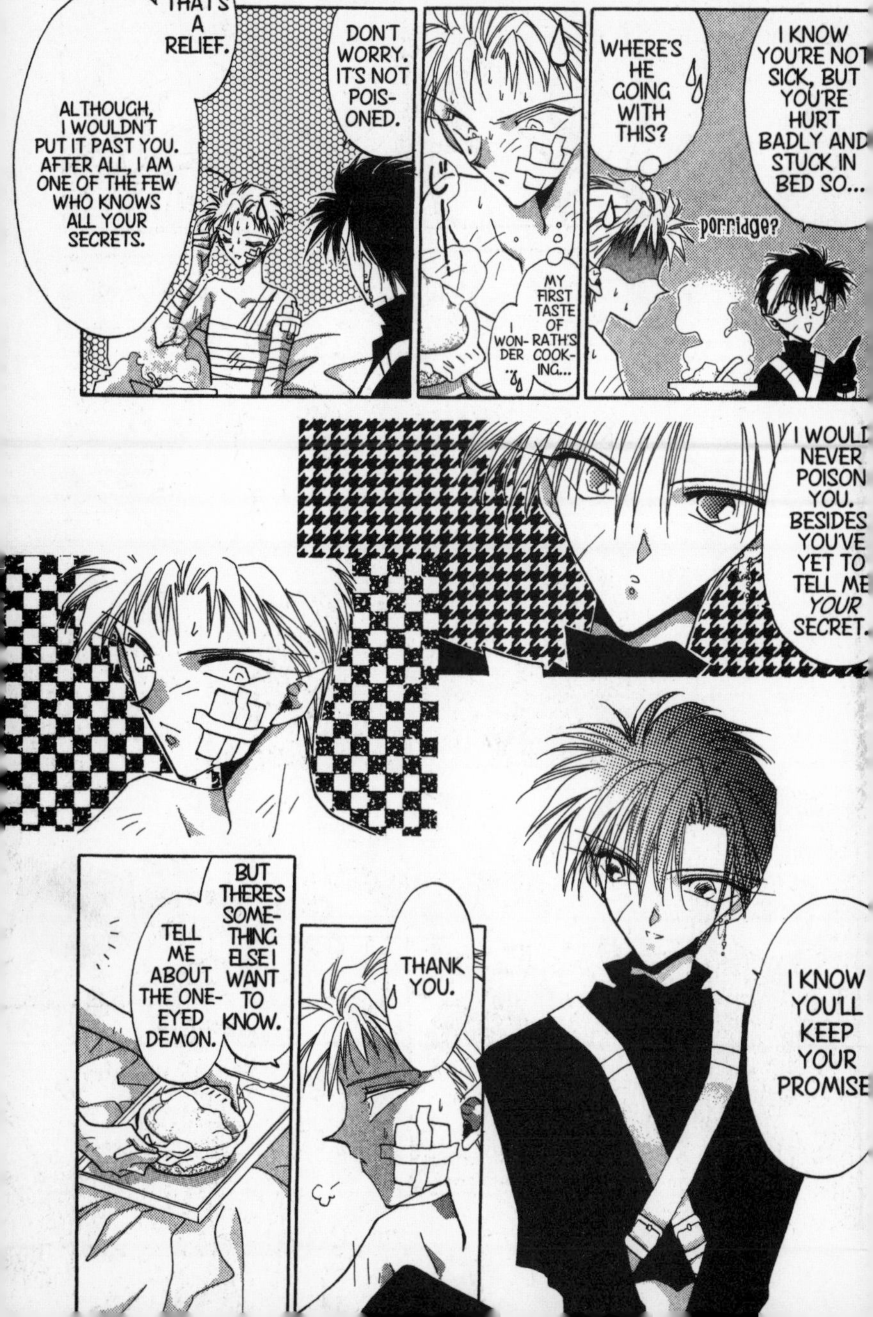

I KNOW YOU'RE NOT SICK, BUT YOU'RE HURT BADLY AND STUCK IN BED SO...
porridge?
WHERE'S HE GOING WITH THIS?
MY FIRST TASTE OF RATH'S COOKING...
I WONDER...
DON'T WORRY. IT'S NOT POISONED.
THAT'S A RELIEF.
ALTHOUGH, I WOULDN'T PUT IT PAST YOU. AFTER ALL, I AM ONE OF THE FEW WHO KNOWS ALL YOUR SECRETS.
I WOULD NEVER POISON YOU. BESIDES YOU'VE YET TO TELL ME *YOUR* SECRET.
I KNOW YOU'LL KEEP YOUR PROMISE
THANK YOU.
BUT THERE'S SOMETHING ELSE I WANT TO KNOW.
TELL ME ABOUT THE ONE-EYED DEMON.

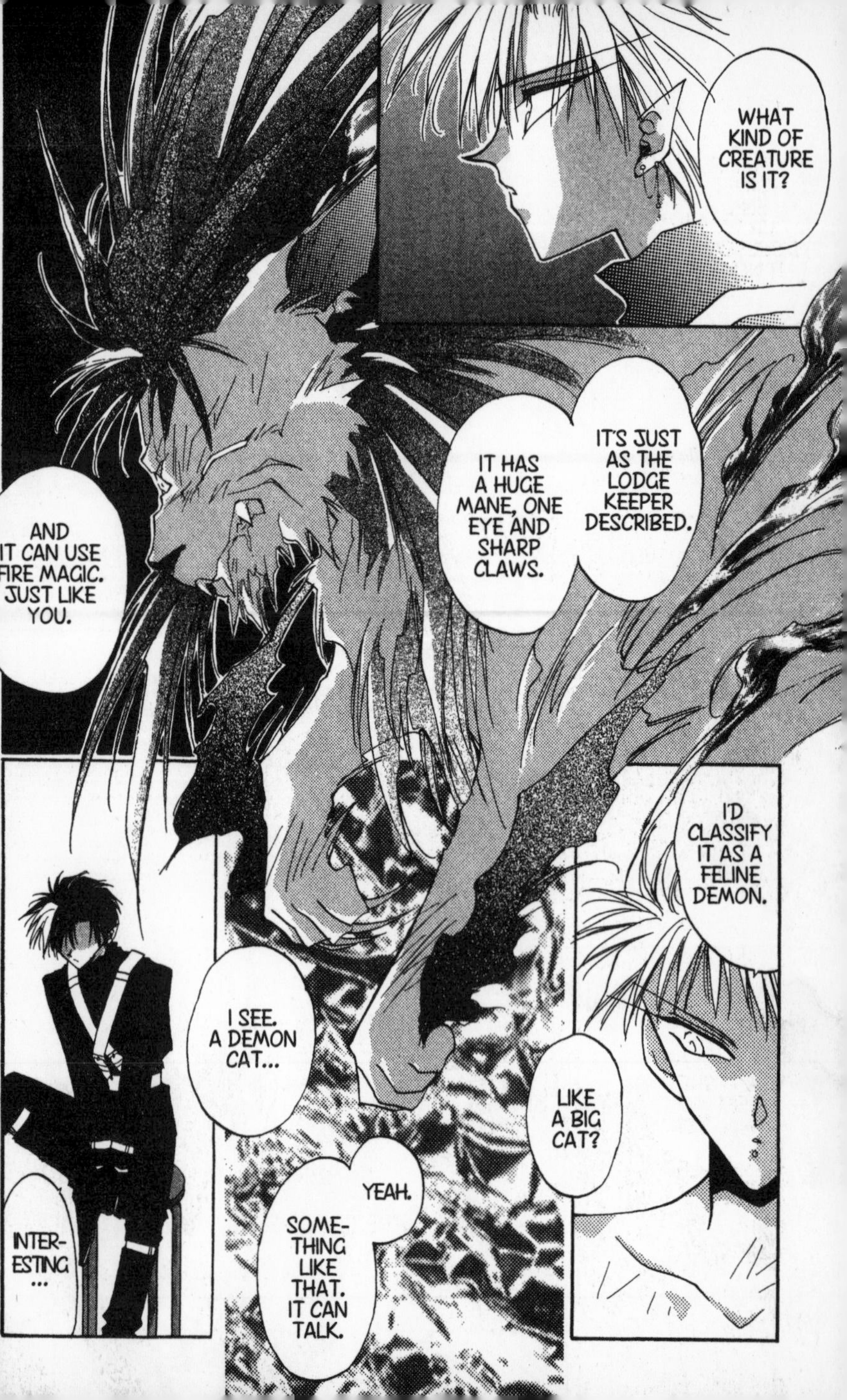
WHAT KIND OF CREATURE IS IT?
IT'S JUST AS THE LODGE KEEPER DESCRIBED.
IT HAS A HUGE MANE, ONE EYE AND SHARP CLAWS.
AND IT CAN USE FIRE MAGIC. JUST LIKE YOU.
I'D CLASSIFY IT AS A FELINE DEMON.
LIKE A BIG CAT?
YEAH.
SOMETHING LIKE THAT. IT CAN TALK.
I SEE. A DEMON CAT...
INTERESTING...

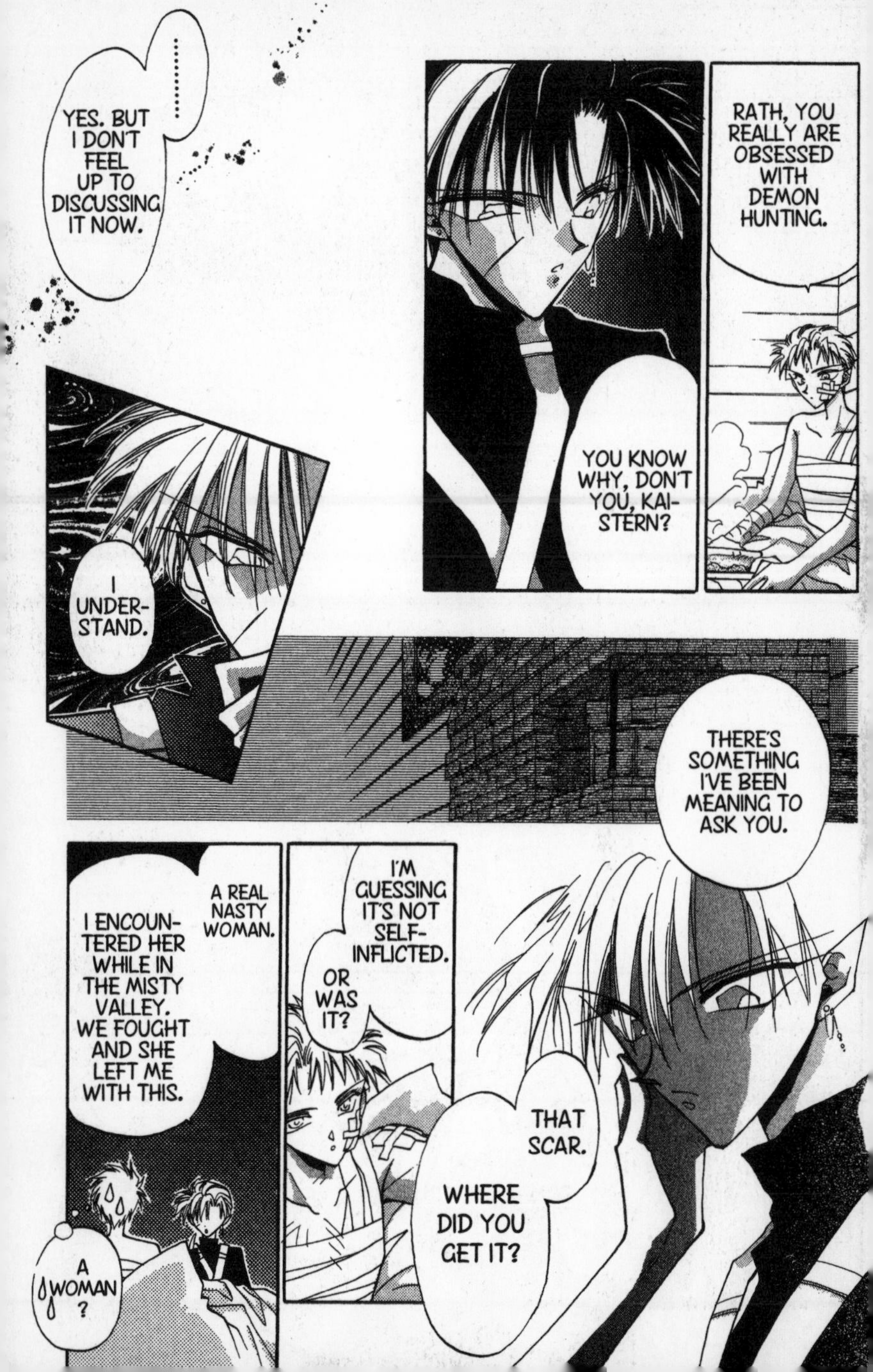
RATH, YOU REALLY ARE OBSESSED WITH DEMON HUNTING.
YOU KNOW WHY, DON'T YOU, KAI-STERN?
......
YES. BUT I DON'T FEEL UP TO DISCUSSING IT NOW.
I UNDER-STAND.
THERE'S SOMETHING I'VE BEEN MEANING TO ASK YOU.
THAT SCAR.
WHERE DID YOU GET IT?
I'M GUESSING IT'S NOT SELF-INFLICTED.
OR WAS IT?
A REAL NASTY WOMAN.
I ENCOUN-TERED HER WHILE IN THE MISTY VALLEY. WE FOUGHT AND SHE LEFT ME WITH THIS.
A WOMAN?

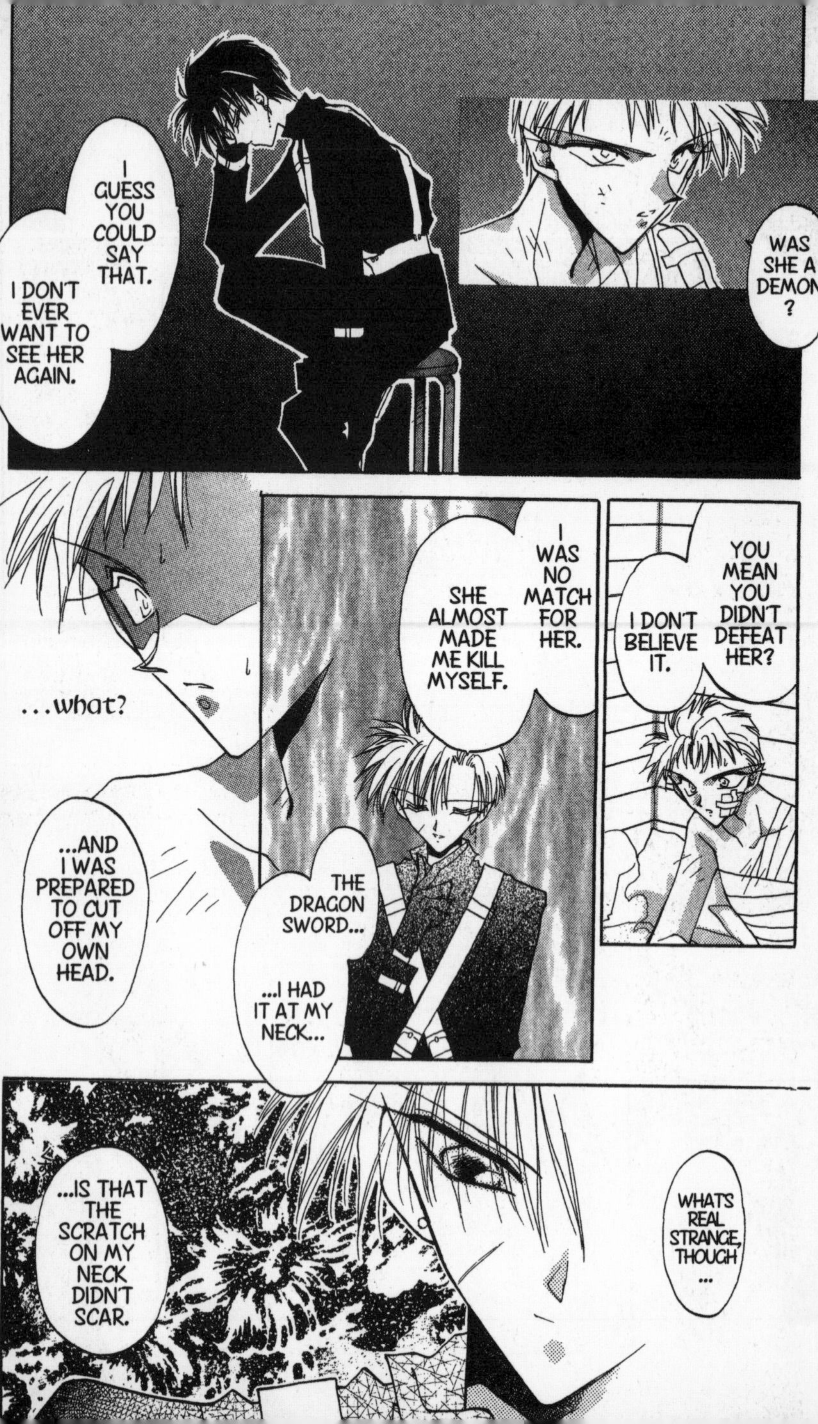
WAS SHE A DEMON?
I GUESS YOU COULD SAY THAT.
I DON'T EVER WANT TO SEE HER AGAIN.
YOU MEAN YOU DIDN'T DEFEAT HER?
I DON'T BELIEVE IT.
I WAS NO MATCH FOR HER.
SHE ALMOST MADE ME KILL MYSELF.
THE DRAGON SWORD...
...I HAD IT AT MY NECK...
...what?
...AND I WAS PREPARED TO CUT OFF MY OWN HEAD.
WHAT'S REAL STRANGE, THOUGH...
...IS THAT THE SCRATCH ON MY NECK DIDN'T SCAR.

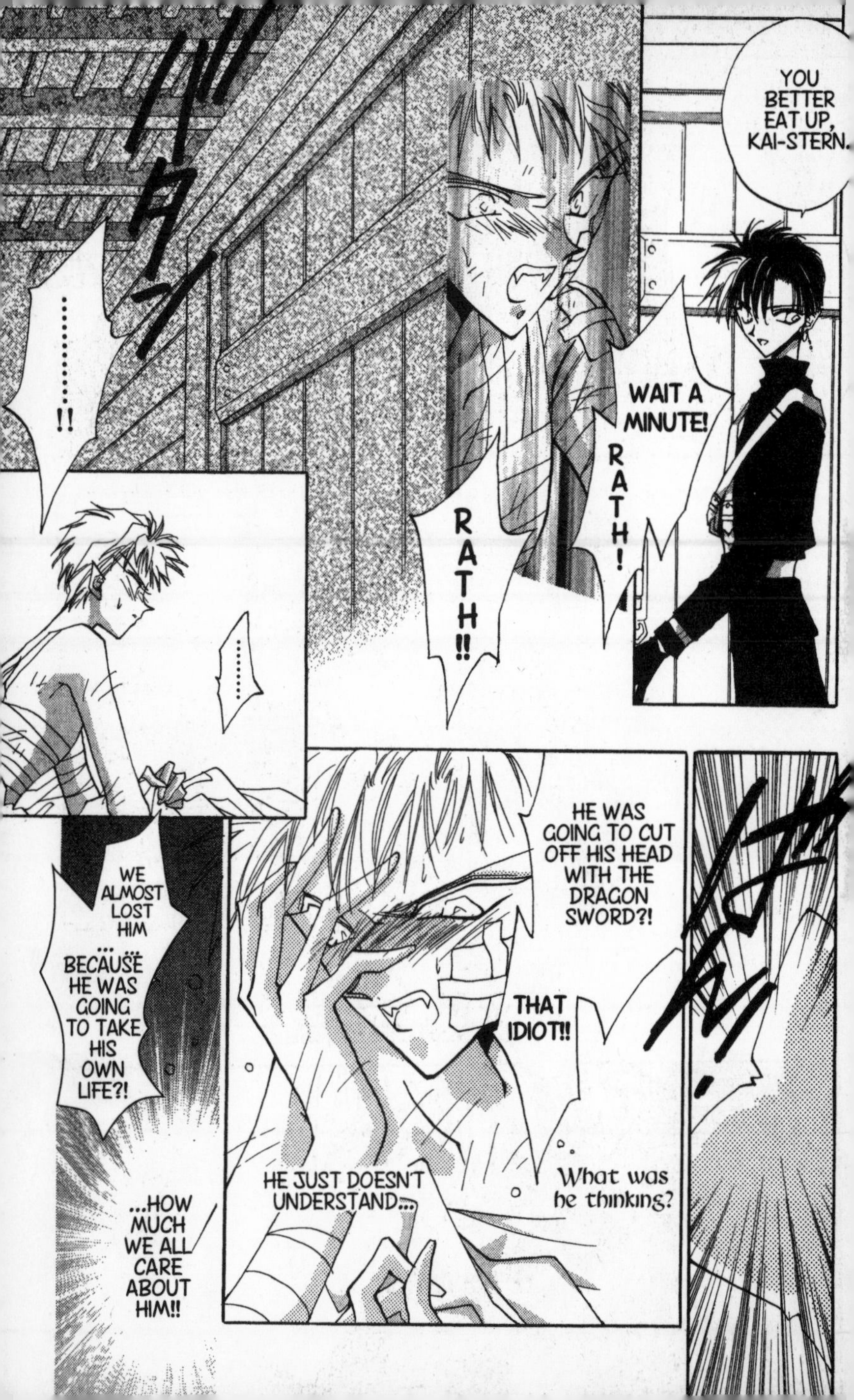
YOU BETTER EAT UP, KAI-STERN.
WAIT A MINUTE!
RATH!
RATH!!
......!!
......
HE WAS GOING TO CUT OFF HIS HEAD WITH THE DRAGON SWORD?!
THAT IDIOT!!
What was he thinking?
HE JUST DOESN'T UNDERSTAND...
WE ALMOST LOST HIM ... ...BECAUSE HE WAS GOING TO TAKE HIS OWN LIFE?!
...HOW MUCH WE ALL CARE ABOUT HIM!!

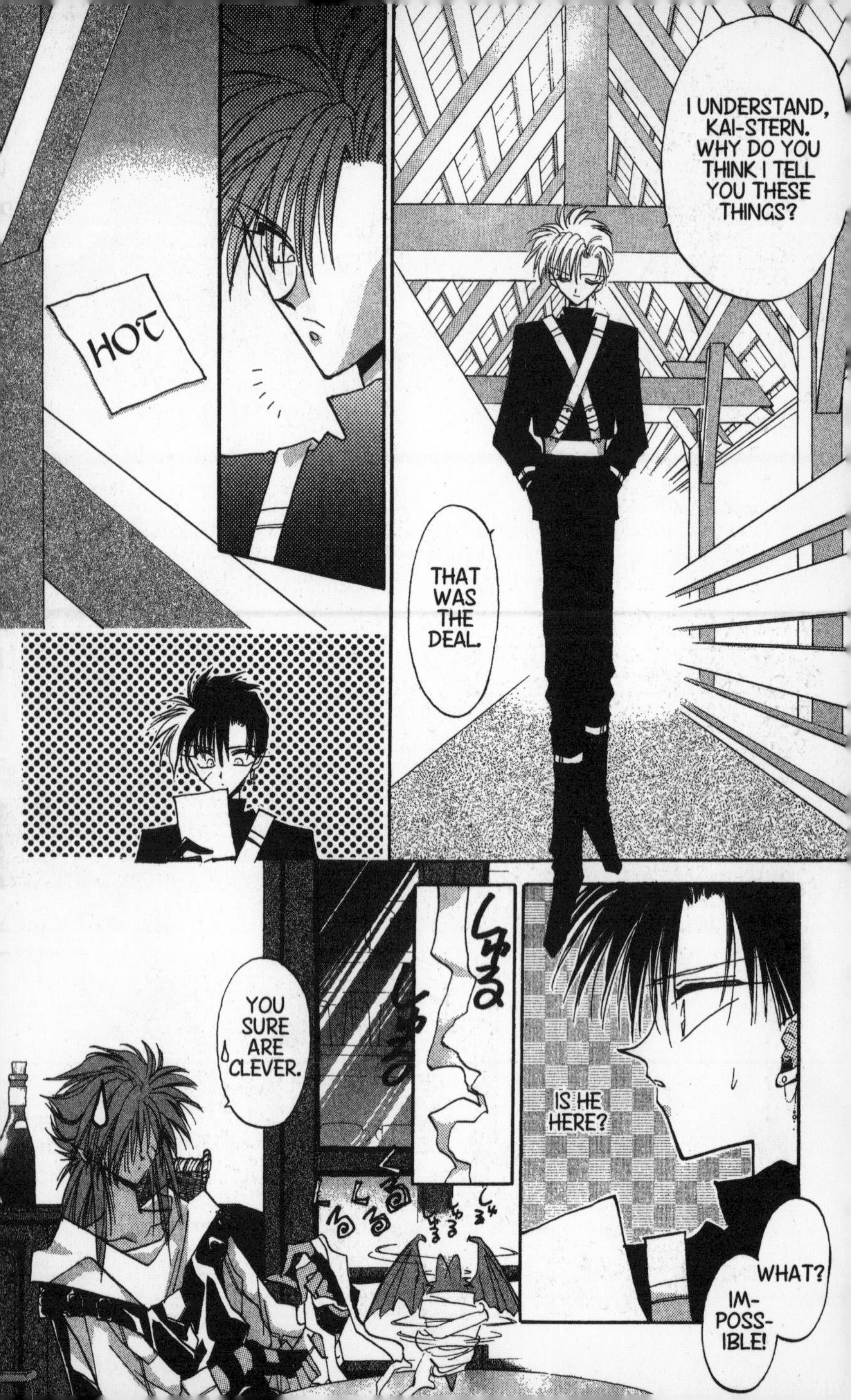
I UNDERSTAND, KAI-STERN. WHY DO YOU THINK I TELL YOU THESE THINGS?
THAT WAS THE DEAL.
HOT
IS HE HERE?
WHAT? IM-POSS-IBLE!
YOU SURE ARE CLEVER.

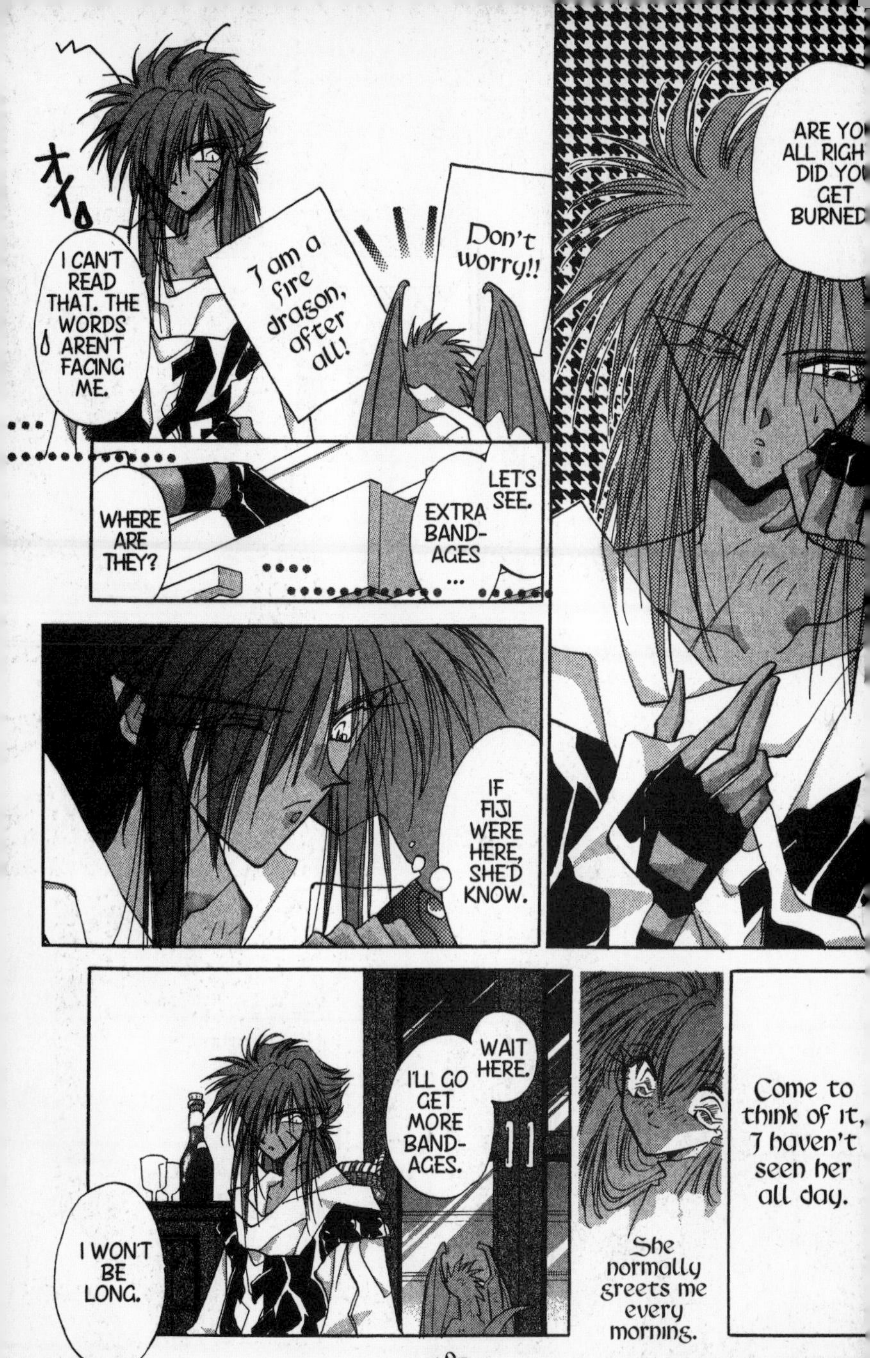

ARE YO ALL RIGH DID YO GET BURNED
Don't worry!!
I am a fire dragon, after all!
オイ
I CAN'T READ THAT. THE WORDS AREN'T FACING ME.
...
LET'S SEE.
EXTRA BANDAGES...
WHERE ARE THEY?
IF FIJI WERE HERE, SHE'D KNOW.
Come to think of it, I haven't seen her all day.
She normally greets me every morning.
WAIT HERE.
I'LL GO GET MORE BANDAGES.
I WON'T BE LONG.

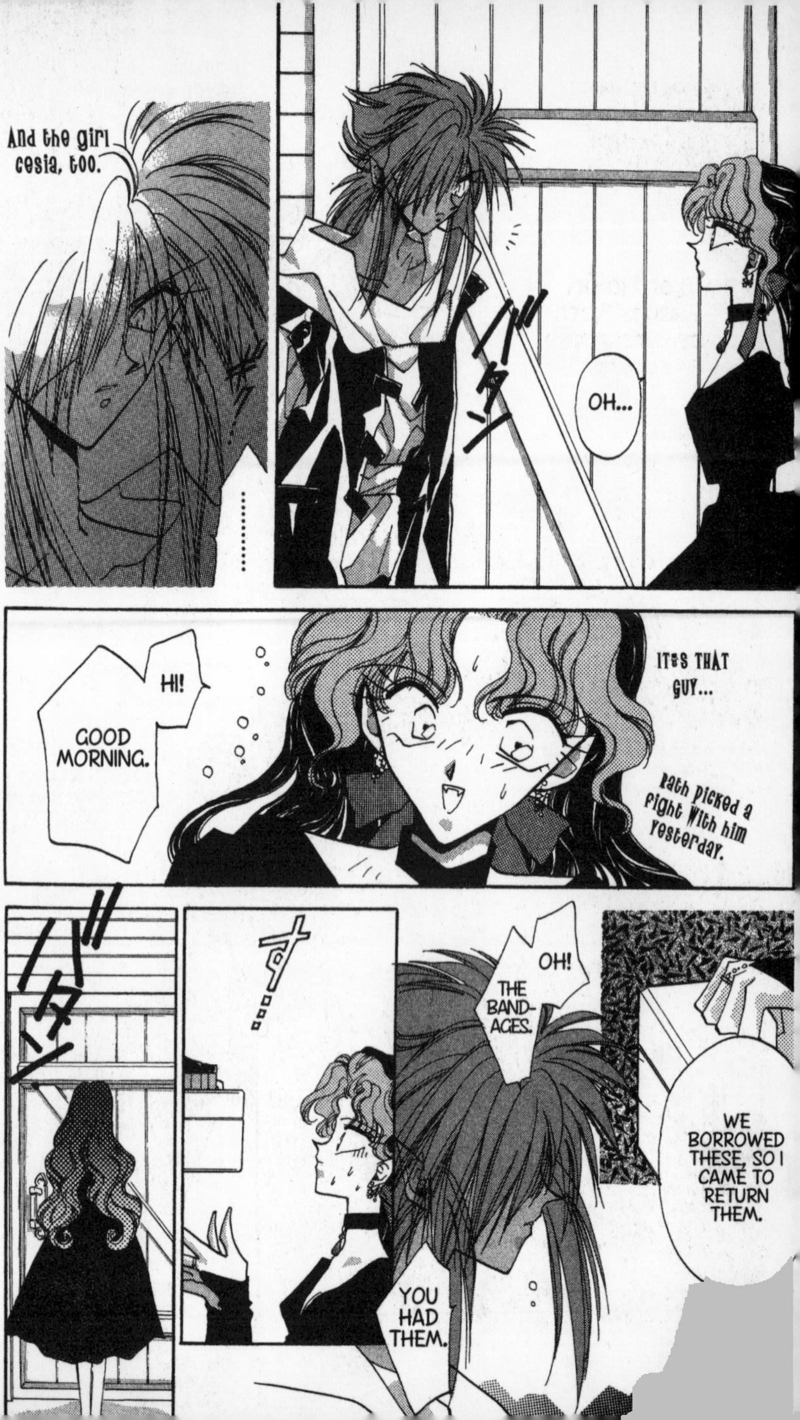
OH...
バタン
And the girl cesia, too.
......
IT'S THAT GUY...
Rath picked a fight with him yesterday.
HI!
GOOD MORNING.
OH!
THE BAND-AGES.
WE BORROWED THESE, SO I CAME TO RETURN THEM.
YOU HAD THEM.
す...
バタン

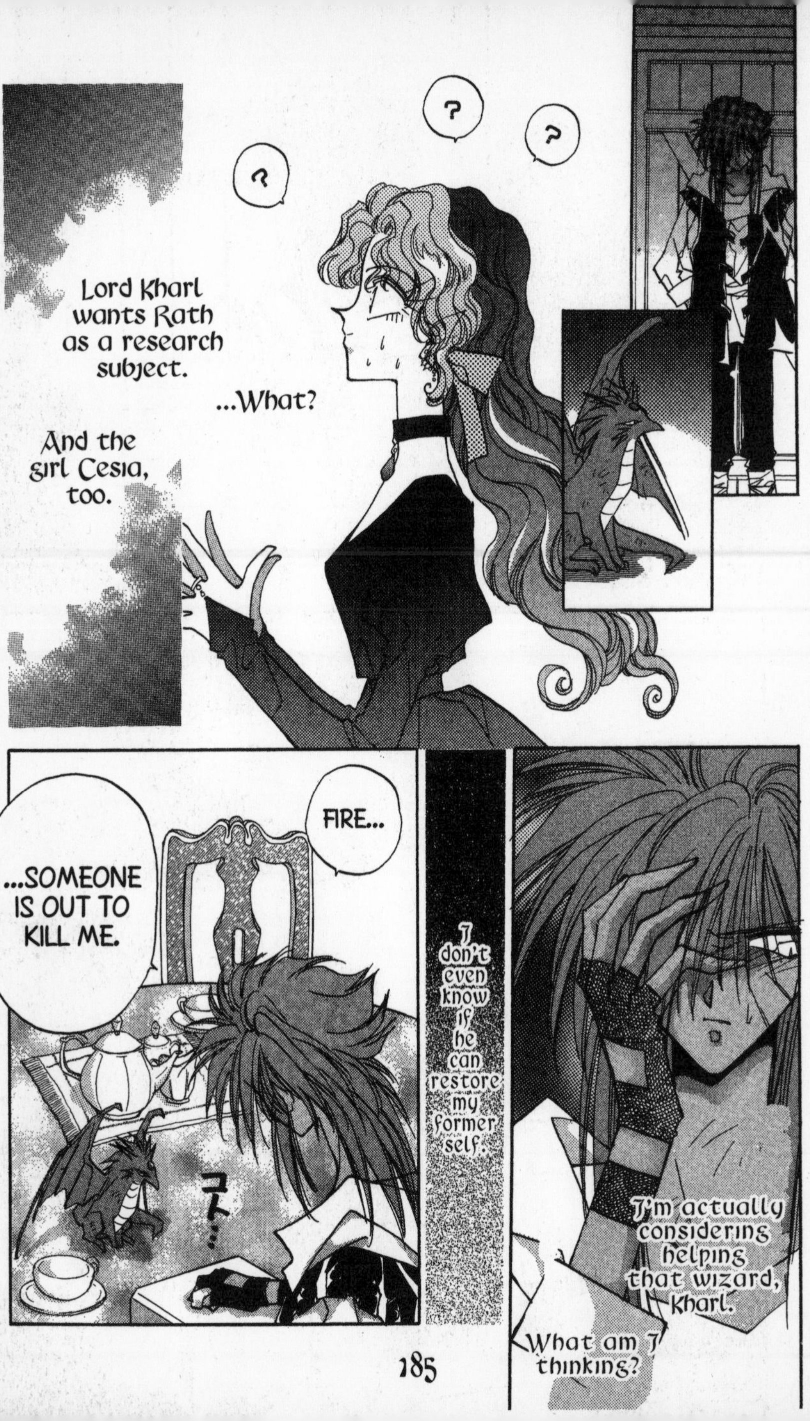
?
?
?
Lord Kharl wants Rath as a research subject.
...What?
And the girl Cesia, too.
I'm actually considering helping that wizard, Kharl.
What am I thinking?
I don't even know if he can restore my former self.
FIRE...
...SOMEONE IS OUT TO KILL ME.
コト...

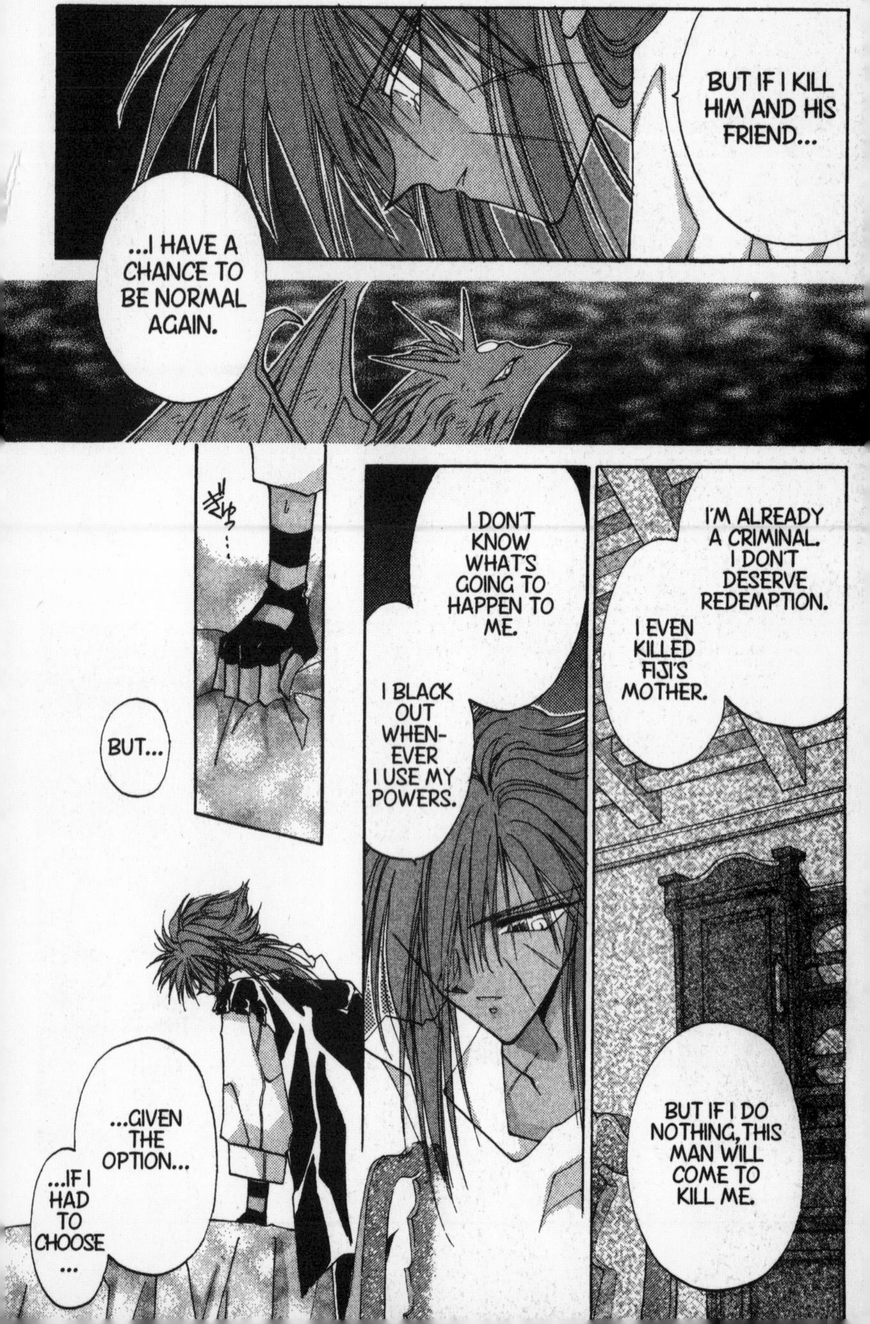
BUT IF I KILL HIM AND HIS FRIEND...
...I HAVE A CHANCE TO BE NORMAL AGAIN.
I'M ALREADY A CRIMINAL. I DON'T DESERVE REDEMPTION.
I EVEN KILLED FIJI'S MOTHER.
I DON'T KNOW WHAT'S GOING TO HAPPEN TO ME.
I BLACK OUT WHEN-EVER I USE MY POWERS.
BUT...
BUT IF I DO NOTHING, THIS MAN WILL COME TO KILL ME.
...GIVEN THE OPTION...
...IF I HAD TO CHOOSE...

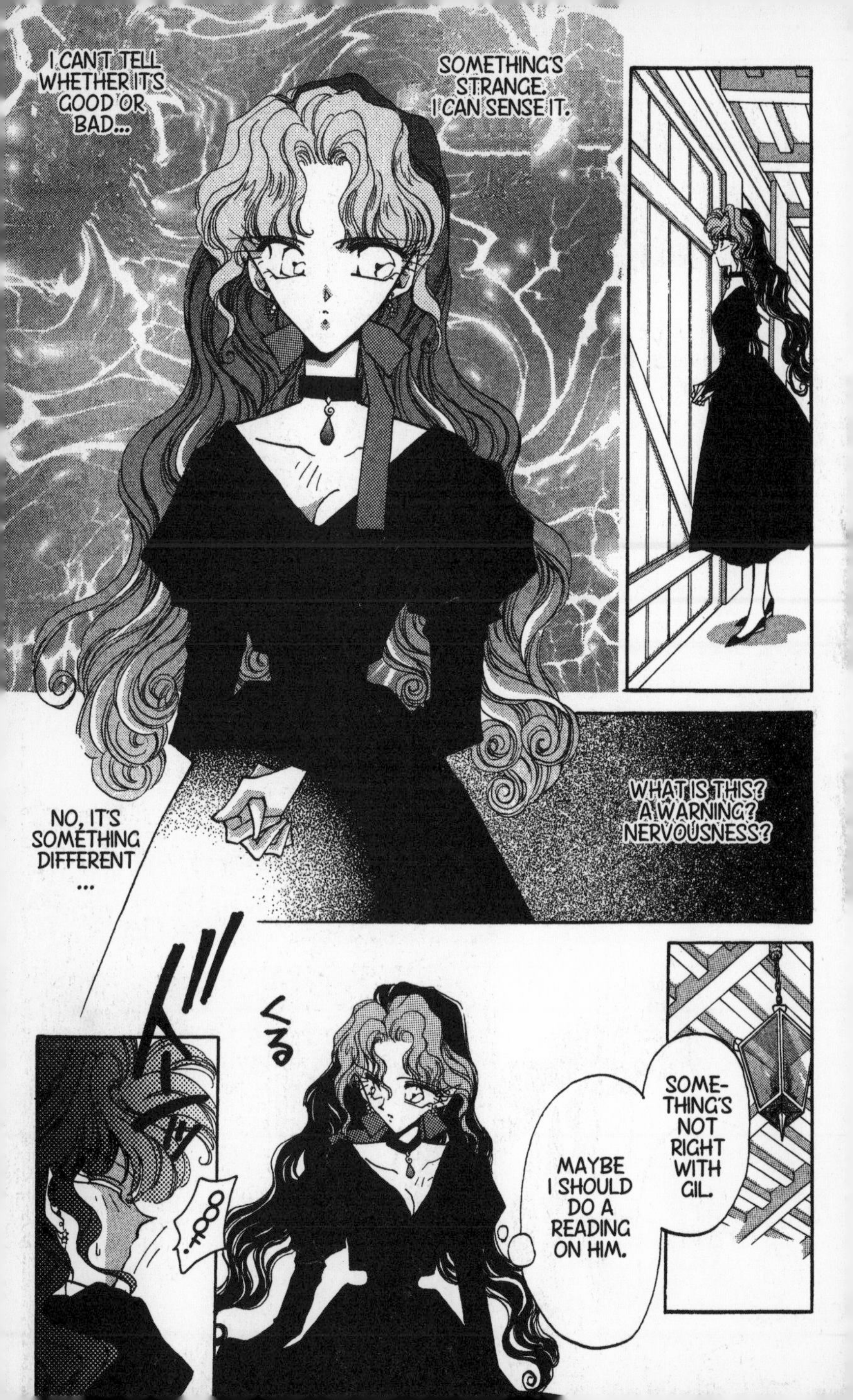
SOMETHING'S STRANGE. I CAN SENSE IT.
I CAN'T TELL WHETHER IT'S GOOD OR BAD...
WHAT IS THIS? A WARNING? NERVOUSNESS?
NO, IT'S SOMETHING DIFFERENT ...
SOME-THING'S NOT RIGHT WITH GIL.
MAYBE I SHOULD DO A READING ON HIM.
OOOF...

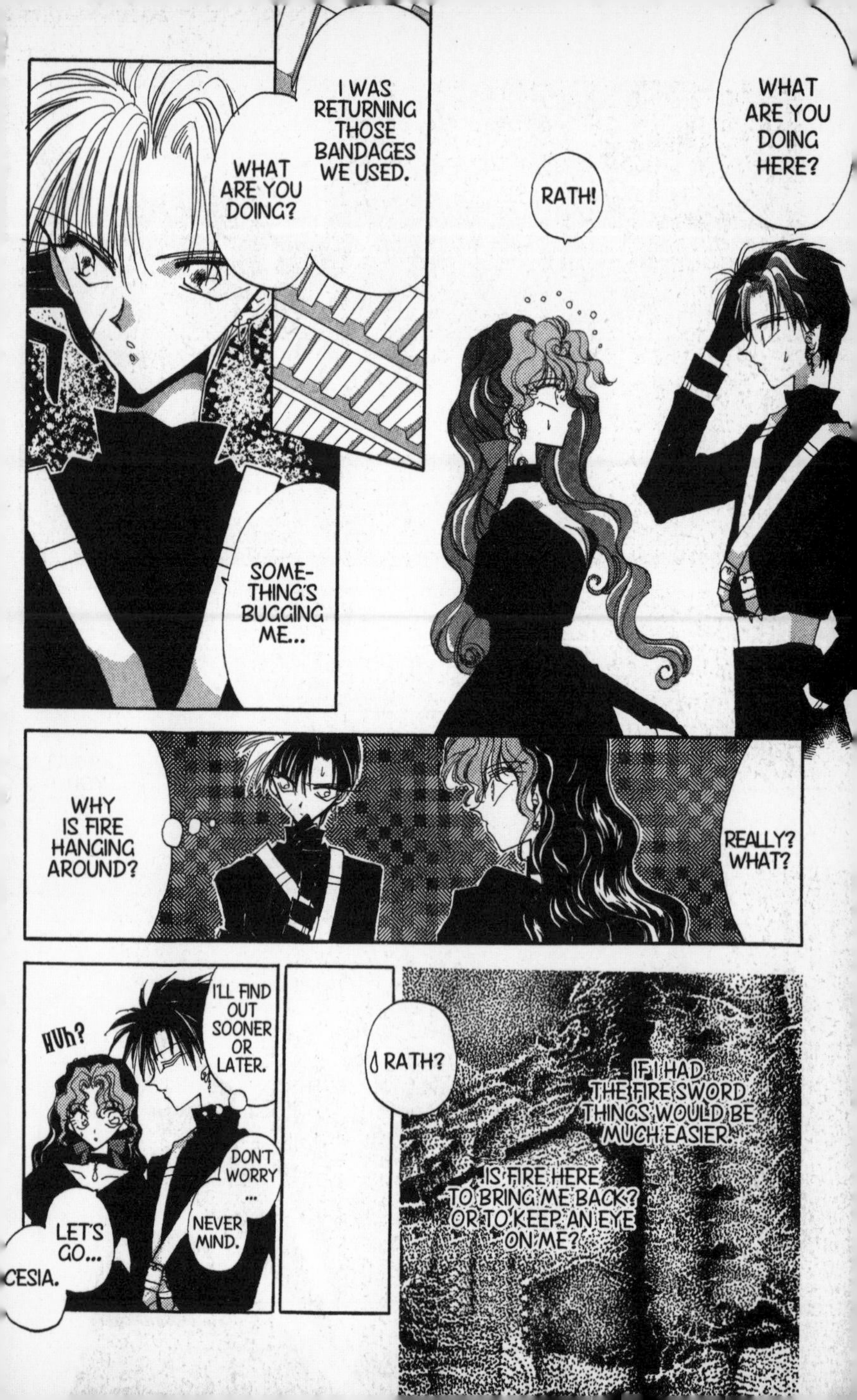
WHAT ARE YOU DOING HERE?
RATH!
I WAS RETURNING THOSE BANDAGES WE USED.
WHAT ARE YOU DOING?
SOME-THING'S BUGGING ME...
REALLY? WHAT?
WHY IS FIRE HANGING AROUND?
IF I HAD THE FIRE SWORD THINGS WOULD BE MUCH EASIER.
IS FIRE HERE TO BRING ME BACK? OR TO KEEP AN EYE ON ME?
RATH?
I'LL FIND OUT SOONER OR LATER.
HUh?
DON'T WORRY ...
NEVER MIND.
LET'S GO... CESIA.

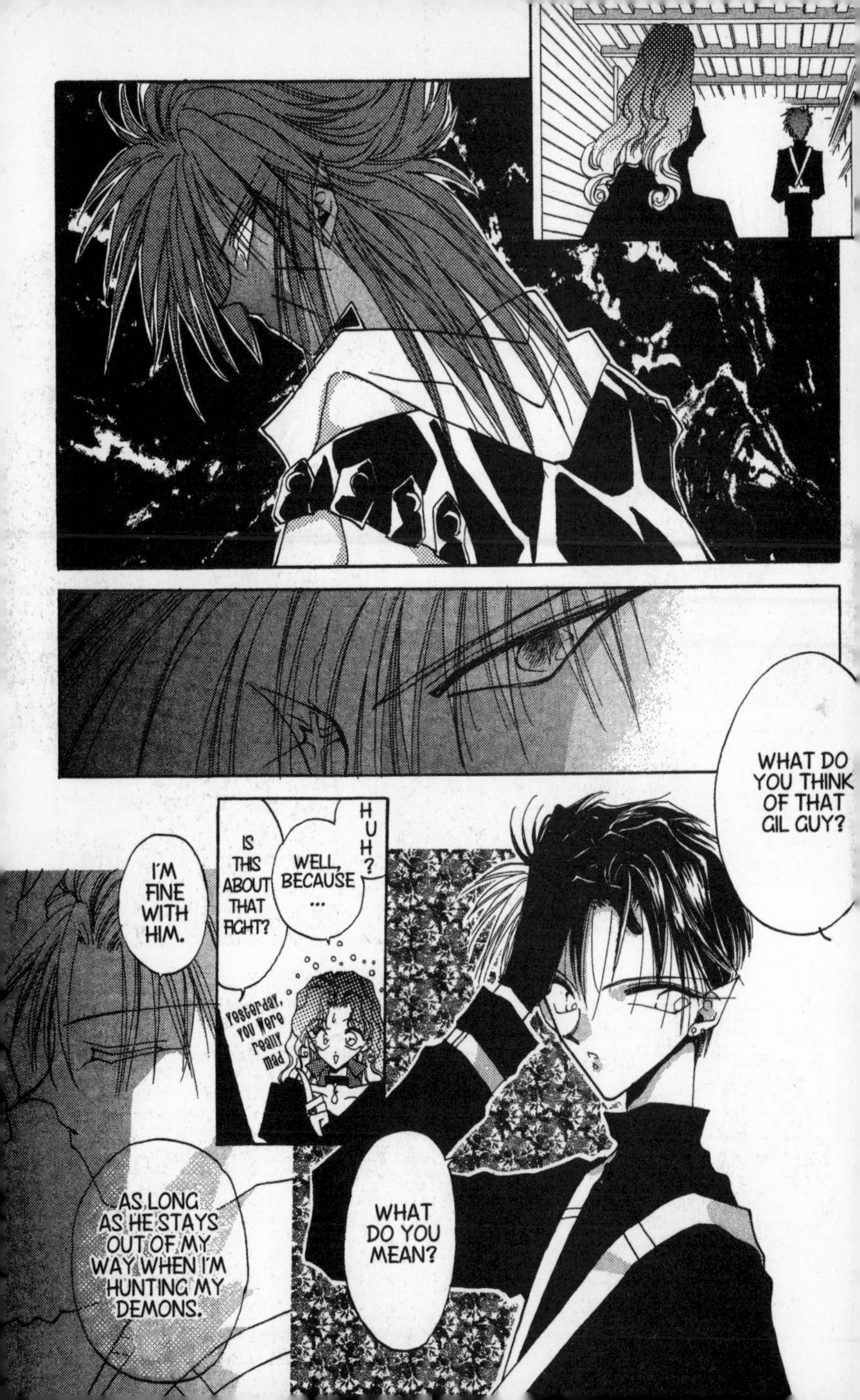
WHAT DO YOU THINK OF THAT GIL GUY?
HUH?
WELL, BECAUSE ...
IS THIS ABOUT THAT FIGHT?
Yesterday, you were really mad
I'M FINE WITH HIM.
WHAT DO YOU MEAN?
AS LONG AS HE STAYS OUT OF MY WAY WHEN I'M HUNTING MY DEMONS.

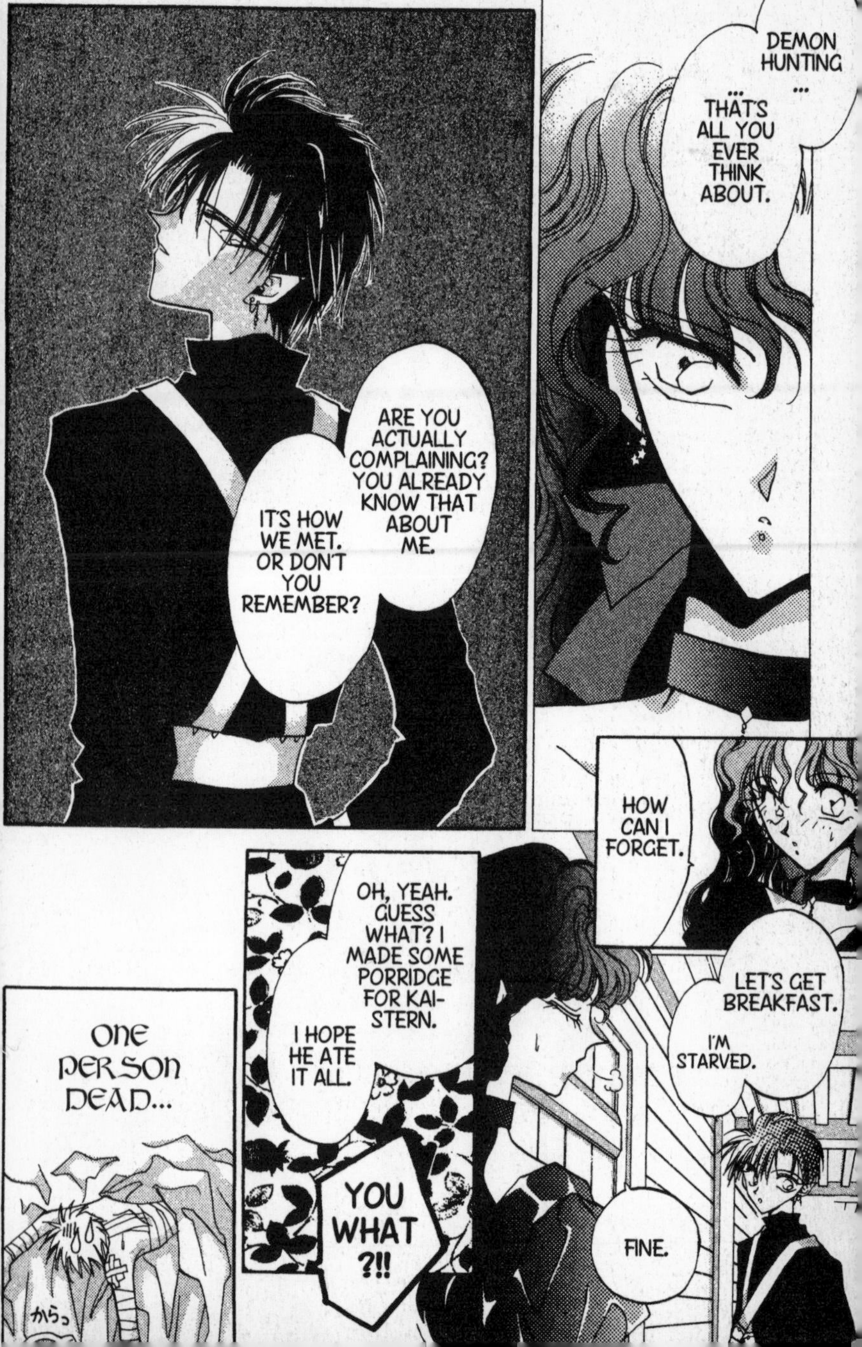
DEMON HUNTING ...
... THAT'S ALL YOU EVER THINK ABOUT.
ARE YOU ACTUALLY COMPLAINING? YOU ALREADY KNOW THAT ABOUT ME.
IT'S HOW WE MET. OR DON'T YOU REMEMBER?
HOW CAN I FORGET.
LET'S GET BREAKFAST.
I'M STARVED.
FINE.
OH, YEAH. GUESS WHAT? I MADE SOME PORRIDGE FOR KAI-STERN.
I HOPE HE ATE IT ALL.
YOU WHAT ?!!
ONE PERSON DEAD...
からっ

Dragon Knights

In Volume 9:

In a deep, and perhaps long overdue, conversation, Kai-Stern reveals to Cesia that he is searching feverishly for the Wind Dragon, the Dragon with the power to restore life. He wants to save the dying Rath.

Cesia, too, wants to find the Wind Dragon in the hopes of reviving Crewger. But the two of them agree to keep this information from Rath, who they fear might be consumed with senseless anger, as he is prone to do.

But their desire to keep Rath calm in the mind becomes shattered when they meet up with Shydeman and Shyrendora accompanied by hordes of demon agents.

In the midst of this madness, who will Rath destory? And what is the secret he has been hiding for so long?

Mineko Ohkami

STOP!

This is the back of the book.
You wouldn't want to spoil a great ending!

This book is printed "manga-style," in the authentic Japanese right-to-left format. Since none of the artwork has been flipped or altered, readers get to experience the story just as the creator intended. You've been asking for it, so TOKYOPOP® delivered: authentic, hot-off-the-press, and far more fun!

DIRECTIONS

If this is your first time reading manga-style, here's a quick guide to help you understand how it works.

It's easy... just start in the top right panel and follow the numbers. Have fun, and look for more 100% authentic manga from TOKYOPOP®!

100% AUTHENTIC MANGA